OCR AS
PSYCHOLOGY

Matt Jarvis • Julia Russell •
Lizzie Gauntlett • Penny Crooks

OXFORD

Great Clarendon Street, Oxford OX2 6DP

Oxford University Press is a department of the University of Oxford.

It furthers the University's objective of excellence in research, scholarship, and education by publishing worldwide in
Oxford   New York   Auckland   Cape Town   Dar es Salaam   Hong Kong
Karachi   Kuala Lumpur   Madrid   Melbourne   Mexico City   Nairobi
New Delhi   Shanghai   Taipei   Toronto

With offices in
Argentina   Austria   Brazil   Chile   Czech Republic   France   Greece
Guatemala   Hungary   Italy   Japan   Poland   Portugal   Singapore
South Korea   Switzerland   Thailand   Turkey   Ukraine   Vietnam

Oxford is a registered trade mark of Oxford University Press
in the UK and in certain other countries

British Library Cataloguing in Publication Data

Data available

978 019 912988 1

10 9 8 7 6 5 4 3 2 1

Printed by Bell & Bain Ltd., Glasgow

Paper used in the production of this book is a natural, recyclable product made from wood grown in sustainable forests. The manufacturing process conforms to the environmental regulations of the country of origin.

Acknowledgements

The authors and publishers would like to thank the following teachers and their students for their help, advice and input:
Becky Hawkins and Sian Izzet, Richard Huish College, Taunton, Somerset
Dawn Knox and Miriam Pedder, Alun School, Mold, Flintshire
Fiona Lintern, Walford and North Shropshire College and Glyndŵr University
Alex Price, Ousedale School, Newport Pagnell, Buckinghamshire

The publishers would like to thank the following for permission to reproduce photographs: **p.5**: Sebastian Kaulitzki/Shutterstock; **p.6**: Pavel Vorobyev/Fotolia; **p.7**: With kind permission from Elizabeth Loftus; **p.8**: Image Source/Alamy; **p.9**: Deyan Georgiev/Fotolia; **p.15**: Brian Harris/Rex Features; **p.15**: Jasmin Merdan/Fotolia; **p.16**: Baron-Cohen, S., Joliffe, T. Mortimore, C. & Robertson, M. (1997) "Another advanced test of theory of mind: evidence from very high functioning adults with autism or Asperger Syndrome." *Journal of Child Psychology & Psychiatry 38, 813-822*; **p.24–31**: With kind permission from Liz Rubert-Pugh; **p.47**: Dmitriy Shironosov/Shutterstock; **p.48**: Bill Anderson/Science Photo Library; **p.49**: Doug Goodman/Science Photo Library; **p.50**: Joel Sartore/Getty Images; **p.51**: Laura Dwight Photography; **p.61–63**: With kind permission from Professor Albert Bandura; **p.71**: Mary Evans Picture Library/Sigmund Freud Copyrights; **p.72**: Yuri Arcurs/Fotolia; **p.73**: Franz Pfluegl/Shutterstock; **p.74**: Paul Banton/Shutterstock; **p.84**: Patrick Landmann/Science Photo Library; **p.85**: Bruce MacQueen/Shutterstock; **p.86**: Bikeworldtravel/Shutterstock; **p.87**: Geoff Tompkinson/Science Photo Library; **p.88**: Pasieka/Science Photo Library; **p.89l**: Medimage/Science Photo Library; **p.89r**: Arthur Glauberman/Science Photo Library; **p.106**: Christine Boyd/Telegraph Media Group Limited 2004; **p.126**: J Neurosci. 2008 June 18; 28(25): 6453–6458. doi: 10.1523/JNEUROSCI.0573-08.2008; **p.135**: sculpies/Shutterstock; **p.136**: scabam/Fotolia; **p.137**: With kind permission from Alexandra Milgram; **p.140**: Subject receives a sample shock. From the film *Obedience* © 1968 by Stanley Milgram © renewed 1993 by Alexandra Milgram and distributed by Penn State Media Sales; **p.140**: Obedient subject in Touch-Proximity Condition. From the film *Obedience* © 1968 by Stanley Milgram © renewed 1993 by Alexandra Milgram and distributed by Penn State Media Sales; **p.149**: Philip G. Zimbardo, Inc.; **p.149**: With kind permission from Alex Haslam and Steve Reicher; **p.150**: Philip G. Zimbardo, Inc.; **p.151–155**: With kind permission from Alex Haslam and Steve Reicher; **p.162**: courtesy Vincent Genovese; **p.164**: Professor Bop/Flickr; **p.176**: Caroline Purser/Getty Images; **p.177**: CinemaPhoto/Corbis; **p.179**: Ed Souza/Stanford News Service; **p.180**: Konstantin L/Shutterstock; **p.181**: Boris Mrdja/Shutterstock; **p.182**: Photoroller/Shutterstock; **p.189**: AF archive/Alamy; **p.191**: Oleg Golovnev/Shutterstock; **p.192**: James Steidl/Fotolia; **p.193**: Janos Radler/Flickr/Getty Images; **p.194**: Markus Gann/Shutterstock; **p.195**: dule964/Fotolia; **p.197**: John Springer Collection/Corbis; **p.203t**: Sean Gladwell/Fotolia; **p.203b**: ilker canikligil/Shutterstock; **p.204**: Image Source/Alamy; **p.205**: Comstock/Getty Images; **p.214**: _Lonely_/Shutterstock; **p.221**: Eric Isselée/Fotolia; **p.222**: With kind permission from Alex Haslam and Steve Reicher; **p.224**: Ace Stock Limited/Alamy; **p.224**: nsphotography/Fotolia; **p.231**: Daniel Bramich / Alamy; **p.233**: Lee Martin / Alamy; **p.235**: Roman Pyshchyk/Fotolia; **p.238**: Image Source/Alamy; **p.243**: Monika Wisniewska/Shutterstock; **p.244**: Gabe Palmer/Alamy; **p.253**: Janine Wiedel Photolibrary/Alamy; **p.254**: Monkey Business/Fotolia; **p.257**: Radius Images/Alamy; **p.258**: Corbis Super RF/Alamy; **p.260**: STOCK4B GmbH/Alamy; **p.263**: Burntlight/Alamy; **p.273**: _Lonely_/Shutterstock; **p.280**: James Holmes/Science Photo Library; **p.282**: Patrice Latron/Look At Sciences/Science Photo Library; **p.285**: i love images/Alamy; **p.286**: Jacek Chabraszewski/Fotolia; **p.287**: Ariel Skelley/Getty Images; **p.289**: Tomasz Trojanowski/Fotolia; **p.298**: Dessie/Fotolia

Artwork: Q2A; John Hallett; Barking Dog Art; Patricia Briggs

Cover photo by Tischenko Irina/Shutterstock

The authors and publisher are grateful to the following for permission to reprint copyright material:
Elsevier for tables from E F Lotus and J C Palmer: 'Reconstruction of automobile destruction: an example of the interaction between language and memory', 13(5) *Journal of Verbal Learning and Verbal Behaviour* 585 (1974), copyright © Elsevier 1974.

Mirrorpix (Mirror Syndication International) for report, 'Brain structure snapshots reveal science behind why only half of London taxi trainees pass the Knowledge test', *The Mirror*, 8.12.2011, copyright © Mirrorpix 2011.

Telegraph Media Group for extract from report, 'A Dangerous Sleep' by Judith Woods, *The Daily Telegraph*, 18.10.2004, copyright © Telegraph Media Group Ltd 2004.

John Wiley and Sons for figures from M Griffiths: 'The role of cognitive bias and skill in fruit machine gambling', 85(3) *The British Journals of Psychology* 361(1994), copyright © The British Psychological Society 1994.

Every effort has been made to contact copyright holders of material reproduced in this book. If notified, the publishers will be pleased to rectify any errors or omissions at the earliest opportunity.

CONTENTS

INTRODUCTION

Welcome to our book!

The OCR AS-level focuses on core studies, a selection of studies that have been of particular historical importance in psychology, and on the methods of psychology research. These core studies are grouped according to the British Psychological Society's classification of the approaches to psychology, and we devote a chapter to each of these approaches:

The OCR specification also includes a whole unit on research methodology, and you can find all you need to know about carrying out psychological research in Chapter 6.

We have oriented the features in this book towards exam preparation. For every core study there are summaries, to make sure you have a good grasp of the basics before getting into the finer detail of studies; exam tips, in the Question Spotlight feature; and sample questions, answers and comments.

Some, but please note not all, of the questions in the Exam Focus feature are from past OCR exam questions. Where we have suggested marks that answers would achieve it is important to note that these are marks the authors think the questions might gain. These marks are not attributable to OCR or any of their assessors.

If you enjoy psychology and are thinking about taking it further, check out 'To A2 and beyond!' on page 299, where we offer some careers advice.

Good luck and enjoy!

C1

COGNITIVE

PSYCHOLOGY

Cognitive psychology is concerned with the mental processes that allow us to deal with information. In this chapter we will look at three classic studies from cognitive psychology:

1 Loftus and Palmer's study of eyewitness testimony. This was a laboratory experiment in which the researchers tested the idea that they could distort participants' memory of a car accident by asking them misleading questions.

2 Baron-Cohen *et al.'s* study of mind-reading (the ability to correctly interpret other people's mental states) in adults with autistic spectrum disorders. This was compared to mind-reading ability in adults with Tourette's syndrome and a control group with no diagnosis.

3 Savage-Rumbaugh *et al.'s* study of language acquisition in pygmy chimps – humans' nearest relative. Pygmy chimps were compared to common chimps in their ability to pick up the meanings of spoken words and written symbols, and to put symbols together to convey meanings.

We will now look at each of these studies in detail, before using them to explore the nature of cognitive psychology and to think about its strengths and limitations.

LOFTUS AND PALMER'S STUDY OF DISTORTION OF WITNESS MEMORY

KEY IDEAS

An **eyewitness** is someone who sees an event such as a crime or an accident. Technically, someone who hears the incident is an 'earwitness' and someone who, for example, smells gas prior to an explosion would be a 'nosewitness'. This study is concerned with the accuracy of **eyewitness memory** and, by implication, the usefulness of **eyewitness testimony** – the accounts given by witnesses to the Police and in court.

WEB WATCH @

Test your own skill as an eyewitness. Go to www.youramazingbrain.org and click on 'Test yourself'.

Figure 1.1
We are generally poor at estimating the speed of cars in a crash

Loftus, E.F. and Palmer, J.C. (1974) Reconstruction of automobile destruction: an example of the interaction between language and memory. *Journal of Verbal Learning & Verbal Behaviour,* **13**, 585–9.

CONTEXT

How well do you remember events you have seen and experienced? Psychologists have been concerned with the accuracy of our memory of events for many years. As far back as 1909, G.M. Whipple reviewed evidence and concluded that **eyewitnesses**' memory of events is considerably less accurate that we would like to believe. This may be particularly true when we are asked to recall numerical values, such as time, distance or speed. By the 1970s, several studies had shown that people tend to over-estimate the time and speed involved in complex events. In one study, Marshall (1969) asked Air Force personnel to estimate the speed of a car that they had been watching. Although the participants knew that they would be questioned, their responses varied wildly and were inaccurate (their estimates were between 10–50mph, whereas the actual speed was 12mph).

Loftus and Palmer proposed that: 'Given the inaccuracies in estimates of speed, it seems likely that there are variables which are potentially powerful in terms of influencing these estimates' (1974: 585). In other words, if we are poor at judging speed, then there must be factors other than the actual speed that influence our judgement. Fillmore (1971) had suggested that one such factor might be the language used to describe the motion, and that using words such as 'smashed', rather than more neutral words, such as 'hit', could lead people to judge speed to be greater.

The inaccuracy of **eyewitness memory**, and the potential for memories to be distorted by the use of language, have important practical applications. In particular, the Police and the courts often rely on **eyewitness testimony** in order to make decisions about what actually took place and who was responsible for what happened. By the 1970s, there was concern in legal circles about the use of leading questions, and the likelihood that such questions can lead to inaccurate eyewitness testimony. Loftus and Palmer define a leading question as 'one that, either by its form or content, suggests to the witness what answer is desired or leads him to the desired answer' (1974: 585). The present study is concerned with the effect on eyewitness memory of asking leading questions about the speed of a car.

GENERAL AIM

The overall aim of the study was to test whether the phrasing of questions about a car accident could alter participants' memory of an event.

EXPERIMENT 1

AIM

The aim of the first experiment was to see whether using different verbs to describe a collision between two cars would affect estimates of the speed at which they were travelling when the crash took place.

METHOD

Participants
Forty-five students took part in the first experiment. No details of age or gender were recorded.

Design and procedure
The study was a laboratory experiment using an independent measures design. Participants were shown seven films of car crashes, taken from training films used by the Seattle Police Department and the Evergreen Safety Council. In four of the films the speed of the car was known because the crashes were staged for training purposes. The speeds in these four films were 20mph, 30mph, 40mph and 40mph. After watching the films, all participants were asked to write an account of the accident and

Figure 1.2
Elizabeth Loftus

IN BRIEF ❗

Aim: To investigate the effect of questionning on witness memory for a car accident.

Experiment 1: 45 students watched film of car crashes. They were then asked to estimate the cars' speed, using different verbs to describe the crash. Estimated speed varied according to the verb used, with 'smashed' leading to the highest estimates.

Experiment 2: 150 students underwent a similar procedure but were asked about broken glass at the scene. Where the word 'smashed' was used, participants still estimated a higher speed, but, in addition, they wrongly remembered seeing broken glass at the scene of the crash.

Conclusion: Wording of questions can alter witness memories for events.

STRETCH & CHALLENGE ◎

Normally, more participant details are reported in psychological studies. Suggest a reason why this might be less important in cognitive psychology than in some other areas, such as social psychology or individual differences.

KEY IDEAS

Laboratory experiments take place under controlled conditions. They test cause and effect by comparing two or more conditions. The **independent variable (IV)** is the thing that varies between the conditions. The **dependent variable (DV)** is the thing that is measured for the results.

Figure 1.3 Eyewitness testimony is important in many criminal cases

Film number	Actual speed	Estimated speed
1	20mph	37.7mph
2	30mph	36.2mph
3	40mph	39.7mph
4	40mph	36.1mph

TABLE 1.1 MEAN ESTIMATES AND ACTUAL SPEED IN FOUR CRASHES

then to answer a series of questions. All but one of the questions were fillers, designed to make it harder to work out the aim of the experiment. The other question was a *critical* question, meaning that it was closely concerned with the aim of the study. This question was: 'About how fast were the cars going when they hit each other?'

The independent variable was the verb used in the critical question. For one group this was 'hit'. The other groups received the same question but with the verb 'contacted', 'bumped', 'collided' or 'smashed' instead of 'hit'. The dependent variable was the mean estimated speed of the car.

RESULTS

Results were in the form of quantitative data. Participants' estimates of the speed at which the cars were travelling were not affected by the actual speed. The mean estimates for each of the crashes in which the speed was known are shown in Table 1.1. This shows that we are generally poor at estimating speed. However, estimates of the cars' speeds did vary according to the verb used in the critical question. These results are shown in Table 1.2.

CONCLUSIONS

Participants' estimates of the speed at which the cars were travelling when the accident took place varied according to the verb used to describe the crash. There are two possible reasons for this:

1 *Response bias.* When a participant is unclear what speed to estimate, the verb gives them a clue as to whether they should estimate a high or low figure.
2 *Memory distortion.* The verb used in the question actually alters a participant's memory of the crash.

EXPERIMENT 2

AIM

The aim of the second experiment was to investigate whether the different speed estimates found in Experiment 1 were, in fact, the result of a distortion in memory. This was achieved by seeing whether participants who heard the words that were associated with high-speed estimates would be more likely to incorrectly remember broken glass at the crash site.

METHOD

Participants

One hundred and fifty students took part in the second experiment. No details of age or gender were recorded.

Design and procedure

As in the first experiment, the method was a laboratory experiment with an independent measures design. All participants watched a film of a car crash. The entire film lasted less than one minute, and the accident itself lasted four seconds. All participants were given a questionnaire that asked them first to describe the accident in their own words, and then to answer a series of questions. As in the first experiment, there was a critical question. The first 50 participants received the question: 'About how fast were the cars going when they smashed into each other?' Another 50 participants received the question: 'About how fast were the cars going when they hit each other?' Finally, a control group of 50 participants received questions that did not ask about the speed of the cars. All 150 participants were asked to estimate speed, as in Experiment 1. A week later, the participants returned and answered a further 10 questions. The critical question was: 'Did you see any broken glass?'

QUESTION SPOTLIGHT!

The Loftus and Palmer procedure has been challenged on the basis of its ecological validity. *Suggest two reasons why this might be an issue.*

TABLE 1.2 MEAN ESTIMATES OF SPEED IN ANSWER TO THE CRITICAL QUESTION

Verb used	Estimated speed
Smashed	40.5
Collided	39.3
Bumped	38.1
Hit	34.0
Contacted	31.8

Source: Loftus and Palmer (1974), p. 586.

RESULTS

As in Experiment 1, participants who heard the word 'smashed' in the critical question estimated a higher speed (10.46mph as opposed to 8.0mph in the 'hit' condition). The numbers of participants reporting that they had seen broken glass in each condition is shown in Table 1.3. More than twice as many people incorrectly remembered seeing broken glass having heard the word 'smashed' in the question.

Figure 1.4
Is there broken glass?

TABLE 1.3 NUMBERS OF PARTICIPANTS REPORTING SEEING BROKEN GLASS IN EACH VERB CONDITION

Response	'smashed'	'hit'	'control'
yes	16	7	6
no	34	43	44

Source: Loftus and Palmer (1974), p. 587.

QUESTION SPOTLIGHT!

Understanding the purpose of Experiment 2 is crucial to being able to write about the study. *Explain the purpose of Experiment 2.*

QUESTION SPOTLIGHT!

If you offer an answer evaluating the research method for this study, make sure your answer makes reference to the study itself. A generic answer will gain limited credit.

CONCLUSIONS

The general conclusion from the two experiments is that the way in which questions about events are worded can affect the way in which those events are remembered. The results of Experiment 2 are important because they strongly suggest that this is not simply due to response bias. Instead it seems that post-event questions actually become part of the memory for that event. Therefore, the wording of questions can actually distort event memory.

STUDY 1

LOFTUS AND PALMER'S STUDY OF DISTORTION OF WITNESS MEMORY

SUMMARY

EXPERIMENT 1

AIM

To investigate the effect of question phrasing on witness memory of a car crash.

METHOD

A laboratory experiment carried out on 45 students. They were shown footage of seven crashes and asked how fast the cars were travelling when they contacted, bumped, collided, smashed or hit each other, depending on the condition.

RESULTS

The average estimated speed varied according to the verb, with 'smashed' leading to the highest speed estimates, and 'contacted' the lowest.

CONCLUSION

The phrasing of questions actually distorted witnesses' memory of the crash.

EXPERIMENT 2

AIM

To establish whether the memories of the participants were actually distorted by the phrasing of the question, by seeing if a false memory of broken glass was created in the 'smashed' condition.

METHOD

A laboratory experiment carried out on 150 students. They were shown the same filmed crash and asked to estimate how fast the cars were travelling when they smashed or hit. A week later they were asked if they remembered seeing broken glass.

RESULTS

More than twice as many participants remembered broken glass if they had heard 'smashed' in the question.

EVALUATION

This is a straightforward laboratory experiment, with minimal ethical issues but more interesting methodological ones.

THE SAMPLE AND SAMPLING METHOD

The participants were all American students, not chosen by any representative sampling method. This means that they were unlikely to be truly representative of the population. They were predominantly white, middle-class and within a narrow age-range, and all had the same occupation. This is important for the following reasons:

- Because their teachers were running the study, the students could have been particularly vulnerable to demand characteristics. In other words, they might have been strongly influenced by cues suggesting what the researchers expected to find. However, the independent measures design would possibly have elimited the worst of this problem.

- Because the participants were all students, they were very used to taking in information and being tested on it.

- The participants were less likely to be drivers than the population as a whole, and their speed estimates might have been less accurate as a result of their lack of experience with cars.

These characteristics could mean that the results were partly a product of the sample itself.

THE RESEARCH METHOD

The study was a laboratory experiment. Laboratory experiments come with a set of strengths and limitations. Because the procedure takes place in a highly controlled environment it is possible to eliminate many extraneous variables and to be reasonably confident that it is the independent variable we are interested in that is affecting the dependent variable. Laboratory procedures are straightforward to replicate, which makes them reliable. The potential weaknesses of laboratory studies such as that of Loftus and Palmer lie in the realism of the environment and the participants' tasks. It is hard to set up laboratory procedures in such a way as to ensure that people behave as they would in real life. In this case, watching a film is not quite the same experience as witnessing a real event.

ECOLOGICAL VALIDITY

As just said, a potential problem with laboratory experiments such as Loftus and Palmer's is their realism. In this case, both the environment and the task were quite artificial. Participants had a better view of the crash than is typical in real-life situations, but they were probably more relaxed and less motivated to remember details, given that they were in a familiar and safe situation and knew that they were taking part in a study. Remember that it can be quite upsetting to witness an accident in real life, and this emotional response can make the event more memorable. It is possible that the participants' memory was artificially poor in the study for these reasons.

QUALITATIVE AND QUANTITATIVE DATA

The data gathered in this study were quantitative. This is both a strength and a weakness. On the plus side, the statistics allow easy comparison of the conditions, clearly showing that memory is affected by the wording of questions. On the other hand, there was no opportunity for participants to comment either on what they remembered, or on their experience of being questioned in this way. Such qualitative data might have added to the completeness of the findings.

PRACTICAL APPLICATIONS

Studies like this are extremely important in helping the authorities to understand how to question witnesses to important events such as accidents and crimes. Following the work of Loftus and her colleagues, the use of leading questions – both by the Police immediately after an event, and later in the courtroom – is now tightly controlled.

EXAM FOCUS

We now show you some of the sorts of questions that could be asked about the Loftus and Palmer study in your exam. We will then show you some examples of the sorts of answers we believe might be successful and less successful, and point out some classic traps to avoid.

SECTION A

1 Describe the procedure in the second experiment conducted by Loftus and Palmer on eyewitness testimony. *(4 marks)*

2 The Loftus and Palmer study used two laboratory experiments.
   (a) Identify the two experimental groups in Experiment 2. *(2 marks)*
   (b) Outline one difference between the responses given by the two experimental groups in Experiment 2. *(2 marks)*

3 The Loftus and Palmer study on eyewitness testimony involved the experimental method. Describe one strength and one weakness of the experimental method as used in this study. *(4 marks)*

4 From the study by Loftus and Palmer on eyewitness testimony, outline two ways in which the procedure was standardised. *(4 marks)*

5 **(a)** Identify the independent variable (IV) in the first experiment conducted by Loftus and Palmer on eyewitness testimony. *(2 marks)*
   (b) Outline how the independent variable was manipulated in this experiment. *(2 marks)*

6 In Experiment 2 of the Loftus and Palmer study on eyewitness testimony:
   (a) What was the result for the 'hit' and the control groups? *(2 marks)*
   (b) Give one reason why these participants saw broken glass. *(2 marks)*

7 In the study by Loftus and Palmer on eyewitness testimony, the participants were shown film clips of car accidents. Outline two differences between witnessing these film clips and witnessing a real accident. *(4 marks)*

8 **(a)** What was the effect of changing the verb on the critical question in Experiment 1 in the study by Loftus and Palmer on eyewitness testimony? *(2 marks)*

   (b) State one conclusion that can be drawn from the results of Experiment 1 in the study by Loftus and Palmer. *(2 marks)*

SECTION B

(a) State one of the hypotheses investigated in the study by Loftus and Palmer. *(2 marks)*

(b) Describe the sample used in the study by Loftus and Palmer, and suggest one weakness of using this sample. *(6 marks)*

(c) Outline two of the quantitative measures recorded in the study by Loftus and Palmer. *(6 marks)*

(d) With reference to the study by Loftus and Palmer, suggest one strength and one weakness of quantitative data. *(6 marks)*

(e) Outline the results of the study by Loftus and Palmer. *(8 marks)*

(f) Suggest one change to the procedure of the study by Loftus and Palmer, and explain how this might affect the results. *(8 marks)*

SECTION C

(a) Outline one assumption of the cognitive approach. *(2 marks)*

(b) Explain how the cognitive approach could explain the inaccuracy of eyewitness testimony. *(4 marks)*

(c) Describe one similarity and one difference between any studies that use the cognitive approach. *(6 marks)*

(d) Discuss strengths and weaknesses of the cognitive approach using examples from any studies that take this approach. *(12 marks)*

SOME ANSWERS AND COMMENTS

SECTION A 6(b) Give one reason why these participants saw broken glass. *(2 marks)*

Drake's answer:

They got confused and thought it was there because they were asked a question.

> **We say:** 1 mark.
> Drake, this is too vague and not very psychological. Bring in the concept of leading questions in the explanation, as just saying that they were asked a question does not really explain why they saw broken glass.

Chelsea's answer:

The participants were asked a leading question with the use of the verb 'smashed', or 'hit', which altered their memory, as they would imagine, and thus remember, a more violent accident, confabulating the broken glass.

> **We say:** 2 marks.
> Chelsea, you have used some good psychological terminology here. Your answer clearly explains the memory processes involved and makes clear what the reasons for seeing the broken glass were. Well written.

SECTION A 7 In the study by Loftus and Palmer on eyewitness testimony, the participants were shown film clips of car accidents. Outline two differences between witnessing these film clips and witnessing a real accident. *(4 marks)*

Conor's answer:

In real life you would be stressed and would not be waiting for it to happen. The weather might also be bad which would be distracting.

> **We say:** 2 marks.
> Conor, remember that this answer is worth four marks, so you do need to have more detail overall to get all these marks. Your first sentence is quite short but seems to have two separate points in it. If you expanded your sentence and explained why we would be stressed seeing an accident compared to a video, and explained that accidents are unexpected but video clips are not, then you would have a good answer. The weather is not relevant here!

Aoife's answer:

One difference between watching a real-life accident and a film is that real-life causes emotions such as fear, as well as an accompanying physiological response like adrenaline, which would have a strong effect on you and your recollection of events. This is not the case in a video.

Another difference is that you would not be expecting the accident to happen in real-life – it would be a surprise that you would not have been preparing yourself for. However, in the lab, you would be waiting for the accident to show on the video, so are less surprised.

> **We say:** 4 marks.
> Aoife, two well set out points here. Each is clear and detailed and outlines what the differences are. You mention both the real-life accident and the video clip to highlight how they differ, and you draw an explicit comparison, as requested in the question.

SECTION B (e) Outline the results of the study by Loftus and Palmer. (8 marks)

Monique's answer:

Participants were asked what speed the car was going when the accident happened that they saw on video. Different verbs were used and this made people guess at higher speeds. In the second experiment, people were asked about broken glass and more people said yes with 'smashed'. As a result, people have bad memories but this is not ecologically valid as it was in a lab and so the results are not good.

We say: 3 marks.
Monique, you have not fully focused on the results here and have a bit on the procedure and some evaluation as well. You should make some clear statements on what Loftus and Palmer found in each of the two parts of the study, i.e. you could say which of the verbs produced the fastest estimate. Do not be too general, as to get the eight marks you need to be specific and accurate and explain exactly what they found.

Jan's answer:

After watching the video of an accident, participants were placed in different groups, each with a different verb. When asked how fast the car was going, the speed estimates increased as the verbs became more violent. 'Smashed' had the highest estimate at 40.8mph. Contacted was the lowest, at 31.8mph. The difference was statistically significant. Memory can be altered by information after the event. In the second experiment, where only 'smashed' and 'hit' were used, and participants were asked if they saw any broken glass. More people said yes when 'smashed' was used compared to when 'hit' was used. A few people in the control group answered yes.

We say: 6 marks.
Jan, you have revised this study well and have some accurate facts on the results, and some fine detail, which is what you need for good marks. You illustrate the answer with some figures for Experiment 1. For Experiment 2, it would make an even better answer if you could add the numbers of people recalling glass in each condition. If asked for results, just give the findings and data, there is no need to interpret it and draw conclusions.

SECTION C (a) Outline one assumption of the cognitive approach. (2 marks)

Bryn's answer:

The cognitive approach looks at how we think about things and is to do with our minds.

We say: 0 marks.
Bryn, this is too general – you have been more descriptive and not addressed an actual assumption. You show general knowledge but it is not clear. If you said, 'the cognitive approach says we need to investigate thinking and our minds', that would get you a mark.

Alan's answer:

The cognitive approach in psychology suggests people are like computers and are constantly taking in information from around them and processing it like computers do when we input information to them and they are thinking.

We say: 1 mark.
Alan, you are on the right lines, but in stating an assumption for a perspective or approach you must really talk more about our actions or the things we do in terms of our behaviour in relation to the approach. Do try to include the word 'behaviour' in your answer, e.g. 'The cognitive approach states our behaviour is due to....' This would be one way to answer the question and would get the two marks if well written.

BARON-COHEN *et al.'s* STUDY OF ADVANCED THEORY OF MIND

Baron-Cohen, S., Joliffe, T., Mortimore, C. and Robertson, M. (1997) Another advanced test of theory of mind: evidence from very high functioning adults with autism or Asperger Syndrome. *Journal of Child Psychology & Psychiatry*, **38**, 813–22.

*Figure 1.5
Autism researcher
Simon Baron-Cohen*

CONTEXT

This study is concerned with the autistic spectrum. Autism is a life-long disorder usually diagnosed in childhood. A diagnosis of an autistic spectrum disorder requires that a person has difficulties in communication, relationships with other people and imagination. Children on the autistic spectrum struggle to understand other people's behaviour, and this in turn leads to difficulties in forming friendships and getting on with peers. Usually there is some degree of language delay, and because they lack imagination, they can fail to appreciate hazards and put themselves in dangerous situations.

Because individuals vary so much in their symptoms, it is usual now to refer to the 'autistic spectrum' rather than to 'autism'. Most people with autistic spectrum disorders are below average in intelligence, but this is not always the case. There are some people on the spectrum who have a small number of well-developed cognitive abilities, who are known as savants, and others with a range of well-developed abilities, who are known as 'high-functioning' individuals. This study is concerned with individuals on the spectrum who are said to be 'high functioning', and those with Asperger Syndrome, a particular autistic spectrum disorder in which language development is mildly or not at all affected, yet the individual is still impaired in their social development.

*Figure 1.6
Children on the autistic spectrum struggle with peer relations*

KEY IDEAS

Tourette's Syndrome is a condition that, like autism, is usually diagnosed in childhood, and that can cause severe disruption to education and peer relations. The main symptom is tics or involuntary movements. These can include vocal tics in which the patient involuntarily says socially inappropriate things.

THEORY OF MIND AND AUTISM

Among autism researchers there is some debate as to what exactly causes autism. Simon Baron-Cohen and colleagues have suggested that a problem in 'theory of mind' – i.e. the ability to perceive mental states in other people – underlies difficulties in communication and social development. Baron-Cohen points out that if we cannot read other people's minds, we cannot have meaningful interactions with them, and without such interaction we cannot expect to develop normal language or form friendships.

There is considerable evidence to suggest that people on the autistic spectrum struggle with theory of mind tasks. However, this has been challenged by other researchers who have found that high-functioning adults with autism and Asperger Syndrome can usually succeed in standard theory of mind tasks. Baron-Cohen and colleagues answered this by suggesting that the standard theory of mind tests are too easy for high-functioning adults, and that if a more difficult test for theory of mind could be devised, then they would still be able to demonstrate a deficit in theory of mind when compared with adults who have no clinical condition, and adults with a different developmental problem. This is the idea underlying the current study.

AIM

The aim of the study was to test whether high-functioning adults with autism and Asperger Syndrome would struggle with a new and more difficult test for theory of mind. This new test, known as the 'Eyes Task,' involves reading emotion from photographs of eyes. In order to see whether this difficult test for theory of mind was particularly hard for people on the autistic spectrum, their results were compared with those of matched groups with no clinical condition and with a different disorder, **Tourette's Syndrome**.

QUESTION SPOTLIGHT!

Make sure you can explain clearly the purpose of both the 'normal' and Tourette's conditions.

Figure 1.7
Examples of items from the Eyes Task
(from Baron-Cohen et al.'s original paper)

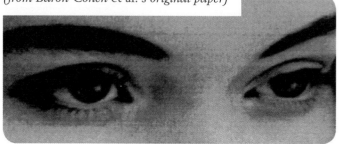

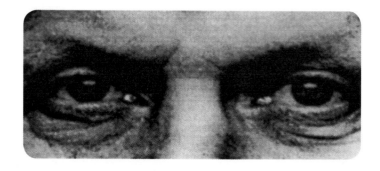

METHOD

Participants

The autism group consisted of 13 men and three women of normal intelligence and with a diagnosis of high-functioning autism or Asperger Syndrome. They were a volunteer sample recruited through their doctors and in response to an advert in the National Autistic Society's magazine. The control group was made up of 25 men and 25 women with no autism diagnosis. There was no test of IQ, but it was assumed that all were of normal intelligence. In addition, eight men and two women with Tourette's Syndrome took part in the study as a second control group. This was important because Tourette's has several key elements in common with autism. It exists in childhood and causes disruption to schooling and peer relations. Like autism, it is also believed to be associated with a biological problem in the frontal lobes of the brain. If theory of mind deficit is specifically a problem with autism, as opposed to being simply the result of a childhood disrupted by a psychological condition, the autism group would be expected to do worse than the Tourette's group on the Eyes Task.

Design and procedure

Participants were shown 25 black-and-white photographs of eyes for three seconds each, and asked to choose between two mental states represented by the photographs. Some of these mental states were basic emotions, such as 'sad or afraid'. Others were more complex, such as 'fantasising or noticing'. The list of choices is shown in Table 1.4.

Control task

In order to eliminate the possibility that the autism group simply had a visual problem that meant that they could not process the photographs, all participants were also asked to name the gender of the eyes.

Validation of the Eyes Task

It was believed that the Eyes Task actually measures theory of mind ability. However, as it was a new test it was important to check this idea. In order to do this, participants in the autism and Tourette's groups also took another quite difficult test, **Happe's Strange Stories.** If the Eyes Task really measures theory of mind ability, then those who struggle with it should also score less well in the Strange Stories test.

IN BRIEF !

Aim: To test whether high-functioning adults with autistic spectrum disorders struggle to identify emotions from photographs of eyes (the Eyes Task).

Method: 16 adult volunteers with an autistic spectrum disorder were shown 25 photographs of pairs of eyes, and were asked to identify the emotions in them. Control groups of 50 adults with no diagnosis, and 10 adults with Tourette's, carried out the same task.

Results: The autism group did significantly worse than the control groups in identifying the emotions.

Conclusion: Even high-functioning adults with autism struggle to recognise mental states in others.

KEY IDEAS

Happe's Strange Stories is a fairly advanced test for theory of mind, aimed at older children. It involves asking children questions about the emotions and intentions of characters in unfamiliar stories.

WEB WATCH @

You can download the Eyes Task from www.autismresearchcentre. com (click on 'Tests'), or run a version online at http://glennrow.net (click on 'Male-female test').

TABLE 1.4 THE 25 PAIRS OF CHOICES IN THE EYE TASK

No.	Target team	Foil	No.	Target team	Foil
1	Concerned	Unconcerned	14	Cautious about something over there	Relaxed about something over there
2	Noticing you	Ignoring you	15	Noticing someone else	Noticing you
3	Attraction	Repulsion	16	Calm	Anxious
4	Relaxed	Worried	17	Dominant	Submissive
5	Serious message	Playful message	18	Fantasising	Noticing
6	Interested	Disinterested	19	Observing	Daydreaming
7	Friendly	Hostile	20	Desire for you	Desire for someone else
8	Sad reflection	Happy reflection	21	Ignoring you	Noticing you
9	Sad thought	Happy thought	22	Nervous about you	Interested in you
10	Certain	Uncertain	23	Flirtatious	Disinterested
11	Far away focus	Near focus	24	Sympathetic	Unsympathetic
12	Reflective	Unreflective	25	Decisive	Indecisive
13	Reflective	Unreflective			

TABLE 1.5 SCORES IN THE EYES TASK

Condition	Mean score out of 25	Range of scores
Autism	16.3	13–23
None	20.3	16–25
Tourette's	20.4	16–25

Results

On the control tasks, all groups performed normally. However, in the Eyes Task, the autism group did significantly worse than the two control groups. This is shown in Table 1.5. Although 16.3 out of 25 might appear to be a reasonable score, bear in mind that the participants had a 50% chance of guessing each emotion correctly. A result of 16.3 out of 25 is barely above what we would expect from chance.

No participants in the Tourette's group were incorrect in any of their Strange Stories responses, but the autism group struggled. The fact that the same participants struggled with the Eyes Task and the Strange Stories is evidence for the validity of the Eyes Task.

Conclusions

There are two main conclusions that can be drawn from the study.

1 Even high-functioning adults with autism, including those with Asperger Syndrome, have a significant problem with their theory of mind. In other words, they find it hard to read mental states in other people. This supports the idea that theory of mind deficit is central to understanding autism, and might even directly cause its main symptoms.

2 The Eyes Task is a valid test of theory of mind suitable for high-functioning adults with autism.

QUESTION SPOTLIGHT!

If you offer an answer evaluating the research method for this study, make sure your answer makes reference to the study itself. A generic answer will gain limited credit.

STUDY 2

BARON-COHEN *et al.'s* STUDY OF ADVANCED THEORY OF MIND

SUMMARY

AIM

To test whether a new and more difficult test for theory of mind would be hard for high-functioning adults with autism.

METHOD

A group of high-functioning adults with autism were compared on the Eyes Task with a group of adults with no diagnosis and a group with Tourette's Syndrome. The Eyes Task is a new and advanced test for theory of mind that involves recognising the emotion on faces where just the eyes are visible.

RESULTS

The autism group did significantly worse than the two control groups on the Eyes Task.

CONCLUSIONS

When a difficult test for theory of mind is used, even high-functioning adults with autism struggle.

EVALUATION

Studies such as this have to meet very high ethical standards because of the use of vulnerable adults as participants. The participants were volunteers, they were not deceived, and they experienced no distress beyond that which they could expect in their daily lives. However, there are some interesting methodological issues.

THE SAMPLE AND SAMPLING METHOD

The sample of adults on the autistic spectrum was quite small, at 16, and only three of these were female. This small sample size makes it hard to assume that this was a representative group of high-functioning adults with autism. Generalisability is therefore a problem. This is made worse by the fact that they were a volunteer sample, generally one of the less representative sampling methods. The sample of Tourette's participants was even smaller, at 10. This means that the sample and sampling method are weaknesses of the study.

THE RESEARCH METHOD

The study was carried out in a laboratory, so environmental conditions were well controlled, which is a strength. On the other hand, the ecological validity is poor because the situation was so different from an everyday real-life social situation and because the experience of looking at the Eyes Task is so different to that of judging emotion in faces in real life. A further problem is that this is a quasi-experiment, not a true experiment, because three naturally occurring groups were being compared. This means that the groups might not have been well-matched for all the relevant variables. This is made worse by the fact that the control group without a diagnosis were not rigorously tested to make sure they were comparable with the autism and Tourette's groups.

VALIDITY OF THE EYES TASK

This can also be seen as a weakness of the study. The Eyes Task is carried out under controlled conditions, and the experience of judging emotion by looking at an isolated pair of eyes is very different from the real-life experience of judging emotions in whole moving faces with additional information such as body language and speech. On the other hand, the researchers did include a test for validity when they gave participants the Strange Stories task, and this supported the validity of the Eyes Task. Including such a test of validity is a strength of the study.

QUALITATIVE AND QUANTITATIVE DATA

The data gathered in this study were quantitative. This is both a strength and a weakness. On the plus side, the numbers allow easy comparison of the conditions, clearly showing that theory of mind is worse in the autism group. On the other hand, there was no opportunity for participants to comment on what they experienced when they looked at the eyes, or on what they found difficult about the task. Such qualitative data might have added to the completeness of the findings.

PRACTICAL APPLICATIONS

If we accept that this study, in spite of its methodological limitations, demonstrates that even high-functioning adults with autism have problems when it comes to reading emotions in faces, then this could open up practical ways forward in helping high-functioning people with autism manage their condition. For example, it might be possible to teach people on the spectrum to make use of different visual cues to judge emotion, or to teach those interacting with people on the spectrum to give very clear visual and verbal cues to signal what they are feeling.

EXAM FOCUS

We now show you some of the sorts of questions that could be asked about the Baron-Cohen *et al.* study in your exam. We will then show you some examples of the sorts of answers we believe might be successful and less successful, and point out some classic traps to avoid.

SECTION A

1 From Baron-Cohen *et al.*'s study on autism in adults:
   (a) Identify the two control groups used. *(2 marks)*
   (b) Explain why one of these groups was used. *(2 marks)*

2 From the study by Baron-Cohen *et al.* on autism in adults, describe how two of the groups of participants were selected. *(4 marks)*

3 In the Baron-Cohen *et al.* study on autism in adults:
   (a) Identify one of the word pairs in the Eyes Task. *(2 marks)*
   (b) Outline one finding from the Eyes Task. *(2 marks)*

4 In the study by Baron-Cohen *et al.*, the autistic and Asperger Syndrome participants were found to be unimpaired on two control tasks. Describe these two control tasks. *(4 marks)*

5 From the study by Baron-Cohen *et al.* on autism in adults:
   (a) Identify one difference between the performance of the adults with autism and the adults with Tourette's Syndrome. *(2 marks)*
   (b) Outline what this study tells us about advanced theory of mind. *(2 marks)*

6 The study by Baron-Cohen *et al.* on autism involved three groups of participants. Describe two of these groups. *(4 marks)*

7 From the study by Baron-Cohen *et al.* on autism:
   (a) Briefly describes the Eyes Task. *(2 marks)*
   (b) Describe how the validity of this task was checked. *(2 marks)*

8 **(a)** Describe what type of data was gathered in Baron-Cohen *et al.*'s study on autism in adults. *(2 marks)*
   (b) Give one advantage of this type of data. *(2 marks)*

SECTION B

(a) Briefly outline the previous research or event that was the stimulus for the study by Baron-Cohen *et al.* *(2 marks)*

(b) Describe how the sample in the study by Baron-Cohen *et al.* was selected, and suggest one advantage of using this sample. *(6 marks)*

(c) Explain why the study by Baron-Cohen *et al.* can be considered a laboratory experiment. *(6 marks)*

(d) Give one advantage and one disadvantage of conducting the study by Baron-Cohen *et al.* in a laboratory. *(6 marks)*

(e) Suggest how the study by Baron-Cohen *et al.* can be improved. *(8 marks)*

(f) Outline the implications of the improvements you have suggested for the study by Baron-Cohen *et al.* *(8 marks)*

SECTION C

(a) Outline one assumption of the cognitive approach. *(2 marks)*

(b) Describe how the cognitive approach could explain the lack of a theory of mind in autism. *(4 marks)*

(c) Describe one similarity and one difference between any studies that take the cognitive approach. *(6 marks)*

(d) Discuss strengths and weaknesses of the cognitive approach, using examples from any studies that take this approach. *(12 marks)*

SOME ANSWERS AND COMMENTS

SECTION A 1 (b) Explain why one of these groups was used. (2 marks)

Jane's answer:

To compare to people with another disorder.

We say: 0 marks.
Jane, this answer is really brief. The groups were used as a comparison, but you need to actually identify one of the groups and specifically say why it was used.

Alan's answer:

The Tourette's Syndrome group were used to compare autism to another mental disorder, to see if a lack of theory of mind is a problem only in autism, or in lots of disorders.

We say: 2 marks.
Well done, Alan, for naming one group. You have also identified a reason for the comparison and explained this clearly.

SECTION A 5 (a) Identify one difference between the performance of the adults with autism and the adults with Tourette's Syndrome. (2 marks)

Mark's answer:

The Tourette's group scored better on the eyes task.

We say: 1 mark.
Mark, you have only said what one of the groups did, so this is not actually a clear comparison. Say who they actually did better than, or the answer is incomplete.

Stacey's answer:

The Tourette's Syndrome group did better and guessed more emotions correctly in the eyes task than the autism group. This suggests that they are more able to recognise emotions than the autistic group.

We say: 2 marks.
Stacey, you have written a clear comparison that mentions both the groups in the question, and you have explained what the results mean – this clearly answers the question.

SECTION B (d) Give one advantage and one disadvantage of conducting the study by Baron-Cohen et al. in a laboratory. (6 marks)

Brian's answer:

In the lab, more controls can be used, so you can control what participants do in your study so nothing bad happens and you get results. A negative is that it is less useful as it is not in a real-life setting, it's in your lab, meaning that the task is not like you get in real life.

We say: 3 marks.
Brian, this is a fairly basic answer. Try to use some more psychological terminology here to show the examiner what you know. You have not mentioned the study, so have no context, and the question does ask you to look at using a laboratory in your chosen study. Explain your points in a bit more detail.

Amir's answer:

An advantage of doing this experiment in a laboratory is that strict controls can be administered so that you can be sure of what you are testing. In this study, autistic adults, Tourette's adults and adults with no mental disorder were asked to identify emotions from pictures of eyes, with no distractions. Doing this test in a lab setting allowed the researchers to control all confounding variables so that the true abilities of the individuals could show, so firm conclusions could be drawn.

A disadvantage of conducting a laboratory study is the lack of ecological validity. In this experiment, participants were asked to identify emotions from pictures of just eyes. This is not how people read emotions in real life, as there are other cues, e.g. social setting and body language. This means that the test did not fully reflect the real-life task of identifying emotions.

We say: 6 marks.
Amir, you have clearly explained and commented on an advantage and a disadvantage using psychological terminology. You have also used examples to back up your points. Excellent answer!

SECTION C (b) Describe how the cognitive approach could explain the lack of a theory of mind in autism. *(4 marks)*

Aaron's answer:

Baron-Cohen says that people lack a theory of mind as they cannot really read what other people feel by looking at their eyes. This is a problem for them in their daily lives.

We say: 1 mark.
Aaron, you have looked at a study here when the question is asking you about behaviour more generally. You can use the study to help you, and to illustrate your answer, but you need to look at what features of the cognitive approach might explain the behaviour. To be more focused on the question, you could talk about information-processing and input and output with regard to emotions and feelings.

Eshe's answer:

It can explain the lack of a theory of mind as the cognitive approach looks at the mind like a computer. It sees people as taking in information about other people from around them, like data-inputting in a computer. If the processing has problems, then this causes problems for the person, and, in autism, information about others' feelings might not be processed clearly.

We say: 3 marks.
Eshe, you have the right idea here, and have picked out some features of the cognitive approach itself to help explain theory of mind. There is some detail in your answer. To get four marks you could just have made your link from the approach to theory of mind a bit clearer, but it is quite a good attempt.

SAVAGE-RUMBAUGH *et al.'s* STUDY OF CHIMP LANGUAGE

 KEY IDEAS

Sign language is a true language, it isn't just a way to represent an existing spoken language manually, or merely a set of simple physical movements related to their meanings. Like any other language, it is a symbolic representation of ideas that can be linked together to add to the meaning of an utterance, using its own set of rules.

Savage-Rumbaugh, S., McDonald, K., Sevcik, R.A., Hopkins, W.D. and Rubert, E. (1986) Spontaneous Symbol Acquisition and Communicative Use by Pygmy Chimpanzees *(Pan paniscus)*. *Journal of Experimental Psychology: General*, **115**(3), 211–35.

CONTEXT

Naming versus knowing: what indicates a language has been learned?

Prior to this study, the acquisition of language by animals had been studied in a range of ways. Chimpanzees had been shown to have some capacity to learn languages based on American Sign Language (ASL), symbols, or plastic tokens, using rewards. Furthermore, such chimps

WEB WATCH @

You can see footage of the pygmy chimp Kanzi on YouTube, for example:

www.youtube.com/watch?v=wRM7vTrIlis

www.youtube.com/watch?v=2Dhc2zePJFE

www.youtube.com/watch?v=KxmvRpnVXJQ

Figure 1.8
Austin and Sherman, two common chimps whose test results were used for comparison with those of the pygmy chimps

demonstrated communication skills including requesting, labelling and comprehending, and, without further training, their language extended from associative references about the present to include:

- referential symbol usage, and
- communicating about what they intended to do (i.e. in the future).

In these respects, the acquisition of language by apes resembles that of young children. However, some aspects of the language acquisition of apes differ from that of children, particularly in the need for repeated exposure and reinforcement to learn associations between symbols and their meaning.

Children make the transition between **associative** and **referential** use spontaneously and quickly (Lock, 1980). If a child asks for a teddy, and the mother holds up a duck and says 'what's this?' the child can answer, because they do not become confused between the symbol (the words 'teddy' and 'duck') and their respective referents. In contrast, Savage-Rumbaugh (1986) reports that two common chimps – Sherman and Austin – could request things they were unable to name, and name things they were unable to request. They required reinforced training to make the cognitive step to distinguish between naming and requesting.

Following their training in referential symbol use and retrieving unseen objects, Sherman and Austin began to show spontaneous representational symbol use. This then appeared to follow the same pattern as is observed in children:

- They began to initiate word games by selecting objects and offering the correct symbol without prompting.
- They generalised symbol usage beyond the original context. For example, Austin referred to a chimp screaming outside with the symbol 'scare', which had been learned through a game involving pretend 'scaring', using a mask over the face.
- Like Kanzi, they acquired some symbols without explicit training.
- They assigned new symbols to foods and tools they had not encountered before.
- They could make categorical judgements based on symbolic information only. For example, the 'apple' symbol would be placed in the 'fruit' category, even when no actual apples were present.

KEY IDEAS

Apes and young children are both capable of **associative naming**. This is the ability to link, or associate, certain symbols (e.g. sounds or signs) with specific objects. In contrast, **referential naming** is the ability to use these symbols to refer to those objects or activities. Although children rapidly acquire this language skill, it is unclear whether apes are capable of developing such understanding.

QUESTION SPOTLIGHT!

Savage-Rumbaugh reports that Fouts *et al.* (1976) taught Ally the chimpanzee 10 different behaviours, which were, after training, consistently produced in response to 10 different spoken English phrases. *Can you explain how is this different from the method used by Savage-Rumbaugh, and why this difference is important?*

IN BRIEF !

Aim: To investigate the capacity of pygmy chimpanzees to learn language without being trained.

Method: Two pygmy chimps – Kanzi and Mulika – were exposed to a language environment (using symbols) without specific training or reinforcement. Their progress was compared to that of previously trained common chimpanzees. Spontaneous, behaviourally verified vocabulary development was tracked, and controlled tests of spoken English comprehension and lexigram use were conducted.

Results: The pygmy chimps learned to use symbols to communicate with humans and demonstrated more complex language skills than common chimps. They developed large vocabularies, showing the ability to produce and comprehend symbols and to combine them, as well as to respond to equivalent spoken words. They showed patterns of development similar to those of children, such as imitation.

Conclusion: Pygmy chimps (like children) acquire symbol use spontaneously, develop reception first, and use new words accurately, but common chimps do not. Pygmy chimps can also use word combinations to express interactions between individuals other than themselves, and to add rather than repeat information. Both species use symbols referentially and generalise their meanings, but only pygmy chimps can comprehend spoken English and discriminate between specific referents within narrow categories.

KEY IDEAS

Of the four species of great ape, the **pygmy chimpanzee (bonobo)** uses the most eye contact, gestures and vocalisations. They also have closer male–female bonds, more male infant care and food-sharing between adults, and appear to have greater cognitive abilities than common chimpanzees. These features suggest that they are the most likely species to be able to acquire language.

Listen and learn: difference in language learning between children and apes

Apes lack the vocal apparatus to produce spoken language, and there is little evidence to suggest that apes can understand spoken language. One reason for this might be that the ability of a species to analyse sounds is related to its capacity to produce those sounds. Because chimps cannot produce human speech, the limits to their understanding are unsurprising.

The key difference, therefore, is that children learn to extract words from the speech they hear in order to comprehend their meaning, and they learn to reproduce those words in context, without reinforcement. This has not been observed in apes. However, even though apes are unable to produce spoken language, evidence of spontaneous development of comprehension would indicate a level of cognitive equivalence with human language ability.

AIM

The aim of the study was to compare acquisition of language by **pygmy chimps** in relation to common chimps, and in the absence of formal teaching.

METHOD

Design

This study reports findings relating to four animals. Each animal is the feature of a detailed case study. The data from each study are used in a comparison between two chimpanzee species (*Pan paniscus* and *Pan troglodytes*). They were compared on various measures of the dependant variable of language acquisition, including vocabulary development and comprehension of spoken language. The study involved ongoing inclusion of the pygmy chimps into human daily living, offering exposure to symbol use and human speech. In addition, formal, controlled systematic testing of language acquisition was employed.

Participants

The primary focus was on Kanzi, a male pygmy chimp (*Pan paniscus*). It was noticed that Kanzi had begun to spontaneously acquire symbol use at two-and-a-half years of age, and he was studied in detail over the subsequent 17 months. Kanzi was four years old on completion of the study. His younger half-sister, Mulika, began using symbols at 11 months and was also studied. Both of these animals were born in captivity and were mothered by Matata, who had also been a participant in language-learning studies. Previous findings relating to Sherman and Austin, two common chimps (*Pan troglodytes*), are reported for comparison, as they used the same symbol-based language system. Sherman and Austin had been actively taught to use the language over an eight-year period.

Procedure

Kanzi and Mulika were raised at the Language Research Center, an American facility dedicated to studying primate language. Within the centre, Kanzi and Mulika were exposed to humans using spoken English, lexigrams, and some American Sign Language (ASL). When the lexigrams were used, meanings were repeated clearly using speech. Although the animals had a large feeding area that they roamed by day with their human companions, they were also given extensive access to human company and activities, such as cooking, cleaning and watching television. The young chimps had daily access to their mother, Matata (e.g. for play and affection), although they chose to spend more time in human company. In his early life (6–30 months, after which Matata was removed for breeding), Kanzi had access to his mother during her language training. This training was initially informal but later systematic. At first, Kanzi was discouraged from staying with her (as he distracted her), and he

Figure 1.9
Sue Savage-Rumbaugh with Kanzi's son, Teco, who is also learning to communicate and who might one day surpass his father, experts believe

Figure 1.10
Kanzi's half-sister, Mulika

KEY IDEAS

All four apes communicated using a
lexigram board, a visual symbol system
consisting of a board with arbitrary
pictorial images that represent words.
The main boards had symbols that lit up
when touched. A voice synthesiser was
added to Kanzi's board to generate the
corresponding spoken word when each
symbol was touched. Battery-powered
ones were not sufficiently robust for use
in the field, so simple laminated 'pointing
boards' were used that could be carried
easily. Although Kanzi, Mulika and humans
could all use these, the common chimps
were unable to do so because their
pointing was too inaccurate to tell which
symbol they had chosen.

seemed disinterested in requesting food. However, by the age of 18
months he had begun to sporadically light keys on the **lexigram board**,
and he would run to the vending machine, suggesting that he had learned
an association between touching symbols and the appearance
of food. He did not appear to associate specific symbols with specific foods,
although at the end of this period he did use the symbol for 'chase',
or his own spontaneous hand-clapping gesture, to initiate chasing.
Mulika did not observe Matata's language training, but could observe
Kanzi's language use.

Similarities between pygmy and common chimp treatment

There were some key similarities in the treatment of the pygmy and
common chimps. These included:

*   Use of a visual version of English, produced using symbol-based
    lexigrams on a board
*   Extent of exposure to accompanying human use of speech and
    informal gestures
*   Use of this system throughout the day in a range of contexts
*   Exposure to many of the same teachers
*   Opportunities to interact with and observe people
*   Exposure to photographs, novel objects, opportunities to watch
    television, discipline, and types of formal testing
*   Indoor free-time activities, such as playing games.

Differences between pygmy and common chimp treatment

There were also differences in the way pygmy and common chimps were
treated. These are listed in Table 1.6.

Figure 1.11
The chimps could select their play
activities, such as watching videos

TABLE 1.6 DIFFERENCES BETWEEN PYGMY AND COMMON CHIMP TREATMENT

Feature	Sherman and Austin	Kanzi and Mulika
Setting for introduction to lexigrams	One year's training without the opportunity to observe	Kanzi – observation of Matata's training Mulika – observation of Kanzi and other lexigram users
Use of food rewards	Yes	No
Opportunities for observing lexigram use	Following first year of training	From outset of project
Speech synthesiser	Not added to lexigram board as no indication of understanding of spoken words	Added to Kanzi's electronic lexigram board
Locations for lexigram use	Only in the laboratory	Anywhere

Chimp environments

Most of the pygmy chimps' daytime hours in warm weather were spent outdoors, moving between 17 feeding stations within a 55-acre forested area. They did this accompanied by researchers, and carrying laminated pointing boards of lexigrams. Initially, they also carried photographs. No food was available in the laboratory, but the chimps could select a desired food or location by pointing to a photo or a symbol.

Indoors, the pygmy chimps were asked to assist with activities, such as changing bed sheets, doing laundry and preparing food. They frequently attempted to engage others in games, such as hide, chase, grab or tickle. They also spontaneously helped in activities such as wiping up spills, washing dishes, spraying the hose, or scrubbing the floor. Play activities for the chimps included using clay, making bubbles, and watching video tapes ('subtitled' with lexigram symbols) of familiar people doing interesting things.

Data collection

A complete record of all keyboard utterances was maintained for Kanzi from 30 to 47 months, and for Mulika from 11 to 21 months. This was done electronically by the keyboards when indoors, and by hand when using the pointing-boards outside. Each utterance was scored in terms of :

- Accuracy:
  - Correct
  - Incorrect
- Context:
  - Spontaneous (without a prompt)
  - Imitated (containing any part of a companion's prior utterance)
  - Structured (e.g. by a question, request or being shown an object).

QUESTION SPOTLIGHT!

Could you classify the following examples of utterances:
- A query from Kanzi about something he had seen in the wood
- A response by Mulika to the question 'Which do you want?'

STRETCH & CHALLENGE ◎

Look through the appendix of Savage-Rumbaugh's original article. Find and copy out one example of each of the context types that were used to classify Kanzi's utterances, i.e. spontaneous, imitated and structured. If you can, show your examples to a partner without giving them the contexts. Can they identify which is which?

The inclusion of a word in a chimp's vocabulary was operationalised by the following criteria:

- Context-appropriate (i.e. it made sense in that situation)
- Naturally occurring situations
- Spontaneously produced (not prompted) on 9 out of 10 occasions (but not necessarily on consecutive days)
- Verified by behavioural concordance (i.e. that the chimp responded to the subsequent situation in a way that indicated the word had been used correctly – for example, if Kanzi asked to go to the treehouse, the word 'treehouse' would be added to his vocabulary only if he then led the experimenter there)
- Behavioural concordance was achieved on 9 out of 10 occasions (in addition to the spontaneous 9 out of 10)
- Behavioural concordance was not inevitable (i.e. it had to be possible for the chimp to give an incorrect response – for example, if Kanzi asked for bananas from the backpack and it contained only bananas, the utterance would not be scored)
- Words for which behavioural correspondence fell below the 0.9 criterion were removed from the individual's vocabulary.

To ensure that the recording of vocabulary items was reliable, 4.5 hours of video tape, which had been scored by a real-time coder, was watched separately by two other observers. (The real-time coder was unaware that the tape would be used in this way.) Their scoring identified 37 utterances by Kanzi, including all those originally scored. The original coder and two new observers achieved 100% agreement on which symbols Kanzi used and whether they were in a correct context. There was one disagreement between the new observers about whether an utterance was spontaneous or structured, and nine utterances were identified by the new observers that were not originally identified in the real-time observation. This was probably because the flow of social interaction is too rapid for every utterance to be acknowledged. All nine of these utterances were correct, and eight were spontaneous.

Informal testing employed the words the chimps already knew. This included situations such as asking an individual chimp to pick up items one-by-one by name, or asking which keys they were playing with if they were spontaneously engaged with the keyboard. These situations did not use rewards and, if errors were made, the chimps were corrected.

Formal testing was also conducted, on Kanzi aged 46 to 47 months, and Mulika aged 18 to 21 months. There were four tests (see Table 1.7), two of which were also conducted on Austin and Sherman (with a somewhat different selection of symbols). The common chimps, unlike Kanzi and Mulika, were given food rewards during testing, as they appeared to anticipate receiving the item they were asked to label in the test, and became confused if they did not then receive it.

Controls ensured that the chimps' test responses were valid. These controls included:

- *Order and presentation of stimuli.* This was varied to avoid unintentional cuing of responses by context. The same stimulus was never presented consecutively on two trials, and was only repeated in a different test context within the same set of trials.
- *Number of alternatives.* Three or four choices were given for possible responses on each trial. The correct choice was always present.
- *Photographs of target items.* These were varied so that each item (e.g. food type) appeared slightly differently in different photographs.
- *Response items could not be seen by the experimenter.* The response choices were hidden behind a blind so that they could be seen by the chimp but not the researcher conducting the test, to avoid unintentional cuing of responses by gestures such as glances.
- *Voice synthesiser.* One of the four tests conducted on Kanzi used a voice synthesiser to ensure that he was responding to spoken words rather than to human intonation.

Figure 1.12
Part of Kanzi's lexigram

QUESTION SPOTLIGHT!

What does the accuracy and spontaneity of Kanzi's utterances in the reliability check indicate about validity? Is it likely that the observers were over-estimating the chimp's accurate use of language?

TABLE 1.7 FORMAL TESTING OF LANGUAGE COMPREHENSION BY PYGMY AND COMMON CHIMPS

Test of matching:	Procedure	Scoring
photograph to lexigram	Chimp shown a photograph and given three lexigrams.	The experimenter dropped the blind to check whether the chimp had pointed to the correct lexigram.
spoken English to photograph	Chimp heard an experimenter speak an English word in context, then repeat it, then given three photographs.	The experimenter dropped the blind to check whether the chimp had pointed to the correct photograph.
spoken English to lexigram	Chimp heard an experimenter speak an English word in context, then repeat it, then given three lexigrams (Kanzi and Mulika only).	The experimenter dropped the blind to check whether the chimp had pointed to the correct lexigram.
synthesised speech to lexigram	Chimp heard a synthesised voice rather than actual speech, then given three lexigrams (Kanzi only).	The experimenter dropped the blind to check whether the chimp had pointed to the correct lexigram.

WEB WATCH @

To learn more about language use in chimps, try the following sites:
http://panbloglodytes.wordpress.com (a chimp blog)
www.facebook.com/cwuchci (Chimpanzee and Human Communication Institute Facebook page)
www.friendsofwashoe.org/visit/chimpcams.html (Washoe webcams)
http://kanzi.bvu.edu (videos of several language-learning apes)

RESULTS

Quantitative and qualitative data were gathered and are presented in comparison to equivalent data from common chimps.

Observational data

Kanzi and Mulika both began to use gestures spontaneously, for example to obtain help. They often vocalised to draw attention from human companions. The gestures were iconic, i.e. directly representing the request (such as twisting movements to gain help opening a jar, or hitting motions to gain help opening a nut). This use of iconic gestures began between 6 and 16 months of age, whereas Sherman and Austin did not use them until 24 to 48 months and they were not accompanied by vocalisation. Furthermore, the pygmy chimps' gestures were more informative. For example, if Mulika wanted a balloon blown up, she would put it in a person's hand, point to their mouth, and push the hand holding the balloon towards their mouth.

Spontaneous keyboard use

After Matata was removed, Kanzi began to light symbols on the keyboard more often. It had been assumed that his use was not referential, as he had not actively 'searched' the board for specific keys previously. However, responses from the researchers were based on an interpretation of his actions as if his utterances were intentional. Kanzi quickly started to search for keys deliberately, and these appeared to be referential. For example, if he used the 'apple' key and was offered three fruits (e.g. banana, apple and orange), he would select an apple and ignore the others. If asked in English to name the other foods by pointing to the correct key, he could do this, even though didn't want to eat the foods. His use of keys was not always for requests. For example, he would touch the 'apple' and 'chase' symbols, then run around with the apple.

Mulika began using the keyboard earlier than Kanzi (at 12 months), and for the first two months did so differently, using one symbol ('milk') in a generalised way. This suggested that she understood that the keyboard was for communication (but not the one-to-one correspondence between symbols and their meaning). 'Milk' was used, for example, to ask to be picked up, for attention, and to go to different places, as well as for milk and other foods. Because she could obtain what she wanted without using the keyboard – e.g. by pointing – it is unlikely that she was using the keyboard just to make things happen. Furthermore, she would imitate the use of other keys, but her spontaneous use was limited to 'milk', and this was the case regardless of the keyboard being used or the location of the key.

After this two-month period, Mulika expanded her use of lexigrams to include other symbols, such as 'surprise', 'Matata', 'peanut', 'hotdog', 'coke', 'mushroom', 'melon', 'cherry', 'banana', 'jelly', 'go' and 'blueberry'. These were all used for specific and appropriate referents, and her use of 'milk' also became specific unless she was uncertain, when she would revert to selecting the 'milk' lexigram before making her request clear.

Kanzi and Mulika, in common with children, often used new symbols in an associative way before demonstrating a referential understanding. For example, Kanzi was introduced to the 'strawberry' symbol in the context of eating mushrooms on the 'mushroom trail'. He imitated the use of the symbol immediately, followed his human companions to the strawberry site, and ate the new fruit readily. Following this, he used the 'strawberry' symbol only when on the mushroom trail, then later began to use the symbol to request that they eat at the strawberry site. During this initial stage of symbol acquisition, his usage was limited to a particular routine. Finally, he moved on to an independent comprehension of the symbol and its meaning that was not context-driven. At this stage, he could also respond to the spoken word 'strawberry'. Savage-Rumbaugh *et al.* suggest that this happens because, with increasingly diverse contexts for symbol use, the only thing they have in common is the meaning of the symbol, so it is possible to extract the common element – the meaning of the symbol – as a referent.

Spontaneous development of symbol use was not seen in Sherman or Austin. Furthermore, even after an association was taught between a symbol and its referent, the common chimps did not go on to acquire the distinction between naming and requesting, as Kanzi and Mulika did without further formal training. Receptive understanding in Kanzi and Mulika typically appeared before their production, unlike Sherman and Austin, who needed to be taught to respond to the requests of others (reception) after they had been taught the association between a symbol and its meaning. Finally, like children, Kanzi and Mulika tended to produce the words accurately from their first use, because they had acquired the meaning of them already. Sherman and Austin, in contrast, tended to use new words inaccurately at first, or ceased to use them, before they became an established part of their vocabulary.

Vocabulary development

The data in Figure 1.13 suggest that Kanzi's **receptive use** (comprehension) was acquired more quickly than his **productive use** of symbols. This pattern is the same as is typically seen in children and was true for 63% of Kanzi's vocabulary – i.e. not all of it. As receptive use

KEY IDEAS

Lock (1980) suggests that children's language learning progresses because adults treat their utterances as if they are intentional, even before they actually have meaning. This **guided reinvention** serves to help the child to understand the communicative purpose of language. The same strategy was employed by all staff working with Kanzi, Mulika, Sherman and Austin.

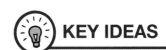

KEY IDEAS

There are two criteria of usage that new symbols must reach. **Productive use** is demonstrated when the chimp can use symbols in the appropriate way. **Receptive use** is shown when the chimp demonstrates an understanding of the use of the symbol (or word) by others.

was not tested as often as productive use, Kanzi's receptive use could have been underestimated. This is likely because in formal tests Mulika's receptive ability far exceeded her production. It is clear that Kanzi did understand English words he did not use himself, so his receptive vocabulary could well have developed well in advance of his production. This is illustrated in the Appendix of Savage-Rumbaugh *et al.*'s paper. In one example, Kanzi was told by Bill following a request to travel outside ('go peaches') that they would do so 'later', using the English word and symbol. This Kanzi appeared to understand because he did not repeat the request, yet 'later' was not a symbol that he himself used.

Mulika initially engaged in less spontaneous and more imitative symbol use (the reverse of the pattern shown by Kanzi in testing) and she understood more symbols than she used for many months. There are two possible explanations for these differences:

*   Kanzi's symbol use appeared later than Mulika's.
*   In Kanzi's early exposure to the keyboard there were only eight symbols, the number grew as his vocabulary needed to expand. Mulika was presented with a much harder task: 256 symbols from the start.

Symbol combination

Kanzi began combining symbols within a month of his first spontaneous symbol use. Although combinations represented only 6% of Kanzi's utterances during the 17-month period (i.e. they were much less common than single words), he made 2540 non-imitative combinations (plus another 265 that were prompted or partially imitated). All except ten of the non-imitative combinations were understood by his human companions, and 764 of them were produced only once (i.e. they were unique).

Some of Kanzi's two-word utterances were just combinations of two distinct things he wanted, for example, 'hotdog coke'. However, sometimes he gestured that he wanted the two things mixed together, suggesting that the two-word utterance could have had more meaning.

In 36% of his three-word combination, Kanzi made reference to other individuals. For example, he might use the keyboard to express 'chase grab' then take one person's hand and push it towards another. He would sometimes reverse such roles, requesting the 'chased' to become the 'chaser'. This development is interesting because, until this point, all keyboard requests (e.g. for food or tickles) would have indicated Kanzi as the recipient. However, in the absence of any syntax in lexigram use, these meanings had to be indicated gesturally. Tables 1.8 and 1.9 present comparisons of word combinations used by Kanzi and by Nim, a common chimp who was taught ASL, and who learned to combine signs (Terrace, 1979). Like Nim, Sherman

QUESTION SPOTLIGHT!

Look at the graphs in Figures 1.13 and 1.14, showing the acquisition of single words by Kanzi and Mulika. From the difference in shape, Savage Rumbaugh concludes that Kanzi must have acquired many things that had not been identified prior to his separation from his mother.
What aspect of the graph led her to this conclusion?
She also offers an alternative explanation: that Mulika wasn't asked to demonstrate behavioural concordance as often as Kanzi had been. *How could this have led to an underestimation of Mulika's progress?*

Figure 1.13
Kanzi's receptive and productive vocabularies

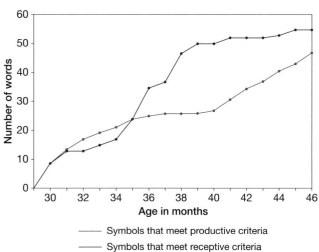

Figure 1.14
Mulika's productive vocabulary

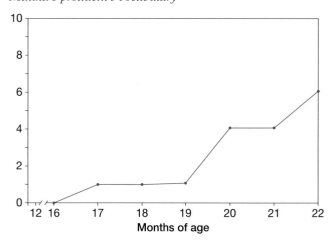

Source: Savage-Rumbaugh et al. (1986), Fig. 3, p. 222.

Source: Savage-Rumbaugh et al. (1986), Fig. 2, p. 222.

and Austin never used combinations that requested an interaction between two individuals that did not include themselves. Savage-Rumbaugh *et al.* speculate that this ability to conceptualise and initiate complex interactions between others through the use of symbols might be a precursor to, or even be the basis for, syntax itself.

TABLE 1.8 COMPARISON OF COMMON TWO-WORD COMBINATIONS

Kanzi	Nim
chase(g) person(g)	play me
person(g) chase(g)	me Nim
person(g) pat(g)	tickle me
chase bite	eat Nim
chase Kanzi	more eat
person(g) come(g)	me eat
tickle ball	Nim eat
chase Sue	finish hug
chase Sue	tea drink

TABLE 1.9 COMPARISON OF COMMON THREE-WORD COMBINATIONS

Kanzi	Nim
chase(g) person1(g) person2(g)	play me Nim
person1(g) pat(g) person2(g)	eat me Nim
person1(g) person2(g) pat(g)	eat Nim eat
person1(g) chase person2(g)	tickle me Nim
Kanzi chase person(g)	grape Nim eat
chase Kanzi person(g)	Nim eat me
Kanzi person(g) chase	me more eat
Sue bite person(g)	give me eat

(g) indicates use of a gesture, not a lexigram

Formal test performance

Kanzi and Mulika performed very accurately on all tests conducted (Mulika was not tested using synthesised speech). The greatest proportion of errors were made on trials involving synthesised speech. Here, Kanzi's mistakes were confined to a small number of items and, for many of these, human listeners found the words difficult to understand too. Sherman and Austin found the tests using speech distressing, which they indicated by scratching their bodies and vocalising. The results clearly show that both common and pygmy chimps can acquire the referential meaning of symbols (see Table 1.10). They also clearly demonstrate that pygmy chimps (but not common chimps) can learn to comprehend spoken English. This is especially significant as no attempt had been made to teach English words, the meanings had been extracted from the speech that Kanzi and Mulika heard around them. The only responses to English words made by Sherman and Austin were when the words were accompanied by non-verbal glances and gestures from which the meaning could be guessed. The development of an association between spoken words and their meanings so early led to Kanzi and Mulika's acquiring lexigram use in a fundamentally different way from Sherman and Austin. For the pygmy chimps the task was a much easier one – they simply had to learn to 'read' the symbols, associating them with a concept (a spoken word) that they already knew.

Communicating travel plans

After four months of visiting a food site, Kanzi was able to identify it by a photograph or symbol. He could indicate which of the 17 places he

TABLE 1.10 RESULTS OF FORMAL TESTING OF LANGUAGE COMPREHENSION BY PYGMY AND COMMON CHIMPS

	Proportion of correct items	
Test of matching:	**Kanzi and Mulika**	**Sherman and Austin**
photograph to lexigram	Kanzi 66/66 Mulika 41/42	Sherman 30/30 Austin 30/30
spoken English to photograph	Kanzi 58/59 Mulika 30/35	Sherman 2/30 Austin 3/30
spoken English to lexigram	Kanzi 56/59 Mulika 41/42	Not tested
synthesised speech to lexigram	Kanzi 51/66 Mulika not tested	Not tested

wanted to go to, quickly understanding that by choosing from laid-out photographs he could select a location to travel to. He would make certain his choice had been seen and would often point to the photo or symbol during the journey as if to remind himself or the experimenter of their destination. At the time of testing, Mulika was too young to travel without Kanzi and, when Kanzi was present, he typically led the way.

One test of Kanzi's ability to lead someone to a food site he had selected used a 'blind' (naïve) experimenter. On a journey around the outdoor area and feeding stations, Kanzi selected a site with a photo five times, with a symbol seven times, and by selecting both the symbol and photo a further three times. He did not select an incorrect photo or symbol on any occasion. In every case except one he led the experimenter, by the most direct route possible, to the location he had indicated by his selection. On the exception, he appeared to take advantage of the experimenter's innocence and led her to the next site via a 30-minute detour to the 'back fence', part of the 55-acre site that he was not normally allowed to visit! Having visited 15 sites, Kanzi no longer wanted to go anywhere, but when asked by the experimenter, using English, to take her to the two remaining sites, he did so via the most direct route.

Generalisation of referents

Like other chimps, Kanzi and Mulika demonstrate generalisation – that is, the ability to extend the use of a symbol beyond the typical referent to include other, similar objects or activities. Table 1.11 presents a selection of such generalisations. For example, 'clover' was used to include another ground plant and red tree blossom. In contrast, some referents were used only in their narrow sense, such as 'pine needles'.

For Kanzi, place names seemed to have a wider area of reference than for people. For example, 'Sue's office' included the outdoor area around it. When away from the lab, Kanzi would express the desire to return using a range of referents, such as 'Sue's office' or 'bedroom' even though these would be used to specify locations more precisely when he was within the lab itself.

Sherman and Austin also generalised the use of symbols, but did so in a different way. Although they could discriminate between broad categories, such as 'drinks' or 'eating', they found distinctions within such categories more difficult, so tended to use a single symbol to refer to all examples within a category. For example, while Kanzi and Mulika learned without effort that 'coke' and 'juice' were different, Sherman and Austin tended to use referents such as 'orange drink', 'strawberry drink', 'coke' and 'juice' interchangeably, even with ongoing training. For the common chimps, these symbols seemed not to refer to significantly different items.

QUESTION SPOTLIGHT!

Can you explain why it was important to use a 'blind' experimenter to test Kanzi's communication skills?

TABLE 1.11 GENERALISATIONS

Symbol	Generalised to include
coke	all brands of dark, fizzy drinks
rain	water sprinkled from a hose
tomato	small, round, red soft fruits, e.g. strawberries and cherries
bread	all varieties, including taco shells
hamburger	all cuts of beef, raw or cooked
hide	to hide, find or explore
chase	following and games of tag
apple*	plums
paint*	crayons
peas*	green beans

used by Mulika rather than Kanzi

STRETCH & CHALLENGE

Look at Figure 6 in Savage-Rumbaugh *et al.*'s original paper. Why is it unlikely that Kanzi's detour to the back fence was simply an error?

Other examples of symbol use

Kanzi would often use the keyboard alone, for example pointing to the lexigram for 'pine needle', then collecting a handful of pine needles. If an experimenter tried to interact with him during such activities, he rejected their company and left.

The lexigram board was also used by Kanzi to express intentions to change his behaviour. When disciplined for eating wild mushrooms (by being kept indoors) he touched the symbols for 'no bite mushrooms'. When ask whether he would be good outside, he responded with positive vocalisations, and behaved appropriately when allowed out.

CONCLUSIONS

Savage-Rumbaugh *et al.* drew four main conclusions from this study:

1 Spontaneous development of symbol use occurs only in pygmy chimps. Common chimps require formal training to develop both receptive understanding and production. Like children, but unlike common chimps, the pygmy chimps develop reception first and use new words accurately.

2 Kanzi's word combinations, unlike those of Nim, Sherman or Austin, often requested an interaction between two individuals other than himself, and his combinations added information rather than simply repeating concepts.

3 Both common and pygmy chimps acquire referential meanings for symbols, but only pygmy chimps can learn to comprehend spoken English. This might lead them to develop lexigram use in a different way, by simply associating a new symbol with a known English word.

4 Both common and pygmy chimps generalise symbol use, but do so differently. Common chimps tend to discriminate only between broad categories, often referring to all examples within a category using one symbol, whereas pygmy chimps discriminate between specific referents within categories.

STRETCH & CHALLENGE ◎

Kanzi sometimes indicated the desire to visit a site by indicating the food commonly found there (e.g. using 'juice' for the treehouse). On arrival, Kanzi would play on the ropes or in the trees and ignore any juice offered. However, if asked to identify 'juice' from a selection of foods, or asked to name it when a bottle was held up, he could do so. How does this indicate that this is an example of generalisation rather than an error?

SAVAGE-RUMBAUGH *et al.*'S STUDY OF CHIMP LANGUAGE

SUMMARY

AIM

To find out whether pygmy chimps can acquire language spontaneously – that is, without being trained.

METHOD

The early environment of two pygmy chimps, Kanzi and Mulika, exposed them to spoken English and symbolic language, using lexigrams. Their development was compared to common chimps. Vocabulary development was measured by scoring spontaneous, behaviourally verified use of symbols and in controlled tests of spoken English and lexigram use.

RESULTS

- Kanzi and Mulika learned to communicate with humans, and developed large vocabularies.
- They could produce, comprehend and combine symbols, and respond to spoken words (getting 100% or close to it correct on tests matching photos/lexigrams/English words). The common chimps performed as well on photograph/ lexigram matching but performed no better than chance on matching photos to English words.
- Kanzi and Mulika's development was similar to that of children, for example, in their imitation.

CONCLUSIONS

- Pygmy chimps (but not common chimps), like children, spontaneously learn to use symbols and comprehend spoken English.
- Pygmy chimps, like children, develop reception before production, and use new words accurately.
- Pygmy chimps combine words to express interactions about individuals other than themselves, and to add rather than repeat information.
- Both species use symbols referentially and generalise their meanings, but only pygmy chimps discriminate between referents within narrow categories.

EVALUATION

Unlike any other study discussed in this book, this study raises ethical issues relating to animals. It is important to recognise that, in the USA, where this research was conducted, as well as in the United Kingdom, the controlling standards that determine the way in which researchers use animals are different from those that determine the use of human participants. The appropriate ethical standards for working with humans in research are indicated by ethical guidelines, which are advisory. In contrast, when studying animals, ethical procedures in research are governed by law. In addition, bodies such as the American Psychological Association (APA) and the British Psychological Society (BPS) publish guidelines that psychologists are required to follow.

As well as raising different ethical questions, this study also offers some unique methodological issues.

ETHICAL ISSUES

The current APA ethical principles raise several issues relevant to Savage-Rumbaugh *et al.*'s research. Importantly, they observe that while consideration for animal welfare should be incorporated into the design and conduct of studies, including the use of the minimum number of animals possible, it is also essential to remember that the primary goal of science is to produce sound, replicable data. That only two chimps were used, and that they were able to communicate such needs as food, being carried, company, or solitude, demonstrate that this research gave consideration to the ethical treatment of the animals. The discussion below, which includes the methodological strengths of the study, illustrates the extent to which it was designed to be scientifically rigorous.

> You can read the APA ethical guidelines here:
> www.apa.org/science/leadership/care/
> guidelines.aspx
> and an interesting article here:
> www.nature.com/embor/journal/v8/n6/full/7400996.
> html

In terms of the pain or distress potentially caused by the study, the means for disciplining the chimps clearly offers a interesting illustration. Two examples of discipline include being kept indoors for eating wild mushrooms (see page 38), and, when seen taking his shirt off in the cold, he was told (in English) that if he did not come down and put his shirt on, everyone would go away and leave him there alone, in response to which he came down and put it back on. These disciplinary measures are like those used with children, so they can be seen to be ethical. Furthermore, as young chimps, Kanzi and Mulika had daily access to their mother.

The current (1999) APA guidelines say: 'In addition to the federal requirements to provide for the psychological well-being of nonhuman primates used in research, psychologists are encouraged to consider enriching the environments of their laboratory animals and should keep abreast of literature on well-being and enrichment for the species with which they work.' There can be no doubt that the chimpanzees discussed here benefitted from a highly enriched social and physical environment relative to other research animals.

METHODOLOGICAL ISSUES
The sample and sampling method

The sample investigated in this paper consisted of two pygmy chimpanzees whose development was compared to that of similarly reared, previously studied, common chimps. The sample therefore comprises only two animals, which may not be representative of their species, but Savage-Rumbaugh *et al.* observe that there is no reason to suppose that they were not representative.

The research method

The surprising findings, demonstrating important differences between the chimpanzees, were obtained through the case-study method, which provided detailed and long-term data collection. They could not have been obtained in any other way. Savage-Rumbaugh *et al.* observe that such comparisons between species are important to developing an understanding of the evolution of advanced cognition, such as language.

Reliability

Remember that reliability means consistency. A procedure is reliable if we can precisely replicate it, and when doing so consistently leads to the same results. We have said that laboratory procedures are generally easy to replicate and many steps were taken to achieve consistency both in the way the animals were reared and in the collection of data. All four chimps were exposed to a language-filled environment in which people used the keyboard and spoke to each other – and the chimps – in English.

In testing learning, several measures ensured that there was consistency between chimps, between researchers, and over time. In the scoring of observational data, utterances were categorised by accuracy (correct or incorrect) and context (spontaneous, imitated or structured) each of which was, itself, defined. In addition, context-appropriateness and naturally occurring situations were also operationalised. To ensure that the words scored were used consistently, a criterion of 9/10 occasions was imposed for spontaneous production and behavioural concordance (and if words fell below the latter criterion they were removed from the individual's vocabulary). The inter-observer reliability for records of vocabulary items was high, with 100% agreement on symbols used and the correctness of context. The reliability for spontaneous/structured was also high, with only one difference between the observers.

There were also some inconsistencies in rearing and in data collection. The most important difference was that the common chimps were reinforced for language learning, while the pygmy chimps were not. This cannot, however, be considered a weakness of the study as it was necessary to reinforce the common chimps in order to demonstrate that they could acquire language at all. The keyboards used for the common and pygmy chimps were also different. This arose inevitably because the chimps acquired different meanings – and Kanzi learned many more, so had a much more extensive array of lexigrams to use. Finally, although using only two animals is ethically sound, it limits the reliability of the findings.

Validity

Remember that validity is about being sure that a study measures what it claims to measure. In order to be sure that a full and fair record of Kanzi and Mulika's language use was obtained, the research records from this study (unlike previous research) include all of the chimps' utterances, and span a significant length of time, so are likely to be representative. As a consequence, the findings are less likely to be biased by the subjective recording of selected aspects of the data. Two other differences from previous research were the recording of the accuracy of the chimps' utterances, and ongoing tests of their reception (rather than just their production) of language.

Another aspect of the procedure that improved validity was the need for confirmation of comprehension by behaviour. This showed that the chimp's use of a symbol was not just imitative or coincidental. Importantly, behavioural concordance was not inevitable – that is, it was possible for the chimp to give an incorrect response. For example, if Kanzi asked for 'bananas'

from the backpack, and it contained only bananas, the utterance would not be scored. Furthermore, changing the arrangement of the lexigrams on the keyboard helped to confirm that the chimps were responding to the arbitrary symbols, not to their locations.

In the recording of observational data with Kanzi, receptive use was not tested as often as productive use. This means that his receptive use could have been underestimated. As formal tests of Mulika's receptive ability showed that it far exceeded her production, it is possible that there is an issue with the validity of Kanzi's data.

Many controls were imposed in the formal testing of the chimps' understanding. The most significant of these were the use of an experimenter who was working 'blind', to ensure they could not cue the chimp's response, and the use of a voice-synthesiser test with Kanzi, to ensure that he was not responding to non-language cues, such as tone or rhythm. In addition, items were excluded if there was not a good photograph, so errors were more likely to be the result of a failure to comprehend language than a misperception of the stimuli.

Matata – like Sherman and Austin – did not acquire symbol use spontaneously, so one conclusion is that there is a critical period for acquisition of a symbolic system in chimps, as there is in humans. Alternatively, other variables affecting the chimps' rearing environments might account for the apparent species differences. The only way to test this effectively would be to rear individuals from the two species in identical ways (which is currently being done).

Qualitative and quantitative data

A strength of Savage-Rumbaugh *et al.*'s study was the recording of both qualitative and quantitative data. It thus has the strengths of both types of data (see p.215 for a discussion). As the details seen in the Appendix of the paper illustrate, the context in which the utterances occur is critical to determining the extent to which an utterance can be viewed as context-appropriate and spontaneous. In contrast, the precise quantitative data, such as the numbers of symbols understood in each formal test, offer direct comparisons between the species.

EXAM FOCUS

We now show you some of the sorts of questions that could be asked about the Savage-Rumbaugh *et al.* study in your exam. We will then show you some examples of the sorts of answers we believe might be successful and less successful, and point out some classic traps to avoid.

SECTION A

1 Describe two of the formal tests conducted by Savage-Rumbaugh *et al.* to assess Kanzi's language acquisition. *(4 marks)*

2 From Savage-Rumbaugh *et al.*'s study into symbol acquisition by pygmy chimpanzees:
   (a) What were the names of the two pygmy chimps studied? *(2 marks)*
   (b) Explain why these pygmy chimps might not have been representative of their own species. *(2 marks)*

3 In the Savage-Rumbaugh *et al.* study into symbol acquisition by pygmy chimpanzees:
   (a) Identify two ways in which quantitative data was gathered. *(2 marks)*
   (b) Give two examples of quantitative data collected in this study. *(2 marks)*

4 Savage-Rumbaugh *et al.* studied symbol acquisition by pygmy chimpanzees.
   (a) Identify two symbols Kanzi identified correctly using the lexigram keyboard before any training. *(2 marks)*
   (b) Explain why Kanzi was able to identify these symbols without training. *(2 marks)*

5 From the study by Savage-Rumbaugh *et al.*:
   (a) Identify one reason why Kanzi was taught symbol acquisition as a means of communication. *(2 marks)*
   (b) Outline one way in which the researchers recorded Kanzi's symbol acquisition. *(2 marks)*

6 From the study by Savage-Rumbaugh *et al.*, identify two pieces of evidence that suggest pygmy chimps have a greater aptitude for symbol acquisition than common chimpanzees. *(4 marks)*

7 Outline two ethical issues raised in Savage-Rumbaugh *et al.*'s study into symbol acquisition by pygmy chimpanzees. *(4 marks)*

8 Give two reasons why pygmy chimpanzees were chosen as opposed to other apes in Savage-Rumbaugh *et al.*'s study into symbol acquisition. *(4 marks)*

SECTION B

(a) What was the aim of the study by Savage-Rumbaugh *et al.*? *(2 marks)*

(b) Describe why the sample was selected for the study by Savage-Rumbaugh *et al.*, and suggest one disadvantage of this sample. *(6 marks)*

(c) Give two advantages of the case-study method as used in the study by Savage-Rumbaugh *et al.* *(6 marks)*

(d) Give two disadvantages of the case-study method as used in the study by Savage-Rumbaugh *et al.* *(6 marks)*

(e) Outline the results of the study by Savage-Rumbaugh *et al.* *(8 marks)*

(f) Suggest how the study by Savage-Rumbaugh *et al.* could be improved. Give reasons for your answers. *(8 marks)*

SECTION C

(a) Outline one assumption of the cognitive approach. *(2 marks)*

(b) Describe how the cognitive approach could explain the acquisition of language. *(4 marks)*

(c) Describe one similarity and one difference between any studies that take the cognitive approach. *(6 marks)*

(d) Discuss strengths and weaknesses of the cognitive approach using examples from any studies that take this approach. *(12 marks)*

SOME ANSWERS AND COMMENTS

SECTION A 5 (b) Outline one way in which the researchers recorded Kanzi's symbol acquisition. *(2 marks)*

David's answer:

Symbols that Kanzi did during the day were written down

Ken's answer:

For a period of 17 months, any signage or utterance made by Kanzi could be recorded on the lexigram attached to the computer so there was a record of it. Researchers could then work out if it was correct or incorrect in the situation.

We say: 1 mark.
David, it is true that the symbols were written down, but you need to explain that this was when the lexigram was used outdoors and then they were added to the computer. To get all the marks, be sure to explain your point in a bit more detail.

We say: 2 marks.
Ken, this shows knowledge of the study and the specific detail from it. You show exactly how the signs were noted, as, although Kanzi used the lexigram, the signs he used still needed to be recorded.

SECTION A 6 From the study by Savage-Rumbaugh *et al.,* identify two pieces of evidence that suggest pygmy chimps have a greater aptitude for symbol acquisition than common chimpanzees. *(4 marks)*

Susanne's answer:

Kanzi and Mulika used signs more spontaneously and were able to refer to other people.

Carol's answer:

First, Kanzi and Mulika were able to ask for things that were for someone other than themselves, which common chimps seem unable to do – they have only been shown to ask for themselves. Second, Kanzi and Mulika were far more specific in their signs/lexigram. They were able to identify symbols within categories, whereas common chimps can only communicate with broad categories.

We say: 1 mark.
Suzanne, the question asks for a comparison, and you have mentioned only one of the groups of chimps. When comparing, you should make sure you mention both groups so that it is clear what each of their abilities are. Your points are also too brief.

We say: 4 marks.
Carol, you have identified two different pieces of evidence from the study, described them well, and have specific points of comparison. A four-mark question does need some detail.
Well done.

SECTION B (a) What was the aim of the study by Savage-Rumbaugh et al.? (2 marks)

Sam's answer:

To teach a monkey language.

We say: 0 marks.
Sam, Kanzi is a chimpanzee, not a monkey! The aim is also not clear and too general, as it was to examine language capability rather than to actually teach language.

Sara's answer:

To observe language acquisition in pygmy chimps compared with that of 'common chimps'. Also to detail how a non-human species has obtained symbols without formal training.

We say: 2 marks.
Good knowledge of the study here, Sara. It is well explained, focused and to the point. Aims should avoid being too general.

SECTION C (c) Describe one similarity and one difference between any studies that take the cognitive approach. (6 marks)

Neil's answer:

One similarity is that both the study on autism and the study on eyewitness testimony have numerical data for results, and a difference is that Kanzi is a chimp and the other studies use people and not chimps.

We say: 2 marks.
Neil, remember there are six marks available here. Your answer is quite short. Try to use psychological terms, such as 'quantitative data' for numerical. Give an example from each study – for example, Loftus and Palmer had speed estimates in mph – as a clear illustration to support your point. Have an example for each of the two studies. Do this for both parts of the answer and you will get far better marks here. Name the studies if you can as well.

Vanessa's answer:

One similarity is that both Baron-Cohen and Savage-Rumbaugh used different groups of participants in their studies and compared them and their behaviour. Baron-Cohen had people with Tourette's and autism and clinically normal people to compare for theory of mind, and Savage-Rumbaugh used the pygmy chimps and common chimps to compare for language.

A difference is that they both use quite different sample sizes for their studies. Baron-Cohen used 16 participants with autism, 50 clinically normal adults, and some people with Tourette's syndrome, so it was large. Savage-Rumbaugh used just two pygmy chimps and two common chimps, so quite small.

We say: 6 marks.
A well-written answer, Vanessa. You have clearly done a lot of revision and know the studies well. The fact that you have pointed out the similarity and difference shows you know what you are talking about. To get good marks here you need to outline a similarity/difference, and then illustrate this by picking out a relevant bit from each of the two studies, which you have done. Good work.

THE COGNITIVE APPROACH TO PSYCHOLOGY

We have now looked in some detail at three cognitive studies. Based on these studies, let's see what we can tease out about the cognitive approach to psychology. We have already said that cognitive psychology is concerned with mental processes. Breaking that down a bit, we can identify some assumptions underlying the approach.

1. **Mental (cognitive) processes are key to understanding human behaviour**

    Cognitive psychology emphasises the importance of cognitive processes such as perception, memory, language and thinking. Cognitive processes are important in all human activity. We feel and behave in particular ways because we perceive what is happening around us, remember what has already happened, and think about these things. We use language as a tool for thinking about ideas ourselves, and for communicating them to others. Therefore, language is also an important cognitive process.

    In the Loftus and Palmer study we looked at an aspect of human memory – the fact that memories for events can be altered by information received after the event itself. In the Baron-Cohen *et al.* study we looked at perception of emotion in the facial expression of other people, and the fact that people on the autistic spectrum seem to be impaired in this perceptual ability. Psychologists have wondered for a long time about whether language is unique to humans, and, through the Savage-Rumbaugh *et al.* study, we explored one approach to investigating this – teaching a non-human species to use language.

2. **We can understand the mind as an information processor**

    Before cognitive psychology, psychologists were much more likely to just look at a stimulus (an aspect of the environment that people respond to) and our response to it. This stimulus-response psychology was sometimes called the 'black-box approach', because it treated the mind as something we could not see into. By understanding mental processes, cognitive psychologists are opening up the black box.

We input information through the senses and make sense of it. Throughput involves memory and thinking. Output might be in the form of a behaviour, a decision or an emotional response. The Loftus and Palmer study is concerned with the effect of how later input of information about an event affects memory for that event. This alteration to the information in the mind affects output, in the form of decision-making about the speed at which cars were travelling and the presence of broken glass. The Baron-Cohen *et al.* study reveals a particular problem with throughput of information about facial expression in people with autistic-spectrum disorders.

This way of looking at the human mind as an information processor makes use of the computer analogy. In other words we are looking at the mind as if it were a computer, which we understand in terms of input, throughput and output of information. This is not to say that cognitive psychologists believe that the mind works exactly like a computer, but rather that computers provide a useful way of trying to understand what happens in the mind.

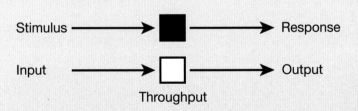

Figure 1.15
The black-box approach versus the cognitive approach

STRENGTHS AND WEAKNESSES OF THE COGNITIVE APPROACH

Strengths

- **Good scientific status.** The cognitive approach has many of the features of good science. Most research is experimental and takes place as far as possible in controlled conditions where extraneous variables can be controlled. Theories and ideas are open to being tested by researchers. For example, the Baron-Cohen *et al.* study tested the idea that difficulty in processing information about states of mind in others is central to autism. Loftus and Palmer tested the idea that recall involves reconstructing a memory using all the information we have available to us, rather than playing back an event like a video. Both of these studies provide clear information that supports these ideas.

- **Opening up the 'black box' has extended our understanding of people.** Before cognitive psychology existed, psychologists had some understanding of human behaviour and human emotion. However, how we think, remember, speak and make sense of the world around us are also essential aspects of human psychology, and without a cognitive approach we simply can't look at those. A cognitive understanding of psychology has opened up a range of practical applications. For example, there are now psychological therapies that work by altering how people think about things that are bothering them. Legal procedures involving witness testimony have evolved to incorporate a modern cognitive understanding of memory.

Weaknesses

- **The computer analogy breaks down.** Adopting an information-processing approach to psychology makes the assumption that the human mind processes information in the same way as a computer. In some ways this is true: like a computer, we receive, recognise, store and retrieve information and we use language to make that information easier to work with. However, unlike a computer, we are emotional, intuitive and influenced by instinct as well as logic. These things alter considerably what happens to information in the mind. We are much slower than computers in our processing of information but we are much better at making use of mental short cuts. We are therefore only partly justified in treating the mind as an information-processing machine.

- **Cognitive reductionism.** When we focus on mental processes we ignore many other important aspects of human psychology. The mind is emotional and instinctive as well as logical, and it is influenced by unconscious factors that cannot easily be explained by a cognitive approach. Perhaps more importantly, as individuals, we never process information in isolation but always within a social context, influenced by individuals and groups around us. By focusing on a particular set of mental processes within the individual mind, the cognitive approach neglects these important parts of human psychology and so is guilty of reductionism.

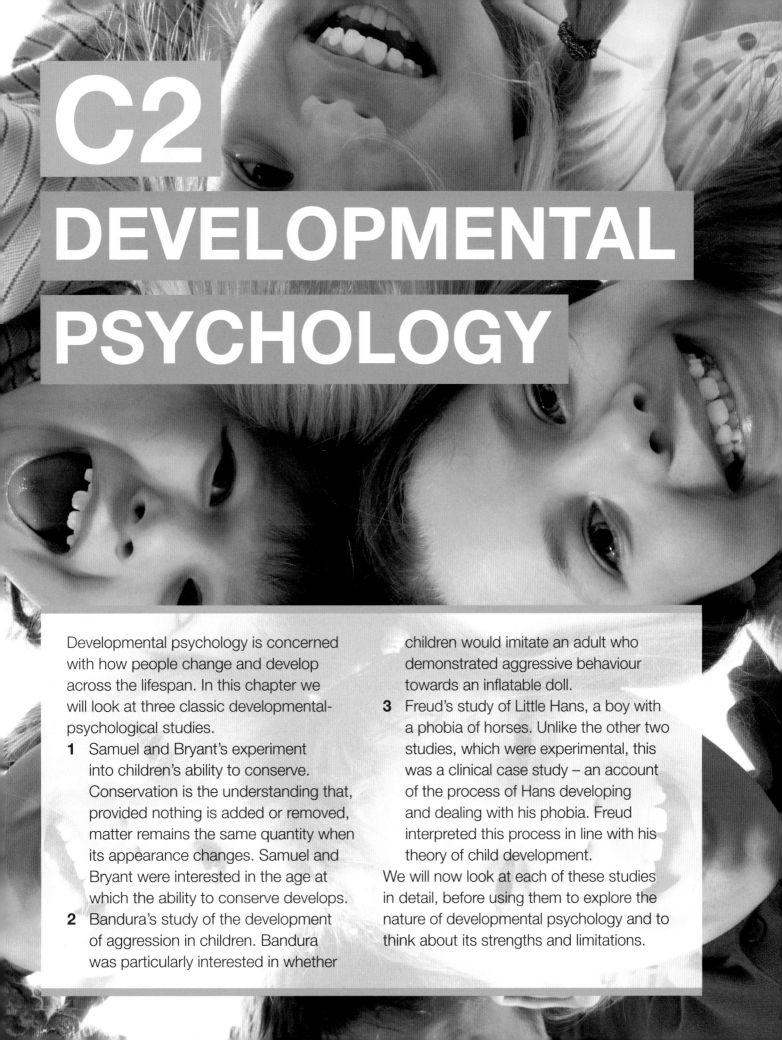

C2

DEVELOPMENTAL PSYCHOLOGY

Developmental psychology is concerned with how people change and develop across the lifespan. In this chapter we will look at three classic developmental-psychological studies.

1 Samuel and Bryant's experiment into children's ability to conserve. Conservation is the understanding that, provided nothing is added or removed, matter remains the same quantity when its appearance changes. Samuel and Bryant were interested in the age at which the ability to conserve develops.

2 Bandura's study of the development of aggression in children. Bandura was particularly interested in whether children would imitate an adult who demonstrated aggressive behaviour towards an inflatable doll.

3 Freud's study of Little Hans, a boy with a phobia of horses. Unlike the other two studies, which were experimental, this was a clinical case study – an account of the process of Hans developing and dealing with his phobia. Freud interpreted this process in line with his theory of child development.

We will now look at each of these studies in detail, before using them to explore the nature of developmental psychology and to think about its strengths and limitations.

SAMUEL AND BRYANT'S STUDY OF CONSERVATION IN CHILDREN

KEY IDEAS

Piaget placed great importance on a child's ability to **conserve** as a measure of cognitive development. A child can conserve when they recognise that the quantity of a substance stays the same when its appearance changes.

Samuel, J. and Bryant, P. (1984) Asking only one question in the conservation experiment. *Journal of Child Psychology and Psychiatry*, **25**, 315–18.

CONTEXT

One of the most important aspects of developmental psychology is the study of how children come to think and to perceive information in the same way as adults. For a long time it had been assumed that children simply knew less than adults. For example, elsewhere in this chapter Bandura demonstrates his theory of social learning, which is based on the idea that knowledge and skills increase over time through a process of observation and imitation. Development therefore is seen as quantitative, as what is known by the child simply adds up as they grow older. Swiss psychologist Jean Piaget (1896–1980) was one of the first to study cognitive development in a systematic, structured way. He developed a theory of cognitive development which proposed that children are born with basic mental structures upon which all other knowledge and skills are based. Piaget used a range of different ways to explore how children's thinking evolved and became more sophisticated over time. This approach considers that children's thinking undergoes a qualitative change, emphasising that children do not think about the world in the same way as adults do.

A range of methodologies were used by Piaget to identify recognisable stages of change, including specially designed tests, clinical interviews, and observations of children of different ages. He even used his own children to explore his ideas about the abilities that individuals develop over time. From this work, he proposed a four-stage model of cognitive development, wherein each stage is characterised by the emergence of different skills and knowledge, as well as certain flaws in thinking (see Table 2.1).

Figure 2.1 Jean Piaget

TABLE 2.1 PIAGET'S STAGE OF COGNITIVE DEVELOPMENT

Name of stage	Age	Key feature of cognitive development
Sensori-Motor	0–2 years	• explores environment using senses such as touch • develops motor skills • develops a sense of object permanence
Pre-Operational	2–7 years	• develops language skills • has ability to mentally represent objects and events • is egocentric and cannot conserve
Concrete Operational	7–11 years	• has ability to decentre and conserve • has ability to think about the world as it is; finds it difficult to think about how it might be
Formal Operational	11+ years	• is capable of forming and testing hypotheses • understands rules of formal logic • is able to reason about abstract concepts

Figure 2.2
A baby participating in a study of object permanence

One key cognitive skill is the ability to **conserve**. Piaget theorised that children who were in the Pre-Operational stage of cognitive development had yet to grasp the concept. Piaget and Szeminska (1952) devised a series of experiments which demonstrated that children below the ages of seven or eight years (in other words, those in the Pre-Operational stage) are unable to distinguish a perceptual change in quantity from a real change in quantity. By lengthening a ball of clay or a row of counters, the psychologists were able to identify differences in the children's abilities to conserve quantities in the form of number, mass and volume.

In Piaget's original experiment, children were shown two identical rows of counters side by side. They were asked if the rows were the same in number. Then, one of the rows was 'transformed' by spreading out the counters. Although it now looked different, clearly no counters had been added. The children were then asked the same question about whether the rows were the same in number post-transformation. It was found that most children in the Pre-Operational stage incorrectly answered that the transformed row was larger in number post-transformation, whereas older children correctly asserted that the rows remained the same in number. This finding was true of other measures of quantity, such as transforming mass (using balls of clay) and volume (using liquid-filled beakers of different sizes).

WEB WATCH @

You can watch demonstrations of the different conservations task at: www.simplypsychology.org

Figure 2.3
Games such as peek-a-boo
help babies develop a sense of
object permanence

Over time, Piaget's work has been subject to criticism by those who believe the nature of his tasks confuses children and may lead to biased responses. Rose and Blank (1974) replicated Piaget's task of conservation of number using a sample of six-year-olds. Instead of the two-question model, they asked the participants to compare the quantity only post-transformation. They found that some of the children correctly answered that the rows were still the same, contradicting Piaget's previous findings. One reason for this might be that asking two questions in the original experiment is confusing for children and created **demand characteristics**. The children might answer differently the second time not because they cannot conserve, but because they think the experimenter wants a different answer. As well as bringing Piaget's methodology into question, this also highlights problems with using young children as participants in psychological research.

ACTIVITY

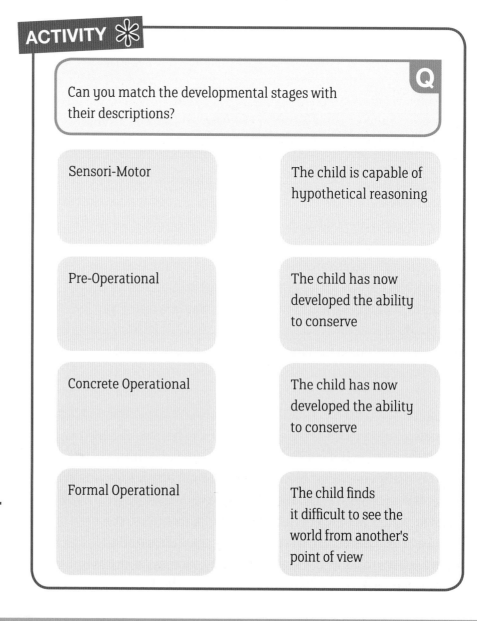

Q

Can you match the developmental stages with their descriptions?

Sensori-Motor	The child is capable of hypothetical reasoning
Pre-Operational	The child has now developed the ability to conserve
Concrete Operational	The child has now developed the ability to conserve
Formal Operational	The child finds it difficult to see the world from another's point of view

KEY IDEAS

Demand characteristics – These are cues to which the participant might be exposed, and which reveal the real aim of the study.

IN BRIEF !

Aim: To challenge Piaget's findings by altering his method for assessing conservation abilities in children.

Method: 252 male and female participants were sourced from primary schools in Devon. Participants were between five and eight-and-a-half years of age. They were divided into four groups by age, then into three age-matched groups for the conditions of the experiment. This was a laboratory experiment, as it was a controlled, artificial task involving manipulated variables. The independent variables were age (naturally occurring), condition (standard Piagetian, one question, and fixed array) and type of material (counters, play dough or liquid). The standard condition involved asking the child whether the amounts of the materials were the same both before and after the transformation took place. In the one-question condition, this question was only asked once, post-transformation. In the fixed-array condition, the child was shown the materials only post-transformation and then asked whether they were the same in amount. This was the control condition. The materials used tested different types of conservation: counters were used to assess ability to conserve number, play dough to assess conservation of mass, and liquid to assess conservation of volume. Participants completed four trials of each material. The dependent variable measured by researchers was the number of errors made by each child across the various conditions.

Results: The one-question condition produced fewer errors in the judgement of participants than either the standard or fixed-array conditions. Overall, younger children made more errors than older children.

Conclusion: Although older children are better at conserving number, mass and volume, the way in which children are asked to make judgements affects the quality of their judgements – children can become confused when asked a question more than once. Therefore, it seems that children can conserve at a younger age than Piaget believed.

Figure 2.4
A child in the Pre-Operational stage carrying out the task of conservation of volume

AIM

Piaget's previous research was the stimulus for Samuel and Bryant's study. Their aim was to challenge Piaget's findings by changing the method used to investigate conservation in children. They wanted to extend the scope of the critical research carried out by Rose and Blank to participants of a wider age range and using other versions of the conservation task.

 **KEY IDEAS**

Independent measures – This is a type of experimental design that uses different participants for each condition of the experiment.

Control condition – This is the group that, instead of being manipulated, is kept as the basis for comparison against the other experimental group or groups.

METHOD

Participants

The participants used in this study were 252 boys and girls aged between five and eight-and-a-half years. The sample was drawn from primary schools and playgroups in and around Crediton, in Devon. They were then divided into four groups of 63 participants in each group, whose mean ages were five years and three months; six years and three months; seven years and three months; and eight years and three months, respectively. The groups were then further divided into three groups, closely matched to control for age in order as they completed the conditions of the experiment.

Design and procedure

Samuel and Bryant's study can be considered a laboratory experiment. As you might remember, this kind of research method manipulates the independent variable (IV) and measures the outcome or dependent variable (DV). This study uses three independent variables:

- the age of the participants
- the task conditions, and
- the type of material used.

The first IV – the age of the participants – is naturally occurring, which means that this experiment can also be considered a quasi-experiment. There were four levels of this IV, corresponding to the four age categories. The second IV is the task conditions, which are outlined here:

1 *Standard condition.* The traditional method used by Piaget in which children are asked about the quantity or size of the materials both before and after they are changed.

2 *One-question condition.* The task is the same as the standard Piagetian task, but children are posed only one question about the quantity of the objects post-transformation.

3 *Fixed-array condition.* This is the **control condition**. The child sees no transformation being made. They are shown the objects only post-transformation, already looking different from one another.

Researchers wanted to compare Piaget's original method of asking two questions with an alternative method. Piaget's technique is called the 'standard' condition. Samuel and Bryant use this condition in their experiment to show that children who fail the traditional conservation task do not always fail because they cannot conserve. It is a way of allowing a direct comparison with Piaget's work, to see whether their experimental condition of asking the question only once would produce a difference in results. Samuel and Bryant introduce the fixed-array control condition to assess whether children who had answered the post-transformation question correctly had done so only by using the information brought over from the pre-transformation display. As different groups of children were used for each condition, this study can be said to use an **independent measures** design.

The third IV is the type of material used in the task. Three kinds of materials were used in the trials to assess number, mass and volume (see Table 2.2).

TABLE 2.2 MATERIALS FOR THE CONSERVATION TASKS USED BY SAMUEL AND BRYANT		
Type of task	**Material**	**Procedure**
Number	Plastic counters	In both the standard and one-question condition, children were shown two rows of six counters in an identical display. Then one row was spread out. In the fixed-array control, children saw only the post-transformation display.
Mass	Play dough (plasticine)	In both the standard and one-question condition, children were shown two equal and identical balls of play dough. Then one ball was squashed. In the fixed-array control, children saw only the post-transformation display.
Volume	Glasses of liquid	In both the standard and one-question condition, children were shown two equal and identical glasses of liquid. Then the liquid from one glass was poured into a narrower glass. In the fixed-array control, children saw only the post-transformation display.

Each participant undertook four trials using each type of material. The order in which they did the tests, and the order of the materials, systematically varied for each child.

The experimenters collected quantitative data only, in the form of the dependent variable (DV), which was the number of errors made by the children. Errors were made when a participant wrongly judged the quantities to have changed post-transformation.

RESULTS

The results of this research revealed significant differences between conditions of age, condition and type of materials used. Their key finding was that the one-question condition was typically easier than the standard conservation task and the fixed-array controls. As Table 2.3 shows, this was true of all three types of materials, and of all four age groups. They also noticed that fewer errors were made by children aged 8 in all three conditions, compared to children aged 5.

TABLE 2.3 RESULTS BY MEAN NUMBER OF ERRORS

Age (years)	Condition		
	Standard	One question	Fixed array
5	8.5	7.3	8.6
6	5.7	4.3	6.4
7	3.2	2.6	4.9
8	1.7	1.3	3.3

TABLE 2.4 RESULTS BY MEAN NUMBER OF ERRORS

Material	Condition		
	Standard	One question	Fixed array
Number	1.5	1.0	1.5
Mass	1.5	1.2	1.7
Volume	1.8	1.6	2.5

The fixed-array condition produced the highest number of errors in all age groups. This shows that children of all ages have difficulty conserving (mass, number and volume) if they do not observe the transformation. It is also noticeable that some materials were more prone to producing errors in judgement than others, as volume was the material that produced the most errors in the conservation task.

CONCLUSIONS

Samuel and Bryant were right to question Piaget's use of two questions. Children are more able to show their ability to conserve when they are not asked the same question twice, because children of all ages made fewer errors in the one-question condition than in the standard two-question condition. However, it seems likely that the ability to conserve increases with age.

EXPLANATIONS FOR THE FINDINGS

Samuel and Bryant attempt to explain the difference between the numbers of errors children made on the one-question conservation task compared to the standard conservation task. They argue that the pre-transformation question entices the child to give the wrong answer by asking the same question twice. This repetitive questioning leads the child to believe that they should be giving a different answer the second time around. In this study, Samuel and Bryant have shown that children are capable of conserving at an earlier age than that which was previously assumed.

Nonetheless, their findings support Piaget's basic assertion that conservation is a cognitive skill that develops with age. They have established that, as children grow older, they are less likely to make errors relating to the conservation of number, mass and volume. Furthermore, they also confirm Piaget's finding that children learn to conserve number before they learn to conserve mass and volume (this is supported by the differences in errors made by children using the variety of materials).

Importantly, Samuel and Bryant's research extended the critical studies undertaken by, among others, Rose and Blank, who had found reason to question the methodology used by Piaget. It raises issues around how easily experimenters can influence participants' behaviour. This is perhaps most true of younger children, who can be more susceptible to suggestions and eager to please grown-ups engaging with them on tasks.

STUDY 1

SAMUEL AND BRYANT'S STUDY OF CONSERVATION IN CHILDREN

SUMMARY

AIM

- To challenge the methodology used by Piaget by asking only one question in the conservation task.

METHOD

- 252 children between the ages of five and eight-and-a-half took part in one of three conditions: the standard task, the one-question task, and the fixed-array task.
- Participants completed four trials of their condition with each of the three materials, making judgements on number, mass and volume.
- Researchers recorded the number of errors made by each child across each condition.

RESULTS

- Children made fewest errors in the one-question condition, compared to the other conditions.
- Older children performed significantly better than young children.
- Participants made fewest errors when judging number, compared to the other materials.

CONCLUSIONS

- The ability to conserve develops as children grow older.
- Children make more errors when asked questions twice in the conservation task.

EVALUATION

ETHICAL ISSUES

The study used children as participants, which means its researchers should be especially careful in applying ethical considerations. The tasks in this study, while not typical activities for children, were not harmful or distressing to the participants, so it can be considered fairly ethically sound. However, Samuel and Bryant do not make it explicit whether they sought assent from the children to take part in the study – there is a risk that the children might have felt obliged to complete the set tasks. When conducting research with those under the age of 16, psychologists must obtain consent from the adult responsible for each child.

METHODOLOGICAL ISSUES
The sample and sampling method

Findings from a sample as large as 252 children can be generalised with some confidence to a wider target population. Unlike Rose and Blank's research, participants of various ages were used, so the researchers could note how conservation skills develop with age.

However, the entire sample was drawn from one small geographical region in Devon, which limits the representativeness of the sample. Despite this, we have no reason to assume that teaching practice in Devon varies considerably from elsewhere in the UK, and so it is likely that the sample is representative of children in other counties. It could be that in countries with different education systems, the findings might be different, so we should exercise caution in generalising the findings of the research beyond Western Europe.

The research method

The research method employed by Samuel and Bryant was a laboratory experiment, so they could directly compare different levels of the IV, such as the age of the participants. By manipulating variables in this way they were able to demonstrate a clear cause-and-effect relationship. For example, the experiment clearly shows that as children grow older; their ability to conserve improves – as shown by the reduction of errors in the older age groups.

Although Samuel and Bryant intended to reduce demand characteristics, there is a risk that, when participants are aware that they are being tested, this might affect their performance. If the children felt nervous doing the tasks, this might have impeded their abilities to reason about the task. It is conceivable that this might have affected younger, less-confident children more than older participants.

Validity

Using a laboratory experiment allowed researchers to control for possible confounding variables. For example, they systematically varied the order in which tasks were presented to ensure participants were not influenced by the order in which stimuli were shown.

Perhaps an obvious disadvantage to the study is that it lacked ecological validity. Repetitively estimating quantities of materials while being questioned by an unfamiliar adult was an unfamiliar task and was perhaps not a true reflection of their cognitive abilities.

Reliability

The children had four attempts to complete each conservation task. This reduces the possibility that one answer was a mistake, or the result of chance. In other words, it makes the findings more reliable. Furthermore, the procedure used by researchers was standardised, with the only change being the conditions and materials assigned to each trial. This makes the study highly replicable.

Qualitative and quantitative data

Researchers in this study recorded the number of errors made by participants across all groups and tasks. This quantitative data was then analysed to see whether differences between conditions was significant. The advantage of this technique was that a large amount of data was collected fairly quickly; it made for a robust analysis allowing Samuel and Bryant to confidently conclude that the one-question condition produced fewer conservation errors than the standard or fixed-array conditions. If researchers had gathered qualitative data – for example by questioning children on the reasons behind their judgements – this might have given additional insight into the reasons behind errors in the different tasks.

PRACTICAL APPLICATIONS

Finally, we must consider the impact this study has had on how we understand children's cognitive development. Samuel and Bryant have demonstrated that Piaget is likely to have underestimated the abilities of young children to conserve. It might be that they are more capable of performing internalised operations than was once thought. Furthermore, they have shown that children are influence by adults in their development and display of cognitive abilities. Therefore a deeper appreciation of the qualitative differences between adult thinking and child thinking should inform teaching method and the educational environment.

EXAM FOCUS

We now show you some of the sorts of questions that could be asked about the Samuel and Bryant study in your exam. We will then show you some examples of the sorts of answers we believe might be successful and less successful, and point out some classic traps to avoid.

SECTION A

1 In the study by Samuel and Bryant on conservation, in the one-question condition, children were asked the question about number, mass or volume only after they had seen the transformation.

   (a) Identify the other two conditions of this experiment. *(2 marks)*

   (b) In addition to these conditions, two other factors affected the children's ability to conserve. Identify both of these factors. *(2 marks)*

2 Describe two of the conservation tasks the children were asked to perform in the Samuel and Bryant study. *(4 marks)*

3 From the study by Samuel and Bryant:

   (a) Describe how the participants' age affected their ability to conserve. *(2 marks)*

   (b) Describe how the type of task affected the participants' ability to conserve. *(2 marks)*

4 Outline two of the experimental conditions from the study on conservation by Samuel and Bryant. *(4 marks)*

5 Describe two of the independent variables that were tested in the study by Samuel and Bryant. *(4 marks)*

6 Briefly explain why Samuel and Bryant conducted their study of cognitive development. *(4 marks)*

7 Describe two controls that were used in the study on conservation by Samuel and Bryant. *(4 marks)*

8 From Samuel and Bryant's study on conservation:

   (a) Give one piece of evidence that supports Piaget's claims about children's ability to conserve. *(2 marks)*

   (b) Give one piece of evidence that challenges Piaget's claims. *(2 marks)*

SECTION B

(a) Briefly outline the research method in the study by Samuel and Bryant. *(2 marks)*

(b) Explain why the study by Samuel and Bryant can be considered a snapshot study. *(4 marks)*

(c) With reference to the study by Samuel and Bryant, suggest one strength and one weakness of conducting snapshot studies. *(6 marks)*

(d) Describe the procedure followed in the study by Samuel and Bryant. *(8 marks)*

(e) Suggest how the procedure followed in the study by Samuel and Bryant could be improved. *(8 marks)*

(f) Outline the implications of the procedural changes you have suggested for the study by Samuel and Bryant. *(8 marks)*

SECTION C

(a) Outline one assumption of the developmental approach. *(2 marks)*

(b) Explain how the developmental approach could explain conservation in children's cognitive development. *(4 marks)*

(c) Describe one similarity and one difference between any core studies that take the developmental approach. *(6 marks)*

(d) Discuss strengths and weaknesses of the developmental approach using examples from any core studies that take this approach. *(12 marks)*

SOME ANSWERS AND COMMENTS

SECTION A 2 Describe two of the conservation tasks the children were asked to perform in the Samuel and Bryant study. (4 marks)

Fran's answer:

They were asked to do maths where they had to count counters and space them out. They also had to watch water in a tall jug and a fat jug.

We say: 2 marks.
Fran, you have the basic idea of part of what the children were doing, however you do need to describe what they were conserving here for both the examples. Explain that the first task is on number and then outline what the children had to do, and the same for the second task of volume. This shows your psychological knowledge of conservation more clearly.

Kate's answer:

The children were asked to do a volume test that consisted of watching water from a tall thin container be poured into a short, wide container. They then had to say if the volume had changed. They also had a task where the same numbers of counters were shown and then one row was spaced out differently. The task being that they had to say if there was a difference of number.

We say: 4 marks.
Kate, in your answer you name a type of conservation task, showing familiarity with the study, and then you go on to describe what the children have to do. This is good, as for a four-mark question you do need to have detail to show that you understand and can talk about conservation generally, and how it was assessed in this particular study.

SECTION A 3 From the study by Samuel and Bryant:
(b) Describe how the type of task affected the participants' ability to conserve. (2 marks)

Tina's answer:

They found the water task hard and could do the counting task.

We say: 1 mark.
Tina, make sure your answer always gives a full explanation that answers the question. You do not really do that here. Rather than just saying one task was easy and one hard, you need to say that the tasks test different aspects of conservation, and that children find some aspects of conservation easier to acquire than others. Then you can say that volume (water) was hard, and number (counters) easy. Do not be too brief.

Tony's answer:

The conservation tasks were varying in difficulty and the harder the task, the less able the child would be to conserve. The easiest task was number, with less errors, then shape, and the hardest was volume, with more errors.

We say: 2 marks.
Tony, this is a clear answer to the question. You describe the differences in the types of task and then have a sentence on the effect on the children's abilities. This is focused on exactly what the question requires and well written.

SECTION B (b) Explain why the study by Samuel and Bryant can be considered a snapshot study. *(4 marks)*

Ruth's answer:

The study can be considered a snapshot study because it was done quickly. There was not a long period of time over which the study took place. The researchers only asked the children to do the study then.

We say: 2 marks.
Ruth, you have some basic points of the essentials but have not fully explained it enough for four marks. Rather than saying it was not a long period of time and done quickly, describe how it is done only once on the participants, and that they are not studied extensively. We look at their behaviour and capture it at that point – like a snapshot with a camera. So, say the children did the conservation tasks only once at that age and were not followed up.

Frankie's answer:

The study is a snapshot study as the participants had their abilities at the conservation tasks assessed once, as opposed to continuously over a period of time like in a longitudinal study. They were tested on number, mass and volume at one point in their lives at that particular age, so the study is a snapshot of their abilities at that point in time.

We say: 4 marks.
Frankie, you have included detail from the study itself in the answer, which is good, as the question does say '…in the study by Samuel and Bryant'. Do always link the answer to the study for top marks.
You summarise the key points of a snapshot study succinctly and have a quick comparison to highlight your points. Good thinking.

SECTION C (c) Describe one similarity and one difference between any core studies that take the developmental approach. *(6 marks)*

Darrell's answer:

Samuel and Bryant and Bandura use children in their studies, so are very similar in this. Bandura encourages children to be aggressive, but Samuel and Bryant do not do this and their children do not see a bobo doll.

We say: 1 mark.
Darrell, a better style for the answer is to set out clearly what your main point is. Developmental studies commonly use children, so this point is rather weak. You could talk about how many children they use, making sample size the point. Your difference is more to do with what the studies are about – it is true that they look at different things, but so do most studies! Look at issues such as methods or ethics to make a clear point of difference.

Mary-Lou's answer:

A similarity is Bandura and Samuel and Bryant use laboratory experiments. Bandura uses a lab to look at the aggression in the children and has different types of role models, and Samuel and Bryant have a lab study with different conservation tasks for the children to do, like number. One difference is that of ethical issues, and Bandura is really unethical but Samuel and Bryant are not. This is because Bandura makes the children see aggression and so they are psychologically harmed and distressed by it all.

We say: 5 marks.
Mary-Lou, you have set out your answer in a straightforward way here. We like how you identify your point and in your similarity have some detail from both the studies you are using. The difference is a really good point, but what a pity you had some detailed evidence only from Bandura and not from Samuel and Bryant. You needed that to get up to top marks.

BANDURA *et al.*'s STUDY OF CHILDREN'S IMITATION OF ADULT AGGRESSION

Bandura, A., Ross, D. and Ross, S.A. (1961) Transmission of aggression through aggressive models. *Journal of Abnormal & Social Psychology*, 63, 575–82.

CONTEXT

This study is concerned with the tendency of children to imitate adult social behaviour, specifically aggression. Learning behaviour by imitating others is called **observational learning**. Several studies had already demonstrated that children are influenced by witnessing adult behaviour. However, previous studies had tended to show children repeating adult behaviour in the same situation and in the presence of the adult that modelled the behaviour. Although this suggests that children **identify** with adult **models**, it does not show whether they will go on to repeat the observed behaviour in other situations and without the adult present. One purpose of the study, therefore, was to test whether children will reproduce observed behaviour in a new situation and in the absence of the model.

This study is also concerned with the learning of gender-specific behaviour. Previous studies had shown that children are sensitive to gender-specific behaviours. For example, children see their parents as preferring gender-stereotyped behaviour. Aggression is a good example of a gendered social behaviour, being associated with masculinity.

A further purpose of this study was to investigate whether boys were more likely to imitate aggression than girls, and whether they would be more likely to imitate male than female models.

 **KEY IDEAS**

Observational learning is learning behaviour through observation of that behaviour in another individual, known as the **model**. Observational learning can be seen in many species. Albert Bandura and colleagues demonstrated observational learning in humans and built the idea into social learning theory.

Identification is another idea from social learning theory. We identify with a model when we adopt their behaviour in order to become like them.

Figure 2.5
Albert Bandura

QUESTION SPOTLIGHT! ⭐

Be clear on the distinction between aims and hypotheses. *Outline one aim and one hypothesis from this study.*

IN BRIEF ❗

Aim: To investigate the extent to which children would imitate aggression modelled by an adult, and to investigate the effects of gender on imitation.

Method: 72 children were divided into three groups. One group saw an adult attack an inflatable doll (a bobo doll) in a play room. A second group saw an adult behave non-aggressively, and a third group did not see an adult playing. All the children were then frustrated by being banned from playing with attractive toys and left to play in a room containing a bobo doll.

Results: Children who had witnessed the aggressive adult were more likely to play aggressively with the bobo doll. Boys were more likely than girls to imitate physical aggression, especially from a male model.

Conclusion: Children can acquire aggression through observation of adults modelling aggression. They selectively imitate gender-specific behaviour and boys imitate male models, at least selectively.

AIMS AND HYPOTHESES

The overall aim of the study was to investigate observational learning of aggression. Specifically, the study aimed to see whether children would reproduce aggressive behaviour when the model was no longer present, and to look for gender differences in learning of aggression. Several hypothese were tested:

1. Participants exposed to an aggressive model would be more likely to reproduce similar aggression than those exposed to a non-aggressive model and those who did not see a model at all.

2. Participants exposed to a non-aggressive model would be less aggressive than those not exposed to a model at all.

3. Participants would imitate aggression modelled by a same-sex adult more than that modelled by an opposite-sex adult.

4. Boys would be more inclined than girls to imitate aggression.

METHOD

PARTICIPANTS

There was a total of 72 participants: 36 male and 36 female. All were selected from the nursery school of Stanford University. Ages ranged from 37 months (just over three years) to 69 months (five-and-three-quarter years). The mean age was 52 months (four years and four months).

DESIGN

This was a laboratory experiment, using an independent measures design. The effect of three independent variables was tested:

- The behaviour of the model – aggressive or non-aggressive;
- The sex of the model; and
- The sex of the children.

There were eight conditions in all. The children in each condition were matched for their aggression levels, so that this did not become a confounding variable. This was achieved by the experimenter and a nursery teacher independently rating 51 of the children on scales of 0 to 5. Very good agreement between the two raters was achieved (0.89). The conditions were as follows:

1. 12 boys and 12 girls were exposed to an aggressive model. Six boys and six girls saw aggression modelled by a same-sex model, while the rest saw it modelled by an opposite-sex model.

2 12 boys and 12 girls were exposed to a non-aggressive model. Six boys and six girls saw non-aggression modelled by a same-sex model, while the rest saw it modelled by an opposite-sex model.

3 A control group of 12 boys and 12 girls did not see a model display any behaviour, aggressive or otherwise.

Figure 2.6
Aggression is modelled and imitated

PROCEDURE

The procedure consisted of three stages.

1 *Modelling the behaviour.* Each child was brought individually into a play room and invited to join in a game. This lasted for 10 minutes. In the first two conditions there was also an additional adult present in the room. In the aggressive condition, this adult demonstrated aggression towards a 5-foot tall inflatable bobo doll, kicking and hitting it, including with a hammer. They also said aggressive things, such as 'kick him ... pow ... sock him on the nose'. In the non-aggressive condition, the adult assembled toys and did not interact with the doll. In the control condition, there was no additional adult in the room.

2 *Aggression arousal.* In order to annoy the children and increase the chances of aggressive behaviour, all the children were then taken to a different play room with some very attractive toys. After being allowed to play with these for around two minutes, the participants were told they were not allowed to play with them any more as they were 'the very best' toys and they were going to be reserved for other children.

QUESTION SPOTLIGHT!

Identify two controls in the design of the Bandura *et al.* study.
Explain how one of these controls is helpful in avoiding the effects of extraneous variables.

WEB WATCH @

You can read the original research paper here:
psychclassics.yorku.ca/Bandura/bobo.htm
You can also see footage of the study here:
http://www.youtube.com/watch?v=Pr0OTCVtHbU

3   *Testing for delayed imitation.* Children were then observed playing for the next 20 minutes as the experimenter remained in the room but busied herself with paperwork. Two more observers watched through a two-way mirror. The room contained a range of toys including a smaller bobo doll. The observers were unaware, while observing, which condition the child was in. This helped eliminate bias.

Three types of aggression were recorded by observers:

1   Imitative aggression – physical and verbal aggression identical to that modelled in stage 1;

2   Partially imitative aggression – similar behaviour to that carried out by the model;

3   Non-imitative aggression – new aggressive acts not demonstrated by the model.

RESULTS

Quantitative data was recorded. This showed significant differences in levels of imitative aggression between the group that witnessed aggression and the other two groups. This was true of physical and verbal aggression. To a lesser extent this was also true of partial imitation and non-imitative aggression. Significantly more non-aggressive play was recorded in the non-aggressive model condition.

TABLE 2.5 MEAN AGGRESSION SCORES RECORDED BY OBSERVERS

Participant group	Aggressive male model	Aggressive female model	Non-aggressive male model	Non-aggressive female model	No model
Male imitative physical aggression	25.4	12.8	1.5	0.2	2.0
Female imitative physical aggression	7.2	5.5	0.0	2.5	1.2
Male imitative verbal aggression	12.7	4.3	0.0	1.1	1.7
Female imitative verbal aggression	2.0	13.7	0.0	0.3	0.7
Male non-imitative aggression	36.7	17.2	22.3	26.1	24.6
Female non-imitative aggression	8.4	21.3	1.4	7.2	6.1

In terms of the hypotheses tested:

1   Children who had witnessed an aggressive model were significantly more aggressive themselves.
2   Overall, there was very little difference between aggression in the control group and that in the non-aggressive modelling condition.
3   Boys were significantly more likely to imitate aggressive male models. The difference for girls was much smaller.
4   Boys were significantly more physically aggressive than girls. Girls were slightly more verbally aggressive.

CONCLUSIONS

1   Witnessing aggression in a model can be enough to produce aggression by an observer. This is important because it had been widely believed prior to this study that learning aggression was a more gradual process in which a learner experimented with aggression and was rewarded in some way for doing so.
2   Children selectively imitate gender-specific behaviour. Thus boys are more likely to imitate physical aggression, while girls are more likely to imitate verbal aggression. Because boys but not girls were more likely to imitate aggression in a same-sex model, it could be concluded only cautiously that children selectively imitate same-sex models. It could not be ruled out that this process is specific to boys.

There is more than one possible explanation for these findings. One suggestion was that children were not learning aggression at all, but that they were just disinhibited by witnessing the adult aggression. In other words, they already knew how to aggress but it became okay when the adult did it. However, if this were true, we would expect that children would be aggressive to the doll in a wide range of ways. In fact, although there was non-imitative aggression, they tended to imitate exactly the style of aggression modelled by the adult. This suggests that they were actually learning the aggression.

Figure 2.7
All the children who had witnessed an aggressive model became more aggressive, but boys showed significantly more aggression than girls

STUDY 2
BANDURA *et al.'s* STUDY OF CHILDREN'S IMITATION OF ADULT AGGRESSION

SUMMARY

AIM

To investigate children's learning of aggressive behaviour through imitation of adult models.

METHOD

Seventy-two children from a university nursery school witnessed an adult behaving aggressively towards a bobo doll (aggression modelling condition); an adult behaving non-aggressively (non-aggressive model condition); or no adult (no-model condition). They were then annoyed and left in a room containing a bobo doll.

RESULTS

Children in the aggressive modelling condition were more aggressive to the bobo doll than those in the other conditions. Boys were more physically aggressive than girls, particularly when they witnessed aggression in a male model.

CONCLUSIONS

Aggression can be learned by imitation of a model. However, children selectively imitate gender-specific behaviour, so boys are more influenced by seeing physical aggression modelled by men.

EVALUATION

This is a classic example of a laboratory experiment, strong on experimental control but weaker on ecological validity.

ETHICAL ISSUES

All studies making use of children raise additional ethical issues above and beyond those conducted on adults. This is because, unlike adults, children cannot really give informed consent to take part in studies, nor can they withdraw as easily. A typical response to these issues is to get parental permission. Although in their research paper Bandura *et al.* thank the head teacher of the nursery school, they do not make it clear what steps they took to ensure parental permission. In this case, children were not doing anything substantially different from their everyday activities so there is little risk of real harm or serious distress, although they were deliberately annoyed by not being allowed to play with the nicest toys. Mild distress was therefore caused, and this is an ethical issue. A more serious issue would be any lasting change to the children's behaviour. However, the type and level of violence children witnessed here was similar to that which they would expect in cartoons, so it is highly unlikely that any child was left more aggressive by participating.

METHODOLOGICAL ISSUES
The sample and sampling method
Sample size was quite large for a laboratory experiment. At first glance this appears to be a strength of the study.

However, consider the number of conditions. By the time we get down to, say, boys imitating a male aggressive model, there are only six participants in that condition. That is quite a small group, and any confounding participant variables could have quite a large effect. A larger sample would have helped avoid this. Bandura *et al.* do not say how their sample was selected from the nursery school, but drawing a sample from a single nursery school is problematic in itself. The nursery used for this study was attended by the children of academics, who are not representative of the population at large. This means that there could difficulties in generalising results.

The research method

This study was a classic laboratory experiment, with the strengths and weaknesses that typically go with laboratory experiments. On the positive side, there are many excellent controls that cut down the risk posed by extraneous variables. All participants had very much the same experience, with the same rooms and toys being used in all conditions. This is a particular strength of the design. However, like many laboratory experiments, this one lacks a degree of realism. Hitting a bobo doll is very different from hitting a person, and we should be cautious about applying results obtained in this experimental situation to more life-like situations.

Reliability

Reliability was excellent. Conditions were closely controlled and we can take it that all participants had very much the same experience. The most relevant participant variable – prior aggression – was also controlled, by assessing each child for aggression and matching the levels of aggression between the groups. The reliability of observers was assessed and found to be very good. Reliability was therefore a strength of the study.

Ecological validity

We have already said that realism is often a problem for lab experiments. This is for two reasons: first, the environment differs from real life; and second, the tasks carried out by participants tend to differ from those they carry out in real life. This study took place in two play rooms similar to those in which children played in other situations, so the fact that they were technically in a laboratory is not too much of a problem. However, being asked to play with a strange adult in an unfamiliar room is not a typical everyday task. More importantly, the experience of hitting a bobo doll is very different from hitting a real person because it does not react. Understanding real-life violence is more complex, because our hitting a person has a range of consequences – both external (e.g. they might hit back, or cry) and internal (e.g. we feel some degree of empathy with the pain of being hit). Studying aggression against a doll lacks realism and so the procedure lacks ecological validity.

Quantitative data

Typically for a laboratory experiment, only quantitative data were gathered in this study. This is both a strength and a weakness. On the plus side, numbers allow us to easily compare the levels of aggression in each condition. As long as we are concerned with observable behaviour we are on safe ground in rating what we observe quanitatively. However, what we don't get from this data is much indication of what is happening in the minds of the children doing the imitating. If you watch the film of Bandura's participants, you can see that some seem to have quite powerful emotional responses to the situation. It would have been really interesting to have qualitative data about what they thought and felt when hitting the doll.

Practical applications

This study has interesting applications in settings where we are concerned with children's learning of aggression. Child psychologists and social workers work with children who have witnessed domestic violence. Bandura's work informs this work by emphasising the likelihood of children imitating the sort of violence they observe in their parents. This study also has important implications for understanding the link between media violence and children's aggression, suggesting that children, particularly boys, are likely to imitate physical aggression when it is modelled by a male adult.

EXAM FOCUS

We now show you some of the sorts of questions that could be asked about the Bandura study in your exam. We will then show you some examples of the sorts of answers we believe might be successful and less successful, and point out some classic traps to avoid.

SECTION A

1 One of the independent variables (IVs) in the study of aggression by Bandura *et al.* was the behaviour of the model (aggressive or non aggressive).

    (a) Identify the other two independent variables. *(2 marks)*

    (b) Outline how the behaviour of the model was manipulated. *(2 marks)*

2 Describe two ethical problems in the study of aggression by Bandura *et al.* *(4 marks)*

3 The participants in the study of aggression by Bandura *et al.* were children.

    (a) Identify two other characteristics of the sample used in this study. *(2 marks)*

    (b) Outline one difficulty which may arise when psychologists study children. *(2 marks)*

4 Outline two findings from the study of aggression by Bandura *et al.* *(4 marks)*

5 In their study of aggression, Bandura *et al.* used a matched pairs experimental design.

    (a) How were the children matched in this study? *(2 marks)*

    (b) Outline why the children were matched in this study. *(2 marks)*

6 In the study by Bandura *et al.*, all the participants were taken individually into a second room and subjected to mild aggression arousal.

    (a) Describe how the children's aggression was aroused in this room. *(2 marks)*

    (b) Explain why the researcher felt that this was necessary. *(2 marks)*

7 From the study of aggression by Bandura *et al.*:

    (a) Identify two of the categories of aggression that were measured. *(2 marks)*

    (b) Outline the findings for one of these categories. *(2 marks)*

8 The study by Bandura *et al.* on the imitation of aggression used a number of experimental controls. Describe how two variables were controlled. *(4 marks)*

SECTION B

(a) Give the aim of the study by Bandura *et al.* *(2 marks)*

(b) Describe the sample used in the study by Bandura *et al.* and outline one problem of generalising from it. *(6 marks)*

(c) Describe how observational data was gathered in your chosen study and outline one problem in generalising from it. *(6 marks)*

(d) Outline one advantage and one disadvantage of using observation in the study by Bandura *et al.* *(6 marks)*

(e) Suggest two changes to the study by Bandura *et al.* *(8 marks)*

(f) Discuss the effect that these changes may have on the results in the study by Bandura *et al.* *(8 marks)*

SECTION C

(a) Outline one assumption of the developmental approach. *(2 marks)*

(b) Describe how the developmental approach could explain aggression. *(4 marks)*

(c) Describe one similarity and one difference between any core studies that take the developmental approach. *(6 marks)*

(d) Discuss strengths and weaknesses of the developmental approach using examples from any core studies that take this approach. *(12 marks)*

SOME ANSWERS AND COMMENTS

SECTION A 2 Describe two ethical problems in the study of aggression by Bandura *et al.* (4 marks)

Celine's answer:

They attacked the bobo doll with weapons which is aggressive and made young people angry. The participants were very young too and should not have been used because of this.

Maria's answer:

The use of children is an ethical issue. If they are aged under sixteen you should have parental consent and try to explain the study simply to the children. Also, winding children up in the aggression arousal part is mean and unethical as it causes psychological harm and stress, which is against the ethical guidelines.

We say: 2 marks.
Celine, in any question on ethics you should identify the ethical guideline you are saying is broken. You have not done this in your answer, but have described more generally what was wrong. It would get you more marks to say, 'The children were exposed to psychological harm as they say an adult attack a bobo doll with weapons', and then expand on this. Do the same with the point on being too young, to get up to four marks.

We say: 4 marks.
Maria, well done on clearly naming some appropriate ethical guidelines here. You have a very good answer as not only do you name them, you then go on to explain how they are broken in the study with some detail from the procedure. This shows really good knowledge of the study.

SECTION A 7 From the study of aggression by Bandura *et al.*:
(a) Identify two of the categories of aggression that were measured. (2 marks)

Samuel's answer:
Verbal and physical.

Rina's answer:
Imitative verbal aggression is one, which is where what the adult does to the bobo was copied. Non-imitative aggressive was also looked at, and gun play, where the child used a toy gun, was one category.

We say: 0 marks.
Samuel, you are obviously a man of few words, but that is not so good in an exam answer! This is much too short and vague. There were no physical and verbal categories. Be specific and explain that as the study was looking for imitation of behaviour, the categories were imitative physical aggression (any act that the child particularly copied) and imitative verbal aggression (where they copied any phrase the role model had said). Unfortunately, as yours were not actual categories, you get no credit.

We say: 2 marks.
A spot-on answer. There are two distinct and clear categories that were used in the study to record the data during the observation, with a little bit of explanation. Full marks to you, Rina.

SECTION B (d) Outline one advantage and one disadvantage of using observation in the study by Bandura *et al*. *(6 marks)*

Lauren's answer:

One advantage of observations is that you can obtain qualitative data which is rich in detail so you get a great understanding of your chosen topic, like in Bandura where they wrote down what the children said towards the bobo. A bad thing is that the children may not do anything at all.

We say: 2 marks.
Lauren, while you give an advantage and a disadvantage, they do not relate as clearly to observations as they could. Your first point is true, but rather general, and you should explain how you get the qualitative data from observations as the question is not just about data. Remember the study, and go on to give a detailed example to explain the point further. The second point is not particularly relevant to observations, so, sadly, you gain no marks for that.

Zach's answer:

An advantage of carrying out an observation is that there are no demand characteristics if people don't know they are being observed like the children with the bobo doll; the behaviour seen is true to life and therefore ecologically valid. For example, in Bandura, the children were not told that researchers were behind the mirror recording their actions. A disadvantage is that you could miss some behaviour that is shown, like by the children towards the bobo doll, as you cannot necessarily record it all.

We say: 5 marks.
Zach, a really nicely written advantage with detail, and some psychological terminology. We like the way you have detail in the example to back up your point. The disadvantage is not bad, but needs a bit more explanation. Adding another sentence saying why this is a problem and giving specific detail from the study would really show the examiner your knowledge.

SECTION C (b) Describe how the developmental approach could explain aggression. *(4 marks)*

Asha's answer:

It explains aggression as it shows that when the children actually see a bobo doll being attacked by an aggressive adult model then they copy it. This means the children are now aggressive. As they were children it is developmental.

We say: 2 marks.
Asha, your answer is talking more about what happened in the study. The question is not asking you about one of the studies but rather to explain some behaviour that is looked at by a study in the approach. Make the focus on examining this aspect of behaviour very clearly in your study, and do not focus on findings from a study.

Bevan's answer:

Social learning theory teaches children to be aggressive. If a child sees some aggression in important role models around them, they will remember this. It may be that later on they get angry with another child and they will recall what they have seen and so imitate it, as the children did in Bandura's study. They have learned the aggression as part of their growing up.

We say: 4 marks.
Bevan, you have quite a bit of relevant detail here and show understanding of the process in the answer. You have looked at the behaviour of aggression and explained it clearly. You have a brief link to a study but the answer concentrates on the mechanisms by which the approach could explain the behaviour. Good thinking here.

FREUD'S CASE STUDY OF LITTLE HANS

Freud, S. (1909) Analysis of a phobia in a five-year-old boy. In Strachey, J. (Ed) *The Standard Edition of the Complete Psychological Works: Two Case Histories.* Volume X. London, Hogarth Press.

CONTEXT

Sigmund Freud remains the most famous psychologist, even more than 70 years after his death. Freud wrote from the 1890s until the 1930s. His approach to psychological theory and therapy – called psychoanalysis – forms the basis of the psychodynamic approach to psychology. Freud had a number of important ideas, some more controversial than others. Most controversially of all he proposed that childhood can be seen as a series of psychosexual stages. Each stage is characterised by a fixation on an area of the body and a distinct pattern of relationships to parents.

The oral stage takes place in the first year of life. The mouth is the main focus of pleasure at this stage, as the child is suckling and weaning. At this stage, they are totally dependent on their main carer, and they acquire the ability to accept nurture and have close relationships. From around one to three years of age, the child goes through the anal stage. Here the focus of pleasure is the anus, as the child learns to retain and expel faeces at will. This is also the time at which the parents start to exert control over the child's behaviour by potty-training them, and this is when the child acquires a pattern of relating to authority.

The third and most crucial Freudian stage of development is the phallic stage (from the word phallus, meaning penis), which lasts from around three to six years of age. In the phallic stage, children go through the **Oedipus Complex**. This involves the development of a strong attachment to the opposite-sex parent, and a sense of the same-sex parent as a rival for their affection. Freud came to this conclusion after a period of self-analysis. He revealed his own Oedipus Complex in a letter to a friend:

KEY IDEAS

The **Oedipus Complex** is Freud's term to describe the three-way relationship dynamic between a child and the two parents, in which the child attaches strongly to the opposite-sex parent, and starts to see the same-sex parent as a rival. The name 'Oedipus' comes from Sophocles' play, *Oedipus Rex*, which was itself based on a Greek legend. In this play, Laius of Thebes is told he will one day be killed by his son, Oedipus, so he abandons him. However, Oedipus survives, and, as an adult, ends up killing his father and marrying his mother, unaware of who they are. Freud believed that we all react powerfully to this story because it triggers memories of our own Oedipus Complex.

Figure 2.8
Sigmund Freud

Figure 2.9
According to Freud, this
family can soon expect to
experience Oedipal conflict

IN BRIEF ❶

Aim: To record a case of the Oedipus Complex.

Method: A boy was followed through the course of a phobia of horses, to the end of the phobia. His dreams, anxieties and fantasies were recorded by his father and passed on to Freud, who interpreted them in line with his idea of the Oedipus Complex.

Results: Hans' fear of horses was interpreted as anxiety caused by a threat to castrate him and about his father banning him from his parents' bed. Dreams and fantasies were interpreted in the light of this theoretical position.

Conclusion: Hans experienced castration anxiety and the Oedipus Complex, but resolved this through his fantasies.

'I have found in my own case too being in love with my mother and jealous of my father, and now I consider it a universal event in early childhood.'

One of Freud's most famous cases is that of Little Hans, whom Freud believed to be going through the Oedipus Complex.

AIM

To give an account of a boy who was suffering from a phobia of horses and a range of other symptoms, and to use this case to illustrate the existence of the Oedipus Complex.

METHOD

Participant

The participant was a Jewish boy from Vienna, Austria. He was five years old at the start of the study, although some events were recorded from a couple of years earlier. He was called Little Hans in the study, however his real name, Herbert Graf, was well known. Little Hans was suffering from a phobia of horses. His father, a fan of Freud's work, referred the case to Freud and went on to provide much of the case information.

Design

The study was a clinical case study. This means that the participant is a patient undergoing therapy. In this case, Freud's direct input in the therapy was very limited. Accounts of how often Freud saw Little Hans vary a little, but it almost certainly was not more than twice. Hans' father conducted regular discussions with Hans and passed these on to Freud, who analysed them in line with his theory. The results consist of Freud's analysis.

Case history

From around three years of age, Hans developed a great interest in his penis – his 'widdler' as he called it – and it was reported that he played with it regularly. Eventually, his mother became so cross that she threatened to cut it off if he didn't stop. Hans was very disturbed by this and developed a fear of castration. At around the same time, Hans saw a horse collapse and die in the street, and he was very upset as a result. At three-and-a-half years of age, Hans' baby sister was born and he was separated from her for a while when she was hospitalised.

Shortly after this, when Hans was four years old, he developed a phobia of horses. Specifically, he was afraid that a white horse would bite him. When reporting this to Freud, Hans' father noted that the fear of horses seemed to relate to their large penises. At around the same time as the phobia of horses developed, a conflict developed between Hans and his father. Hans had been in the habit for some time of getting into his parents' bed in the morning and cuddling his mother. However, his father began to object to this. Hans' phobia worsened to the extent that he would not leave the family house. At this point, he also suffered attacks of generalised anxiety. By the age of five, Hans' phobia lessened, initially becoming limited to white horses with black nosebands, then disappearing altogether. The end of the phobia was marked by two fantasies:

- Hans fantasised that he had several children. When his father asked who their mother was Hans replied 'Why Mummy, and you're the Granddaddy' (p. 238).
- The next day, Hans fantasised that a plumber had come and removed his bottom and penis, replacing them with new and larger ones.

RESULTS

Freud interpreted the case as an example of the Oedipus Complex. More specifically:

- Horses represented Hans' father. White horses with black nosebands were the most feared because they resembled the moustached father. Horses also made good father symbols because they have large penises.
- The anxiety Hans felt was really castration anxiety triggered by his mother's threat to cut off his 'widdler' and fear of his father caused by his banishing Hans from the parental bed.
- The giraffes in Hans' dream represent his parents. The large

KEY IDEAS

Hans reported a dream to his father. Hans dreamed that there were two giraffes in his room at night. One was large and the other 'crumpled.' Hans took the crumpled giraffe away from the large one, which cried out. He then sat on the crumpled giraffe.

QUESTION SPOTLIGHT!

You could be asked to outline one dream, day-dream or phobia. Be really clear that castration anxiety is not a phobia – go for the fear of horses if you see that question. Also, be clear that the giraffe dream is a true dream. Day-dreams, such as the plumber, are fantasies, not dreams.

Figure 2.10
Hans particularly feared white horses with nosebands

Figure 2.11
Giraffes with their long necks
could represent penises

giraffe that cried out represented Hans' father objecting to Hans. The crumpled giraffe represented Hans' mother, the crumpling representing her genitals. The large giraffe, with its erect neck could have been a penis symbol.

- The children fantasy represents a relatively friendly resolution of the Oedipus Complex in which Hans replaces his father as his mother's main love object, but the father still has a role as grandfather.
- The plumber fantasy represents identification with the father. By this we mean that Hans could see himself growing a large penis like his father's and becoming like him.

CONCLUSIONS

Hans suffered a phobia of horses because he was suffering from castration anxiety and going through the Oedipus Complex. Dreams and fantasies helped express this conflict and eventually he resolved his Oedipus Complex by fantasising himself taking on his father's role and placing his father in the role of grandfather.

STUDY 3

FREUD'S CASE STUDY OF LITTLE HANS

SUMMARY

AIM

To provide an account of a case of a young boy experiencing anxiety – specifically a phobia of horses – as a result of the Oedipus Complex.

METHOD

A clinical case study was carried out on a single participant – a Viennese male child, known as Little Hans. Hans' father recorded events, including details of the phobia and other anxieties, dreams and fantasies, and passed them on to Freud, who interpreted these events.

RESULTS

Freud interpreted Hans' symptoms and behaviour as the result of castration anxiety and the Oedipus Complex. For example, two giraffes in a dream represented Hans' parents and his fantasy of having children with his mother, and his father taking the role of grandfather represented the resolution of the Oedipus Complex.

CONCLUSIONS

Hans' symptoms were the result of castration anxiety and the Oedipus Compex. When he successfully resolved the complex, his symptoms disappeared.

EVALUATION

Although interesting and, at least on the surface, relevant to understanding Freud's idea of the Oedipus Complex, in general we would have to say that the Little Hans study is methodologically weak, especially if taken as evidence for Freudian theory. There are also some ethical issues, although these pale in comparison with the methodological problems.

ETHICAL ISSUES

There was no deceit in the case study. Although Hans did not give formal consent to take part in a study, his father did, and parental consent is quite normal for participants of Hans' age. Hans was not put through any experimental procedure that might cause harm or distress. There are issues however around confidentiality and privacy. Although Freud used the name Little Hans, the boy's real identity was well known in Vienna, where he and Freud lived. Hans' real name was Herbert Graf, and he went on to be a successful operatic director. It is not well known whether being the subject of Freud's study ever caused him later problems, but we might regard it as dodgy that his identity is public knowledge when he was linked to something as socially sensitive as the Oedipus Complex.

METHODOLOGICAL ISSUES
Sampling and research method

Throughout this book we consider sampling and the general issues with the research method separately. In this case, the sampling is the problem with the method! That is, case studies such as this have a particular problem with their sample. By definition, they use very small numbers of participants, and, almost by definition, these participants are unusual enough to be sufficiently interesting to be worth writing about. Small samples of unusual people are a problem in psychology because it is hard to generalise from them to the population as a whole. Even if we accept that Little Hans had a full-blown Oedipus Complex, this does not mean that everyone has one, which is Freud's claim.

Reliability and validity issues

Reliability is always a problem for clinical case studies because they are one-offs and cannot be replicated. The Little Hans study also raises particular problems of validity. First, the way the data was collected could have affected validity. Hans' father was a fan of Freud's work, and it is hard to know if this distorted his perception of the events he passed on to Freud. A further validity issue concerns making theoretical interpretations. Interpretation, by definition, involves going way beyond the information available to an observer. This is subjective, and good science requires an attempt at objectivity.

Qualitative data

The data analysed in this study were exclusively qualitative, and the study has the strengths associated with qualitative data. There is a large volume of rich information in Freud's account of the Little Hans case. Freud meticulously recorded very detailed information, and this has allowed later researchers to offer alternative interpretations of the case. However, compare the data recorded in the Little Hans case to that in the Eve study (see Chapter 5). Where Thigpen and Cleckley used tools such as IQ tests and EEGs to gather quantitative data to supplement their account of the case, Freud relied purely on a qualitative account. This means that we have very little concrete information about Hans.

Practical applications

As an illustration of the Oedipus Complex, the Little Hans case has been extensively used by psychotherapists for training purposes. An important aspect of such training is in-depth study of cases. This means that the study has an important practical application. A related strength of the study is its theoretical importance. It is hard to study the Oedipus Complex, and this case gives some evidence, however imperfect. It therefore has good theoretical importance.

EXAM FOCUS

We now show you some of the sorts of questions that could be asked about the Freud study in your exam. We will then show you some examples of the sorts of answers we believe might be successful and less successful, and point out some classic traps to avoid.

SECTION A

1 From Freud's study of Little Hans:
  (a) Describe one of Hans' phobias. *(2 marks)*
  (b) Describe Freud's interpretations of one of Hans' phobias. *(2 marks)*

2 From Freud's study of Little Hans, outline one strength and one weakness of the way in which the data was gathered. *(4 marks)*

3 Freud's study of Little Hans was a case study:
  (a) Outline one strength of the case study research method used by Freud. *(2 marks)*
  (b) Outline one weakness of the case study research method used by Freud. *(2 marks)*

4 From Freud's study of Little Hans:
  (a) Describe how the data was collected. *(2 marks)*
  (b) Suggest one reason why this data may not be considered valid. *(2 marks)*

5 Outline two pieces of evidence used by Freud to suggest that Hans's fear of horses was symbolic of a fear of his father. *(4 marks)*

6 From Freud's study of Little Hans:
  (a) Briefly describe one of little Hans' dreams or fantasies. *(2 marks)*
  (b) Outline Freud's explanation of this dream or fantasy. *(2 marks)*

7 In the study by Freud, Little Hans is referred to as a little Oedipus.
  (a) Identify two features of the Oedipus Complex. *(2 marks)*
  (b) Outline one piece of evidence from the study that supports the suggestion that Hans was a little Oedipus. *(2 marks)*

8 The study by Freud is an example of 'action research', where the researcher collects evidence at the same time as attempting to bring about a change in the situation. Using the case study of Little Hans as an example, give two problems with conducting action research. *(4 marks)*

SECTION B

(a) Briefly outline the research method in Freud's study of Little Hans. *(2 marks)*

(b) Explain why Freud's study of Little Hans can be considered a longitudinal study. *(4 marks)*

(c) With reference to Freud's study of Little Hans, suggest one strength and one weakness of conducting longitudinal studies. *(6 marks)*

(d) Describe the procedure followed in Freud's study of Little Hans. *(8 marks)*

(e) Suggest two changes to the procedure in Freud's study of Little Hans. *(8 marks)*

(f) Outline the implications of the procedural changes you have suggested for Freud's study of Little Hans. *(8 marks)*

SECTION C

(a) Outline one assumption of the psychodynamic perspective. *(2 marks)*

(b) Describe how the psychodynamic perspective could explain phobias. *(4 marks)*

(c) Describe one similarity and one difference between any studies that could be viewed from the psychodynamic perspective. *(6 marks)*

(d) Discuss strengths and weaknesses of the psychodynamic perspective using examples from any studies that could be viewed from this perspective. *(12 marks)*

SOME ANSWERS AND COMMENTS

SECTION A 4 From Freud's study of Little Hans:
(a) Describe how the data was collected. *(2 marks)*

Aaron's answer: Little Hans was asked by his dad about his problems, who then told Freud.

We say: 1 mark.
Aaron, this is really rather brief and you do not communicate that Freud collected his data from correspondence, based on questioning by the father. The dad did not tell Freud directly! You have attempted to explain what was done, but it is not at all clear.

Daniel's answer: By self-report. Hans' father would ask little Hans about his dreams, phobias and troubles. This would then be sent to Freud for analysis

We say: 2 marks
You have the key idea of the data collection here, Daniel. You identify the fact that it was self-report and then go on to say exactly how this was done, with the passing of information on to Freud.

SECTION A 7 In the study by Freud, Little Hans is referred to as a little Oedipus.
(a) Identify two features of the Oedipus Complex. *(2 marks)*

Gavin's answer: Hating your little sister and your Dad.

We say: 1 mark.
Gavin, part of the complex is jealousy, so hatred of your father is correct up to a point. But your answer is far too brief and not focused on the central features of the complex.

Steve's answer: Two features are, the really huge jealousy of your father for taking up your mother's time, and the love of your mother so you do not want to share her at all with anyone else.

We say: 2 marks.
You have grasped the main components of the complex here, Steve, and have explained them pretty thoroughly. There is nothing else you would really need to add. Good work.

SECTION B (f) Outline the implications of the procedural changes you have suggested for Freud's study of Little Hans. *(8 marks)*

Tracy's answer: If Freud was to have questioned Little Hans directly himself it would have been better, as Freud would have seen Little Hans' dreams in person and so would get to analyse the actual dreams and other issues first hand rather than having them go through the middle man of Hans' father. This would make the data better for analysis and would make the study more ecologically valid as Freud would have studied Hans in real life.

We say: 3 marks.
Tracy, some fair comment here. You identify what would happen if Freud himself were doing the study. I like the point that you cut out the middle man, but you should tell me exactly why having the middle man is not good. Saying data is 'better' is not very clear; always say how it would be better, to have more detail in the answer. Your big problem is that you should have two changes to discuss and you have only one – so, unfortunately, half the marks cannot be awarded.

Al's answer:

Having Freud study Little Hans in person would enable him to obtain the true data from Hans directly. This cuts out the unreliability of Hans' father asking Hans questions and then relating to Freud, which is open to a lot of unreliability as it all depends on how Hans' dad (a non-psychologist) asks Hans questions and what information he chooses to tell to Freud. Having Freud study Hans directly would mean Freud could ascertain all the important information he wanted and build up a more accurate case scenario for Little Hans.

Secondly, studying Little Hans for the much longer period of time until adolescence would give us a lot more data, and we would be able to see if he really had resolved the complex fully and whether he got any more phobias from later problems related to this.

We say: 6 marks.
Al, you are being very critical here and picking out what would actually happen if you change the procedure. I like the comments on reliability which show good understanding and relate well to your first change. You have thought through possible implications and make them relevant to the study. The second point is less well discussed and you need more analysis here. Tell us what we would gain from all the extra data more carefully. Explain the implications rather than just outlining them.

SECTION C (d) Discuss strengths and weaknesses of the psychodynamic perspective using examples from any studies that could be viewed from this perspective. (12 marks)

Jade's answer:

One strength of the perspective is it produces lots of qualitative data.

An example is Freud used this in his study of Hans from the letters written to Freud.

One weakness is that is often seen as not really very scientific at all. This is because you do not do controlled lab studies but it is more on case studies of individuals.

An example is Freud and Little Hans which has lots of letters written by the father on the dreams and phobias. He could say what he liked about his son and it might not be always true. It has no real control at all.

Another strength is that it can make real-life therapies and help people. Freud shows how we can understand phobias and the conflict that caused them and so treat them, like Hans.

We say: 7 marks.
Jade, this is a reasonably detailed answer. Try to get a balance so that you have two strengths and weaknesses each. You first strength was correct, but you do need to expand a little on the example as it is quite brief here. The weakness was well explained and you have a more detailed example in support. You do go on to comment further on this point, and this is a good idea but your comment could be a little clearer. The last strength is another relevant point. However, again is a bit brief and the example does not contain much detail. Remember this is worth 12 marks.

THE DEVELOPMENTAL APPROACH TO PSYCHOLOGY

We have now looked in detail at three developmental studies. You can probably see from these that the developmental approach to psychology is very wide-ranging. We have already said that developmental psychology is concerned with how people change and develop across the lifespan. This is really the only assumption that binds the field together.

People change with age (they develop)

Other approaches to psychology focus on psychological processes in adults. Cognitive psychology looks at cognition taking place in the mind of the adult individual, and social psychology looks at social processes taking place between adults. However, our everyday experience tells us that people change with age. What happens in the mind of a child is not entirely the same as what happens in the mind of an adult, and groups of young adults do not necessarily behave socially like groups of older adults.

Two of the studies in this chapter have looked at age-specific processes. Samuel and Bryant were concerned with changes in children's ability to judge quantities from five to eight years. Freud was concerned with the Oedipus Complex, which he believed took place during the phallic stage between three and six years. Samuel and Bryant and Freud were investigating particular stages of development. However, Bandura's study is different because it is concerned with the process of social learning, which is not limited to a particular age or stage of development.

STRENGTHS AND WEAKNESSES OF THE DEVELOPMENTAL APPROACH

The developmental approach is so diverse that it does not really have strengths and weaknesses that apply to the whole approach in the same way as the other approaches. However, we can use the core studies from this chapter to draw out some evaluation points.

- **Strength: developmental psychology has improved our understanding of people at different ages and stages of development.** Understanding that people are different at different ages has improved our understanding of human behaviour, cognition and emotion. This has changed our whole view as a society about, for example, what a child is. Prior to people like Freud exploring emotional development, and Piaget exploring cognitive development, children were largely thought of as little adults. Developmental psychologists have shown us that children, adolescents and adults each have their own psychological characteristics. This in turn has led to our better appreciating children's needs, and treating children better.

- **Weakness: some aspects of development are hard to study scientifically, so there is some dodgy theory and methodology around.** Freud's study of Little Hans is a good example of this. Although emotional development is clearly important, it has proved harder to study than cognitive development (like Samuel and Bryant) or behavioural development (like Bandura). This means that key theoretical ideas about development – such as Freud's Oedipus Complex – lack solid evidence. A theoretical idea that is hard to test scientifically is also a poor theory, so we can say that some aspects of developmental psychology are lacking in both good theory and good research.

PERSPECTIVES ON PSYCHOLOGY

As well as the approaches to psychology you need to know about two perspectives. Each approach is concerned with particular aspects of psychology, so developmental psychology is about how we change with age, and individual differences is about the ways in which people vary from one another. Perspectives are different because they are theoretical approaches to understanding human psychology. Here, we are going to consider two perspectives: behavioural and psychodynamic.

THE BEHAVIOURAL PERSPECTIVE

This approach dominated psychology for the first half of the 20th century. More than anyone else it was the behaviourists that established psychology as a scientific discipline. Few psychologists describe themselves as behaviourists nowadays, however the influence of behaviourism remains strong because behaviourists made many discoveries that still hold true. The following are some of the main assumptions of the behavioural perspective.

1. The proper subject matter of psychology is observable behaviour. The early behaviourists were determined to make psychology a respectable science. One way in which they tried to do this was to ignore the mind and focus on behaviour. This is because we cannot see directly into the mind, and the behaviourists believed that good science required that psychologists should study only what they could see in front of them. Behaviourism is sometimes called 'black box' psychology, because it treats the mind as a closed box that we cannot see into. Instead, what is studied is stimulus and response. A stimulus is anything in the environment that is detected by one of the senses. A response is the behaviour that results from detecting the stimulus. We can show this in the form of a diagram –

Figure 2.12
The 'black box' model of behaviourism

Modern behaviourists tend to take a less extreme view on this, but the emphasis is still on studying stimulus and response rather than mental processes.

2. We are products of our environment. In the nature–nurture debate, behaviourists fall on the nurture side. In fact, the early behaviourists believed that human behaviour was entirely a product of environmental influences. John Watson, the founder of behaviourism, once said:

'Give me a dozen healthy infants, well-formed, and my own specified world to bring them up in and I'll guarantee to take any one at random and train him to become any type of specialist I might select—doctor, lawyer, artist, merchant-chief and, yes, even beggar-man and thief, regardless of his talents, penchants, tendencies, abilities, vocations, and race of his ancestors.' (Watson, 1930)

By this, Watson meant that we are entirely products of environment and that if we can control someone's environment we can control their development. Modern behaviourists take a slightly less extreme view. For example, behaviourists studying the learning of phobias have identified the phenomenon of preparedness – we seem to be hard-wired to learn fear of some things but not others, for example, we can easily acquire phobias of snakes and spiders, but not of cars or guns, which are actually much more dangerous. However, behaviourists still study the influence of the environment on behaviour.

3. We acquire our behaviour through learning. According to the behaviourists we learn our behaviour. In particular, behaviourists are concerned with three types of learning.

- **Classical conditioning.** Learning to associate a stimulus that already triggers a response (called an unconditioned stimulus) with another stimulus (a neutral stimulus), so that the latter comes to trigger the same response. For example, we might fear muggers but have no feeling about bus stops. If we are mugged at a bus stop we are likely to associate the bus stop with the mugging and learn to be wary of bus stops. Classical conditioning can explain how some simple responses – fear, salivation, sexual arousal, etc. are learned.

- **Operant conditioning**. This is learning by the consequences of our actions. When we perform a behaviour and this has a good consequence we become more likely to repeat that behaviour. This is called reinforcement. Similarly, when something we do has a bad consequence we are less likely to do it again. This is called punishment. Operant conditioning can explain the development of quite complex behaviours, but not necessarily where the behaviour originated (we have to try a behaviour first before it can be reinforced or punished).

- **Observational learning**. This is a much more recently discovered type of learning than the previous two, and takes place when an observer imitates behaviour modelled by another individual. Observational or social learning is sometimes described as 'neo-behaviourist' rather than behaviourist, because the theory makes reference to cognitive processes. For observational learning to take place, the observer must attend to the behaviour being demonstrated and retain it in their memory. Attention and memory are cognitive processes and a true behaviourist would probably not place so much emphasis on this type of process.

Core studies that can be understood from the behaviourist approach include the following:

1   **Bandura *et al*. (1961)** (p. 61). Bandura explained the results of his study in terms of observational learning. Children learned to aggress towards the bobo doll by imitating the model.

2   **Piliavin *et al*. (1969)** (p.162). Piliavin explained the results in terms of a cost-reward model. In other words, they received reinforcement or punishment according to their actions as a bystander. People received reinforcement in the form of a reduction in arousal levels when they helped, moved away from or dismissed the victim's need for help.

STRENGTHS AND WEAKNESSES OF THE BEHAVIOURAL PERSPECTIVE

Strengths

- **Scientific status.** The kinds of research carried out by behaviourists conform closely to the standards of good science. Most studies are experimental and carried out under laboratory conditions. They are therefore highly reliable. Behavioural ideas are easily testable because they concern easily oberved behaviour and there is an absolute minimum of inferring what is happening in the mind from behaviour that can be observed.

- **Practical applications.** Behaviourism has many practical applications in the real world. Understanding the role of observational learning in developing aggression has informed the debate about violence in the media, and the intervention in families where children observe domestic violence. Classical and operant conditioning also have important applications. We can for example use classical conditioning therapies to understand and treat mental disorders. Classical conditioning can be used to desensitise people to phobic stimuli (things they are afraid of). Operant conditioning can be used to modify behaviour in a range of situations, including the rehabilitation of long-term psychiatric patients.

Weaknesses

- **It is reductionist.** Reductionism takes place when we look at something complex and reduce it to something much simpler in order to be able to study and explain it. By ignoring most mental processes and focusing instead on just stimulus and response, behavioural theories are generally guilty of reductionism. Even social learning explanations of aggression are reductionist. There are many aspects to human aggression, including biological (hormones, evolution), cognitive (perception of the situation) and social (group membership, culture). In the light of this complexity it is very reductionist to look at aggression simply as a learned response.

- **It raises ethical issues.** Behavioural techniques are extremely powerful in altering human behaviour, giving some people tremendous power over the behaviour of others. While this makes behaviourism very useful, it also raises ethical issues. Under what circumstances is it okay to forcibly alter behaviour? Aversion is a classical conditioning technique that can be used to eliminate undesirable responses by teaching the patient to associate the stimulus that triggers the response with an unpleasant stimulus, such as a painful electric shock. This is used to treat paedophiles, replacing their arousal response to children with a fear response. This may or may not seem controversial to you, but then consider that aversion was used for some time to 'treat' gay men. It was also reportedly used under the apartheid system in South Africa to 'treat' white men who had relationships with black women. These hideous misuses of aversion show how open to misuse behavioural techniques are.

THE PSYCHODYNAMIC PERSPECTIVE

Like the behavioural perspective, the psychodynamic perspective is one of the older ways of thinking about psychology. However, in every other way it could not be more different! Where the behavioural approach is highly scientific and helped establish psychology as a science, the psychodynamic approach uses very different methods and is much more theoretical. As a result, it has never been accepted as part of mainstream psychology. The psychodynamic approach has the following assumptions:

1. We are strongly influenced by our unconscious mind. The 'unconscious mind' is the aspects of the mind that we are not consciously aware of. According to the psychodynamic approach we are constantly affected by unconscious mental processes. Different psychodynamic theorists have different views on the nature of the unconscious. To Freud, who developed the approach and carried out the Little Hans study, the unconscious mind contains memories of early experiences and powerful instinctive drives, most

importantly sexual and aggressive. Freud believed that from birth our behaviour is influenced by sexual and aggressive instincts. We can see this in the Oedipus Complex (e.g. Little Hans), in which boys target their sexual instinct towards their mother and their aggressive instinct towards their father.

2. Our development is affected by early relationships. According to Freud and other psychodynamic theorists, the most crucial factor affecting our psychological development is our early experiences, and the most important early experiences centre around the quality of relationships with parents. In Freudian theory the most important aspect of parental relationships is the Oedipus Complex, as illustrated by the Little Hans case. In the Oedipus Complex, children attach strongly to the opposite-sex parent and see the same-sex parent as a rival for their affection. On an unconscious level this involves targeting sexual and aggressive instincts towards the parents. How parents handle this situation has an impact on the child's later development. According to Freud, a badly handled Oedipus Complex can leave a child sexually over- or under-confident, or with a too strict or too lax sense of morality.

3. Important information can be found in dreams, slips of the tongue and what patients say in therapy. The psychodynamic approach stands aside from the rest of psychology in terms of its approach to research. Where other perspectives and approaches try to be as scientific as they can, this is not possible for those working in a psychodynamic way. This is because the focus is the unconscious mind, which is extremely difficult to study scientifically. Instead, psychodynamic psychologists look for clues about what is happening in the unconscious in phenomena such as slips of the tongue, dreams and what patients spontaneously say when letting their mind drift in therapy. Little Hans revealed his classic 'giraffe' dream, interpreted by Freud as sexual in nature. The emergence of Eve's personalities can also be seen as important information. Sometimes, dissociation appears to be an unconscious response to childhood trauma, so the existence of multiple personalities is a clue that the individual might have suffered such trauma.

Core studies that can be understood from the psychodynamic approach include the following:

- **Freud (1909)** (p. 71): Freud explained Hans' phobia as the result of anxiety from the Oedipus Complex, and the end of the phobia as the resolution of the Oedipus Complex.
- **Thigpen and Cleckley (1954)** (p. 189): Although the authors are cautious about explaining the causes of Eve's condition, there is some evidence that parental rejection and sibling rivalry were the childhood relationship difficulties that gave rise to her dissociation into different adult personalities.

STRENGTHS AND WEAKNESSES OF THE PSYCHODYNAMIC PERSPECTIVE

Strengths

- **Explanatory power.** The psychodynamic approach can be used to explain a wide variety of behaviours, including the more bizarre ones, such as multiple personalities, dreams of crumpling giraffes, and day-dreams of being fitted with big penises by a plumber! This is a serious point, because all these things are very difficult to explain using other perspectives or approaches. One contemporary application of Freudian theory is in understanding adult baby syndrome, in which adults take on infant behaviours, dressing in nappies and sometimes paying specialist prostitutes to feed and change them. In Freudian terms, this is straightforward to explain – the adult babies are regressing to an early stage of development at which their development stalled due to something going wrong with their key relationships. There is no other explanation for adult baby syndrome that so neatly explains the phenomenon.
- **Occupies the middle ground on key debates.** Unlike behaviourism, which can be thought of as reductionst, determinist and taking an extreme nurture view in the nature–nurture debate, the psychodynamic perspective takes account of both innate instincts (nature), and environment too, in the form of parenting (nurture). This means that it allows for the influence of both nature and nurture, and it is not too reductionist because it looks at more than one aspect of our psychological functioning. As regards determinism, the psychodynamic perspective explains that we are strongly influenced by unconscious factors, but that once we become aware of these – e.g. through therapy – we can exert our free will.

Weaknesses

- **Poor research methodology.** The kind of research carried out in the psychodynamic approach often fails to live up to the standards of good science. By definition, case studies involve very small samples, and the samples are always unrepresentative because they involve patients in psychological distress who have undertaken psychotherapy. Most people don't have therapy, so generalising from those who do to the whole population is problematic. Case studies cannot be replicated, so they lack reliability. Actually, some of Freud's ideas came not from case studies but from self-analysis. This is even dodgier. For example, the idea of the Oedipus Complex came from an intensive period of reflection on Freud's own childhood. Essentially he was saying that he had been through the Oedipus Complex, and therefore everyone else must have done. The Little Hans case was meant to illustrate this.
- **Theoretical ideas are sometimes vague and hard to test.** Two of the 'gold standards' of a sound scientific theory are that it has clear concepts, and that it can be scientifically tested. Some aspects of Freud's theory fall down on both of these. Ideas such as the unconscious and the Oedipus Complex are very hard to pin down precisely or to measure. It is also pretty much impossible to design a study to test whether such things really exist. Of course attempts have been made to do this, and there is some supporting evidence, but compared to other approaches and perspectives the psychodynamic perspective is weak on precision and testability.

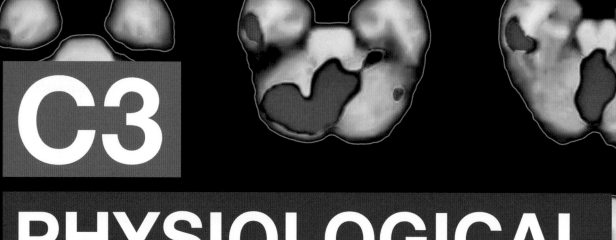

C3
PHYSIOLOGICAL PSYCHOLOGY

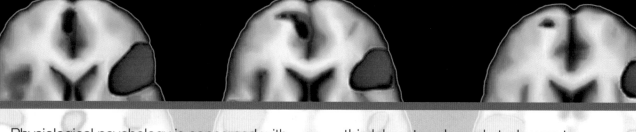

Physiological psychology is concerned with the action of genes, the nervous system and hormones on our behaviour, emotions and cognition. In this chapter we will look at three classic studies from physiological psychology.

1. Maguire *et al.*'s study of taxi drivers' brains. This was a laboratory-based study investigating the role of a brain area called the hippocampus in navigation. The participants were taxi drivers who had been working for different lengths of time. Their brains were scanned to explore differences in the size of the hippocampus.

2. Dement and Kleitman's study of sleep and dreaming. The aim of this laboratory-based study was to investigate how eye movements during sleep relate to dreaming.

3. Sperry's study of split-brain patients. Like the first two studies, this was also a laboratory-based investigation, but in this case the participants were deliberately selected because they had all had an operation to separate the left and right halves of the brain. The aim was to see how this 'split-brain' procedure affected their cognition.

We will now look at each of these studies in detail, before using them to explore the nature of physiological psychology and to think about its strengths and limitations.

MAGUIRE *et al.*'s STUDY OF TAXI DRIVERS' BRAINS

Maguire, E.A., Gadian, D.G., Johnsrude, I.S., Good, C.D., Ashburner, J., Frackowiak, R.S. & Frith, C.D. (2000) Navigation-related structural changes in the hippocampi of taxi drivers. *Proceedings of the National Academy of Science*, USA. **97**: 4398–4403R.

💡 KEY IDEAS

Localisation refers to the restriction of a particular brain function to a particular structure. **Plasticity** refers to the brain's ability to change in response to use.

CONTEXT

The concept of **localisation** of function is central to this study, as it illustrates a role of the hippocampus in navigation. The hippocampus appears to provide a 'cognitive map' – that is, a mental representation of spatial relationships. This role is well documented in previous research both on humans and on animals, as is the change in size of the hippocampus with use. This is neural **plasticity**, the idea that brain structure and function can change with experience. In a review of research into hippocampal variations in nature, Lee *et al.* (1998) found that the hippocampus in birds and mammals, unlike most brain tissue, retains its ability to make new cells. So, when seasonal behaviours occur that use the hippocampus, such as homing or caching food, the hippocampus changes – growing more cells and getting bigger. For example, Smulders *et al.* (1995) found that in birds such as the black-capped chickadee, which bury their excess food in the autumn and then retrieve it in winter, the hippocampus increases in size during the period when they are learning food-store locations. Such evidence suggests that people who make greater use of their navigational skills might also develop larger hippocampi.

Figure 3.1
The hippocampus of the black-capped chickadee increases during the food-storing season

ACTIVITY ✳

Figure 3.2 Only around half of trainees finally make the grade as London taxi drivers by passing the Knowledge test.

BRAIN STRUCTURE SNAPSHOTS REVEAL SCIENCE BEHIND WHY ONLY HALF OF LONDON TAXI TRAINEES PASS THE KNOWLEDGE TEST

Scientists followed a group of 79 trainee drivers and a 'control group' of 31 non-taxi drivers. **Magnetic Resonance Imaging (MRI)** scans were used to take brain structure 'snapshots' of the volunteers, who were also given certain memory tasks.

At the start of the study, there were no obvious differences between participants' brains. Three to four years later, significant differences were seen. The 39 trainees who qualified had greater volumes of grey matter in their posterior hippocampus than the 40 who failed, or the non-taxi drivers.

In memory tasks, both qualified and non-qualified trainees performed better in tests involving London landmarks than non-taxi drivers. However, the qualified trainees – but not those who failed to qualify – were worse at other tasks, such as recalling complex visual information, than the controls. This suggests there might be a price to pay for the extra effort involved in acquiring the Knowledge, said the researchers.

They speculate that the findings may reflect an increase in the rate at which new neurons are generated and survive when faced with a significant mental challenge. The hippocampus is one of the few brain areas where new neurons continue to be born in adults.

Prof Maguire said: 'What is not clear is whether those trainees who became fully-fledged taxi drivers had some biological advantage over those who failed. Could it be, for example, that they have a genetic predisposition towards having a more adaptable "plastic" brain? In other words, the perennial question of "nature versus nurture" is still open.'

Source: The Mirror, *8 December 2011*

Q

1 Explain the finding that the trainees who qualified had greater volumes of grey matter in the posterior hippocampus than either those who did not qualify, or the control group.
2 What does Maguire mean by 'plastic' brains?
3 Why does she say that the 'perennial question of "nature versus nurture" is still open'?

AIM

The aim of the study was to investigate whether there was a difference in hippocampal volume between individuals who did, or did not, have extensive navigational experience.

IN BRIEF ❶

Aim: To investigate whether doing a job that demands navigational experience, and spending more years in that job, affect the volume of the hippocampus.

Method: The experimental analysis compared 16 right-handed male taxi drivers and 50 non-taxi-driving controls (IV), matched for gender, handedness and age range. The DV was hippocampal volume, measured with an MRI scan.

The correlational analysis explored a relationship between the measured variables of time spent as a taxi driver (between 1.5 and 28 years) and hippocampal volume, using 15 of the 16 taxi drivers, excluding the oldest.

Results: The posterior region (i.e. the back) of the hippocampus was larger in taxi drivers, and the anterior region was larger in non-taxi drivers. For the taxi drivers, the correlation between hippocampal size and number of years spent driving a taxi was positive for the posterior region, and negative for the anterior region.

Conclusion: The distribution of grey matter in the hippocampus changes with use. The posterior hippocampus appears to store spatial information about the environment and to grow larger when used more.

STRETCH & CHALLENGE ◎

Maguire *et al.* (2000) refer to an earlier review article (Maguire *et al.*, 1999) which discusses issues in navigation research, including human and animal studies, sex differences and the use of different methodologies e.g. virtual reality and brain scanning. A free full-text copy is available at: http://wexler.free.fr (Click on 'library' and then scroll down and click on 'Maguire 1999: Human spatial navigation'.) Read the article and produce a poster to illustrate one aspect of the review, explaining how it relates to the present study.

METHOD

Design

Although this study was based in a laboratory setting, the method used was a natural or 'quasi' experiment, because the participants already belonged to the existing groups of 'taxi drivers' and 'controls' – that is, they could not be allocated to the conditions by the researchers.

A correlational analysis was also conducted, which considered the variables of hippocampal volume and time spent as a taxi driver.

Participants

The experimental group consisted of 16 right-handed male taxi drivers with a mean age of 44 years (range 32–62 years). Their experience as licensed London taxi drivers varied between 1.5 and 42 years (mean 14.3 years). Their training (i.e. time on 'the Knowledge') had taken on average 2 years (range 10 months-3.5 years, some part-, some full-time). All were medically, neurologically and psychiatrically healthy. The matched control group consisted of people on the MRI-scan database held at the unit where the experimental participants were scanned. From this group, females, left-handed males, those under 32 or over 62, and those

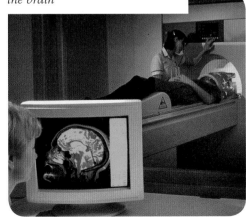

Figure 3.3
A Magnetic Resonance Imaging (MRI) scanner uses a powerful magnet to produce images of the brain

KEY IDEAS

In a **Magnetic Resonance Imaging** (MRI) scanner, a powerful magnetic field affects water molecules, and the changes in these molecules, which are detected by the scanner, produce a very detailed image that presents different brain areas in shades of black, grey and white. The technique of **voxel-based morphometry (VBM)** takes images in 1.5x1.5x1.5 mm 'blocks' (called voxels). This allows the volume of grey matter in small brain areas to be measured precisely. **Pixel counting** is an image analysis technique in which the number of pixels in a known area occupied by a particular tissue type (in this case hippocampal tissue) are counted and converted into a volume.

KEY IDEAS

A researcher is described as working **blind** when they do not know which level of the IV a participant they are testing belongs to. This helps to avoid experimenter bias.

QUESTION SPOTLIGHT!

This study used a detailed matching procedure. Make sure you could answer a question asking for the ways in which the groups were matched.

with health problems, were excluded. This left scans of 50 people, which were used as the non-taxi-driving controls. The experimental and control groups did not differ in mean or range of age, and the spread of ages in each decade of life was similar in both groups.

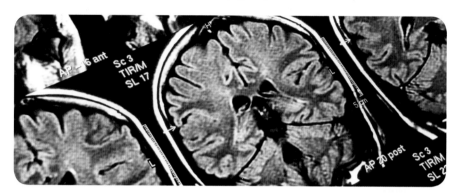

Figure 3.4
MRI scans are detailed images of brains structure

Procedure

In the experimental part of the study an independent groups design was used. The independent variable was whether the individuals were London taxi drivers or were non-taxi drivers. Taxi drivers were chosen as their job demands a dependence on navigational skill and they are required to demonstrate a very high level of spatial understanding of locations and routes in London (the Knowledge). The dependent variable was the volume of the hippocampus (on the left and right side). This was assessed using measurements from MRI scans. There were several controls. These included:

- matching the samples in terms of age, gender and handedness.
- measurements of brain volume being done by one experienced individual who, in order to ensure that the assessments were consistent, was unaware of each participants' condition (i.e. they were working '**blind**')
- both experimental and control participants being scanned in the same MRI scanner.

The scans from 13 of the control group were used to produce an image 'template' against which all scans were judged using a technique called **voxel-based morphometry (VBM)**. These measures were used to calculate the volume of grey matter in different regions of the brain.

An image-analysis technique called **pixel counting** was used to compare 16 taxi drivers with 16 precisely age-matched controls. The total hippocampal volume on the left and right was measured using three-dimensional information from at least 26 visual 'slices' of each hippocampus, taken at 1.5mm intervals (therefore covering a total

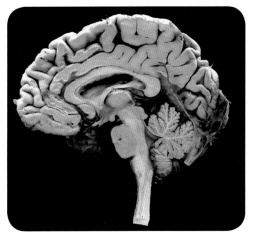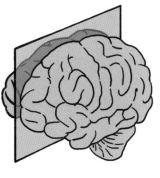

sagittal plane

WEB WATCH @

You can find out about the
Knowledge here:
www.taxiknowledge.co.uk
and do a mock test here:
www.the-knowledge.org.uk

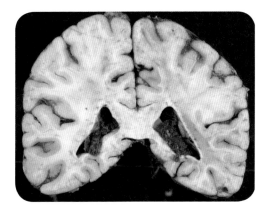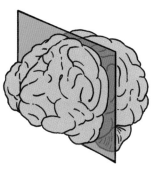

coronal plane

Figure 3.5
Brain sections

length of about 4cm). These slices were taken in 'cross sections' of the
hippocampus on a **coronal plane** – that is, at right angles to the longest
length of the hippocampus (Figure 3.5b). The images were analysed by
counting the number of pixels occupied by hippocampal tissue, which
was then converted into a volume. This volume was corrected for total
intracranial volume – the size of the person's brain – (based on
measurements from slices on a **sagittal plane** – Figure 3.5a) to make all
participants' data comparable. The same experienced researcher counted
the pixels on all scans (both experimental and control) but was 'blind' to
each participant's condition.

In the correlational analysis, a possible link between the two variables
of time spent as a taxi driver (both in training on the Knowledge, and
subsequently) and hippocampal volume was explored. One participant
was excluded from this analysis as he had been a taxi driver for much
longer than all the others (42 years, compared to 28 years for the next
nearest participant).

QUESTION SPOTLIGHT! ⭐

*Can you explain why was it important
that the researcher assessing the
scans was 'blind' to the group to
which each participant belonged?*

RESULTS

This study collected only quantitative data. From the experimental investigation, the VBM data showed that the only brain areas with a significant difference between taxi drivers and the control group were the left and right hippocampi. The difference demonstrated by this technique was significant for the left and right posterior hippocampus (the back part), but not the left and right anterior hippocampus (the front part). The amount of grey matter in the hippocampus of taxi drivers was significantly different from that of non-taxi drivers.

The total hippocampal volumes measured by pixel counting were smaller on every measure for the controls, but the differences were not significant (see Table 3.1). Further statistical analysis, however, found differences between specific hippocampal areas and the left and right sides between taxi drivers and the controls. These differences were similar to those in Table 3.1, but were significant (see Figure 3.6).

TABLE 3.1 PIXEL-COUNTING ESTIMATES OF HIPPOCAMPAL VOLUME

Side of brain	Intracranial volume correction	Hippocampal volume (mm³)	
		Taxi drivers	Controls
Right	corrected	4159	4080
	uncorrected	4300	4255
Left	corrected	3977	3918
	uncorrected	4155	4092

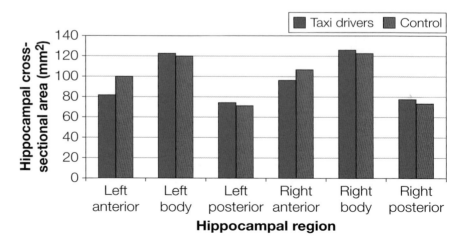

Figure 3.6
Comparison of hippocampal regions using data from pixel counting

Figure 3.6 shows several differences that were significant:

- Controls had larger anterior hippocampi than taxi drivers.
- For both groups, the right hippocampus was larger than the left.
- The posterior hippocampi of taxi drivers were significantly greater in volume.

However posterior hippocampal volume did not differ between the left and right sides.

In the correlational investigation, a significant relationship was found between time spent as a taxi driver and right-posterior hippocampal volume. Correlation coefficients of $r = 0.6$ (based on VBM) and $r = 0.5$ (based on pixel counting) both indicated a positive correlation (see Figure 3.7). The pixel-counting data also revealed a correlation between anterior hippocampal volume and time spent working as a taxi driver. Here, the correlation coefficient of $r = -0.6$ indicated a negative correlation. The data from the driver whose scores were omitted from this analysis also conformed to the pattern, for example with 42 years' experience, his VBM measure was 13.7.

STRETCH & CHALLENGE ◉

Maguire *et al.* (2003) tested navigation in an unfamiliar virtual environment and found better navigators did not have bigger hippocampi. This supports the idea that level of navigational experience and the consequent brain changes, rather than innate navigational skill due to brain differences at birth, account for the navigational ability of taxi drivers. Explain why.

If you want to read about this, look here:

http://cream.fil.ion.ucl.ac.uk/Maguire/Maguire2003.pdf

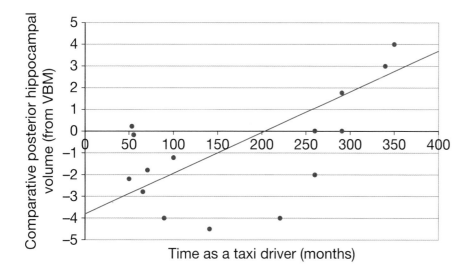

Figure 3.7
Positive correlation between time spent taxi-driving and posterior hippocampal volume.
Source: Maguire et al. (2000), fig. 3b, p.4401

CONCLUSIONS

The results suggest that the distribution of grey matter in the hippocampus changes with use because the posterior hippocampus stores information about spatial relations in the environment, so it grows in response to demand for navigational skills. This explanation is more likely than the idea that people with a large posterior hippocampus choose to be taxi drivers. This is because the correlational data show that, as taxi drivers developed a better understanding of routes and locations, improving their cognitive maps over time, the volume of the posterior hippocampus increased.

QUESTION SPOTLIGHT! ⯈

Sketch the graph in Figure 3.7 onto graph paper with an extended scale to cover the omitted taxi driver, and include these data. *Can you explain how these data support the general pattern?*

STUDY 1

MAGUIRE *et al.*'s STUDY OF TAXI DRIVERS' BRAINS

SUMMARY

AIM

To find out whether the navigational experience of taxi driving affects hippocampal volume.

METHOD

An experiment used MRI scans to measure hippocampal volume (DV) in 16 right-handed male taxi drivers and 50 matched controls (IV) of the same gender, handedness and age spread. In a correlational analysis, two variables were measured in 15 taxi drivers and 15 matched controls: time spent as a taxi driver (between 1.5 and 28 years) and hippocampal volume.

RESULTS

Posterior hippocampal volume was greater in taxi drivers; the anterior region was larger in non-taxi drivers. The taxi drivers' hippocampal size showed two relationships: a positive correlation between hippocampal size and years spent driving a taxi for the posterior region, and a negative correlation for the anterior region.

CONCLUSIONS

The posterior hippocampus stores spatial information and grows when used more.

EVALUATION

This study raises few ethical issues, but several methodological ones.

ETHICAL ISSUES

The ethical issues of informed consent and competence were important in relation to the taxi drivers. Although MRI scanning is not in itself dangerous, it does carry risks for some individuals. An MRI scanner generates a powerful magnetic field, so it is therefore dangerous for people with metal implants, such as pacemakers or pinned bones. It would have been important for the ethical conduct of the study to ensure that the taxi drivers were not putting themselves at any greater risk than in their normal lives by offering to be scanned. Also, an MRI scanner is a confined space and it is noisy. Some people

find this unpleasant or frightening. The participants would need to have been given sufficient details of the intended procedure to be 'informed', and given the option to be included in the study or not, i.e. to 'consent'. The control participants were not given unnecessary brain scans as their data were retrieved from an existing store, thereby avoiding the potential for additional distress in this group.

METHODOLOGICAL ISSUES
The sample

The experimental sample of 16 taxi drivers was quite large given that they had to be willing to undergo MRI scanning. As they were all London taxi drivers, they all lived in the same area, although there is no reason to suppose that men from any other city would differ.

As the sample was all male right handers, this might limit the generalisability of the findings, as navigation by females, or left-handed people, may differ. However, the age spread, the range and the nature of training (full time or part time), and time in the job all contributed to a varied sample. The matching of experimental to control participants used several important criteria (age, gender and handedness).

The research method

This research was a laboratory-based study, so many of the typical strengths and limitations apply (see page 134). The scanning procedure took place in a highly controlled environment, and the sample was carefully selected. This eliminated many extraneous variables, such as the possibility that the hippocampus gets bigger (or smaller) with age, or that any differences in the size of the left and right hippocampi were a function of handedness. Maguire *et al.* could therefore be reasonably confident that it was the independent variable (navigational experience) that was affecting the dependent variable (hippocampal size). Laboratory procedures are generally straightforward to replicate, as the controls and standardised procedures make them reliable.

Reliability

Reliability means consistency, so a procedure is reliable if it can be precisely replicated and always produces the same results. To achieve consistency in the way in which the hippocampal volumes were recorded from the brain scans, one experienced individual assessed all of the images. The same scanner was also used for both control and experimental participants.

Validity

A potential weakness in laboratory experiments is often a lack of ecological validity, but the realism of the environment and task are not at issue here. The participants did not have to perform a task and, although the scanner is clearly a highly artificial environment, this cannot affect the size of a brain area – that is, the participants cannot have responded to demand

characteristics. In addition, the researcher assessing the scans was unaware of the participants' condition, thus increasing the validity of the measure of the DV, as they were less likely to be biased.

The comparison of taxi drivers and a separate control group could, however, be questioned. As the occupations and interests of the control group were not considered, it is possible that this group included individuals with other reasons for a high demand on navigational skills – such as people who go orienteering, or happened to drive to lots of different places for their work. In fact, it is unlikely that this was a problem, as the correlational analysis demonstrated an increase in hippocampal volume with experience.

Quantitative data

A strength of Maguire *et al.*'s study was the use of quantitative data that could be analysed statistically, allowing the researchers to be more certain about their conclusions. Measurements of length and volume are highly objective, assuming the individual applying the criteria for measurement is reliable and independent of experimenter bias (see above).

STRETCH & CHALLENGE ◎

Why might Maguire *et al.*'s findings be unlikely to generalise to females? Search the internet for scientific evidence for gender differences in navigational ability.

EXAM FOCUS

We now show you some of the sorts of questions that could be asked about the Maguire *et al.* study in your exam. We will then show you some examples of the sorts of answers we believe might be successful and less successful, and point out some classic traps to avoid.

SECTION A

1 The Maguire *et al.* study on taxi drivers used MRI (Magnetic Resonance Imaging) scans.
   (a) Explain what an MRI scan measured in this study. *(2 marks)*
   (b) Outline one piece of evidence that suggests the brains of taxi drivers are different from those of non-taxi drivers. *(2 marks)*

2 From Maguire *et al.*'s study on taxi drivers:
   (a) Describe two features of the sample. *(2 marks)*
   (b) Outline one limitation of this sample. *(2 marks)*

3 Maguire *et al.* investigated structural changes in the hippocampi of taxi drivers.
   (a) Identify the independent variable and the dependent variable in this experiment. *(2 marks)*
   (b) Describe one effect the independent variable had on the dependent variable in this experiment. *(2 marks)*

4 From Maguire *et al.*'s study on taxi drivers:
   (a) Identify two of the criteria used to select the taxi drivers in this study. *(2 marks)*
   (b) Explain why Maguire *et al.* could not manipulate the independent variable. *(2 marks)*

5 From Maguire *et al.*'s study on taxi drivers:
   (a) Identify two controls used in this study. *(2 marks)*
   (b) Explain the importance of using controls in this study. *(2 marks)*

6 Describe two findings from Maguire *et al.*'s study on taxi drivers. *(4 marks)*

7 From Maguire *et al.*'s study on taxi drivers:
   (a) Describe how participants were matched in this study. *(2 marks)*
   (b) Explain why it was important to match the participants. *(2 marks)*

8 Maguire *et al.* carried out a correlation between hippocampal volume and the amount of time spent as a taxi driver as part of their study.
   (a) Explain what the results of this correlational analysis showed. *(2 marks)*
   (b) Give one criticism of using a correlation in the study by Maguire *et al.* *(2 marks)*

SECTION B

(a) What was the aim of the study by Maguire *et al.*? *(2 marks)*

(b) Describe the method used in the study by Maguire *et al.*, and suggest one advantage of using this method. *(6 marks)*

(c) Outline two quantitative measures recorded in the study by Maguire *et al.* *(6 marks)*

(d) Assess the reliability of these measures from the study by Maguire *et al.* *(6 marks)*

(e) Outline the results of the study by Maguire *et al.* *(8 marks)*

(f) Suggest one way in which the study by Maguire *et al.* could be improved, and outline the effect this may have on the results. *(8 marks)*

SECTION C

(a) Outline one assumption of the physiological approach. *(2 marks)*

(b) Describe how the physiological approach could explain structural changes in the brain. *(4 marks)*

(c) Describe one similarity and one difference between any studies that use the physiological approach. *(6 marks)*

(d) Discuss strengths and weaknesses of the physiological approach using examples from any studies that take this approach. *(12 marks)*

SOME ANSWERS & COMMENTS

SECTION A 2 From Maguire *et al.*'s study on taxi drivers:
(b) Outline one limitation of this sample. *(2 marks)*

Kay's answer:
They are taxi drivers, which means it's unreliable.

Linda's answer:
It was actually a very small sample, with just 16 taxi drivers and 16 in the control group. This means it is hard to generalise and be representative. We do not know if they are different to other taxi drivers, as there are hundreds in London.

We say: 0 marks.
Kay, you have not really made a clear point here. They had to be taxi drivers as that was the purpose of the study. Saying that they are unreliable tells us nothing, as you would have to explain how they were not reliable – but this is not actually appropriate here. Focus on features of the sample to criticise it – such as the number, or how they were selected – but not who they are if the study is examining one special group.

We say: 2 marks.
Well done, Linda. You have identified a key criticism of the sample (that of the number), explained why it is a criticism, and clearly linked your answer to the study. There is nothing else you needed to do to get the marks.

SECTION A 4 From Maguire *et al.*'s study on taxi drivers:
(a) Identify two of the criteria used to select the taxi drivers in this study. *(2 marks)*

Glen's answer:
MRI scans and age was limited, with no young new drivers or really old ones.

Doris's answer:
All were men, as most taxi drivers in London are men, so no women were included, and all were right handed, in case this was a variable affecting brain organisation and so the scan.

We say: 1 mark.
Glen, there is a little confusion here as the control group was made up of the ones who had previously had an MRI. For your point on age, try to give an idea of the age range to show detailed knowledge – otherwise, it's just a bit vague.

We say: 2 marks.
Very clear, Doris. Two criteria are stated and you explain relevant details about them. It is nice and clear and to the point.

SECTION B (b) Describe the method used in the study by Maguire *et al.*, and suggest one advantage of using this method. *(6 marks)*

Bryn's answer:
This study scanned taxi drivers and other people to see if taxi driver brains were bigger or not. This was good

Continued

because there are lots of taxi drivers around, making it easy to do.

Gwen's answer:

This study used a quasi-experimental method, as the groups were naturally occurring, being male taxi drivers and male non-taxi drivers, where the hippocampus of taxi drivers was compared with a control group to see the difference. They did this with the MRI scans and looked at the pixel counting and VBMs. This was a good method, as it allowed easy comparison of a group who had naturally occurring differences in memory capacity and use. This meant no manipulation was necessary, meaning that the study is ecologically valid.

We say: 0 marks.
Bryn, think about the detail your examiner is looking for in a six-mark answer, and think about whether you have enough here. The answer is too general and does not focus on the key points about the method. Remember, the brain scan was to look at the hippocampus in particular, so tell us about that and the idea of greater volume. Avoid saying 'bigger' as it is really not psychological. You could state that it is a quasi-experiment. The advantage should be to do with the method, not the sample and how many people were in it.

We say: 5 marks.
Good use of terminology in naming the type of method used here, Gwen. You then went on to explain how this was carried out with nice detail from the study. Add a bit more technical detail to further illustrate the point, such as what the IV and DV are. The advantage was clear and relevant here, but in explaining it remember to link this clearly to the study itself as well, to avoid your point being too general.

SECTION C (c) Describe one similarity and one difference between any studies that use the physiological approach. *(6 marks)*

Neil's answer:

Maguire and Dement and Kleitman, both had equipment to measure participants' brains, and Sperry and Dement and Kleitman used small samples in their research.

Mei's answer:

A difference is that the methods are different, as Maguire is a quasi-experiment and Dement and Kleitman is not comparing two groups. Maguire was a quasi-study as there were London taxi drivers and a control group who were not taxi drivers. Dement and Kleitman used one group of people to study sleep in the laboratory, and there was no comparison group.
A similarity is that Maguire and Dement and Kleitman both gathered quantitative data from scientific equipment that they used. Maguire used MRI scans of the hippocampus and had data from the pixel counting, which is quantitative. Dement and Kleitman used the EEG scans to record the brain activity and how many of the different stages of sleep there were in each night, which is also quantitative.

We say: 2 marks.
Neil, you really need to make your answer clearer here. In a question on a similarity and a difference, do signpost for your examiner which one is which – do not leave them to guess. Start a sentence by saying, 'A similarity is…', as this makes it very clear. Having done this, you then need to support this with some detailed evidence from each of the studies you are using in the point. Show the examiner your knowledge of the studies, or you cannot get much credit.

We say: 6 marks.
A really well-written answer, Mei. It is a good style to set out what your point is at the start, and to identify it as a similarity or difference. Showing that you know the studies well by picking out examples that fit your point tells the examiner you know what you are talking about. This is a good way to pick up marks.

DEMENT AND KLEITMAN'S STUDY OF SLEEP AND DREAMING

Dement, W. and Kleitman, N. (1957) The relation of eye movements during sleep to dream activity: an objective method for the study of dreaming. *Journal of Experimental Psychology,* **53**: 339-46.

CONTEXT

KEY IDEAS

Rapid eye movement (REM) is a state of sleep during which the sleeper's eyes move quickly beneath the eyelids. If woken during this time, the sleeper typically reports having a vivid, visual dream.

The topics of sleep and dreaming are clearly hard to investigate because the participant is necessarily asleep and so can't communicate with the researcher. Even when participants are awake, only self-report data can be obtained about dream content, and these alone might not be valid, as they are subjective. The study of sleep and dreaming became more scientifically rigorous with the invention of physiological techniques to measure brain activity that indicated dreaming (the **electro-encephalograph**, or **EEG**) and allowed the electrical recording of eye movements (the **electro-oculogram**, or **EOG**) rather than their direct observation (see Key Ideas, p. 98). These techniques were used by Dement and Kleitman (1955) to trace the cyclical changes that occur in brain activity and eye movements during a night's sleep (summarised in Figure 3.8). The cycle alternates between a stage in which there are eye movements, and several stages during which there are none.

In the dream or **rapid eye movement (REM)** sleep stage, our eyes move under the lids (hence 'rapid eye movements'). In Aserinsky and Kleitman's (1955) study, participants woken from this stage were more likely to report a vivid, visual dream, than participants woken from **non-rapid eye movement (nREM)** sleep. Non-rapid eye movement sleep can be broken down into four stages (1 to 4), of which 1 is the lightest and 4 the deepest.

REM sleep resembles wakefulness in some ways: our eyes move, we often experience vivid (if bizarre) thoughts in the form of dreams, and

KEY IDEAS

An **electro-encephalograph (EEG)** detects and records tiny electrical changes associated with nerve and muscle activity. The EEG machine produces a chart (an encephalogram) that shows **brain waves** (see Figure 6.22, p. 280). These change with the frequency and amplitude (i.e. the 'height', which indicates the voltage) of electrical output from the brain over time. In REM sleep, the EEG is relatively low voltage, high amplitude. Non-REM sleep has either high voltage and slow (low amplitude) waves, or frequent 'sleep spindles', which are short-lived high-voltage, high-frequency waves. Modern EEG machines are entirely computerised, whereas Dement and Kleitman's EEG had continuously running paper. The faster the paper moved, the more detail could be recorded. The paper was usually moving at 3 or 6mm per second, although a faster speed of 3cm per second was used for detailed analysis. To remember the meaning of EEG it can help to break the word down:

*E*lectro (electric)

*E*n cephalo (in head)

*G*raph (writing).

The same EEG electrodes and machine can also be used to record eye movements. The output – called an **electro-oculogram (EOG)** – indicates the presence or absence of eye movements, their size and their direction (horizontal or vertical).

our brains are active. However, in other ways it is very different from wakefulness: we are quite difficult to wake up, we are fairly insensitive to external stimuli, and we are paralysed. As REM sleep presents these contradictions, it is also known as *paradoxical sleep*.

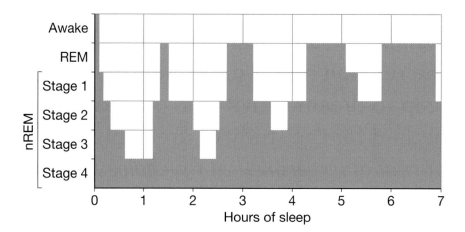

Figure 3.8
A summary of sleep stages over the course of a night

AIM

The aim of the study was to investigate dreaming in an objective way by looking for relationships between eye movements in sleep and the dreamer's recall. Three approaches were used to investigate this, with the aim of finding out whether:

1 dream recall differs between REM and nREM sleep;

2 there is a positive correlation between subjective estimates of dream duration and the length of the REM period; and

3 eye-movement patterns are related to dream content.

METHOD

This study included several laboratory investigations with different designs. Three specific approaches were used to test the three aims:

1 *To test whether dream recall differs between REM and nREM sleep*: participants were woken either in REM or nREM, but were not told which stage of sleep they had been in prior to waking. They confirmed whether they had been having a dream and, if so, described the content into a recorder.

2   *To test whether subjective estimates of dream duration are related to the length of the REM period*: participants were woken following either 5 or 15 minutes in REM sleep. They were asked to choose whether they thought they had been dreaming for 5 or 15 minutes. Longer REM periods were also tested. Again, they gave a report of dream content and the number of words in the dream narrative was counted.

3   *To test whether eye-movement patterns represent the visual experience of the dream content or whether they are simply random movements arising from the activation of the central nervous system during dream sleep*: the direction of eye movements was detected using electrodes around the eyes (EOG). The participant was woken after exhibiting a single eye-movement pattern for longer than one minute. Again, they were asked to report their dream.

IN BRIEF ❶

Aim: To investigate: dream recall in REM and nREM sleep (1); estimation of dream duration (2); and the relationship of dream content to eye movements (3).

Method: 7 male and 2 female participants ate normally (but without caffeine or alcohol), then slept overnight in a laboratory. They had electrodes stuck beside their eyes (EOG) and on the scalp (EEG), and were woken by a doorbell during the night (either in REM or nREM, but they were not told which). They recalled any dream into a voice recorder (1). If awoken following either 5 or 15 minutes of REM sleep, they chose which duration they had been woken up after, and the number of words in their dream narrative was counted (2). The direction of eye movements was detected and participants were woken following a one-minute long pattern that was mainly vertical, mainly horizontal, both vertical and horizontal, or that had very little or no eye movement (3).

Findings: The dream phase of the sleep cycle lasted 20 minutes on average. Dreams were frequently described when woken from REM, but rarely when woken from nREM sleep (1), and participants could accurately estimate 5- or 15-minute REM durations. This duration also correlated with the number of words in the participants' dream narrative (2). Eye-movement patterns were related to dream content (3).

Conclusion: Dreaming is reported from REM but not nREM sleep, the length of a dream can be accurately judged, and eye movements relate to dream content.

Design

Dement and Kleitman described this series of studies as experiments. Approach 1 was a natural experiment in a lab setting, and Approach 2 was a true experiment,, with each participant being tested in both conditions, i.e. they used a repeated measures design. Approach 2 also included a correlation.

- Approach 1: the levels of the IV were REM sleep/non-REM sleep and the DVs were whether a dream was reported and, if so, the detail.
- Approach 2: the data were used in both experimental and correlational designs.
  - experimental analysis: the levels of the IV were waking after 5 or 15 minutes, and the dependent variable was the participant's choice of 5 or 15 minutes.
  - correlational analysis: the two variables were the participant's time estimate and the number of words in the dream narrative.
- Approach 3: the IV of eye-movement pattern type could not be manipulated by the experimenters, so this was also a natural experiment (conducted in a laboratory). The DV was the report of dream content.

Participants

Nine adult participants were used in this study (seven male and two female). Four of these were mainly used to confirm the data from five who were studied in detail. Those studied in detail spent between 6 and 17 nights in the lab and were tested with 50–77 awakenings, those used to confirm the findings stayed only 1 or 2 nights and were awoken between 4 and 10 times in total. Each participant was identified by a pair of initials.

Procedure

During the daytime prior to arrival at the laboratory, each participant ate normally (excluding drinks containing alcohol or caffeine). They arrived at the laboratory just before their normal bedtime and were fitted with electrical recording apparatus. This included electrodes attached near the eyes (to record eye movements) and on the scalp (to record **brain waves**). Once in bed in a quiet, dark room, wires from the electrodes (which fed to the EEG in the experimenter's room) were gathered into a 'pony tail' from the participant's head, to allow them freedom of movement. The EEG ran continuously through the night to monitor the participant's sleep stages and to inform the experimenters when they should be woken up. Participants were woken by a doorbell that was loud enough to rouse them from any sleep stage. This meant that the experimenter did not have to enter the room to wake the participant, and thus they were all treated in exactly the same way. The doorbell was rung at various times during the night and participants indicated whether they had been dreaming prior to being woken and, if so, described their dream into a voice recorder. They then returned to sleep (typically within 5 minutes). Occasionally, the experimenter entered the room after the participant had finished speaking in order to ask questions. When the narrative was analysed, it was considered to be a dream only if it was a coherent, fairly detailed description of the content (i.e. vague, fragmentary impressions were not scored as dreams).

The patterns of REM and nREM wakings differed between different participants. For PM and KC, they were determined randomly to eliminate any possibility of an unintentional pattern. WD was treated in the same way, although he was told that he would be woken only from dream sleep. DN was woken in a repeating pattern of three REM followed by three non-REM awakenings. The waking of IR from REM or nREM was chosen by the experimenter.

WEB WATCH @

This website describes sleep stages and has links to videos about sleep stages:
http://healthysleep.med.harvard.edu
Click on 'The Science of Sleep'.
You can download from this site an app that will track your sleep stages and produce a graph like an EEG, showing your REM and nREM stages:
http://mdlabs.se/sleepcycle/

RESULTS

Quantitative and qualitative data were gathered in response to Approaches 1 and 2. Only qualitative data were gathered for Approach 3.

Results for Approach 1: Does dream recall differ between REM and nREM sleep?

As Table 3.2 shows, participants described dreams often when woken in REM but rarely from nREM sleep (although there were some individual differences). This pattern was consistent over the night. When awakened from nREM, participants tended to describe feelings (eg pleasantness, anxiety, detachment) but this did not relate to specific dream content.

TABLE 3.2 INSTANCES OF DREAM RECALL FOLLOWING WAKINGS FROM REM AND NON-REM SLEEP

Sleep stage (level of independent variable)	REM-sleep awakenings		Non-REM-sleep awakenings	
	Dream recall	No recall	Dream recall	No recall
Number of times participants reported the presence or absence of a dream (dependent variable)	152	39	11	149

Source: adapted from Dement and Kleitman (1957), table 2, p. 341.

Waking pattern did not affect recall. Specifically, WD was no less accurate despite being misled, and DN was no more accurate even though he might have guessed the pattern of wakings. Recall of dreams during nREM sleep was much more likely when the participant was woken soon after the end of a REM stage (see Table 3.3).

TABLE 3.3 NUMBER OF DREAMS RECALLED FOLLOWING WAKINGS FROM NON-REM SLEEP IMMEDIATELY AFTER, OR MUCH LONGER AFTER, AN REM STAGE		
	Time of waking after REM stage	
	Within 8 minutes	*After 8 minutes*
Number of wakings conducted	17	132
Number of dreams recalled	5	6
Percentage of occasions on which dreams recalled	29	5

So, REM and nREM sleep differ as the vivid, visual dreams are reported only from wakings during, or a short time after, REM sleep.

Results for Approach 2: Are subjective estimates of dream duration related to the length of the REM period?

Initially, Dement and Kleitman had attempted to wake participants after various REM durations to ask them to estimate these. Although the participants' responses weren't wildly wrong, the task was too difficult. When asked instead whether they had been in REM sleep for 5 or 15 minutes, the participants responded more accurately. They were 88% and 78% accurate respectively for 5- or 15-minute REM durations (see Figure 3.9). Although most of the participants were highly accurate (with only 0–3 incorrect responses), one was not. Participant DN frequently found he could recall only the end of his dream, so it seemed shorter than it actually was. Therefore, he consistently underestimated dream duration, often choosing 5 minutes instead of 15. This meant he was accurate on short REM estimates (making only 2 errors over 10 wakings), but inaccurate after 15 minutes' of REM (making 5 errors over 10 wakings).

Using REM periods over a range of durations, narratives from 152 dreams were collected. Twenty six of these could not be used, however, as they were too poorly recorded for accurate transcription. For the remaining dreams (15–35 per participant) the number of words in the dream narrative was counted. Even though this was affected by how expressive the participant was, a significant positive correlation was found between REM duration and number of words in the narrative. The r values varied between 0.4 and 0.71 for different participants.

Dream narratives for very long durations (e.g. 30 or 50 minutes) were not much longer than those for 15 minutes. The participants did report, however, that they felt as though they had been dreaming for a long time, suggesting that they could not recall the early part of the dream.

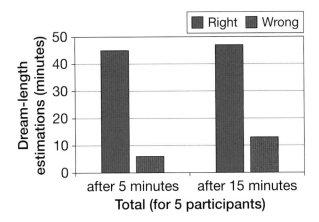

Figure 3.9
Accuracy of dream-length estimations after 5 or 15 minutes of REM sleep

QUESTION SPOTLIGHT! ⟩

You could be given examples to interpret.
What kinds of eye movements would you expect to have been found prior to these two dream reports from Dement and Kleitman?
1   Looking up and down while climbing ladders.
2   Throwing basketballs, watching them go up into the net, and then looking down to take another from the floor.

Results for Approach 3:
Do eye movement patterns in REM sleep represent the visual experience of the dream?

Dement and Kleitman found that participants' narratives were not sufficiently accurate to be matched exactly to the changes in eye-movement patterns over the length of a REM sleep period. Instead, participants were woken after periods of specific eye-movement patterns (vertical, horizontal, both or little movement).

Three of the nine participants showed periods of predominantly vertical eye movements, and each was allied to a narrative about vertical movement. In one, the participant dreamed about standing at the foot of a tall cliff, using a hoist (a kind of winch or pulley). They reported looking up at climbers at various levels on the cliff, and down at the hoist machinery. A single dream followed predominantly horizontal movements. Here, the participant reported dreaming about two people throwing tomatoes at each other.

QUESTION SPOTLIGHT!

Note that 'results' are typically numerical or are quotes from participants that describe the data collected. In contrast, 'conclusions' indicate what those results mean. They are more general and can be linked back to the aims of the study. However, it is not sufficient simply to restate the aim and say 'they found this was true'. You need to explain why, sometimes using the results (for example, if the question says, 'Using the findings from the study by Dement and Kleitman, explain the conclusions about…').

On 10 occasions, participants were woken after little of no eye movement. Here, they reported either watching something in the distance, or staring with their eyes fixed on a single object. In two cases, the participants had been dreaming about driving. Their eyes had been very still, then made several sudden movements to the left just before being woken up. One participant reported a pedestrian standing on the left who hailed him as he drove by, and the other had been startled by a speeding car appearing to his left as he arrived at a junction.

Twenty-one wakings followed mixed eye movements. In these instances, the participants reported looking at people or objects nearby (rather than far away) – for example, in fighting or talking to a group of people.

Dement and Kleitman also recorded the eye movements of people when they were awake (including the five original participants and some other, naïve ones). These findings confirmed that, when awake, our eyes are relatively stable when we are focused on objects in the distance, and show movements of similar amplitude to when we are dreaming of viewing nearby objects (i.e. many small but frequent and predominantly horizontal movements). Few vertical movements were recorded except when the experimenter threw a ball in the air for them to watch (and when they blinked).

Box 3.1
General findings
Dement and Kleitman made some additional observations:
- Participants were more likely to report dreams later in the night than earlier.
- Rapid eye movements were never observed in the initial minutes of sleep, even though the EEG was similar to that seen during REM sleep.
- Although most REM phases were interrupted by testing, when uninterrupted they varied from 3–50 minutes in length (mean: 20 minutes).
- REM stages were longer later in the night.
- Rapid eye movements occurred in bursts of 2–100 movements at a rate of 0.1–0.2 per second.
- Cycle length was consistent within individuals, but varied between them, e.g. 70 minutes for participant DM; 104 for KC (average: 92 minutes).
- When woken from nREM sleep, participants returned to nREM and the next REM stage was not delayed. When woken from REM sleep, participants generally didn't dream again until the next REM phase.

CONCLUSIONS

Dement and Kleitman drew three main conclusions from this study, one in relation to each approach:

1   Dreams probably (although not certainly) occur only during REM sleep, which occurs regularly throughout each night's sleep. Dreams reported when woken from nREM sleep are ones from previous REM episodes. As the REM phases are longer later in the night, dreaming is more likely at this time. Earlier research found that dreams did not occur every night. This study suggests three possible explanations for this difference:

   (a)   If previous recordings were not continuous, they may have failed to 'catch' instances of dream sleep in every participant (if short REM periods occurred between sampling intervals).

   (b)   Equipment might not have detected small eye movements.

   (c)   Participants in whom no dreaming was identified might have had dreams that led to few eye movements, such as those about distant or static objects.

2   It is often believed that dreams happen in an instant. If the length of REM periods is proportional to subjective estimates, this would help to confirm that the two are related and would provide some information about the rate at which dreaming progresses. The finding that the length of a REM period and its estimation by the participant are very similar shows that dreams are not instantaneous events but rather they are experienced in 'real time'.

3   Eye movements during REM sleep correspond to where, and at what, the dreamer is looking in the dream. This suggests that eye movements are not simply random events caused by the activation of the central nervous system during dream sleep, but are directly related to dream imagery. Furthermore, they correspond in amplitude and pattern to those we experience when awake.

QUESTION SPOTLIGHT!

In testing Approach 3, Dement and Kleitman suggest that, rather than being related to dream content, eye movements could be just 'a random motor discharge of a more activated central nervous system'. You need to learn what this phrase means, and learn a piece of evidence that supports it – that is, a piece of evidence that suggests that dream content is random. It is important, too, that you learn some evidence to contradict this view, i.e. which supports Dement and Kleitman's conclusion.

 KEY IDEAS

Neurotransmitters are chemicals that transmit messages from one neuron (nerve cell) to the next. There are many different neurotransmitters found in different parts of the nervous system and which have different functions.

QUESTION SPOTLIGHT!

There are three different aims being tested in this study, each using similar but different techniques. Make sure that you can distinguish between them in terms of their purpose and their method.

ACTIVITY ✳

Figure 3.10
REM sleep behaviour disorder can have disastrous consequences

Physiological studies have told us a great deal about the control of sleep and dreams since Dement and Kleitman's study, including the involvement of specific brain areas and **neurotransmitters**. *The neurotransmitter acetylcholine normally prevents us from acting out the content of our dreams by causing paralysis during REM sleep. However, the article below illustrates what can go wrong with this system when a small area of the brain (called the magnetocellular nucleus) malfunctions.*

A DANGEROUS SLEEP

by Judith Woods

As a teenager, musician Chris Sheldrick's sleepwalking was a great source of amusement to his friends and family.

A former head musician at Eton, his disturbed sleep patterns were well known; he would often wake his fellow boarders with his blood-curdling howls, or be discovered by staff asleep in a cupboard or the laundry room. At youth hostels, he would clamber into strangers' beds in the middle of the night – to their consternation – or stroll through public areas dressed only in his underpants.

But a year ago, Sheldrick's sleepwalking took a tragic turn. One night, while staying with a friend – former BBC Musician of the Year, Guy Johnston– Sheldrick, 23, severed eight tendons, a nerve and an artery in his left arm after punching a window pane. The accident was to spell the end of his promising career as a performer, as he was no longer able to play the clarinet, bassoon or piano properly.

'I couldn't remember what had happened, but by following the trail of blood, it was easy to deduce that I'd smashed the window, then wandered around the house before going outside, where I was stopped by the next-door neighbour,' says Sheldrick.

'He'd heard the glass breaking and thought I was a burglar, but the fact that I was in my boxers convinced him otherwise. He took me into his house and saved my life. Because I had lost so much blood, I was losing consciousness.'

Source: The Daily Telegraph, *18 October 2004*

Q

1 Chris Sheldrick has 'REM sleep behaviour disorder'. According to Dement and Kleitman's proposal, would you expect to find a correlation between the eye movements and behaviours performed by a REM sleep behaviour disorder sufferer during dream sleep?

2 If the length of a period of REM sleep activity was measured in a person with REM sleep behaviour disorder, and if they were woken when the activity ceased, what would you predict about their estimate of the length of time they had been dreaming?

DEMENT AND KLEITMAN'S STUDY OF SLEEP AND DREAMING
SUMMARY

AIM

To test three ideas: (1) whether dream recall differs between REM and nREM sleep; (2) whether we experience dreams in 'real time'; and (3) to explore whether dream content is related to eye movements.

PROCEDURE

Nine participants slept overnight in a laboratory with electrodes around their eyes (to detect eye movements) and on the scalp (to detect sleep stages). They were awoken during REM or nREM sleep. They then: (1) recalled any dream into a voice recorder; (2) guessed whether they had been in REM sleep for 5 or 15 minutes, then gave a dream narrative in which the number of words was counted; and (3) were woken after a one-minute long pattern of mainly vertical, horizontal, mixed or very little eye movement and reported their dream.

RESULTS

- Dreams were much more common in REM than nREM.
- Participants could accurately estimate whether they had been dreaming for 5 or 15 minutes and the number of words in their dream narratives correlated with the length of time they had spent in REM sleep.
- Eye-movement patterns were related to dream content.

CONCLUSIONS

- People dream in REM but not nREM sleep.
- People can judge the duration of their dream accurately.
- Eye movements in dreams relate to dream content.

EVALUATION

This study raises few ethical issues but illustrates several interesting methodological issues.

ETHICAL ISSUES

This study illustrates the use of a strategy to maintain confidentiality. Each participant needed to be identifiable, so, to preserve their anonymity, they were referred to only by their initials. Not all the participants slept well, for example IR, who was awoken 65 times over 12 nights, slept for an average of 4 hours 20 minutes per night. Although this could have been typical for the individual, it is likely that it was less sleep than normal. A reduction in sleep could be unpleasant, thus could raise ethical issues relating to harm and distress. It could have been caused by the repeated wakings, the changes in sleeping environment or diet, or the need to sleep wired up to a machine. Another source of potential stress for the participants would have been the sense of needing to recall a dream so as not to disappoint the experimenters. Indeed, when Dement was a participant himself, he recalled feeling variously 'disappointed', 'upset', 'exhausted' and 'extremely puzzled' (Dement,

QUESTION SPOTLIGHT!

Suggest how studies set in sleep laboratories can raise issues of:

1   Harm and distress
2   Consent
3   Right to withdraw
4   Privacy

Be sure to remember that there is a difference between identifying likely ethical issues and saying that a study was unethical. The conduct of a study is only unethical if the researchers have not responded satisfactorily to the issues raised by the study. Make sure that you can explain not only what the ethical issues are, but also how the researchers tackled those issues.

1978). Because the participants were observed for only 17 nights at most, any such effects would have been short term, so they would have been quickly restored to their previous state. Another potential ethical issue is privacy, as participants might not have wanted to divulge their dream content. Because the experimenters could not check whether the participants were telling the truth, the participants did not have to provide a narrative if they didn't want to – although they might have felt obliged to do so. However, the participants would have known what they were going to do, so had consented to the procedures, although they were occasionally deceived. For example, WD was told that he would be awoken only when he appeared to be dreaming, but in fact his REM and nREM wakings were interspersed.

METHODOLOGICAL ISSUES
The sample and sampling method

The sample was made up of seven men and two women, which is a relatively small sample for a laboratory study. However, given the detail in which each of the five main participants was studied, and the use of a further four to confirm the findings, it is questionnable whether this is a weakness. The fact that the sample consisted mainly of males could make it tricky to generalise from the results to both genders within the wider population, although this is really a problem of sample size rather than the disparity between males and females. In some ways, a small sample should not matter in such a study, as we would expect physiological processes to be very similar for all humans. In fact, this was not the case as, for example, there were marked differences in total sleep time, dream recall and capacity to recall detail of dreams. These differences suggest that the sample size meant that the findings might have been not representative of the range within the wider population.

As the demands on the participants' time and co-operation were quite considerable in this study, it is likely that they were obtained by self-selected or opportunity sampling. Both of these sampling methods are unrepresentative. Most people do not generally volunteer, so, by definition, volunteers are not typical people, and opportunity sampling would have been likely to generate people who were aware of at least some aspects of sleep study. Either method would thus have produced a biased sample.

The research method

The study was a laboratory procedure, but called an experiment by Dement and Kleitman. Aspects of the design were indeed experimental: for example, their comparison of responses following 5 and 15 minute REM durations. Laboratory experiments come with a set of strengths and limitations. Because the procedure takes place in a highly controlled environment it is possible to eliminate many extraneous variables and be reasonably confident that it is the independent variable we are interested in that is affecting the dependent variable. Laboratory procedures are straightforward to replicate, making them reliable. For example, in this case, effects on sleep and dreaming caused by food, drink and location were all controlled. The potential weaknesses with laboratory studies lie in the realism of the environment and participants' tasks. It is hard to set up laboratory procedures in which people behave as they would in real life. This is certainly true of Dement and Kleitman's study, as the participants were sleeping in an unfamiliar and highly unusual situation that would have been likely to affect their sleep patterns, thus reducing validity.

Reliability

Remember that reliability means consistency. A procedure is reliable if we can precisely replicate it and consistently get the same results when we do so. We have said that laboratory experiments are generally easy to replicate. Within the study itself, Dement and Kleitman replicated their findings with their five main participants with four others. Furthermore, some aspects of their results have been replicated many times, such as the predominance of dreams in REM sleep. However, Dement and Kleitman suspected that dreams were not exclusive to REM sleep. Over time it has become clear that this is the case. Although REM sleep remains the most likely time to generate clear recall of active and visual dreams, it is by no means the only time when dream-like cognition occurs during sleep. That our experience of the passage of time in dreams is reasonably accurate is also generally supported, for instance through the use of **lucid dreaming**. The proposed link between eye movements and dream content has not, however, been substantiated. Indeed, it would be unlikely to be the case, because, even when awake, there is no absolute relationship between visualisation and eye movements. For example, some eye movements are related to information processing. So, although many aspects of Dement and Kleitman's procedure had good reliability – for example, the use of the EEG and EOG – some of the findings have not been replicated.

Ecological validity

We have said that a potential weakness in laboratory experiments is their realism. There are two aspects to this realism: the environment and the task. Dement and Kleitman's procedure took place in an artificial environment that was rather different from that in which most people sleep, and the attachment of apparatus would have exacerbated this difference. However, the tasks were not so artificial (how often do you find yourself trying to recall and to re-tell a dream or work out how long it lasted?). Therefore, it can be argued that Dement and Kleitman's study is in some ways low in ecological validity, but in other ways quite high.

Validity

Dement and Kleitman asked participants to abstain from drinks containing drugs that could affect their sleep, such as alcohol (a depressant that reduces REM sleep) or caffeine (a stimulant that reduces the total amount of sleep). On the surface, this would appear to increase validity, as patterns seen in sleep and dreams would be more likely to represent recall differences, rather than differences due to the drugs used. However, changes to eating and drinking patterns also affect sleep, so the sleep patterns of participants who habitually drank coffee or alcohol might have been atypical.

The methods themselves also have strengths and weaknesses in terms of validity. On one hand, EEGs and EOGs clearly distinguish between sleep stages and the types of eye movements, and counting the number of words in a dream narrative is also an objective measure. However, relating the content of a dream narrative to eye-movement pattern is more subjective as it is open to interpretation. This aspect is therefore less valid.

Quantitative and qualitative data

A strength of Dement and Kleitman's study was the recording of both quantitative and qualitative data. It therefore has the strengths of both types of data (see p. 215 for a discussion). In this case, having both types of data was important to enable conclusions to be drawn between dream content (qualitative data) and physiological measures (quantitative data).

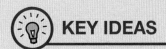 **KEY IDEAS**

In a **lucid dream**, the sleeper is aware that they are experiencing a dream and may be able to control the content of that dream.

EXAM FOCUS

We now show you some of the sorts of questions that could be asked about the Dement and Kleitman study in your exam. We will then show you some examples of the sorts of answers we believe might be successful and less successful, and point out some classic traps to avoid.

SECTION A

1 **(a)** Identify two controls used in the study on sleep and dreaming by Dement and Kleitman. *(2 marks)*

   (b) Explain why one of these controls was used. *(2 marks)*

2 From the study by Dement and Kleitman:

   (a) Outline one way sleep has been measured. *(2 marks)*

   (b) Give one strength of this method of data collection. *(2 marks)*

3 Dement and Kleitman used an electroencephalogram (EEG) to record sleep activity.

   (a) Explain what an EEG measures. *(2 marks)*

   (b) Describe one limitation of using an EEG to investigate dreaming. *(2 marks)*

4 From Dement and Kleitman's study into sleep and dreaming:

   (a) Describe one way in which the study lacked ecological validity. *(2 marks)*

   (b) Explain why it was appropriate for this study to lack ecological validity. *(2 marks)*

5 From Dement and Kleitman's study into sleep and dreaming:

   (a) Identify two substances participants were instructed not to have on the day of the experiment. *(2 marks)*

   (b) Outline one problem with instructing the participants not to have these substances. *(2 marks)*

6 In Dement and Kleitman's study on sleep and dreaming, it is suggested that Rapid Eye Movement (REM) occurs only in dreaming. Give one piece of evidence that supports this suggestion, and one piece of evidence that challenges it. *(4 marks)*

7 From Dement and Kleitman's study on sleep and dreaming, outline two ways in which the data was collected. *(4 marks)*

8 From the study by Dement and Kleitman on sleep and dreaming, give four characteristics of REM sleep. *(4 marks)*

SECTION B

(a) State one of the hypotheses investigated in Dement and Kleitman's study. *(2 marks)*

(b) Describe one of the controls used in Dement and Kleitman's study, and state why it was used. *(6 marks)*

(c) Outline two of the scientific measures used in Dement and Kleitman's study. *(6 marks)*

(d) Give one disadvantage and one advantage of using the scientific method in Dement and Kleitman's study. *(6 marks)*

(e) Explain two ways in which the study by Dement and Kleitman could be improved. *(8 marks)*

(f) Outline the effect on the results for the improvements you have suggested for Dement and Kleitman's study. *(8 marks)*

SECTION C

(a) Outline one assumption of the physiological approach. *(2 marks)*

(b) Describe how the physiological approach could explain dreaming. *(4 marks)*

(c) Describe one similarity and one difference between any studies that use the physiological approach. *(6 marks)*

(d) Discuss strengths and weaknesses of the physiological approach using examples from any studies that take this approach. *(12 marks)*

SECTION A 3 Dement and Kleitman used an electroencephalogram (EEG) to record sleep activity.

(a) Explain what an EEG measures. *(2 marks)*

Nessa's answer:

It measures eye movements behind your eyelids when you are asleep.

We say: 0 marks.
Oh dear, Nessa, unfortunately you have described the EOG and not the EEG, which looks at electrical activity in the brain. Try making a glossary of key terms for each study to help your revision.

Alan's answer:

EEG – Electroencephalograph – measures the level of electrical activity of neurons in the brain by electrodes on the scalp. We can use it to see what stage of sleep we are in as the pattern of activity changes in the stages.

We say: 2 marks.
Spot on, Alan. This is clear and concise and explains an EEG very well.

SECTION A 7 From Dement and Kleitman's study on sleep and dreaming, outline two ways in which the data was collected. *(4 marks)*

Paul's answer:

People slept in a sleep laboratory and were measured while they were there. Data was collected when the doorbell rang as well.

We say: 0 marks.
Paul, being rather vague will unfortunately not get you a lot of credit in the exam. Short-answer questions need you to be very specific and identify precisely what the question asks for. Here, you should identify two actual ways in which data is collected and say what they are. Just saying that they were measured does not tell us anything, and neither does your doorbell point. A better point would be along the lines of 'when the doorbell rang people spoke into a tape recorder to describe their dreams' – this would identify some data collection.

Zena's answer:

First, participants kept a record of the dreams they had. They would speak what they could remember from their dream as soon as they woke up and talked into the tape machine. Second, EOG readings were taken from participants eyes while they slept and recorded on a printout from the machine. This was compared with the sleep records to see if eye movements correlated with dreams.

We say: 4 marks.
Zena, you are certainly knowledgeable about the specific facts of this study, which you have to be to do well in the exam. You have picked out two ways and have a brief but accurate description of each one. It is clear how data was obtained and we can understand what this data actually was.

SECTION B (e) Explain two ways in which the study by Dement and Kleitman could be improved. (8 marks)

Stuart's answer:

This study could have been done in people's houses in their beds as they sleep better there and people would have been less controlled. Also having good beds would make it better because they were probably uncomfortable in the laboratory, so this makes people sleep worse. This means their sleep is not natural so the results are more artificial.

Rick's answer:

First, studying people in their homes would be an improvement on having people come to the laboratory to sleep. They could go about their daily routine, drink caffeine (if this was part of their routine) and not have any restrictions on them. As a result, their daily routine would be identical to every other day, and they would not have to drive to the laboratory at bedtime. They could also keep a diary of what they have done in their day so this could be compared as well.

We say: 2 marks.
Stuart, make sure you read all parts of the question carefully. Part (e) asks you to suggest two improvements, and (f) asks you outline the effects on the results. Therefore, (e) should be just description. You put your ideas very briefly, and then started to evaluate them. That gets no marks, as it is not answering the question. Set out a suggestion that is appropriate for the study (own homes plus nice beds) and then make sure that you fully explain how this would work so that it is a detailed outline that anyone could copy.

We say: 5 marks.
Two very appropriate suggestions here Rick, although the second is brief. Try to explain both in equal detail or you will miss out on marks. Your first idea is fine – you could give a little more explanation on how you could measure them in their homes to make this really clear, but it is just about enough. The one sentence on the diary suggestion is not enough. You need to go on to comment on exactly how this would be used and when it would be filled in.

SECTION C (d) Discuss strengths and weaknesses of the physiological approach using examples from any studies that take this approach. (12 marks)

Salma's answer:

A strength of the physiological approach is that it often produces quantitative data that is objective. This means that your data is very reliable and you can compare the scores very easily. An example is in the study by Dement and Kleitman where we can compare the number of dreams from the participants that occurred in REM sleep and in non-REM sleep when they were woken by the doorbell, which allows us to say clearly in which stage of sleep dreaming is more likely.

Continued

Another strength is that it is very scientific and will use a lot of controls in its studies of how biology affects behaviour. This means that there is far more control over extraneous variables, which can be eliminated and so the results are more accurate and fair. This is seen in Maguire's study where all the participants had to be male and be right-handed, and taxi drivers and non-taxi drivers were scanned on the same MRI scanner. This eliminates problems with different machines scanning differently.

A weakness is that the physiological approach is reductionist. This is because it suggests that all behaviour is due to biological factors and ignores the influence of emotions or social factors that could be important in our behaviour. This could be important because the participants in Maguire's study might have developed their memory skills because people around them helped them to recall the knowledge and continued to help them as they talked to the other drivers while at work. This means that it could be more social and other factors that are at work than biology.

A second weakness is that a lot of studies that take this approach use experiments and so this causes them to be more artificial and have lower ecological validity. In Dement and Kleitman's study, people slept in a sleep laboratory with wires attached to their heads and had to not drink caffeine in the day. This is not like an ordinary day for them and so may affect their sleep so the results we get are not useful as they are not really true behaviour.

We say: 12 marks.
Salma, this is a really excellent answer, well done. You have identified and then explained and commented on each of your strengths and weaknesses, showing real understanding and psychological knowledge. You use some detailed examples, and you pick out precise facts from the studies to go with your points. These examples relate back nicely to the strength/weakness, and really support them. You have covered everything well here.

SPERRY'S STUDY OF SPLIT-BRAIN PATIENTS

 KEY IDEAS

Localisation means the limitation of a particular brain function to a particular *structure*. This is different from **lateralisation**, which limits a particular function to one *side* of the brain, i.e. to one hemisphere.

Sperry, R. (1968) Hemisphere deconnection and unity in consciousness. *American Psychologist.* **23**: 723–33.

CONTEXT

Historically, investigations looking at the anatomy of dead human or animal bodies, and, more recently, brain scanning, have told us about the structure of the brain. This has shown that the brain has clearly defined regions (see Figure 3.11). Other research has explored what the brain does – that is, it has investigated its functional roles. A key area of research is to link these two aspects together – that is, to explore the **localisation** of function. This is the extent to which particular jobs are performed by particular parts of the brain. Some aspects of localisation link functions to specific structures, many of which are replicated in the left and right halves of the brain. In addition, some functions demonstrate

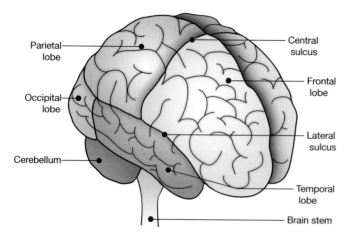

Figure 3.11
Investigations of brain structure show that it is divided into two 'halves' – the cerebral hemispheres – along the central line

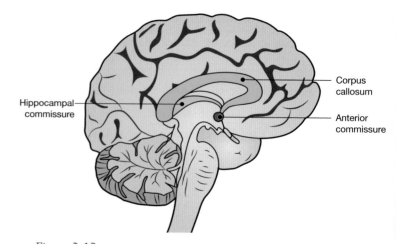

Figure 3.12
Investigations of brain structure show that internally it is divided into smaller structures

lateralisation – that is, there is a difference between the roles of the left and right hemispheres. One example of lateralisation is our language function, which is restricted to the left side of the brain. Another example is the control of movement. Movement of each side of the body is largely controlled by the opposite side of the brain. This is called **contralateral control** (see p. 124).

Structural research shows that there are a number of structures which join the two halves of the brain – the right and left **hemispheres** (see Figure 3.12). This allows for the exchange of information across the brain. These include the corpus callosum (the largest), and the smaller anterior and hippocampal **commissures**. The particular focus of this paper was to explore the effects when the two hemispheres are artificially separated (hemispheric separation). Earlier research into 'split brains' had been conducted by performing surgery on animals to deconnect the hemispheres by cutting through structures such as the **corpus callosum**, and had the effect of preventing 'cross-talk' between the hemispheres – that is, the animals appeared to be unable to exchange information from the left and right halves of their brains.

KEY IDEAS

Along the midline of the brain (in a vertical plane from front to back) there are several structures consisting of nerve fibres that join the left and right sides of the brain together. These are called **commissures**. They include the **corpus callosum**, the hippocampal commissure and the anterior commissure (see Figure 3.12). The cutting of such structures is called a **commissurotomy**.

IN BRIEF

Aim: To investigate the effects of hemispheric deconnection on perception and memory.

Method: Eleven patients who had had **commissurotomies** to separate the left and right hemispheres were tested in a laboratory using apparatus that could display stimuli independently to the left or right visual field. They were required to say, write or find what they had seen. Other tests used objects placed either separately or simultaneously in each hand, which participants had to find or name. Manual tests either required participants to copy hand positions that one hand had been moulded into, or that they had seen identified on a diagram, or required them to locate with a thumb a small area of the hand that they had been shown or that had been touched by the experimenter.

Results: In split-brain patients, each hemisphere can perceive and remember information presented only to that hemisphere. Verbal responses were possible only when information was presented to the left hemisphere (e.g. though the right visual field or right hand).

Conclusion: Hemisphere deconnection causes the two hemispheres to operate independently, each having its own consciousness, including perception and memory. This produces a 'doubling' of conscious awareness, as each hemisphere is unaware of the other. The right hemisphere, although much less linguistic than the left, can use logic.

The aim of the study was to test the effects of hemispheric deconnection in humans. Specifically, to investigate whether cognition, including perception and memory, differs between the hemispheres, and the extent to which the hemispheres would normally interact to achieve these cognitive functions.

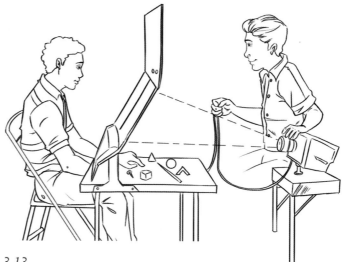

Figure 3.13
Apparatus used for studying lateralisation of visual, tactual, lingual and associated functions in the surgically separated hemispheres
Source: adapted from Sperry (1968), fig. 1, p. 724.

METHOD

DESIGN

Sperry conducted his testing in a laboratory environment with control over specific variables. Some tests were conducted as comparisons between the left and right hemispheres. In essence, these were experimental in method, manipulating the independent variable of hemisphere, and measuring the effect on the individual's performance in tests of cognition (the dependent variable). As each participant could be tested on both the left and right hemisphere, these tests employed a repeated measures design. However, overall, the investigation more closely resembled a collection of case studies.

PARTICIPANTS

The opportunity sample consisted of 11 patients with epilepsy (including at least one woman). They had all had an operation to divide the brain in half down the 'middle' (from front to back) along

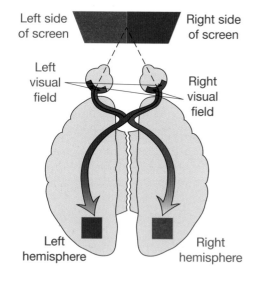

Figure 3.14
In a split-brain patient under experimental conditions, a stimulus presented to one visual field enters only the opposite hemisphere of the brain
Source: adapted from Sperry (1968), fig. 2, p. 725.

the corpus callosum to reduce the spread of epileptic seizures from one side to the other. They needed radical surgery as all had experienced severe symptoms such as seizures and convulsions, for a long time (e.g. over 10 years), and these symptoms could not be controlled with medication. They were evaluated at various times up to 5.5 years post-operatively. The surgery cut through the entire corpus callosum, the anterior commissure, hippocampal commissure and, in some patients, also the massa intermedia. The effect of this was to disconnect the two halves of the brain, thus preventing exchange of information between the left and right hemispheres.

PROCEDURE

The general procedure, using the apparatus shown in Figure 3.13, was to expose one or both hemispheres to a stimulus and to elicit a response. Stimuli were visual, tactual (touch sense) or auditory (sound-based). Controls were employed to reduce input from extraneous variables. In visual tests, controls included covering the non-tested eye, and presenting stimuli to the **left visual field (LVF)** or the **right visual field (RVF)** separately. Each test began by fixing the gaze on the centre line of the screen and presenting stimuli for precisely measured durations (e.g. one-tenth of a second). This latter control was important to ensure that the time available would be insufficient for the participant's eye to move to view the stimulus in the 'other' visual field.

1: Recognition of visual stimuli presented to the left and right hemispheres separately

The visual stimulus of a picture of an object was presented to either the LVF or the RVF (i.e. to one side of the visual field of only one eye). The participant was then shown the same image again to either the same or the other visual field, and asked whether they recognised the object. For example, with the left eye closed, a picture of a ball would be flashed for one-tenth of a second to the left of the fixation point (so the image from the left visual field of the right eye would enter the right hemisphere). The participant would then see the same image flashed either to the left or to the right of the fixation point (so the image would reach the right or left hemisphere respectively).

2: Responding with speech to visual stimuli presented to the left and right hemispheres separately

A visual stimulus was presented to either the LVF or the RVF. The participant was then asked to describe the visual stimulus. For example, with the left eye closed, a picture of a spoon would be flashed to the left

KEY IDEAS

Each hemisphere receives input from the opposite visual field. It is important to understand that this is different from the view from each eye. Read and follow these instructions:

Shut one eye and stare at something small in front of you in the room, such as a mug or a door handle (this is your fixation point). Then, without moving your eye away from the object, decide what else you can see. You will be able to see a little either side of the object. The area to the left is in the **left visual field (LVF)** for the eye you have open. The area to the right is in the **right visual field (RVF)** for that eye. You can do the same for the other eye.

You will have demonstrated for yourself that what you can see to the left of a fixation point is in your left visual field, and what you can see to the right of a fixation point is in your right visual field.

In some of Sperry's experiments it was important to cover one eye, as an exchange of visual information between the left and right eyes occurs before it reaches the brain (at the optic chiasm). If both eyes are open (in normal people or in split-brain patients) information from the left visual fields of both the left and right eyes is passed to the right hemisphere. Similarly, the information from the right visual fields of both the left and right eyes is passed to the left hemisphere. This transfer occurs across the optic chiasm. It is important to note that in Sperry's studies, the split-brain patients were typically exposed to stimuli presented to only one visual field (and only one eye), and thus only one hemisphere received information about the stimulus. This is illustrated in Figure 3.14.

KEY IDEAS

One example of lateralisation is in language. In typical right-handed people (and in the majority of left-handers too) language functions are largely restricted to the left hemisphere. Thus, we can talk or write only about things that have entered the left hemisphere.

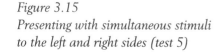

WEB WATCH @

You can see animations and video of Sperry's experiments at www.nobelprize.org (enter 'split brain' into the search box)
and
http://www.youtube.com/watch?v=aCv4K5aStdU

Figure 3.15
Presenting with simultaneous stimuli to the left and right sides (test 5)

of the fixation point (so the image from the left visual field would enter the right hemisphere). Alternatively, with the left eye closed, a picture of a spoon would be flashed to the right of the fixation point (so the image from the right visual field would enter the left hemisphere).

3: Responding in writing to visual stimuli presented to the left and right hemispheres separately

This test was identical to the second test, except that the participant was required to write the name of the stimulus rather than say it. A visual stimulus was presented to either the LVF or the RVF. The participant was then asked to write down what the visual stimulus was. For example, with the right eye closed, a picture of a pear would be flashed to the left visual field and would enter the right hemisphere. Alternatively, a picture of a pear would be flashed to the right visual field and so would enter the left hemisphere.

4. Responding by pointing to visual stimuli presented to the left and right hemispheres separately

The test was also identical to the second test, except that the participant was required to point to the stimulus they had seen. A visual stimulus was presented to either the LVF or the RVF. The participant was then asked to point at the object they had seen, or at a picture of it, with either their left or right hand. For example, with the right eye closed, a picture of a pencil would be flashed to the right visual field of the left eye and would enter the left hemisphere. Such tests are described as cross modal, as they require the participant to receive information though one sense (mode) and respond through another.

5. Recognition of visual stimuli presented to the left and right hemispheres simultaneously

Two different figures were flashed simultaneously, one to the LVF, the other to the RVF. The participant was asked to draw with the left hand what had been seen. The drawing hand was hidden from the participant's visual field which had been used for that test. They then had to say what they had just drawn, still without looking. For example, the participant was shown a dollar sign in the left visual field and a question mark in the right visual field (Figure 3.15). They were then required to draw, out of sight, using their left hand, what they had seen, and finally to say what they had just drawn.

6. Recognition of pairs of related words presented visually and simultaneously to the left and right hemispheres

Words composed of two smaller words were presented to the participants such that half of the word fell in the LVF and half in the RVF. For example, the word 'keycase' was shown so that the LVF saw 'key' and the RVF saw 'case' (see Figure 3.16). There were the three possible ways to indicate recognition: the participant could use one hand to search through a selection of objects hidden from view for the one named by the word they had seen, they could say the name, or they could write the name.

7. Verbal identification of objects placed in the hand (stereognostic somesthetic discrimination)

The participant was prevented from seeing an object placed in either the left or the right hand. They were then asked to say or write the name of the object they had held or to retrieve the object they had held using either the left or the right hand. For example, a cup might be placed in the left hand and the participant asked to identify it by name (in speech or writing), or to find it from among other objects, once it had been taken away.

These tests are summarised, and some further tests conducted by Sperry (tests 8–12) are described, along with their results, in Table 3.4.

 **KEY IDEAS**

Sperry uses several scientific terms. Although they are rather strange, it is helpful to understand them. **Stereognostic** refers to discovering the shape of something by touch. **Somesthetic** means 'the sense of the body', and refers to our ability to sense the position of our body parts. ('Soma' means 'body' and '...sthetic' refers to senses – think 'ana-sthetic' – which blocks sensation.) **Topognosis** is the ability to identify where an object is on the skin.

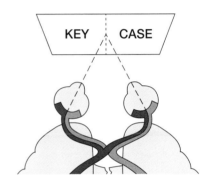

Figure 3.16
Presenting paired words to participants (test 6) Source: adapted from Sperry (1968), fig. 2, p. 725.

Figure 3.17 Hand positions for the symmetric handpose test (test 8)

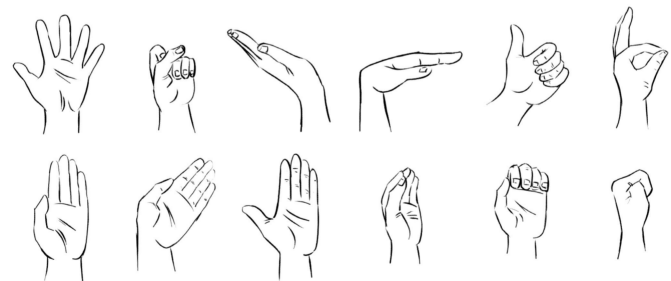

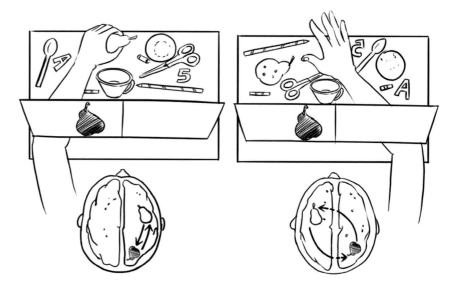

STRETCH & CHALLENGE ◎

Emotionally, the right hemisphere responds like the left. For example, an image of a nude among other images elicits blushing or giggling. When asked to explain the emotional response, the participant – although aware of the arousal – cannot. Why not?

Similarly, when an incorrect verbal response is made by the left hemisphere (e.g. because the correct answer is known only to the right), annoyance is expressed by the right hemisphere through wincing, frowning and head shaking. Explain why.

Figure 3.18
An object felt by one hand will be recognised visually only by the corresponding (i.e. opposite) hemisphere. The pear can be found in (a) as the visual field, the hemisphere and the hand making the response all match. In (b), information from the left visual field enters the right hemisphere and cannot cross to the left hemisphere to instruct the right hand to find the pear.

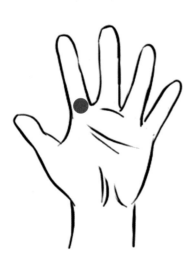

Figure 3.19
Presenting images of locations on hand to participants (test 10)

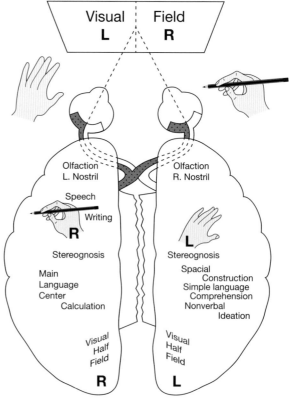

Figure 3.20
Functional lateralisation in split-brain patients.
Source: Sperry (1968), fig. 3, p. 728.

TABLE 3.4 SUMMARY OF THE PROCEDURE AND RESULTS OF SPERRY'S SPLIT-BRAIN INVESTIGATIONS

		Procedure	Results	
			Description	Example
1	Recognition of visual stimuli presented to the left and right hemispheres separately	A picture was flashed to either the LVF or the RVF. The participant was shown the image again to either the same or the other visual field and asked whether they recognised the object.	Pictures of objects were recognised only if they were re-flashed to the same visual field.	The participant sees a picture of a ball in the LVF. They would recognise the ball only if it were presented again in the LVF. This is because memories about stimuli from one visual field cannot cross to the other hemisphere, so cannot be accessed in order to compare them to the stimulus when it is presented the second time, unless it is presented again to the same visual field.
2	Responding with speech to visual stimuli presented to the left and right hemispheres separately	A visual stimulus was flashed to either the LVF or the RVF, and the participant described it.	Participants could describe objects flashed to the RVF only.	A picture of a spoon flashed to the RVF could be named, but if shown to the LVF it could not be. This is because only stimuli presented to the RVF enter the 'speaking' left hemisphere. As speech is controlled only in the left hemisphere, stimuli in the right hemisphere cannot be named.
3	Responding in writing to visual stimuli presented to the left and right hemispheres separately	A visual stimulus was flashed to either the LVF or the RVF, and the participant wrote the name of it.	Participants could write down the name of objects presented to the RVF only.	A participant would be able to write 'pear' if a picture of a pear was flashed to the RVF, but they could not do so if it was shown to the LVF, as it would enter the right hemisphere. This is because writing is a language function so can be controlled only by the left hemisphere. To be able to write down what they have seen, the participant must view the object using the RVF.
4	Responding to visual stimuli by pointing	A visual stimulus was flashed to either the LVF or the RVF. The participant then pointed to that object.	Participants could correctly point to an object presented to the LVF or RVF.	A participant could point to a pencil if a picture of a pencil was flashed to the LVF (so the image entered the right hemisphere). This is because, unlike verbal functions, pointing can be controlled by either hemisphere.
5	Recognition of visual stimuli presented to the left and right hemispheres simultaneously	Two different figures were flashed to the LVF and the RVF. The participant drew what they had seen with the left hand (hidden from view). They then said what they had drawn, without looking.	Participants could draw what they had seen in the LVF, but when asked what they had drawn said whatever entered the RVF.	If shown a dollar sign on the left and a question mark on the right, participants draw a dollar sign but say 'question mark'. This happens because the dollar sign in the LVF goes to the right hemisphere (so can be drawn with the left hand using contralateral control), whereas the question mark, in the RVF, goes to the left hemisphere, so can be named.

6	**Recognition of pairs of related words presented visually and simultaneously to the left and right hemispheres**	Two small words which together made one were flashed so one fell in the LVF and the other in the RVF. Participants indicated recognition by: searching a hidden selection for the object, naming it, or writing the name.	Recognition of simultaneously presented stimuli differed according to the modality of the response.	If the word 'keycase' was shown so that 'key' reached the LVF and right hemisphere, a key would be selected by the left hand. The RVF would see 'case', so the left hemisphere would cause the participant to say or write that they had seen the word 'case'. Verbal responses are produced by the left hemisphere, so verbal recognition occurs only if stimuli are presented to the RVF. The left hand, controlled by the right hemisphere, will respond only to stimuli from the LVF.
7	**Verbal identification of objects placed in the hand**	The participant was asked to say or to write the name of an object they were holding or, to retrieve an object they had held.	Only objects held in the right hand can be named (in speech or writing). Objects held in either hand can be retrieved either immediately or after a delay, but only by the same hand.	If an apple is placed in the right hand, 'apple' can be said or written, but a verbal response could not be given if the apple was in the left hand. An apple could be found in a grab bag, or when among other objects, with either hand as long as it was the same hand that had originally held the object (i.e. there is no cross-retrieval). This happens because verbal functions are confined to the left hemisphere, so can only respond to stimuli in the RVF. Manual recognition can be controlled by either hemisphere, as long as it is the same one that made the initial identification.
8	**Symmetric handpose test**	The participant holds out both hands (where they cannot see them). One hand is put into a certain position and they have to imitate this position with the other hand.	Participants cannot imitate the position of one hand with the other hand unless it is very simple (e.g. a closed fist or a fully open hand).	A normal person asked to copy on their right a hand position with the first two fingers on their left hand crossed can do so, a split-brain patient cannot. This is because the information about the stimulus enters the opposite hemisphere from the hand moved by the researcher. As this is not the hemisphere controlling the other hand, a failure of cross-retrieval prevents access to the information.
9	**Crossed topognosis test and cross integration test**	Crossed topognosis: the participant holds their hands out of sight, palms up. The experimenter touches a point on a finger and the participant touches the same place with the thumb of the same hand. Cross integration: the participant touches the same place with the thumb of the other hand.	When asked to touch a point on the same hand as touched by the experimenter, participants can, but in the cross-integration test, split-brain participants typically fail.	The inability of most split-brain participants to achieve any cross-integration happens because the information about the touched hand enters the opposite hemisphere from the hand they must move, so they cannot access the necessary information to understand the movement required.

10	Ipsilateral and homolateral manual visuognosis test	An image of a black spot on a drawing of the hand is presented to either the LVF or RVF and the participant touches the same place with the thumb of either the left or the right hand.	Success depends on whether the visual field and hand making the response match. If the LVF sees the image, only the left hand can respond (and vice versa with the RVF).	An image shown to the RVF cannot be responded to by the left hand. This is because movement by each hand can be controlled only by the opposite hemisphere, and each hemisphere can receive instructions only from one visual field. When a visual field (e.g. the RVF and, therefore, the left hemisphere) is paired with the requirement for a response from the 'opposite' (e.g. left) hand, this cross-integration is impossible for a split-brain participant.
11	Tactual recognition	Simultaneous presentation: the participant holds out both hands and objects are put simultaneously in the left and right hands. They are removed and scrambled up with other objects. The participant uses both hands to search for the objects without looking. Cross-modal: the participant is shown a picture of an object in the LVF or the RVF, and searches for it with one hand.	Simultaneous presentation: the left and right hands search independently until each finds the object it had held. Cross-modal: the participant can find an object with a hand only if it was seen with the matching visual field.	Simultaneous presentation: if the left hand encounters the object held by the right hand, it will be unrecognised and rejected. This happens because the left and right hemisphere sensory functions, memory and motor control are independent in the split-brain patient. Cross-modal: if the participant sees a picture of a pear in the RVF they can find it with the right hand but not with the left (see Figure 3.19). This difference arises because the RVF, and hence left hemisphere, can control only the right hand.
12	Tests of right hemisphere function	A range of tests similar to those above were conducted to investigate the range of functions in the right hemisphere. These included measures of cross-modal associations, reasoning, use of concepts, arithmetic, language comprehension and emotions.	The right hemisphere cannot perform complex verbal functions as this capacity is lateralised, i.e. it is limited to the left hemisphere.	If a clock is flashed to the LVF, the left hand searches for but fails to find the same object, but the participant will select a logical alternative, such as a wrist watch. This demonstrates that the right hemisphere can understand the concept of 'timepiece' rather than just match shapes. Conceptual thinking by the right hemisphere is also shown by the ability of the left hand to sort objects into logical categories. With block numerals, pointing to answers or writing with the left hand, the right hemisphere can perform simple arithmetic and show simple language comprehension, e.g. being able to find by touch with the left hand an object named by the experimenter.

KEY IDEAS

Movement, or 'motor function', for each side of the body is controlled by the opposite hemisphere. This is called **contralateral** control. This means that each hemisphere can control pointing only by the opposite hand. If Sperry had asked participants to respond by pointing with their left hand to an object that had been seen using the RVF (and so had entered the left hemisphere), they would have been unable to do so, as this hemisphere can control only the right hand. Nerve fibres that stay on the same side of the body are called **homolateral** fibres. Those that (would) cross to the other side are called **ipsilateral** fibres. Contralateral control is governed by ipsilateral fibres. Note that the contralateral control is perfectly normal and is neither a consequence of, nor affected by, split-brain surgery.

KEY IDEAS

Aphasia is a disorder of language. For example, an aphasic individual might not recognise speech or words, or might know what they want to say but be unable to produce the words. The right hemisphere behaves in the same way, being unable to respond in speech or writing, unlike the left hemisphere.

RESULTS

Quantitative and **qualitative** data were gathered. Quantitative data were largely in the form of yes/no results – either the participants could perform a task or they could not. Qualitative data were typically descriptions of the participants' sensations and, in some cases, transcripts of their verbal responses.

1: Recognition of visual stimuli presented to the left and right hemispheres separately

Pictures of objects were recognised only if they were re-presented to the same visual field. This happens as memories about information from one visual field cannot cross the corpus callosum to the other hemisphere. Information therefore cannot be accessed for reference to check against when the stimulus is presented again, unless it is to the same visual field.

2: Responding with speech to visual stimuli presented to the left and right hemispheres separately

Participants could only describe objects presented to the left visual field. This happens because only the left hemisphere is used for speech (because it is a lateralised function), so only stimuli presented to the RVF can be named. The right hemisphere behaves as if it were **aphasic**.

3: Responding in writing to visual stimuli presented to the left and right hemispheres separately

This test was identical to the second test, except that it required writing (another verbal function) so the results were the same, in that participants could write down the name of objects presented to the right visual field only. So pictures shown to the right of the fixation point, in the right visual field, can be responded to in writing, but not those shown to the left visual field (as they enter the right hemisphere). The separation of responses from the left and right hemisphere is further supported by the qualitative data collected (see Box 3.2).

4. Responding by pointing to visual stimuli

This test was also identical to the second test, except that it required pointing (a non-verbal function). The results were therefore different. Participants could correctly point to an object presented to the LVF even though they would not be able to name it. So, if shown a picture in the left visual field (so the image would go to the right hemisphere) the participant could point correctly with their left hand. These results arise because hand movements such as pointing can be controlled by either hemisphere (unlike lateralised language), so a response can be made to a stimulus reaching the right hemisphere.

5. Recognition of visual stimuli presented to the left and right hemispheres simultaneously

Participants appear to have two different streams of consciousness, one relating to the left hemisphere and the other to the right, so respond differently to stimuli presented simultaneously on the left and right. A participant will draw with the left hand what they have seen in the LVF (and entered the right hemisphere), but when questioned about what they have just drawn they describe what they saw with the RVF (which entered the left hemisphere). It is clear that the verbal left hemisphere remains unaware of the actions controlled by the right hemisphere (see Figure 3.21).

6. Recognition of pairs of related words presented visually and simultaneously to the left and right hemispheres

Simultaneously presented stimuli are responded to in different ways, depending on whether the response required is verbal or manual. Either hand can find an object seen by the appropriate hemishere (e.g. LVF, right hemisphere, left hand). However, only the left hemisphere (from the RVF) can respond in speech or writing (see Figure 3.22 on p. 126). If these two tasks occur simultaneously, the two streams of consciousness operate independently and produce entirely separate responses. This is further supported by the qualitative data collected (see Box 3.3)

> **Box 3.3**
> **Qualitative data**
> When asked to say or write down the word they had seen when exposed to the 'keycase' stimulus, participants responded with 'case'. When asked what kind of 'case' they had in mind, replies included: 'in case of fire', 'the case of the missing corpse' or 'a case of beer'. These indicate that the presence of the whole word 'keycase' did not influence the participants' thinking.

7. Verbal identification of objects placed in the hand

Objects placed in the right hand can be identified using words through speech or writing. The names of the same objects placed in the left hand cannot be said or written. However, the object can be retrieved from a grab bag or when scrambled among dozens of other objects, using touch alone. Although this is the case for both immediate recognition and following

> **Box 3.2**
> **Qualitative data**
> When asked to say or to write down the name of objects presented to the right visual field, participants could not do so. They would report having seen a flash of light. They behaved as though they were blind or 'agnostic' i.e. didn't believe that there had been a stimulus at all. But when asked to point to the same object they had denied the existence of, they could do so!

Figure 3.21
Each hemisphere appears to be unaware of the response made by the other hemisphere: the participant would draw a dollar sign (with the left hand) but say they had drawn a question mark

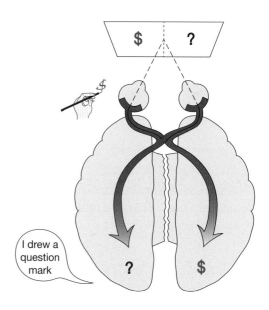

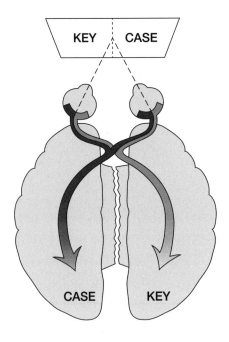

Figure 3.22
The verbal left hemisphere appears to be
unaware of the word perceived by the
right hemisphere
Source: Sperry (1968), fig. 2, p. 725.

Box 3.4
Qualitative data

When first asked to make a spoken or written response to objects in the left hand, participants say that they can't 'work with that hand', that it is 'numb' or that they 'just can't feel anything or can't do anything with it' (although, of course, they can when they are not required to respond verbally). A particularly insightful response was that they 'don't get the message from that hand'. When, in subsequent tests, such individuals correctly retrieve objects that they had said they couldn't feel, they explain the contradiction by saying 'well, I was just guessing', or 'well, I must have done it unconsciously'.

a delay, it can be successfully done only if the same hand (and therefore hemisphere) is used to retrieve the object as was used for initial identification. There is no cross-retrieval – that is, the participant cannot identify the object with one hand and then subsequently recognise it with the other. This inability of information about the stimulus to cross from one hemisphere to the other, which means it cannot be accessed, is called a failure of cross-retrieval. When given both manual and verbal tests, participants experience a contradiction in their ability. The explanations given in these situations are illustrated in Box 3.4.

The results of tests 8–12 are described, along with their procedures, in Table 3.4 (see pp. 121–3).

CONCLUSIONS

In relation to the specific aims of the study, Sperry drew two main conclusions:

1   In split-brain patients, perception in each hemisphere is independent. Information from one visual field or hand passes to only one hemisphere and is not available to the other hemisphere. If the information passes only to the right hemisphere, the individual cannot respond in speech or writing.

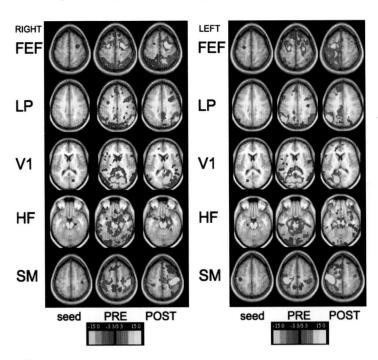

Figure 3.23
Functional magnetic resonance imagery brain scans show
how there is a lack of hemispheric integration in split
brain patients. Source: Johnson et al. (2008), fig. 1.

2 In split-brain patients, memory in each hemisphere is independent. Information from one visual field or hand is remembered only by that hemisphere and cannot be accessed by the other.

In addition, Sperry came to some general conclusions. In day-to-day life, split-brain patients are not obviously impaired. Although the streams of consciousness in their left and right hemispheres are independent, the sensory input is typically the same for both, so the individual is unaware of any difference in experience. Thus, they can interact, watch television and read a newspaper without difficulty. Furthermore, if given two simple, simultaneous tasks, each of which is controlled by a single hemisphere, a split-brain patient will perform at a better-than-normal speed. This is because interference normally caused by trying to attend to both left and right inputs together is eliminated.

Importantly, his findings led him to the overall conclusion that the non-dominant (right) hemisphere has a true stream of consciousness (like that of the left), which includes emotional reactions, and can perform both perceptual and motor functions.

STRETCH & CHALLENGE ◎

Johnson *et al.* (2008) brain-scanned a child before and after corpus callosum surgery for epilepsy. How does the direct physiological evidence from the scans (see Figure 3.23) support Sperry's conclusion about the lack of hemispheric integration in split-brain patients?

STUDY 3
SPERRY'S STUDY OF SPLIT-BRAIN PATIENTS

SUMMARY

AIM

To investigate the effects of hemispheric deconnection on perception and memory.

PROCEDURE

An opportunity sample of 11 split-brain patients were given laboratory tests presenting stimuli independently to the left or right hemispheres (e.g. using the left or right visual field or hand). They then said, wrote or found what they had seen. They also copied hand positions from the experimenter, from their other hand or from pictures.

RESULTS

- Participants could give verbal responses only when objects entered the left hemisphere – e.g. when they were presented to the right visual field or the right hand.
- Participants could find or draw an object they had encountered only if their perception and motor control used the same hemisphere.
- The right hemisphere showed little linguistic ability but understood logic and emotions.

CONCLUSIONS

- Hemisphere deconnection makes the two hemispheres independent, so each has its own consciousness. There is then a 'doubling' of conscious awareness (e.g. of perception and memory) in split-brain patients, although they are usually unaware of this.
- The right hemisphere is logical, understands emotion and has limited understanding of language.

EVALUATION

This is a relatively uncontroversial study in terms of ethics, but raises some methodological issues and has interesting implications.

ETHICAL ISSUES

Although there were considerable ethical issues involved in the surgery itself, these are not issues in terms of the research conducted by Sperry.

METHODOLOGICAL ISSUES
The sample and sampling method

The sample was made up of 11 men and women who had undergone commissurotomies for intractable epilepsy. Although 11 sounds like a small sample, it is quite impressive given the rarity of such patients and the depth to which they were studied, so, overall, it is neither a particular strength nor weakness. Of course, because the participants were all patients suffering from epilepsy who were obtained by opportunity sampling, it is a restricted sample. Generalisation to the whole population might thererfore be invalid, especially as epilepsy is a brain disorder and the findings relate to brain function.

The extent of the deconnection varied between patients, so there were likely to be differences between them. Although Sperry deliberately selected only patients who had had their surgery more than 10 years prior to testing, there were still differences in the duration of individuals' rehabilitation time, which again could have led to variation. In addition, more men than women were tested and, as there are differences in lateralisation of function (especially in terms of language) between men and women, this could make the overall results less typical of women in the general population.

The research method

The study was a laboratory procedure, referred to as an experiment, although only some parts were truly experimental. Where two conditions (levels of the independent variable) were directly compared – such as when the participants' responses to LVF-to-RVF stimuli were tested, or when left- versus right-hand responses were compared – these were experimental. Many comparisons were to non-split-brain people, although these individuals were not part of the sample included in this study. For this study, a control group of non-commissurotomised epileptics would have provided a better comparison.

Experiments come with a set of strengths and limitations that apply here. The procedures took place in a highly controlled environment, so it was possible to eliminate many extraneous variables and be reasonably confident that any independent variable being tested was affecting the dependent variable. For example, the visual restriction imposed ensured that differences between responses to left and right visual field presentations were definitely caused by the failure of communication between the two hemispheres. Laboratory procedures such as the visual and tactile tests used are straightforward to replicate, making them reliable.

Reliability

Remember that reliability means consistency. A procedure is reliable if we can precisely replicate it and consistently get the same results. Laboratory experiments are generally easy to replicate, and Sperry's procedure has been replicated. Although considerable variability between patients has been found (as it was by Sperry), his results have, in general, been supported. However, further evidence of the language ability of the right hemisphere presents some concern. Specifically, damage to the left hemisphere caused by early epilepsy might cause compensation, so that there is some reorganisation of language function to the right hemisphere (Zaidel, 1978). This would make the epileptic sample unrepresentative, and this pattern has been seen in recent brain-scanning studies (Thompson, 2000). Such acquisition might arise in split-brain patients as a consequence of their hemispheric deconnection. Baynes,

Eliassen and Gazzaniga (1997) reported a case of a split-brain patient who, 12 years post-surgery, developed the ability to respond verbally to stimuli presented to the left visual field. Again, this would make Sperry's findings based on the testing of patients a decade post-operatively less generalisible.

Ecological validity

A key potential weaknesses with laboratory studies is the (lack of) realism of the environment and the participants' tasks. It is hard to set up laboratory procedures in which people behave as they would in real life, and Sperry's procedures are clearly utterly unlike real life. The findings therefore reflect this lack of realism and, although Sperry's study was concerned with discovering their problems rather than helping them in the real world, he did note that in day-to-day life, split-brain patients experience little impairment. They use both eyes simultaneously so both hemispheres will receive the same stimuli and the left hemisphere can 'speak out loud' to inform the right hemisphere about its thoughts. As a result, they demonstrate no indication of their two independent, parallel streams of consciousness.

Quantitative and qualitative data

A strength of Sperry's study was the depth and detail of the data he collected, which included both quantitative and qualitative data. It therefore has the strengths of both types of data (see p. 215 for a discussion). In this case, having both types of data was useful in interpreting the findings. For example, the qualitative data supporting tests six and seven help to show that the understanding of the effect of hemispheric deconnection is correct.

Practical applications

The main practical implications of Sperry's work are the demonstration of hemispheric lateralisation and the findings that there are so few debilitating effects of the surgery. This provides an indication for surgical safety: patients receiving even extensive commisurotomies are unlikely to suffer noticeable cognitive effects (although subsequently some side effects on memory have been identified). In contrast, it also offers a warning: that unilateral damage could have profound effects, such as the implications of left-hemisphere surgery on speech.

QUESTION SPOTLIGHT!

Remember that you can be asked to suggest improvements to the studies.

Can you justify three changes you would make to Sperry's sample?

Can you think of a real-world test you could use that would have good ecological validity?

EXAM FOCUS

We now show you some of the sorts of questions that could be asked about the Sperry study in your exam. We will then show you some examples of the sorts of answers we believe might be successful and less successful, and point out some classic traps to avoid.

SECTION A

1 The study by Sperry investigated the psychological effects of hemisphere deconnection in split-brain patients.

    (a) Describe how split-brain patients responded to visual material presented to their right visual field (RVF). *(2 marks)*

    (b) Outline one conclusion from this study. *(2 marks)*

2 From Sperry's split-brain study:

    (a) Identify one difference between split-brain patients and 'normal' people in their ability to identify objects by touch alone. *(2 marks)*

    (b) Outline one reason for this difference. *(2 marks)*

3 Sperry, in his study on hemisphere deconnection, writes '...one hemisphere does not know what the other has been doing'.

    (a) Give one piece of evidence to support this statement. *(2 marks)*

    (b) Explain why in everyday life these patients do not encounter the problems identified in this study. *(2 marks)*

4 The study by Sperry investigated the psychological effects of hemisphere deconnection in split-brain patients.

    (a) Describe what is meant by 'hemisphere deconnection'. *(2 marks)*

    (b) Identify one way in which hemisphere deconnection affected Sperry's participants when they were presented with stimuli to one visual field. *(2 marks)*

5 The study by Sperry investigated the psychological effects of hemisphere deconnection in split-brain patients.

    (a) Give one reason why the participants had previously undergone an operation to disconnect the two hemispheres of the brain. *(2 marks)*

    (b) Outline one problem with generalising from the sample in this study. *(2 marks)*

6 Outline two findings from the split-brain study by Sperry. *(4 marks)*

7 Briefly describe two of the tests carried out on the split-brain patients in the study by Sperry. *(2 marks)*

8 From the paper by Sperry on split-brain patients, outline the evidence which indicates that language is processed in the left hemisphere of the brain. *(4 marks)*

SECTION B

(a) State one of the hypotheses investigated in the study by Sperry. *(2 marks)*

(b) Describe the sample used in the study by Sperry and suggest one weakness of using this sample. *(6 marks)*

(c) Outline two of the qualitative measures recorded in the study by Sperry. *(6 marks)*

(d) With reference to the study by Sperry, suggest one strength and one weakness of qualitative data. *(6 marks)*

(e) Outline the conclusions of the study by Sperry. *(8 marks)*

(f) Suggest one change to the procedure of the study by Sperry and explain how this might affect the results. *(8 marks)*

SECTION C

(a) Outline one assumption of the physiological approach. *(2 marks)*

(b) Describe how the physiological approach could explain organisation within the brain. *(4 marks)*

(c) Describe one similarity and one difference between any studies that use the physiological approach. *(6 marks)*

(d) Discuss strengths and weaknesses of the physiological approach using examples from any studies that take this approach. *(12 marks)*

SECTION A 5 The study by Sperry investigated the psychological effects of hemisphere deconnection in split-brain patients.
(a) Give one reason why the participants had previously undergone an operation to disconnect the two hemispheres of the brain. *(2 marks)*

Jason's answer:

The corpus callosum was cut owing to the fact that they had bad epilepsy, which affected their brains.

We say: 1 mark.
Jason, while it is true that the corpus callosum was cut, and that this is related to their epilepsy, you need to be explicit and tell the examiner that this was to stop seizures spreading to the whole brain. You left us to work that out for ourselves – and you needed to tell us clearly.

Mick's answer:

Participants have had their hemispheres disconnected because if they were having a seizure from their very bad epilepsy it would prevent it spreading to the whole brain. This would be better for them as seizures are dangerous.

We say: 2 marks.
Good knowledge and understanding here, Mick. This is very clear and shows that you know what you are talking about.

SECTION A 6 Outline two findings from the split-brain study by Sperry. *(4 marks)*

Ally's answer:

Brains can't communicate with themselves when the corpus callosum has been cut. This means they can't each remember things if you show an object to one hemisphere of the brain and again to the other. It's like they haven't seen it before. Second, this study was unrepresentative as the participants were unrepresentative of the population as a whole.

We say: 2 marks.
Ally, make certain you know what you are meant to be looking at in the answer and do exactly that! You are asked to outline findings here, and you did that in your first point, but then your second was an evaluation. Findings are the results gathered in the study, so pick out two clear points from this and explain them.

Harvey's answer:

With the divided visual fields, information sent to one hemisphere will be recognised by the same hemisphere only if shown a second time, and not by the other one, as the hemispheres cannot communicate now. When an object is shown to the right visual field it can be described with language as it goes to the left hemisphere language centre. But with the left visual field going to the right hemisphere, it can't be described in language but can be picked out from a selection of objects by hand.

We say: 4 marks.
Some accurate knowledge and description here, Harvey. You give a summary of each of the findings that is quite brief. This is not always easy to do with studies that have descriptive, qualitative results. You have provided comparisons and comment on how each hemisphere would respond to the task, which you should do in this study to make your findings clear.

SECTION B (d) With reference to the study by Sperry, suggest one strength and one weakness of qualitative data. (6 marks)

Pam's answer:

It is good because there are numbers and you can put them into a graph to see the results, making it easy to see if you have proved your hypothesis. It is bad because it is not very detailed and you don't learn a lot from it.

We say: 0 marks.
Check your definitions of qualitative and quantitative data, Pam! You have mixed them up and your points relate to quantitative (numerical) data. This, alas, is not what the question asked, so you gain no credit. It can be an easy mistake; it is important to revise your key terms well.

Sue's answer:

An advantage of qualitative data is that you get rich detail that you cannot get from a number, which allows you a deeper understanding of phenomena like split brains and how they work. For example, in Sperry's study, the way in which the split-brain patients fail at certain tasks like not being able to use language if it goes to the right hemisphere is described in detail. If this was coded into a number, you would not gain the same level of understanding of the split-brain participant's abilities. A disadvantage of qualitative data is that it is not often so cut and dry whether you have proved or disproved a hypothesis. This makes it less scientific as it is hard to do statistical analysis on the data. Sperry's results are just description.

We say: 5 marks.
Sue, your answer shows us that you are very clear about the good and bad points of this type of data. The first point is detailed and accurate, with evidence from the study used throughout. When the question says 'with reference to your chosen study' or a similar phrase, your examiner expects to see you illustrate your more general critical points with specific study related examples – just as you have done. Your second point did not do this quite so well and the example is rather vague, although the point is fine.

SECTION C (a) Outline one assumption of the physiological approach. (2 marks)

Bethan's answer:

It is saying that everything we do is because of biology and biological reasons. We need to understand all about the biology of humans.

We say: 1 mark.
Bethan, you have the basis of the assumption here, but it is not very clearly explained. Try to avoid repeating 'biology' and instead pick out the point that it is explaining all the range of behaviours that we show through biological factors. This would give more clarity to your answer.

Sally's answer:

An assumption is that all our behaviour is caused by our biology and jeans. We need to look at biological factors to explain how people act. An example is in Maguire's study, where the taxi driver's hippocampus changes and they had different behaviour with a huge memory compared to other people.

We say: 2 marks.
Knowledge and understanding are clearly shown here in your outline of this assumption, and your example adds detail. It is not necessary to include one, but if well used, it can show the examiner that you really do understand what you are talking about.

THE PHYSIOLOGICAL APPROACH TO PSYCHOLOGY

We have looked in detail at three studies from physiological psychology. Based on these studies, we will now consider the key aspects of the physiological approach to psychology. We have already said that physiological psychology is concerned with the action of genes, the nervous system and hormones on our behaviour, emotions and cognition. By considering these pieces of research we can outline some key assumptions behind this approach to psychology.

1. We can understand differences in cognition and behaviour in terms of brain differences and changes

The brain is the most complex structure within the nervous system. The human brain is also more complex and, relative-to-body size, bigger than that of any other animal. This makes it important, but also difficult, to study. Although the nervous system is ultimately responsible for all of our emotions, cognitions and behaviours, the brain is in turn affected by other factors, such as our experiences. Sperry's study served to show how the complex structure of the brain is related to its function, and Maguire *et al.*'s study also helped to illustrate the complexity of the brain – how even two small areas, those of the anterior and posterior hippocampus, serve somewhat different functions. It specifically demonstrated how the brain determines behaviour through cognition, by providing evidence for the role of the hippocampus in navigational ability. Furthermore, this study clearly showed how experience affects the brain as more navigational experience leads to an increase in hippocampal volume.

2. Differences in emotion, cognition and behaviour are genetically controlled

Maguire *et al.*'s study is one of many that expose or explore a key question in physiological psychology: the extent to which any characteristic is determined by genetics versus the environment. In the case of Maguire *et al.*'s study, they demonstrated that there were changes in the hippocampus due to the environment, here provided by the Knowledge and subsequent taxi driving. This is an example of the nature-nurture debate, which is central to the physiological approach: nature representing the biological influences, and nurture the environmental ones. It is possible, of course, that some underlying genetic factor predisposed the individuals who became taxi drivers to do so precisely because they were able to learn navigational information. Teasing out the relative importance of the two influences is a central issue for physiological psychology.

3. Brain activity can be studied and related to observable, measureable changes

Until electrical measures were developed in the early 20th century, the only way to study brain activity was by lesioning. This could provide some evidence for brain function as the absence of a behaviour or ability when a brain area was damaged implied that the damaged area was important for that function. However, as we can see from Sperry's study, the absence of the corpus callosum might prevent an individual from saying the answer to a question, even though corpus callosum is not, itself, required for deciding upon or producing verbal response. Sperry's study showed how the absence of the corpus callosum led to a range of clearly observable cognitive deficits in a laboratory setting, and Maguire *et al.* conversely showed that cognitive differences (in navigational skill) were linked to changes in brain structure. Dement and Kleitman used electrical recording of both the brain and eye movements. These illustrated how physiological activity in the brain (which could not previously have been investigated) related to both subjective reports of the cognitive experience of dreams, and to directly observable physiological indicators of dreaming – namely eye movements.

STRENGTHS AND WEAKNESSES OF THE PHYSIOLOGICAL APPROACH
Strengths

1   **Scientific research methods.** All the studies in this chapter have used rigorous procedures. Laboratory experiments are typical of the physiological approach, as is the use of precise, scientific apparatus. Equipment such as that used by Sperry allows researchers to impose stringent controls so that they can be certain that extraneous variables are not responsible for any effects they observe. This helps to ensure that the studies are valid. Techniques such as EEG, EOG and MRI are reliable tools for measurement.

2   **Leads to advances in understanding and practical applications.** By providing an understanding of the biological principles underlying the function of the nervous system, physiological psychology offers a wealth of information that helps us to understand human responses. Furthermore, this can help us to understand what can go wrong with emotional, cognitive and behavioural control, and thus potentially help us to alleviate mental disorders or damage caused by illness or injury. Investigative techniques (such as MRI), drug treatments and some rehabilitation techniques rely on the findings of physiological research.

Weaknesses

1   **Lack of ecological validity.** A common criticism of physiological psychology – precisely because it uses highly controlled laboratory procedures – is that its findings may not relate well to real life. Maguire *et al.* studied brain activity in a small sample of people based on recordings taken inside a brain scanner, yet drew conclusions relating to navigational ability – a particularly 'real-world' behaviour. Sperry explored the cognition of people who had undergone an unusual operation and therefore exhibited an unusual set of observable deficits. In contrast, in the 'real world', these people demonstrated few problems. Dement and Kleitman studied sleep with their participants in an unfamiliar place, attached them to strange equipment, and woke them up often. These factors meant that the participants were unlikely to experience an entirely typical night's sleep. Such criticisms illustrate the way in which physiological studies might be divorced from the tasks of day-to-day life (a lack of mundane realism) and so might not generalise to the experiences of people outside the specific and contrived setting in which they were obtained (a lack of ecological validity).

2   **Reductionism.** It is often argued that the physiological approach is reductionist – because it attempts to explain complex behaviour in terms of genes, brain structure and chemicals. In reality, modern physiological psychologists are exploring the extent to which such factors are important, rather than studying them to the exclusion of other factors. Nevertheless, the physiological approach does not explore, and therefore cannot necessarily explain, how complex systems interact.

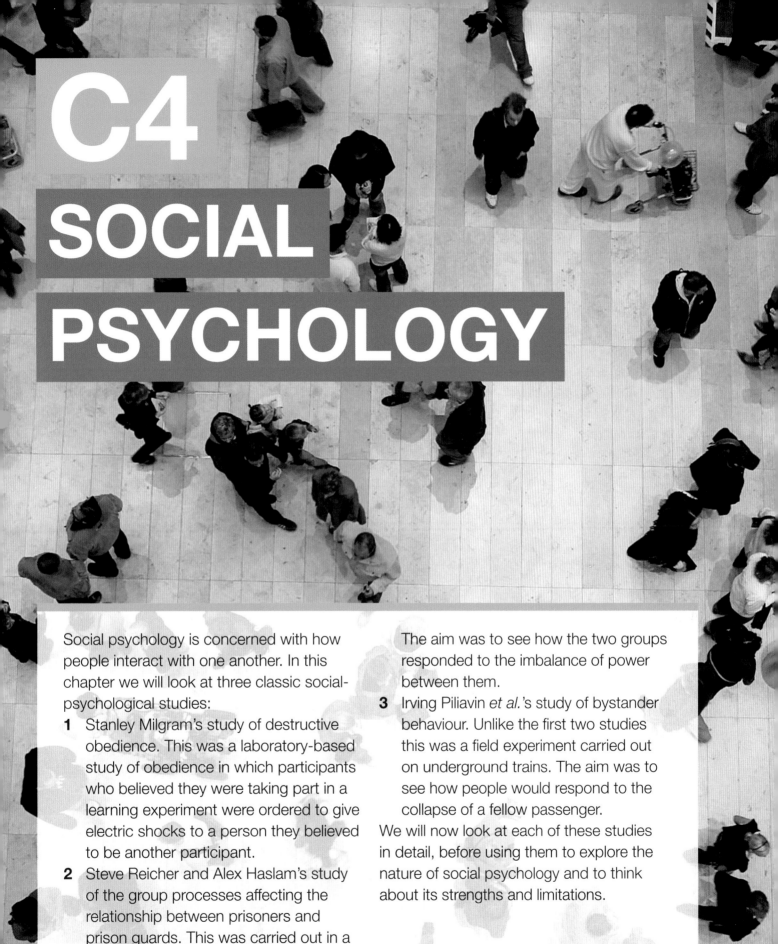

C4

SOCIAL PSYCHOLOGY

Social psychology is concerned with how people interact with one another. In this chapter we will look at three classic social-psychological studies:

1 Stanley Milgram's study of destructive obedience. This was a laboratory-based study of obedience in which participants who believed they were taking part in a learning experiment were ordered to give electric shocks to a person they believed to be another participant.

2 Steve Reicher and Alex Haslam's study of the group processes affecting the relationship between prisoners and prison guards. This was carried out in a simulated prison-like environment.

The aim was to see how the two groups responded to the imbalance of power between them.

3 Irving Piliavin *et al.*'s study of bystander behaviour. Unlike the first two studies this was a field experiment carried out on underground trains. The aim was to see how people would respond to the collapse of a fellow passenger.

We will now look at each of these studies in detail, before using them to explore the nature of social psychology and to think about its strengths and limitations.

MILGRAM'S STUDY OF DESTRUCTIVE OBEDIENCE

 KEY IDEAS

Obedience means following a direct order. This is different from **compliance**, which means going along with what someone wants you to do, or **conformity**, which means behaving in the same way as those around you. Remember that Milgram was studying **destructive obedience**, which means following an order to harm someone. Destructive obedience is generally necessary in order for genocide to take place. **Genocide** is the systematic attempt to wipe out an ethnic group.

Milgram, S. (1963) Behavioural study of obedience. *Journal of Abnormal & Social Psychology*, **67**, 371–8.

CONTEXT

Most of the time we are told that **obedience** is a good thing. If your teacher tells you to get your book out or to answer a question, you might not want to do it but you probably accept that the most socially appropriate behaviour is to obey. You probably also accept that your teacher has the right to give you an instruction of this kind. But what if you were ordered to do something that caused harm or distress to another person? This type of obedience, in which people obey orders to cause harm, is called **destructive obedience**. Social psychologists such as Stanley Milgram have been particularly interested in destructive obedience.

Figure 4.1 Ordinary Germans obeyed orders that led to millions being killed in extermination camps

As the member of a European Jewish family that had left Europe for America, Milgram was profoundly affected by the atrocities committed by Nazi Germany against Jewish people and other minority groups. One of the key features of the Nazi atrocities was the extent to which people displayed destructive obedience. Many ordinary people obeyed destructive orders that led to the systematic mass murder of minority groups, including Jews, Romanies, Communists, Trade Unionists, and people with disabilities.

Early psychological research into the Holocaust focused on the idea that something distinctive about German culture or personality led to the high levels of **conformity** and obedience necessary for **genocide** to take place. This is known as the **dispositional hypothesis**. While Milgram was interested in this idea, he was also interested in the social processes that take place between individuals and within groups. The idea that we can explain events such as the Holocaust by reference to the social processes operating in the situation, rather than the characteristics of the individuals involved, is called the **situational hypothesis**. In his early work Milgram worked with another famous social psychologist Solomon Asch. Together they studied people's tendency to conform to group pressure. Milgram went on to investigate the tendency to obey destructive orders from individuals in positions of authority.

 **KEY IDEAS**

There is a tension in social psychology between explanations that focus on the individuals involved in a social situation and those that focus on the situation itself. These explanations are known respectively as the **dispositional hypothesis** and the **situational hypothesis**.

Figure 4.2
Stanley Milgram

ACTIVITY ✳

It can be hard to picture the sort of real-life situation in which destructive obedience occurs. Read the following account of a massacre that took place in Poland in 1942.

DO AS YOU'RE TOLD

by Nicci Gerrard

C.P. Snow wrote that 'more hideous crimes have been committed in the name of obedience than have ever been committed in the name of rebellion'.

In the early hours of 13 July 1942, the 500 men of the German Reserve Police Force Battalion 101 – middle-aged family men, too old for the army, barely trained and stationed in Poland – were addressed by their leader, Commander Trapp. In a voice shaky with distress he told them of their next assignment: to seek out and kill the 1800 women and children in the nearby village of Jozefow. Then, astonishingly,

Trapp told them he knew what a repugnant task some might find it, and that anyone could stand out with no punishment and no reprisals. Out of 500, only 12 men stood out.

During that terrible day, a further 10–20% managed to evade their duty; many more became distressed but continued to carry out the orders. Quite a few exhibited no signs of distress. A few seemed to enjoy themselves.

Source: The Observer Review, *12 October 1997*

Q

1 How might the behaviour of Battalion 101 be explained using the dispositional hypothesis and the situational hypothesis?
2 What do you think you would have done if you had been in Battalion 101?

KEY IDEAS

STRETCH & CHALLENGE

Design and carry out a study to test what sort of percentage of people nowadays believe they would give a helpless person potentially fatal shocks under orders. How do your results compare to Milgram's, an d what might this tell us?

Figure 4.3 The newspaper advertisement

Public Announcement

WE WILL PAY YOU $4.00 FOR ONE HOUR OF YOUR TIME

Persons Needed for a Study of Memory

*We will pay five hundred New Haven men to help us complete a scientific study of memory and learning. The study is being done at Yale University.

*Each person who participates will be paid $4.00 (plus 50c carfare) for approximately 1 hour's time. We need you for only one hour: there are no further obligations. You may choose the time you would like to come (evenings, weekdays, or weekends).

*No special training, education, or experience is needed. We want:

Factory workers	Businessmen	Construction workers
City employees	Clerks	Salespeople
Laborers	Professional people	White-collar workers
Barbers	Telephone workers	Others

All persons must be between the ages of 20 and 50. High school and college students cannot be used.

*If you meet these qualifications, fill out the coupon below and mail it now to Professor Stanley Milgram, Department of Psychology, Yale University, New Haven. You will be notified later of the specific time and place of the study. We reserve the right to decline any application.

*You will be paid $4.00 (plus 50c carfare) as soon as you arrive at the laboratory.

- -

TO:
PROF. STANLEY MILGRAM, DEPARTMENT OF PSYCHOLOGY, YALE UNIVERSITY, NEW HAVEN, CONN. I want to take part in this study of memory and learning. I am between the ages of 20 and 50. I will be paid $4.00 (plus 50c carfare) if I participate.

NAME: (Please Print). . . . .

ADDRESS . . . .

TELEPHONE NO. . . . . Best time to call you . . . .

AGE. . . . . OCCUPATION. . . . . SEX . . . . .
CAN YOU COME:

WEEKDAYS . . . . EVENINGS . . . . . . WEEKENDS. . . . .

BEFORE THE MAIN PROCEDURE

Before carrying out the main study, Milgram told psychology students about his procedure. This would involve ordering people to give electric shocks to a helpless man (actually an actor) whom they believed to be a fellow participant. The electric shocks would increase in intensity up to 450V. Students estimated that only 3% of participants would obey the orders and give all the shocks.

IN BRIEF

Aim: To investigate the tendency for destructive obedience.

Method: 40 male volunteers were told they were taking part in a learning experiment. They took the role of teacher, giving what they thought were painful shocks to a confederate whom they believed to be a fellow participant taking the role of learner. Shocks increased by 15V for every wrong answer and went up to a maximum of 450V.

Results: 100% of participants gave at least 300V and 65% gave the full 450V. Most participants displayed signs of stress while giving the shocks.

Conclusion: People are surprisingly obedient to orders given by people in authority. However, they become distressed when obeying orders to hurt another person.

AIM

The aim of the study was to investigate how obedient people would be to orders from a person in authority that would result in pain and harm to another person. More specifically, the aim was to see how large an electric shock participants would give to a helpless man when ordered to by a scientist in his own laboratory.

METHOD

Design

Milgram himself described his original study as a laboratory experiment. Technically it might more accurately be called a pre-experiment, because it had only one condition. The results from this condition then served as a baseline for a number of variations in follow-up studies. The independent variable (IV) in the original study was the orders, and the dependent variable (DV) was the obedience. Obedience was operationalised as the maximum voltage given in response to the orders.

Participants

Forty men aged 20–50 were recruited by means of a newspaper advertisement. The sample was therefore mostly a volunteer or self-selecting sample. They were from a range of backgrounds and held a range of jobs: 37.5% were manual labourers, 40% were white-collar workers, and 22.5% were professionals. All were from the New Haven district of North America.

Procedure

Participants were recruited by means of a newspaper advertisement. They were promised $4.50 for their time. It was made clear that payment was for turning up to the study, and was not conditional on completing the procedure. When each participant arrived at Yale University he was introduced to a man he believed to be another participant. The two men were then briefed on the supposed purpose of the experiment, which was described to them as to investigate the effect of punishment on learning.

In fact the other man was working for Milgram. He was a 47-year-old Irish-American accountant. He had been selected for the role because he was mild-mannered and likeable. People who help with experiments in this way are known as confederates or stooges.

The **naïve participant** and the confederate were told that one of them would play the role of teacher and the other the learner. They drew slips of paper from a hat to allocate the roles, but this was fiddled so that the naïve participant was always the teacher and the confederate was always the learner. They were then immediately taken to another room where the learner was strapped into a chair and electrodes were attached to him. They were shown the electric shock generator. This had a row of switches,

WEB WATCH @

You can see footage of Milgram's experiments and various replications online. Videos are sometimes available on YouTube, or try www.psychexchange.co.uk/videos/view/20257

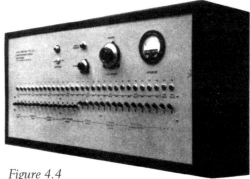

Figure 4.4
The shock generator

QUESTION SPOTLIGHT!

Milgram has been challenged on the ethical issues raised by his procedure. How does his procedure stand up against the following ethical principles?

1 Harm and distress
2 Right to withdraw
3 Real consent
4 Deception
5 Debriefing

See p.169 for an explanation of these principles.

 **KEY IDEAS**

A **naïve participant** is one who does not know the purpose of the procedure in which they are taking part. It is common practice not to explain the purpose of the study they are taking part in so as to reduce the likelihood that their behaviour is affected by their view of the study.

TABLE 4.1 DISTRIBUTION OF MAXIMUM VOLTAGES GIVEN

Voltage	number of participants
0–285	0
300	5
315	4
330	2
345	1
360	1
375	1
390	0
405	0
420	0
435	0
450	26

each labelled with a voltage, rising in 15-volt intervals from 15V up to 450V. Participants were told that the shocks could be extremely painful but not dangerous; they were each given a 45V shock to demonstrate.

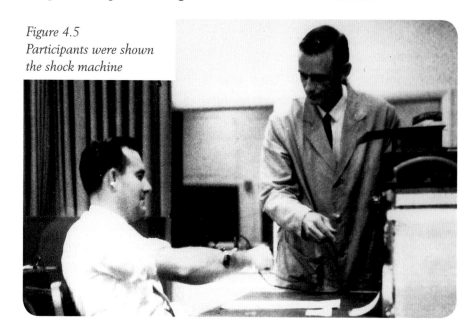

Figure 4.5
Participants were shown
the shock machine

There was a wall between the teacher and learner, so that the teacher could hear but not see the learner. The procedure was administered by an experimenter, played by a 31-year-old male biology teacher. The participant (in the role of teacher) read out word pairs and to test the confederate (in the role of learner) on his recognition of which words went together. Each time the confederate-learner made a mistake, the experimenter ordered the teacher-participant to give a shock. The shock got larger by 15V for each mistake. The confederate-learner did not really receive shocks, but there was no way for the teacher-participant to know this.

Up to 300V the confederate-learner did not signal any response to the shocks. However, at 300V and 315V, he pounded on the wall. He was then silent and did not respond to further questions. This suggested that he was hurt, perhaps unconscious, or even dead. When participants turned to the experimenter for guidance, they were told to treat no response as incorrect and to continue to give the shocks. When they protested, they were given a series of verbal prods to encourage them to continue.

Each participant was considered to have completed the procedure either when they refused to give any more shocks, or when they reached the maximum voltage on the shock machine. They were then interviewed and de-hoaxed. During their interview they were asked to rate on a scale of 0–14 how painful the last few shocks they gave were. They were told that the shocks were not real, that the learner was unharmed, and that the real purpose of the study was to investigate obedience.

Figure 4.6
In a particularly brutal variation
on the basic procedure, participants
were ordered to force the stooge's
hand onto the electrode

RESULTS

Quantitative and qualitative data was gathered. The 'headline figures' were quantitative, in the form of the average voltage that participants went up to, and the number of participants giving each voltage. The average voltage given by participants was 368V. 100% of participants gave 300V or more; 65% gave the full 450V. Remember that psychology students had estimated that only 3% of participants would do this! In their post-experiment interviews, their average rating of how painful the shocks were was 13.42 out of a maximum of 14.

Qualitative data was gathered in the form of the comments and protests participants made during the procedure, and in the form of observations of their body language. Most participants showed signs of tension during the procedure. Signs included groaning, sweating, biting lips, and stuttering. Fourteen giggled nervously. One had a seizure and the procedure was stopped. One observer noted:

'I observed a mature and initially poised business man enter the laboratory smiling and confident. Within 20 minutes he was reduced to a twitching, stuttering wreck, who was rapidly approaching the point of nervous collapse.' (p. 377)

Most participants protested against the procedure, although the verbal prods were in most cases sufficient to get them to continue giving the shocks.

> *"I observed a mature and intially poised business man enter the laboratory smiling and confident. Within 20 minutes he was reduced to a twicthing, stuttering wreck, who was rapidly approaching the point of nervous collapse."*

CONCLUSIONS

Milgram drew two main conclusions from this study:

1   People are much more obedient to destructive orders than we might expect, and considerably more than psychology students suggested in their estimates. In fact, the majority of people are quite willing to obey destructive orders.

2   People find the experience of receiving and obeying destructive orders highly stressful. They obey in spite of their emotional responses. The situation triggers a conflict between two deeply ingrained tendencies: to obey those in authority, and not to harm people.

Results supported the situational hypothesis rather than the dispositional hypothesis.

TABLE 4.2 PERCENTAGE GIVING 450V IN VARIATIONS OF THE MILGRAM PROCEDURE	
Victim is silent throughout	100%
Standard procedure	65%
Location in seedy office	48%
Victim in same room	40%
Orders given by phone	20.5%
No lab coat worn	20%
Fellow participants disobey	10%
Participant chooses voltage	2.5%

EXPLAINING THE HIGH LEVELS OF OBEDIENCE

Milgram identified the following nine possible factors in the situation that might have contributed to the high levels of obedience seen.

1   The study was carried out in the respectable environment of a top university.
2   The aim of the study appeared to be a worthwhile one.
3   The learner appeared to have volunteered and so had an obligation to the experimenter.
4   The teacher also volunteered and so had an obligation to the experimenter.
5   Features of the design, for example payment, increased this sense of obligation.
6   From the perspective of the teacher, he might equally well have been unlucky enough to have been the learner and to have endured the shocks.
7   The rights of participant to withdraw and of the scientist to expect **compliance** were not obvious.
8   The participants were assured that the shocks were not dangerous.
9   The learner appeared to be comfortable with the procedure for the first 300V.

LATER VARIATIONS ON THE PROCEDURE

What we have described here is Milgram's first published study, but over the following 10 years he refined his procedure. (This is why, if you watch footage of the procedure, some details might differ from the original procedure in the first published study.) As well as refining the basic condition, Milgram also tested the effect of a number of variations. Results are shown in the form of the percentage of participants who went to the maximum 450V in each condition. In general, giving the participant greater distance from the learner, or less personal responsibility for decision-making, increased obedience, while reducing the apparent power of the experimenter, or making the situation appear less respectable or scientific, reduced obedience.

These variations have been replicated many times by different researchers. Luttke (2004) reviewed these studies and concluded that Milgram was right about some but not all of his conclusions. In particular, the presence of disobedient participants and the physical closeness of the learner reliably reduces obedience. However, most studies have found that varying the location of the study makes little difference to obedience.

STUDY 1

MILGRAM'S STUDY OF DESTRUCTIVE OBEDIENCE

SUMMARY

AIM

To investigate the extent to which people will obey orders from a figure of authority to inflict severe pain on another person.

PILOT SURVEY

The procedure was explained to psychology students, who were then asked to estimate how many people would obey all the orders. Their estimate was 3%.

METHOD

Volunteers responded to a newspaper advert and came to the laboratory at Yale University. They were told that they were taking part in a learning experiment to investigate the role of pain-avoidance in learning. They took the role of teacher, while a confederate took the role of learner. When the 'learner' made a mistake, the participant was ordered to give them what appeared to be painful shocks. Shocks increased by 15V for every wrong answer and went up to a maximum of 450V. When participants protested against giving the 'learner' large shocks, they were given a series of verbal prods. When they either refused to continue or reached 450V, they were debriefed.

RESULTS

- 100% of participants gave at least 300 volts.
- 65% of participants gave the full 450 volts.
- Most participants showed signs of stress.

CONCLUSIONS

- People are very obedient to those in authority.
- People get distressed when given orders that conflict with their own moral codes.

EVALUATION OF THE STUDY

This is a controversial study for several reasons, both ethical and methodological.

ETHICAL ISSUES

By modern standards, Milgram's procedure raises a number of ethical issues. First, he caused participants considerable distress, if only for a few minutes. He might even have put their health at risk – remember that one participant suffered a seizure. He did not obtain informed consent because participants agreed to take part in a learning experiment not a study of obedience. His payment of participants might also have compromised informed consent because they might have felt obliged to continue once they saw what the procedure involved. Participants were deceived about several things: the purpose of the study, the nature of the confederate, the reality of the 'shocks', and the apparent suffering of the learner. Perhaps most seriously, participants were effectively denied their right to withdraw by the use of the verbal prods. Although they *could* have withdrawn, they didn't *feel* that they could. Only 35% withdrew from giving all the shocks.

At the time of the study Milgram was in the process of applying for membership of the American Psychological Association. His application was suspended while he was investigated over these ethical issues, but he was able to justify his procedure and was found to have acted properly. The following arguments went in his favour:

- Although participants were deceived, this is sometimes allowed within ethical codes provided it is essential for design, and provided participants are fully debriefed at the earliest opportunity. Milgram provided a thorough de-hoax and debrief, and participants generally left the study happy.
- Although participants were distressed for a short time, the vast majority said that they were glad they had taken part and that they had learned something useful.
- Most importantly, the study was an important one, especially given the historical period and the importance of gaining a better understanding of the Holocaust. It is not considered ethically acceptable to replicate the Milgram procedure now.

METHODOLOGICAL ISSUES
The sample and sampling method

The sample was made up of 40 men from the same region in USA. This is a fairly average sample for a laboratory study, neither particularly a strength nor a weakness. The fact that the sample was all male and all came from the same area makes it tricky to generalise from the results of the original study to the whole population. Remember, however, that the intention was always to replicate the study in different populations, so this is not a serious weakness.

The volunteer/snowball sampling method is a more serious problem. Self-selection and snowballing are the most unrepresentative of all the sampling methods. Most people do not volunteer for anything so, by definition, volunteers are not typical people! Allowing snowballing compounds this problem because participants tend to invite other people who are like themselves to take part.

The research method

The study was a laboratory procedure. (It was called an experiment by Milgram, although technically we should now describe it as a pre-experiment.) Laboratory studies come with a set of strengths and limitations. Because the procedure takes place in a highly controlled

STRETCH & CHALLENGE ◎

In groups, design a more ethically acceptable study to test how obedient people are. You will probably find it hard to test destructive obedience ethically, but you might come up with a way to test more mild forms of obedience.

environment it is possible to eliminate many extraneous variables and be reasonably confident that it is the independent variable we are interested in that is affecting the dependent variable. Laboratory procedures are straightforward to replicate, making them reliable. The potential weaknesses with laboratory studies lie in the realism of the environment and participants' tasks. It is hard to set up laboratory procedures in which people behave as they would in real life.

Reliability

Remember that reliability means consistency. A procedure is reliable if we can precisely replicate it, and when we consistently get the same results when we do replicate it. We have said that laboratory experiments are generally easy to replicate, and Milgram's procedure has been replicated many times. Although there is debate over the reliability of some of his variations, the results of the basic procedure have proved to be very consistent. Thus we can say that Milgram's procedure has good reliability.

Ecological validity

We have said that a potential weakness in laboratory experiments is their realism. There are two aspects to this realism: the environment and the task. Milgram's procedure took place in an artificial environment that was rather different to those in which most atrocities take place. On the surface, the task facing Milgram's participants is also artificial – we don't find ourselves operating electric-shock machines very often in real life. Therefore, it can be argued that Milgram's study is low in ecological validity. However, Milgram was clever in selecting both an environment and a task that represent quite well some of the features of the situation in which atrocities take place.

- The situation was respectable and the experimenter was in a position of legitimate authority in that environment. People tend to obey orders to participate in atrocities only when those giving the orders have real status and authority. The experimenter wore the lab coat – the uniform of the scientist – in the same way as military leaders wear uniforms as a visible mark of their authority.

- Participants were told that the experiment was for the advancement of science – a noble aim. When leaders are ordering people to commit atrocities they generally claim that they are for the good of the country or the community. So participants were influenced in the same way as are those who commit atrocities.

- The electric shocks increased in small increments of 15V. In this way, each decision to obey was only a slight move from the one before. This is similar to the 'slippery slope' people find themselves on when receiving orders to act aggressively to their victims in real-life atrocities. For example, people might receive orders at first just to transport victims, then to mistreat them at their new location, then finally to kill them.

Quantitative and qualitative data

A strength of Milgram's study was the recording of both quantitative and qualitative data. It therefore has the strengths of both types of data (see p. 141 for a discussion). In this case, having both types of data was important in drawing the correct conclusions. If we had only the figures for how many people went to what voltage we might conclude that people were uncaring and did not mind harming someone. However, when we add the qualitative data it becomes clear that, although people were highly obedient, they also found the experience highly stressful.

Practical applications

This is an important strength of Milgram's research. Understanding the circumstances in which people will obey destructive orders has proved useful in understanding atrocities, even allowing the International Criminal Court in some cases to predict atrocities before they take place (Alexander, 2009). Understanding obedience has also had some more surprising benefits. Influenced by Milgram's research, Tarnow (2000) analysed records of 37 plane crashes, and suggested that in 25% of cases the crash was a direct result of the pilot's obeying orders from the ground. These results have clear implications for accident prevention.

EXAM FOCUS

We now show you some of the sorts of questions that could be asked about the Milgram study in your exam. We will then show you some examples of the sorts of answers we believe might be successful and less successful, and point out some classic traps to avoid.

SECTION A

1 (a) Describe Milgram's sample. *(2 marks)*
   (b) Outline one limitation of this sample. *(2 marks)*
2 Explain why Milgram's study could be said to be low in ecological validity. *(4 marks)*
3 Suggest two pieces of evidence that suggest that Milgram's participants believed the shocks were real. *(4 marks)*
4 In Milgram's procedure, the experimenter used verbal prods to persuade participants to continue.
   (a) Give one prod that was used. *(2 marks)*
   (b) Suggest one ethical issue raised by the prods. *(2 marks)*
5 (a) What sampling method was used in the Milgram study? *(2 marks)*
   (b) Outline one limitation with this method. *(2 marks)*
6 Outline two reasons why Milgram's participants might have been so obedient. *(4 marks)*
7 Describe how results were recorded in the Milgram study. *(4 marks)*
8 Outline one piece of qualitative data that was recorded in the Milgram study. *(2 marks)*

SECTION B

(a) Briefly outline the previous research or event that was the stimulus for the Milgram study. *(2 marks)*

(b) Milgram described his study as a laboratory experiment. What are the features of a laboratory experiment? Explain why Milgram might have described his procedure as a laboratory experiment. *(6 marks)*
(c) Evaluate laboratory experiments. *(6 marks)*
(d) Describe the findings and conclusions of the Milgram study. *(6 marks)*
(e) Outline how you might improve the Milgram procedure. *(8 marks)*
(f) Explain the implications of these changes for the study. *(8 marks)*

SECTION C

(a) Outline one assumption of the social approach. *(2 marks)*
(b) With reference to the Milgram study, describe how the social approach could explain obedience. *(4 marks)*
(c) Describe one similarity and one difference between any studies that take the social approach. *(6 marks)*
(d) Discuss strengths and weaknesses of the social approach using examples from any studies that take this approach. *(12 marks)*

SOME ANSWERS AND COMMENTS

SECTION A 1. (a) Describe Milgram's sample. *(2 marks)*

Michael says:

Milgram used volunteers for his sample. This is a dodgy sort of sample because it is always unrepresentative.

> **We say:** 0 marks.
> Michael, you have made two classic errors. First, you have confused the sample and the sampling method. Second, you have evaluated when the question just asks you to describe.

Maynard says:

There were 40 participants. All were male and all from the New Haven area in America.

> **We say:** 2 marks.
> There is more you could say, for example about the ages and occupations. However, what is there is fine for two marks. There could always be a three- or four-mark question, of course, so do remember that extra information.

SECTION A 3 Suggest two pieces of evidence that suggest that Milgram's participants believed the shocks were real. *(4 marks)*

Chesney says:

Participants got well stressed when they had to give the shocks.

> **We say:** 1 mark.
> This is true but it's a brief, undeveloped answer and identifies only one source of evidence when the question asks for two.

Chad says:

First, participants displayed signs of stress. Observers said they were sweating and giggling nervously. If they were nervous it was probably because they thought they were really hurting the learner. Second, in the debriefing they estimated the pain level as 13.4 out of 14. If they thought they really caused pain they must have believed the shocks were real.

> **We say:** 4 marks.
> As well as identifying the two pieces of evidence, Chad, you have explained why you suggest that the participants thought the shocks were real. This is a good strategy to be sure you pick up more than the basic marks.

SECTION B (d) Describe the findings and conclusions of the Milgram study. *(6 marks)*

Alexandra says:

Milgram found that most of the participants gave all the shocks. 100% of them gave 300 volts.

> **We say:** 2 marks.
> The first thing to say here, Alexandra, is that this is an awfully short answer for a six-mark question. Second, your answer addresses only the findings, not the conclusion. Even for a description of the findings, your answer lacks detail and reveals a lack of knowledge of some basics. There is no mention of qualitative findings and 'most' is much less precise than '65%' would have been.

Leona says:

65% of participants gave the full 450V, and 100% gave at least 300V. Most either stopped around the 300 mark or carried on to 450V. However, they showed signs of stress such as sweating and giggling nervously. It was concluded from this that people are obedient to orders from an authority figure, but they do not obey the orders happily if they mean going against their own morals.

We say: 5 marks.
Leona, this is a good answer because you have addressed both the findings and conclusions, and because you have made every effort to include a good level of detail. For the full six marks, you need to give a little more detail in the conclusion.

SECTION C (b) With reference to the Milgram study, describe how the social approach could explain obedience. *(4 marks)*

Pete's answer:

The researcher encouraged the participant to carry on with the shocks and so they mainly did. He said 'you have no choice' and similar things. They could not disobey when he said this to them as he looked important in his lab coat and being in the room pressured them.

We say: 2 marks.
Pete, although the question does ask you to refer to Milgram's study, you should still look at obedience in the context of the social approach generally. You have really just made some comments on features of Milgram's results, and the answer is a bit limited. You show some understanding, but needed to say why this makes people obey in order to really explain how the social approach itself explains obedience.

Owen's answer:

It explains it by looking at how other people around you can influence your behaviour. The experimenter was in the room with the participant as they gave the shocks, so his presence was affecting them. Participants felt he was in charge and so were subject to social influences. Other people can affect our behaviour and make us do as we are told if they look like they have power and should be in that place, e.g. here the experimenter was wearing a lab coat and looked like a scientist in a university. Therefore we obey as we are influenced by another person in a social situation who tells us what to do.

We say: 4 marks.
Owen, your answer shows that you understand both the study by Milgram and the social approach itself. You start the answer well, with the context of the social approach. We like the way you pick out a few key points from Milgram's study and discuss these in a clear way, before relating them back to obedience more generally. Good understanding and explanation.

REICHER AND HASLAM'S STUDY OF RELATIONS BETWEEN TWO GROUPS OF UNEQUAL POWER IN A PRISON ENVIRONMENT

Reicher. S., and Haslam, A. (2006) Rethinking the psychology of tyranny: the BBC Prison Study. *British Journal of Social Psychology*, **45**, 1–40.

CONTEXT

Steven Reicher and Alex Haslam are concerned with the phenomenon of tyranny. They define this as 'an unequal social system involving the arbitrary or oppressive use of power by one group or its agents over another' (2006: p. 2). The study of tyranny by social psychologists has been dominated by the belief that tyranny is a basic part of group behaviour. Reicher and Haslam have challenged this view, wishing to show that tyranny is not inevitable.

In order to really understand what Reicher and Haslam were trying to achieve in this study, we need to understand one previous study and one social-psychological theory: the Stanford Prison study, and social identity theory.

WEB WATCH @

You can read the original research paper here:
http://www.prisonexp.org/pdf/ijcp1973.pdf
You can also see footage of the study on YouTube, for example at:
www.youtube.com/watch?v=ZaXXqrUzKHw

Figure 4.7 Philip Zimbardo, lead researcher in the Stanford Prison study

Figure 4.8 Haslam and Reicher

Figure 4.9
A prisoner is punished

Figure 4.10
By day five, the prisoners
were cleaning toilets with
their bare hands

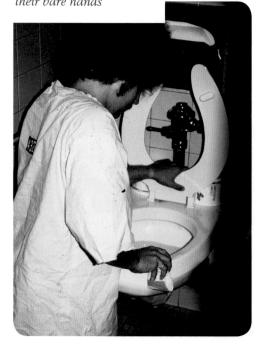

THE STANFORD PRISON STUDY (HANEY, BANKS AND ZIMBARDO, 1973)

This was a famous social-psychological study in the 1970s, which took place in the basement of the psychology department at Stanford University, hence the name. Its aim was to investigate the psychological effect of becoming a prisoner or a prison guard. Eighteen male students were randomly assigned to be either prisoners or guards. The prisoners were arrested at home and taken to the makeshift prison in the university. Each prisoner was strip-searched and de-loused on arrival. They were then made to wear a uniform, a stocking cap to cover their hair, and an ankle chain. They were allowed to refer to themselves and others only by a prisoner number. Guards were not trained; they were allowed to make up the prison rules. Unknown to the participants, the prison area was bugged and monitored 24 hours a day. The lead experimenter, Philip Zimbardo, took the role of Prison Warden.

The results were dramatic. Guards initiated a programme of 'counts' in which prisoners were assembled and ordered to repeat their prisoner number. At first, the prisoners did not take this seriously, however the guards began to use press-ups as punishment. One guard in particular stood on prisoners' backs to make press-ups harder and more painful. For the first day prisoners obeyed, but on the morning of the second day they rebelled, barricading themselves in their cells. The guards forced their way into each cell and stripped the prisoners. They put the ringleaders into solitary confinement. They then tried to divide the prisoners by establishing a 'privilege' cell where those least involved in the rebellion were allowed to live and have such privileges as washing.

By the third day the guards had become more brutal, refusing to let prisoners leave their cells even to go to the toilet. One prisoner started to show extreme anxiety symptoms but he was not allowed to leave until day four. On day five, the guards' aggression increased as they made prisoners clean toilets with their bare hands. At night, when they thought researchers were not looking, they subjected prisoners to sexual humiliation. By day six, their power was almost total and prisoners obeyed without question. A visiting researcher objected strongly and convinced the experimenters to end the study (although she did later marry Zimbardo, so that had a happy ending!).

The authors explained the findings with regard to the power of the social roles in which the prisoners and guards found themselves. Prisoners and guards adopted their roles, which involved an imbalance of power between the groups. Tyranny was the inevitable result.

SOCIAL IDENTITY THEORY

Whereas Zimbardo and his colleagues used the idea of social roles to explain the findings of their study, Reicher and Haslam based their understanding of group behaviour on social identity theory. Tajfel and Turner (1979) proposed social identity theory. It is one of a group of theories that share the idea that we categorise ourselves and others into groups of 'us' and 'them.' We all tend to categorise ourselves by gender and ethnicity, but other groups are particularly relevant to particular people according to their interests or the situation in which they find themselves. What distinguishes social identity theory from other theories is the emphasis on **social identification** with a group. We identify with a group when we become one of them, taking on board their behavioural norms. Social identification is also an emotional process and our self-esteem becomes bound up with the success of the group.

Typically, when there is more than one group, there is inequality between them. One group might be larger, financially better off, or for some other reason have a superior position. Members of the dominant group typically have a positive group identity. Both groups are likely to show some favouritism to members of their own group, but clearly the dominant group has more power to oppress the others. They may or may not do this, according to the norms and values of the dominant group. Members of less dominant groups – known as subordinate groups – *might* act together against the dominant group. This is called collective action. However, whether or not collective action actually takes place depends on two factors. First, if groups are seen as **permeable** (i.e. if people can move from one group to another), members of subordinate groups are less likely to work collectively against the dominant group. **Collective action** becomes more likely once groups become **impermeable**. Second, if the status of the dominant group is seen as unfair or changeable, members of subordinate groups are more likely to act together against the dominant group.

AIMS

There were several aims of the study. Reicher and Haslam point out that their aim was not to replicate the Stanford Prison Experiment, nor to recreate a true prison environment. Instead the idea of the prison-like environment was to create the conditions in which two groups with unequal power could be observed and manipulated. Four specific aims were identified:

KEY IDEAS

Social identification takes place when we start to think of ourselves as part of a group. We take on the appearance and attitudes of the group and show favouritism towards other members of the group. Groups may be **permeable**. This means that it is possible to leave one group and join another. Where it is possible to leave one group and join a group in a superior position people tend to do this. Where groups are **impermeable**, people in the group with lower status tend to identify with their own group. They may then join together in **collective action** against a group in a superior position.

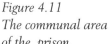

*Figure 4.11
The communal area
of the prison*

IN BRIEF ❗

Aim: To investigate how relations develop between two groups with unequal power. Specifically, to test the prediction that the subordinate group develops a strong identity only once the groups are impermeable.

Method: Fifteen highly selected males spent eight days in a prison-type environment, five taking the role of guards and the remainder that of prisoners. On day three, the groups were made impermeable. On day five, a new prisoner was introduced, and on day six, participants were told that the guards had been selected randomly, not on their merits. This created a new condition of low legitimacy for the guards.

Results: When permeability and legitimacy were high for the first three days, prisoners were dissatisfied and wanted to become guards. When the groups became impermeable they changed behaviour, adopting a strong group identity and acting collectively against the guards. On day six, the prisoners rebelled and the two groups agreed to set up a commune, working together. On day eight, a subgroup tried to impose a new, harsher regime, and the study was halted.

Conclusions: Subordinate groups gain a strong identity only once the groups are impermeable. Tyranny is not inevitable but can result when a group has a weak identity.

1 To see how relations developed between two groups with unequal power and privilege.

2 To test what factors (such as permeability) lead people to identify with their own group and to challenge inequalities between groups. A specific hypothesis was tested: members of the dominant group identify immediately with their group, however members of the subordinate group do so only when the groups become impermeable.

3 To look for relationships between social factors (e.g. group membership), organisational factors (e.g. rules), and clinical factors (e.g. depression) in group behaviour.

4 To develop procedures to allow studies of this type to be carried out in the future both ethically and practically.

METHOD

Selection of participants

Adverts in the national press and a leaflet drop generated a response from 332 males. They underwent three stages of screening, both in order to ascertain as far as possible that those selected were not themselves fragile, and also that they did not pose a danger to others. First, they undertook a battery of psychometric tests designed to measure clinical variables such as depression, aggression and paranoia, and social variables such as racism, social dominance and authoritarianism. Only those low in all these variables were allowed to proceed. Second, applicants were assessed over a whole weekend by a team of clinical psychologists. Third, they underwent police checks and had character references taken up. A total of 27 men got through the screening. Of these, 15 were selected, in order to ensure a reasonable mix of age, social class and ethnic group. They were then grouped into threes, each three closely matched for personality. One person was randomly selected from each three to be a guard.

Design

The researchers described the design as an **experimental case study**. For reasons of cost it was not possible to have separate groups taking part in different conditions. Instead, a series of changes to the situation were made at particular points in the study. Each of these changes involved an independent variable:

- *Permeability/impermeability.* At the start, participants were told that it was possible to move from prisoner to guard (i.e. the groups were permeable). Then, three days into the study, participants were told this was no longer the case (i.e. the groups were now impermeable).

- *Legitimacy/illegitimacy.* At the start, participants were told that the guards had been carefully selected (i.e. their position was legitimate). Then, six days into the study, they were told that in fact selection was random.
- *Changeability.* Five days into the study, a new prisoner was introduced. In real life he was a trade-union official used to asserting people's rights and negotiating change.

The dependent variables in the study were the participants' responses to the situation. These were measured in three ways. Video and audio were recorded continuously. Psychometric tests were used to measure identification with groups, authoritarianism, awareness of possible changes to the relations between groups, self-efficacy and depression. In order to avoid test fatigue, tests were administered during each stage of the study but not daily. Saliva swabs were taken daily to measure levels of cortisol, a stress hormone.

Ethics

This was an ethically sensitive study, especially given the controversy over the Stanford Prison Study. The researchers took several steps to ensure the study was ethical:

1 The three-stage screening to eliminate vulnerable or dangerous individuals
2 A detailed consent form drawing attention to potential risks, discomfort and stress
3 Constant monitoring by two clinical psychologists
4 24-hour security and paramedic cover
5 An independent ethics committee chaired by a Member of Parliament.

Procedure

Prisoners and guards lived together in a prison-like environment built at the BBC's Elstree studios. At the start of the study, participants were randomly allocated to the roles of prisoners and guards.

Guards were told of their role the night before the study began. They were told about the prison rules and regime but were given no information about how to enforce rules other than a no-violence rule. Prisoners arrived one at a time. They had their heads shaved and were given a uniform and a rule list. They were told by loudspeaker that the guards had been selected because of their reliability and initiative. They were also told that if prisoners displayed these characteristics they might be allowed to move to the guards group.

WEB WATCH

You can see footage of the key scenes in the study at www.bbcprisonstudy.org (click on 'view movie map')

QUESTION SPOTLIGHT!

This is a complex set of aims for a study. Make sure you could answer a question asking for the aims to be explained.

QUESTION SPOTLIGHT!

This was an experimental case study. It can be described as experimental because it tests cause and effect. Independent variables are manipulated and their effects noted. However, it was not possible to run this according to strict experimental protocols. In a true experiment, participants are either randomly allocated to different conditions (independent measures design), or they take part in all conditions but not all in the same order (repeated measures design). Neither of these designs was possible in the BBC Prison Study. Instead, behaviour was simply recorded as events unfolded. This was more like the sort of recording that takes place in a case study. Make sure that you can explain why it is a case study and why it is experimental.

In the prison, the prisoners had one cell between three. They slept under a blanket. The guards had more luxurious conditions. On day three, prisoners and guards were told that the groups were now set for the remainder of the study. On day six, they were told that allocation to prisoner and guard groups was in fact random. On day seven, a new prisoner was introduced.

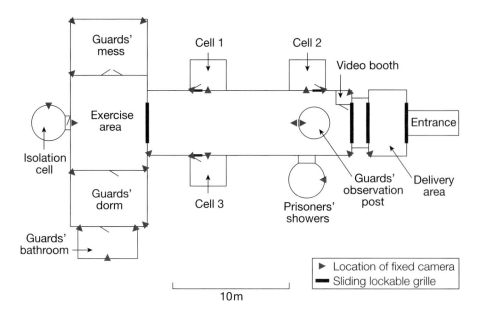

Figure 4.12
The layout of the prison

RESULTS

For the first three days the prisoners were clearly aware of the inequality of the groups. However, they complied with rules, and recorded conversations reveal that their aim was to join the guards: 'I'd like to be a guard because they get all the luxuries' (p. 13). However, once the groups became impermeable this changed and the prisoners began to plan collective action to undermine the guards: 'they've got everything they want and they're not giving two f**ks about you. So think on and f**k *them*' (p. 13). Observations of the guards suggested that they never formed a strong group identity. They could not agree on their priorities and they were wary about using their authority. This got worse rather than better when the groups became impermeable.

Identification scores for prisoners and guards confirmed that prisoners began with a weak group identity but that this strengthened once the groups were impermeable. The guards' group identity was never strong but had begun to pick up before the groups became impermeable. This can be seen in Figure 4.13. Interestingly, depression scores followed a similar pattern (Figure 4.14), being initially high for prisoners and low for guards, but later higher for guards.

Figure 4.13
Social identification scores

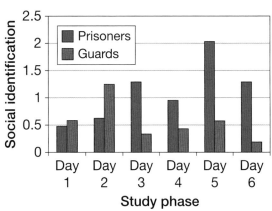

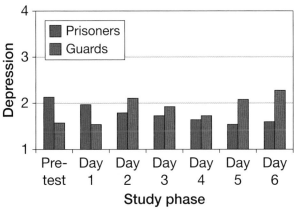

Figure 4.14
Depression scores

Compliance with prison rules declined sharply after day five, when the new prisoner was introduced. This appears to be the result of a change in the prisoners' perception of the changeability of the situation. On day six, when the announcement was made that the division of prisoners and guards was random, the system failed completely. The prisoners broke out of their cells and occupied the guards' quarters. All agreed that the prisoner–guard structure had broken down and they agreed to form a new commune social structure. For a day this worked well, with former enemies among prisoners and guards getting on well and people working harder than before on chores. However, after one day a small group – of one former guard and three former prisoners – called a meeting and proposed a new harsh regime in which they were the guards: 'we want to be the guards and make them toe the f**king line' (p. 22). The study was terminated at this point by the experimenters in order to prevent physical force being used.

Figure 4.15
A prisoner confronts
a guard on day four

ACTIVITY ✳

Designing an ethical prison study in the light of the Stanford Prison Study is tricky. Split into two groups and prepare a debate. One group will represent the research team. Explain your ethical safeguards and justify the case for going ahead. The other group will be an ethics committee. Your job is to interrogate the research team with reference to the British Psychological Society's code of ethics.

CONCLUSIONS

Referring back to the aims of the study:

1 *To see how relations developed between two groups with unequal power and privilege.* It was concluded that tyranny is not the inevitable result of unequal power in two groups. However, tyranny results when group identities fail, as happened when the commune failed.

2 *To test what factors (such as permeability) lead people to identify with their own group and to challenge inequalities between groups.* In line with social identity theory, group identification was low in the subordinate group until the group became impermeable, at which point the group began to use collective action to challenge the inequality. Group identity increased sharply again when the new prisoner introduced the possibility of social change.

3 *To look for relationships between social, organisational and clinical factors in group behaviour.* As social identification increases in the subordinate group and decreases in the dominant group, compliance with rules of the dominant group decreased in the subordinate group. Depression also varies in line with social identification: the stronger the group identity, the less depression can be seen in individuals.

4 *To develop procedures to allow studies of this type to be carried out in the future both ethically and practically.* It is both practical and ethical to carry out large-scale social psychology studies in realistic but controlled environments.

In relation to the Stanford Prison study, Reicher and Haslam agreed with Zimbardo that group processes rather than the personalities of individuals account for tyranny. However they disagreed about the nature of these group processes. Rather than seeing tyranny as the inevitable result of groups having different levels of power, Reicher and Haslam conclude that groups behave according to their identity, which might be pro-social or antisocial. Tyranny, however, can result when a collapse in group identity allows an antisocial minority to gain control. In the Stanford Prison study, it was only when the prisoners' group identity failed that the guards implemented tyranny. Similarly, it was the collapse of the German political system and the resulting confusion that allowed the Nazis to gain power.

STRETCH & CHALLENGE

There are important strengths and weaknesses in the methodology of this study. Rate each strength and each weakness for importance and draw a conclusion about how valid are Reicher and Haslam's conclusions.

STUDY 2

REICHER AND HASLAM'S STUDY OF RELATIONS BETWEEN TWO GROUPS OF UNEQUAL POWER IN A PRISON ENVIRONMENT

SUMMARY

AIM

Generally, to see how relations developed between two groups with unequal power. Specifically, to test the hypothesis: members of the dominant group identify immediately with their group. However, members of the subordinate group do so only when the groups become impermeable.

METHOD

A total of 332 volunteers were recruited through newspaper adverts and carefully screened so that only those considered neither vulnerable nor dangerous were able to take part. Of these, ten were allocated the role of prisoners and five the role of guards. They then spent eight days in a prison-type environment. On day three, the groups were made impermeable; on day five, a new prisoner was introduced; and on day six, participants were told that the guards had been selected only randomly, not on their merits. This created a new condition of low legitimacy for the guards.

RESULTS

When permeability and legitimacy were high, for the first three days, prisoners were dissatisfied and responded by trying to become guards. When the groups became impermeable, prisoners changed behaviour, adopting a stronger group identity and acting collectively against the guards. On day six, the prisoners rebelled and the two groups agreed to set up a commune, working together. On day eight, a subgroup tried to impose a new and much harsher prisoner–guard regime, and the study was halted before violence could result.

CONCLUSIONS

Members of subordinate groups try to join more dominant groups as long as they are permeable. However, they can gain a strong identity of their own when groups are impermeable. Tyranny is not inevitable when there are two groups of unequal power but can result when a group loses its identity.

EVALUATION OF THE STUDY

ETHICAL ISSUES

Studies of this type always raise ethical issues. Participants are likely to experience stress and even risk harm at each others' hands. In this case, one participant was a martial-arts instructor and could certainly have inflicted physical harm had he wished before security staff would have been able to intervene. Even when participants freely give their consent, it is hard at the point of giving consent to know exactly what stresses one is consenting to. Privacy is always an issue when one is being observed over an extended period.

One of the key aims of this study was to demonstrate that it is possible to conduct studies of this type and overcome the ethical issues. The researchers went to great lengths to screen participants before the study, to inform them of the likely consequences of taking part, and to monitor and protect them during the study. The independent ethics panel that monitored the study judged that the ethical conduct was exemplary.

METHODOLOGICAL ISSUES
Sample and sampling

The sample size, at 15, was quite small. As with Milgram's participants, those in the BBC Prison Study were male volunteers of a single nationality recruited by means of newspaper advertisements. They may thus have been an unrepresentative sample. Once they had been screened and only the applicants judged safest to themselves and others were allowed to participate, the representativeness might have been worse. On the other hand, the sample did include a good range of ages and regional and ethnic groups.

The research method

The study was a controlled procedure in an artificial environment. Therefore, although the mock prison is a far cry from what we usually think of as a laboratory, the study has some of the strengths of a laboratory experiment. It is possible to eliminate some extraneous variables and to be fairly confident that it is the independent variables we are interested in that are affecting the dependent variables. Laboratory procedures are generally straightforward to replicate, making them reliable. Remember, however, that Reicher and Haslam described this as an experimental case study rather than an experiment. We can only speculate about how similar the results might be if the procedure were to be repeated with different participants.

Ecological validity

The potential weaknesses with laboratory studies lie in the realism of the environment and participants' tasks. It is hard to set up laboratory procedures in which people behave as they would in real life. In this case, although the environment superficially resembled a prison, the situation was *not* a real prison, and participants were aware that they were not only being observed but televised. It is hard to know what impact this had on their behaviour in this study. If you've ever watched *Big Brother* or *I'm a Celebrity* you'll know that, after a time, most contestants do forget they are on camera and start to behave naturally. The researchers point out that it would be hard to keep up acting for nine days, and that it would also be very hard to fake the psychometric tests.

Quantitative and qualitative data

Like Milgram, Reicher and Haslam gathered both quantitative and qualitative data, and this is a strength of the study. Reicher and Haslam used the different types of data for the purpose of triangulation. Triangulation is achieved when two different sources of information point to the same conclusion: in this case, the quantitative group identification scores, and the qualitative observations of prisoner and guard behaviour and transcripts of their conversations. Both types of data indicated the same rises and falls in group identity in prisoners and guards.

EXAM FOCUS

We now show you some of the sorts of questions that could be asked about the Reicher and Haslam study in your exam. We will then show you some examples of the sorts of answers we believe might be successful and less successful, and point out some classic traps to avoid.

SECTION A

1 Describe how Reicher and Haslam selected their sample. *(4 marks)*

2 **(a)** Identify one ethical issue raised by simulating prison-like environments. *(2 marks)*
   (b) Explain how Reicher and Haslam dealt with this issue. *(2 marks)*

3 Reicher and Haslam described their study as an experimental case study. Explain in what way it was experimental and in what way it was a case study. *(4 marks)*

4 **(a)** Identify two independent variables that were manipulated in the Reicher and Haslam study. *(2 marks)*
   (b) Explain how one of these was operationalised. *(2 marks)*

5 Outline the conclusions reached by Reicher and Haslam. *(4 marks)*

6 Reicher and Haslam obtained both quantitative and qualitative data from their study.
   (a) Outline how qualitative data were obtained. *(2 marks)*
   (b) Identify two ways in which quantitative data were obtained. *(2 marks)*

7 Explain one similarity and one difference between the BBC prison study and the Stanford Prison Study. *(4 marks)*

SECTION B

(a) Outline the event or past research that provided a stimulus for Reicher and Haslam's study. *(2 marks)*

(b) Describe the sampling procedure used by Reicher and Haslam. Explain why this was appropriate for this study. *(6 marks)*

(c) Describe how data was gathered and recorded in the Reicher and Haslam study. *(6 marks)*

(d) Give one strength and one weakness of Reicher and Haslam's procedure. *(6 marks)*

(e) Outline the results and conclusions of the Reicher and Haslam study. *(8 marks)*

(f) Explain how you might improve the Reicher and Haslam procedure. *(8 marks)*

SECTION C

(a) Outline one assumption of the social approach. *(2 marks)*

(b) With reference to Reicher and Haslam's study, describe how the social approach could explain social identity. *(4 marks)*

(c) Describe one similarity and one difference between any studies that take the social approach. *(6 marks)*

(d) Discuss strengths and weaknesses of the social approach using examples from any studies that take this approach. *(12 marks)*

SOME ANSWERS AND COMMENTS

SECTION A 1 Describe how Reicher and Haslam selected their sample. *(4 marks)*

Lily says: They advertised in a newspaper and randomly divided them into prisoners and guards.

We say: 1 mark.
Don't be fooled into thinking that this is an easy question just because it's question 1. There are four marks available here and the procedure was quite a complex one, involving three stages of screening.

Florence says:

332 males responded to newspaper adverts. They went through three stages of screening, involving psychometric tests, meeting clinical psychologists and having police checks. 27 got through and 15 of these went into the sample. They were chosen to give a fair range of age and ethnicity. These were divided randomly into prisoners and guards.

We say: 4 marks.
Not perfect, Florence. You could have said what the psychometric tests were for, and the dividing into prisoners and guards was not entirely random. However, pretty good for someone who has just been studying psychology for a few months.

SECTION A 5 Outline the conclusions reached by Reicher and Haslam. *(4 marks)*

Celine says:

Reicher and Haslam concluded that the prisoners achieved a strong identity and the guards' identity got weaker throughout the study. When the group got impermeable the prisoners' group got stronger, so permeability is important.

We say: 1 mark.
This is a hard question because Reicher and Haslam's conclusions are quite wide-ranging and conceptually difficult. Your first sentence describes results rather than conclusions. The second is appropriate and correct however, so that gets some credit. Not many students would score well on this question.

Cindi says:

Reicher and Haslam conclude that group permeability is important. When groups are impermeable they form better group identities. They also concluded that tyranny is not inevitable. It only happened here when the commune collapsed. This means Zimbardo was wrong. Finally they conclude that it is possible to do studies like this ethically.

We say: 3 marks.
Cindi, you have demonstrated that you understand the conclusions, even if you haven't put them down particularly slickly. A bit more development of the idea about Zimbardo might have got you the fourth mark.

SECTION B (d) Give one strength and one weakness of Reicher and Haslam's procedure. *(6 marks)*

Justin says:

It was a laboratory experiment so lacks ecological validity. It was also unethical because the prisoners were horrible to the guards. Also it was on television so people didn't act naturally. The sample was small and unrepresentative because they were all British men.

We say: 1 mark.
Justin, you should have read the question more closely! You have briefly outlined four weaknesses, but if the question says one strength and one weakness that's what you have to give. (Paying careful attention to question instructions is harder in the exam, when the adrenaline is flowing, than many students realise.) In this case, you will get credit for just one weakness, but as each of these is described only briefly it's only very limited credit.

Jamie says:

One strength of the procedure is the ethical safeguards. Simulating stressful environments like prisons raises ethical issues because of the stress involved. But they screened participants really carefully, and had 24-hour monitoring by psychologists, security staff and a paramedic. They also had a high-powered ethics panel overseeing everything. One weakness is the fact that they were on television so we can't be sure that they were behaving naturally. They might have been playing up for the camera.

We say: 5 marks.
The strength is better developed than the weakness, but overall, Jamie, this is a clear, focused and detailed answer. One tip: if you are selecting a strength and a weakness for a question worth quite a few marks, like this one, be sure to choose a strength and a weakness you can talk about in some detail.

SECTION C (d) Discuss strengths and weaknesses of the social approach using examples from any studies that take this approach. *(12 marks)*

Rose's answer:

One strength of the social approach is that it often carries out studies in real-life settings, like field studies or observations, so as to be more natural.

One study was Piliavin, who looked at helping people on a subway train when they fell to the floor.

Another strength is that it tells us how we are influenced by others in a range of situations so you can use the findings to make practical applications for society.

A weakness is that if you study people in one country it might not apply to people in other countries very well, so it is a poor sample. This is like in Milgram, where he studied people from near Yale University in the USA when seeing if they would go up to 450volts of shock. Lots of them did but they were all from USA and people may well not be like this in other countries, like Sweden, so we cannot really generalise to everyone in the world.

Another weakness is that Reicher and Haslam had a really small sample of all males in their study.

We say: 6 marks.
Rose, you do have some appropriate points here, but need to think about the overall argument and balance of your chosen points. This is a bit variable in your answer. The first point is quite clear but you do not give very much detail on the study you select as an example. Make sure you fully develop the example so that it clearly supports the strength or weakness you are discussing. The second point lacks an example from a study in the approach. Remember that the question asks you to use examples – so please do. The third point on sample is explained, has an appropriate example and discusses the point well overall. You then lose your focus a bit and just have a criticism of a study, and although the study is a social one, you get no credit for just evaluating a study here as the question is on the approach. Look at your point on sample and try to make all your other points similar in style in order to improve your marks.

PILIAVIN *et al.*'s FIELD EXPERIMENT INTO BYSTANDER BEHAVIOUR

KEY IDEAS

The word '**bystander**' is defined differently in different sources. We are using the term broadly to mean anyone who is present at an incident but not directly involved. The terms 'bystander effect' and 'bystander apathy' describe the behaviour of bystanders who do not assist those who need help in an emergency.

Piliavin, I.M., Rodin, J. and Piliavin, J.A. (1969) Good samaritanism: an underground phenomenon? *Journal of Personality & Social Psychology*, **13**, 289–99.

CONTEXT

This study is concerned with **bystander** behaviour. Bystanders are people who witness events and have to choose whether to intervene or not. Recently there has been a lot of debate over 'have-a-go heroes' who put themselves at risk to intervene and attempt to stop crimes taking place. Most of the time, bystanders can help without putting themselves at risk. However, surprisingly often we don't choose to act to help people in need.

THE KITTY GENOVESE MURDER

Psychological research into bystander behaviour was triggered by a murder that took place in New York in 1964. Excerpts from the *New York Times* article describing the incident are shown opposite.

WEB WATCH @

You can watch a report on the Genovese murder and some early research on YouTube, for example www.youtube.com/watch?v=JozmW S6xYEw&feature=related or search for 'Kitty Genovese' you can also see an animation of the Piliavin study here: http://goanimate. com/movie/0CCb_m0Vk5uE/1?utm_ source=gigyabookmark

Figure 4.16
Kitty Genovese

ACTIVITY ✳

THIRTY-EIGHT WHO SAW MURDER DIDN'T CALL THE POLICE

by Martin Gansberg

For more than half an hour 38 respectable, law-abiding citizens in Queens watched a killer stalk and stab a woman in three separate attacks in Kew Gardens. Twice their chatter and the sudden glow of their bedroom lights interrupted him and frightened him off. Each time he returned, sought her out, and stabbed her again. Not one person telephoned the police during the assault; one witness called after the woman was dead.

That was two weeks ago today. Still shocked is Assistant Chief Inspector Frederick M. Lussen, in charge of the borough's detectives and a veteran of 25 years of homicide investigations. He can give a matter-of-fact recitation on many murders. But the Kew Gardens slaying baffles him--not because it is a murder, but because the 'good people' failed to call the police.

This is what the police say happened at 3:20 A.M. in the staid, middle-class, tree-lined Austin Street area: Twenty-eight-year-old Catherine Genovese, who was called Kitty by almost everyone in the neighborhood, was returning home from her job as manager of a bar in Hollis. She parked her red Fiat in a lot adjacent to the Kew Gardens Long Island Railroad Station, facing Mowbray Place.

Miss Genovese noticed a man at the far end of the lot, near a seven-story apartment house at 82–40 Austin Street. She halted. Then, nervously, she headed up Austin Street toward Lefferts Boulevard, where there is a call box to the 102nd Police Precinct in nearby Richmond Hill. She got as far as a street light in front of a bookstore before the man grabbed her. She screamed. Lights went on in the 10-story apartment house at 82-67 Austin Street, which faces the bookstore. Windows slid open and voices punctuated the early-morning stillness.

Miss Genovese screamed: 'Oh, my God, he stabbed me! Please help me! Please help me!' From one of the upper windows in the apartment house, a man called down: 'Let that girl alone!' The assailant looked up at him, shrugged, and walked down Austin Street toward a white sedan parked a short distance away. Miss Genovese struggled to her feet. Lights went out. The killer returned to Miss Genovese, now trying to make her way around the side of the building by the parking lot to get to her apartment. The assailant stabbed her again. 'I'm dying!' she shrieked. 'I'm dying!'

Windows were opened again, and lights went on in many apartments. The assailant got into his car and drove away. Miss Genovese staggered to her feet. A city bus, 0-10, the Lefferts Boulevard line to Kennedy International Airport, passed. It was 3:35 A.M. The assailant returned. By then, Miss Genovese had crawled to the back of the building, where the freshly painted brown doors to the apartment house held out hope for safety. The killer tried the first door; she wasn't there. At the second door, 82–62 Austin Street, he saw her slumped on the floor at the foot of the stairs. He stabbed her a third time—fatally.

Some of the details of the story as it was reported at the time have since been challenged. Given the layout of the block, it would not have been possible for anyone to have seen the whole incident, so each person would have seen just fragments of the event. Also, the area was not actually as quiet as the article implies – one neighbour said that rows between couples leaving a local bar were common late at night. Given these facts, we cannot be sure that 38 people really saw, correctly interpreted, and chose to ignore the murder. However, the Genovese murder captured the public imagination and stimulated psychological research into bystander behaviour.

Source: New York Times, *March 27, 1964*

Q

1 How could you explain these events according to the individual and dispositional hypotheses?
2 What do you think you would have done?

KEY IDEAS

One early explanation for the bystander effect is **diffusion of responsibility**. This occurs when groups of people witness an emergency together and each individual assumes only a fraction of responsibility for helping. The larger the group, the less responsibility placed on each individual, and the less likely anyone is to help.

DIFFUSION OF RESPONSIBILITY

Latane and Darley (1968) proposed that the key issue in deciding whether we help or not is whether we see it as our personal responsibility to do so. One reason why groups of people do not help individuals in need is that responsibility is shared equally among the group so that each person has only a small portion of responsibility. They called this idea **diffusion of responsibility**. In a series of lab experiments they demonstrated that the more people who are present in an emergency, the less likely people are to help.

AIM

The researchers wanted to extend early studies of bystander behaviour in several key ways. First, they wanted to study bystander behaviour outside the laboratory, in a realistic setting where participants would have a clear view of the victim. Second, they wanted to see whether helping behaviour was affected by four variables:

1   The victim's responsibility for being in a situation where they needed help
2   The race of the victim
3   The effect of modelling helping behaviour
4   The size of the group.

By observing variations in the size of the group, they were able to test whether diffusion of responsibility occurred.

METHOD

Participants

An estimated total of around 4,550 passengers travelled in the trains targeted by the researchers. These were all regarded by the researchers as 'unsolicited participants.' An average of 43 were present in each carriage in which the procedure was conducted and an average of eight were in the immediate or 'critical' area. The racial mix of passengers was estimated as 45% black and 55% white.

Design and procedure

The study was a field experiment carried out on trains on the New York subway. The procedure involved a male experimenter faking collapse on a train between stops, in order to see whether he was helped by other passengers. One particular stretch of track was targeted where there was a 7.5 minute gap between two stations.

Figure 4.17
125th Street Station, where the
victim was helped off the train

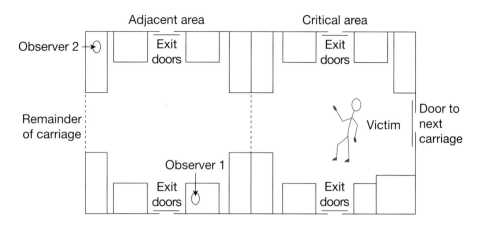

Figure 4.18
The layout of the carriage

Experimenters worked in teams of four, two females to record the results, and two males who would play the roles of victim and model helper. There were four teams, one containing a black male. Each male taking the role of victim took part in both drunk and ill conditions. Seventy seconds after the train left a station the victim would stagger and fall. He then lay still on his back with eyes open, not moving until helped. Between six and eight trials were run each day, between 11am and 3pm. Four independent variables were manipulated in the procedure:

1   Victim's responsibility: operationalised as carrying a cane (ill – low responsibility) or smelling of alcohol and carrying a bottle wrapped in a paper bag (drunk – high responsibility).

2   Victim's race: operationalised as black or white.

3   Presence of a model: operationalised as whether a male confederate; either close to or distant from the victim; helped after 70 or 150 seconds.

4   Number of bystanders: operationalised as however many people were present in the vicinity.

Four males, aged 24–29, and identically dressed in casual clothes, took the role of models of helping behaviour. Four model conditions were applied to both apparently drunk and ill victims:

•   Model stood in the critical area and helped after 70 seconds

•   Model stood in the critical area and helped after 150 seconds

•   Model stood in the adjacent area and helped after 70 seconds

•   Model stood in the adjacent area and helped after 150 seconds.

The dependent variable, helping, was measured in the following ways:

•   Time taken for first passenger to help

•   Total number of passengers who helped.

QUESTION SPOTLIGHT!

What potential extraneous variables might affect results, and what controls did the researchers put into place to counteract these?

Why was it important to fake the collapse in a long gap between stations?

What ethical issues are raised by this type of procedure? How could the researchers have responded to these issues?

Also make sure you know your IVs.

QUESTION SPOTLIGHT!

Most of the data gathered here is quantitative. However, there is some qualitative data too. *Identify the qualitative data and suggest why it was useful.*

In addition, the gender, race and position of each helper was noted. Qualitative data was also gathered in the form of comments from passengers.

RESULTS

Overall, a higher proportion of people helped than was the case in previous laboratory experiments: 78% of victims received spontaneous help from passengers, and in 60% of cases where the victim was helped it was by more than one person. Most helpers were male.

- *Ill versus drunk conditions.* In the cane condition, the victim received help 95% of the time without intervention from a model. In the drunk condition, this was reduced to 50%. People took longer to help the drunk victim than the ill one: over 70 seconds in 83% of the drunk trials, but in only 17% of the cane trials. However the proportion of cases in which more than one person helped was the same.

- *Race of victim.* In the cane condition, black and white victims were equally likely to be helped. However, in the drunk condition, black victims were less likely to receive help. Also, in the drunk condition, there was a slight same-race effect – people were a little more likely to help a drunk of the same race as themselves. The proportion of cases in which help came from more than one person did not vary by race.

- *The effect of modelling.* The model intervening after 70 seconds was more likely to lead to help from other passengers (in nine cases) than the one intervening after 150 seconds (three cases). However, the researchers noted that because passengers helped spontaneously in the vast majority of trials, there were too few cases of helping after modelling to analyse in detail.

- *Number of bystanders.* There was no evidence for diffusion of responsibility. There was a mild effect in the opposite direction – when more passengers were present, people were slightly more likely to receive help.

- *Other observations.* In a significant minority of trials (21 of 103), some passengers moved away from the critical area. More comments were made in drunk trials, and more when no passenger spontaneously helped. The researchers interpreted this as meaning the comments were in response to passengers feeling uncomfortable about the situation.

TABLE 4.3 RESPONSES TO AN ILL OR DRUNK PERSON

	Cane condition	Drunk condition
% helped spontaneously	95	50
% helped in under 70 seconds	83	17

CONCLUSIONS

Piliavin and his colleagues admitted that the situation they set up was unusual in that their participants were trapped in a carriage with a collapsed person and therefore could not simply walk away as they could normally. In this situation:

- An ill person is more likely to receive help than a drunk person.
- Men are more likely to help another man than women are.
- People are slightly more likely to help someone of their own ethnic group, especially when they appear drunk.
- There is no strong relationship between size of group and likelihood of helping. The small correlation between group size and helping behaviour is positive rather than negative. Therefore there is no support for diffusion of responsibility.
- The longer an incident goes on, the less likely people are to help (even if help is modelled), the more likely people are to leave the area, and the more likely they are to discuss the incident.

Explaining the findings

The researchers explained the findings in terms of arousal and the costs and rewards of alternative responses. Perceiving an emergency raises arousal levels. According to the situation, this can be interpreted either as sympathy or as fear and disgust. The closer one is to the emergency and the longer it continues, the more arousal increases. Arousal is also greatest when the bystander can empathise with the victim. The behaviour of bystanders aims to reduce the arousal level. This can be achieved in four ways:

1 helping directly
2 leaving to find help
3 leaving the area
4 dismissing the victim as unworthy of help.

Which of these options is chosen depends on the costs and benefits of helping or not helping. These are shown in Table 4.4. If the benefits of helping and the costs of not helping outweigh the costs of helping and the benefits of not helping, then help will be offered.

This model explains neatly the behaviour of participants. The drunk is helped less because there are greater costs in terms of fear and embarrassment. People help their own ethnic group more because they can feel more empathy with them. Late modelling has less effect than early modelling because people will have found another coping strategy by then.

TABLE 4.4 COSTS AND BENEFITS OF ALTERNATIVE RESPONSES

	Costs	Benefits
Helping	fear, embarrassment, effort, disgust	praise
Not helping	self-blame, blame from other	continuing activities

STUDY 3

PILIAVIN *et al.*'S FIELD EXPERIMENT INTO BYSTANDER BEHAVIOUR

SUMMARY

AIM

To study the factors affecting bystander behaviour. Specifically under what circumstances people would help a collapsed man on the New York underground, whether his race, responsibility for his collapse, number of people present, and modelling of helping behaviour would affect helping.

METHOD

Experimenters faked collapse on New York underground trains, and the number of people helping and the time taken to help were recorded. The race of the victim, the apparent responsibility (ill or drunk) of the victim, the presence of a model helper, and the number of passengers present were varied.

RESULTS

In total, 78% of victims received help. Help was more likely if the victim appeared ill rather than drunk. There was some increased tendency for people to help those of their own race. The number of bystanders present made little difference. Although large groups were more likely to help than smaller groups, most people were helped before the model could initiate helping.

CONCLUSIONS

Provided people are in a closed environment where they cannot simply leave, they are likely to help someone in need. Helping is most likely when the victim is seen as not responsible for the situation and is the same race as helpers. Number of bystanders is not important in this situation.

EVALUATION OF THE STUDY

ETHICAL ISSUES

Field experiments always raise ethical issues because they involve interfering with people going about their business who have not agreed to take part in the study. The following issues are particularly important in this case:

- **Harm and distress.** People observing the collapse felt some anxiety. Those who did not help might have suffered some guilt afterwards. It is also possible that someone might have injured themselves helping a victim up.

- **Consent.** People did not give consent to taking part in an experiment. Nor were they free to choose not to participate.

- **Deception.** People were deceived by the collapse of the actor. They were not informed later that he was an actor or that he was ok.

- **Withdrawal.** People could not ask to have their data removed from the analysis, as they did not know they had taken part in a study.

- **Debriefing.** Participants had no opportunity to be debriefed or de-hoaxed. They might have left the situation in distress and they certainly did not know they had taken part in an experiment.

METHODOLOGICAL ISSUES
Sample and sampling method

The sample was large at around 4,550. The proportion of black and white passengers was also representative of the local population. However, taking the sample from those travelling between 11am and 3pm might have left those at work or in education in the middle of the day under-represented. There was no control over who entered the target carriage or stood in the critical area, therefore the sampling method was opportunity sampling. This is unlikely to be representative.

The research method

The study was a field experiment, and field experiments are associated with particular strengths and weaknesses.

The major strength is the natural environment in which it is conducted and the opportunity to create realistic situations. The weaknesses centre around the difficulty in controlling variables. In this case the researchers put into place a number of controls. The victims were the same age and sex, and dressed identically. They collapsed in the same way. The same stretch of track was used on each trial to ensure that there was always the same time available, and the timings before a model helped were kept the same. Nevertheless, not all conditions could be kept constant. The number and nature of the passengers boarding the particular carriage was unpredictable. Some might have seen the incident several times, and, if so, it is hard to predict how they might have responded to that.

Ecological validity

Remember that there are two aspects to ecological validity: the naturalness of the environment, and the realism of the task or situation. This study does well on both counts. People were in their natural environment on a train, and the situation of seeing an ill or drunk person collapse is an entirely normal one.

Quantitative and qualitative data

Like Milgram and Reicher and Haslam, Piliavin *et al.* collected both quantitative and qualitative data. However, their emphasis was very much on the quantitative. This was appropriate, given the aims of the study. They were interested in *how many* people helped and *how long* it took them to do so under each condition. However, qualitative data in the form of what comments people made about victims collapsing was also useful as an indicator that people were responding to the emergency by justifying why they were not helping. This was important, as this became one of the strategies for reducing arousal levels in Piliavin *et al.*'s model of bystander behaviour.

EXAM FOCUS

We now show you some of the sorts of questions that could be asked about the Piliavin *et al.* study in your exam. We will then show you some examples of the sorts of answers we believe might be successful and less successful, and point out some classic traps to avoid.

SECTION A

1 **(a)** Describe the sample in the Piliavin *et al.* study. *(2 marks)*

   (b) Identify one strength and one weakness of the sample. *(2 marks)*

2 Explain what is meant by diffusion of responsibility and suggest why it was not seen in this study. *(4 marks)*

3 Outline two controls that were used in the Piliavin *et al.* study. *(4 marks)*

4 Outline the researchers' explanation for bystander behaviour. *(4 marks)*

5 **(a)** Describe one finding from the Piliavin *et al.* study. *(2 marks)*

   (b) Explain how this finding is linked to the cost-reward model. *(2 marks)*

6 Describe the ethical issues raised by the Piliavin *et al.* study. *(4 marks)*

7 The Piliavin *et al.* study was a field experiment.

   (a) Outline the features of a field experiment. *(2 marks)*

   (b) Identify one strength and one weakness of a field experiment. *(2 marks)*

8 What conclusions did Piliavin *et al.* draw from their study? *(4 marks)*

SECTION B

(a) Outline the aims of the Piliavin *et al.* study. *(2 marks)*

(b) Explain why the Piliavin *et al.* study can be considered high in ecological validity and give one argument for saying the ecological validity is low. *(6 marks)*

(c) Describe the independent variables varied in the Piliavin *et al.* study and explain how they were operationalised. *(6 marks)*

(d) Outline the findings and conclusions of the Piliavin *et al.* study. *(6 marks)*

(e) Describe the quantitative and qualitative data gathered in the study. Explain why each was useful. *(8 marks)*

(f) Suggest one change to the Piliavin *et al.* study and explain how this might be an improvement. *(8 marks)*

SECTION C

(a) Outline one assumption of the social approach. *(2 marks)*

(b) With reference to Piliavin *et al.*'s study, describe how the social approach could explain bystander behaviour. *(4 marks)*

(c) Describe one similarity and one difference between any studies that take the social approach. *(6 marks)*

(d) Discuss strengths and weaknesses of the social approach using examples from any studies that take this approach. *(12 marks)*

SOME ANSWERS AND COMMENTS

SECTION A 2 Explain what is meant by diffusion of responsibility and suggest why it was not seen in this study. *(4 marks)*

Whitney says:

Diffusion of responsibility is when people don't help. Most people don't help in a emergency, especially when there are lots of people, like in the Kitty Genovese murder. It was not seen in this study because people usually did help.

Veronica says:

Diffusion of responsibility is when people feel less individual responsibility to help people when other people are there. The more people there are, the less responsibility each person has. It wasn't seen in this study because larger groups were actually more likely to help than small groups. This might be because the groups couldn't escape and the more people there are, the more there are to praise you if you help, or disapprove of you if you don't.

We say: 1 mark.
Hmm, a wrong definition is a bad start! Diffusion of responsibility is an explanation for the bystander effect. It is not simply a term used to describe it. By the second sentence, though, you are starting to get somewhere, as you introduce the idea that diffusion of responsibility is associated with larger groups. The final sentence is correct, but you need to give an explanation of why people helped in this study, even in large groups.

We say: 4 marks.
This is a good answer, Veronica, giving a thorough explanation of what diffusion of responsibility is. The second part of the question is ambiguous. Is it testing whether you know that helping increased slightly with group size, or is going a stage further and asking you to explain why that might be? You will often come across questions like this. You have covered all the bases here by doing both. We think that's a really good strategy.

SECTION A 6 Describe the ethical issues raised by the Piliavin *et al.* study. *(4 marks)*

Joe says:

It was unethical because they didn't consent to being in the study. Also they weren't debriefed.

Jello says:

One ethical issue is consent. Because the participants were whoever was on the train there was no chance for them to give consent. They never knew they were being studied. A second issue is debriefing. Normally, participants should be debriefed and de-hoaxed. These however left the scene without ever knowing they had been in a study.

We say: 2 marks.
When deciding how much to write, look at how many marks are available. You have correctly identified two ethical issues and so get some credit. However, for four marks you need to give some kind of elaboration.

We say: 4 marks.
Once the issues are identified, you have plenty of scope for where you get the rest of the marks. Just expand on your first point and you can't go too far wrong.

SECTION B (e) Describe the quantitative and qualitative data gathered in the study. Explain why each was useful. *(8 marks)*

Rick says:

Quantitative data means information in the form of numbers. The strength of quantitative data is that you can make direct comparisons between conditions, so we know that people took longer to respond to the drunk victim than the ill one. Qualitative data is in the form of words. This allows us to see subtle things.

We say: 3 marks.
Rick, you have shown that you understand what quantitative and qualitative mean, and some awareness of their strengths. This is a start, but your answer doesn't really get to grips with the question, which requires discussion of the two types of data in this particular study. You do get some credit, though, for tackling both parts of the question.

Richard says:

They got lots of quantitative data. There were the numbers of people who helped in each condition and how long each person took to help in each condition. Here, numbers allow us to directly compare helping in each condition. We also have numbers like how many people left the critical area and how many helpers were black. Qualitative data comes from what comments were made. This is useful in a different way, as it allows us to judge people's discomfort at the situation.

We say: 6 marks.
This answer makes quite similar points but they are correctly applied to the Piliavin study. This shows understanding of the two types of data and of the study itself. Note that both parts of the question are addressed competently.

SECTION B (c) Describe one similarity and one difference between any studies that take the social approach. *(6 marks)*

Dawn's answer:

A similarity is that of cost and being expensive. It cost money to build a prison in Reicher and Haslam, and it cost Milgram money to build a shock generator and put an ad in the paper.
A difference is to do with the ethics in the studies. Piliavin got no consent from any participants and Reicher and Haslam did when people agreed to be prisoners and guards when they took part in the experiment after being assessed.

We say: 2 marks.
Dawn, you are going for a more minimal style here, which is not a good idea. For six points what is needed is more discussion to show off your psychological knowledge. Your point on cost is not particularly psychological here and not really appropriate. Think about the evaluation issues that you have studied in class – such as samples, type of data, method used – and use one of these as a good basis for points of comparison. Your second point on ethics is a relevant one to use, but is far too brief. You need explicitly to say that the point is that one is unethical and one is not, and follow that up with a clearer example from each study. The examples are relevant to your point – but too short.

Eddie's answer:

A similarity is that both samples of Milgram and Reicher and Haslam use only men in their studies on social psychology. Milgram uses 40 men who replied to an advert placed in the local paper; this is like Reicher and Haslam.

A difference is that of the methods used and how ecologically valid they are, as a field experiment was used by Piliavin, but Reicher used a laboratory experiment/case study. Piliavin did a field experiment on the New York subway where a model pretended to be drunk or disabled. This was high in ecological validity as it was a real-life place for the participants. Reicher and Haslam had a lab experiment as part of the study, as they had a controlled setting in the prison they built. It was not like a real prison as it was very small with nine prisoners and they could go into a video booth to talk to the researchers. This has low ecological validity.

We say: 5 marks.
Some good analysis in your answer, Eddie. You got off to a reasonable start with your point on samples. Having made this clear you should have given an example from both the studies. Milgram is fine, but there is nothing really on Reicher and Haslam. They did recruit from an advert – but rather than just saying 'this is like Reicher and Haslam', you need to explain how, giving details on their particular advert. The difference was very well discussed with detail and examples. Good work here.

THE SOCIAL APPROACH TO PSYCHOLOGY

We have now looked in some detail at three social-psychological studies. Based on these studies, we will now see what we can tease out about the social approach to psychology. We have already said that social psychology is concerned with how people interact with one another. Breaking that down a bit, we can identify some assumptions underlying the approach.

1 **Human behaviour is influenced by the situation as well as by individual characteristics.** Common sense tells us that some people are more helpful, aggressive, obedient, etc., than others. In other words there are individual differences in our social behaviour. However, social psychologists have uncovered a lot of information about something less obvious: the ways in which our social behaviour is influenced by the situation. Take Milgram, for example. Although he started with the hypothesis that the Holocaust was the result of the German national character, he soon realised that in a situation where people are receiving direct orders from a person in a position of authority, the majority of us will obey those orders even though we might suffer distress if this means going against our individual beliefs. Behaviour in this situation was therefore affected by the situation. This does not mean that individual differences are irrelevant – Elms and Milgram (1966) found that people with an authoritarian personality were particularly obedient in the Milgram procedure. It does mean, however, that we are all affected to some extent by the social situation.

2 **We can understand human behaviour in terms of influence by individuals and groups**. The most obvious example of individual influence in the studies we have looked at is in Milgram's study. Here, an individual who has the appearance of legitimate authority influences others by giving them direct orders. This influence is so powerful that the majority of participants obeyed his orders even though they did not want to do so

and although doing so meant going against their own morals. Piliavin *et al.* also attempted to study the influence that an individual can have on others by modelling helping behaviour. This is slightly different because we are talking about an individual influencing a group. Modelling works when one person, the model, demonstrates a behaviour for others to imitate. Modelling certainly can influence behaviour, as Bandura *et al.* showed in their study (see Chapter 3). In the Piliavin study, it didn't really work as planned because the vast majority of the time passengers helped spontaneously before the model had a chance to model helping.

Humans are a social species and we spend much of our time in groups. Understanding how we behave in groups and how we are influenced by group membership is just as important to understanding our social behaviour as is understanding the influence of one individual on another. The studies of Reicher and Haslam and Piliavin *et al.* are both concerned with groups. Reicher and Haslam investigated how two groups with different levels of power developed identities. They also investigated how the relationship developed between the two groups. Some interesting findings emerged about how groups work. For example, it was found that as long as there is a chance for people in the group with less power (the subordinate group) to move to the one with more power (the dominant group), members of the subordinate group will try to do just this. Only when there is no chance of moving to the dominant group will the subordinate group form a strong group identity of its own.

Piliavin *et al.* were also interested in group behaviour. One of their aims was to test the idea that people in groups diffuse responsibility for helping behaviour between all the members so that each member has relatively little responsibility and is unlikely to help. The Piliavin *et al.* study did not support the idea of diffusion of responsibility because larger groups were found to be slightly more likely to provide help than smaller groups (diffusion of responsibility would predict the opposite).

3 **Research can help us understand social issues.** All the researchers we have looked at in this chapter have been inspired by the wish to understand real-life social issues. For Milgram, it was the idea that people commit atrocities, and that one factor influencing atrocities seems to be obedience to orders. Reicher and Haslam were interested in the idea of tyranny – the use of power by a dominant group against a group with less power. Their study tells us some interesting things about tyranny: that a subordinate group with a strong social identity can effectively stick up for themselves, and that when a group has a weak identity, an extremist minority can impose tyranny. Inspired to explain events such as the Kitty Genovese murder, Piliavin *et al.* aimed to explain why people are sometimes helpful to one another in an emergency and sometimes much less so.

STRENGTHS AND WEAKNESSES OF THE SOCIAL APPROACH
Strengths

1 **Real-life relevance.** All the studies in this chapter are clearly relevant to understanding real-life social issues. Some psychological research has been accused of being of interest only to a small group of academics. This cannot be said about social psychology, however. Everyone is affected by obedience, by tyranny, and by helping behaviour.

2 **Good range of research methods.** All the studies we have looked at in this chapter test cause-and-effect relationships, so they are (broadly) experimental. However, social psychologists have been imaginative in the range of experimental methods they have used. Milgram used a highly controlled laboratory setting. Piliavin *et al.* preferred to conduct their experiment in a real-life setting. Reicher and Haslam compromised by setting up a complex living space, neither as artificial as a laboratory nor as uncontrolled as the field. This range of methods is a strength as it means that findings of controlled laboratory studies can be checked out in real-life settings and *vice versa*.

Weaknesses

1 **Social-psychological research often raises ethical issues.** Often it seems that the more relevant to real life a study is, the more it raises ethical problems. All the studies we have looked at in this chapter raise serious ethical issues. Milgram deliberately deceived participants, caused them stress, and denied them their right to withdraw. Piliavin *et al.* involved large numbers of participants without consent or debriefing. In spite of extensive screening and safeguards, Reicher and Haslam put people in a stressful situation. This is not to say that these studies should not have been done, just that we always have to weigh up the benefits of social research against the costs.

2 **Social determinism.** You could be forgiven, after reading about social psychology, for thinking that all our behaviour is simply a product of the social situation and that therefore we have no individual responsibility for our actions. The 'I was just obeying orders' defence is a classic example of this type of thinking. Actually, social situations influence us just as our biology, our development, and our cognitive processes influence us – none of these excuses us when we behave badly, even though they help us make sense of good and bad behaviour.

C5

PSYCHOLOGY OF

INDIVIDUAL

DIFFERENCES

This approach to psychology considers that there are many differences between individuals, as well as similarities. Some of these differences involve behaviour that might be described as 'abnormal'. In this chapter we will look at the following three studies:

1   David Rosenhan's study of the accuracy of psychiatric diagnosis. This research involved participants presenting themselves for admission to real psychiatric hospital settings, and recording their subsequent experiences. The aim was to investigate how well psychiatrists can tell sanity from insanity.

2   Corbett Thigpen and Hervey Cleckley's case study of a young woman whom they diagnosed as experiencing multiple

personality disorder. The aim was both to explore and to treat this controversial mental health disorder through a range of techniques.

3   Mark Griffiths' study of gambling behaviour. This experiment involved monitoring the behaviour and thoughts of participants who gambled regularly and those who did not. It was carried out in an actual arcade and aimed to investigate the cognitive biases involved in gambling.

We will now look at each of these studies in detail, before using them to think about issues of individual differences in psychology. We will then evaluate and explore applications of this approach.

ROSENHAN'S STUDY OF THE RELIABILITY AND VALIDITY OF PSYCHIATRIC DIAGNOSIS

Rosenhan, D.L. (1973) On Being Sane in Insane Places. *Science*, New Series, **179**: 4070, 250–8.

CONTEXT

Abnormal psychology is an area of huge interest for many students approaching the subject for the first time. Psychologists have been arguing for many years about what behaviours can be regarded as abnormal. It is one of the most controversial areas that we will learn about, mainly because of the implications of diagnosing an individual as 'abnormal' or 'mentally ill' on their subsequent treatment.

Attempts to formally classify **abnormality** have been made by psychiatrists – doctors with medical training who consider mental illness as equivalent to other forms of illness. The medical model of mental illness tries to determine the appropriate treatment for an individual by establishing categories of symptoms that form an identifiable disorder. Psychiatrists use the **Diagnostic and Statistical Manual of Mental Disorders (DSM)** to classify abnormal behaviour and diagnose patients.

Rosenhan and others have criticised the medical model of mental illness as part of what is known as the 'anti-psychiatry movement'. While they accept that mental suffering and deviant behaviour *do* exist, they question whether the most useful way of understanding such behaviour is through a rigid system of classification. One of the most serious criticisms levelled at psychiatry is that it actually increases the suffering of those who receive a mental health diagnosis. This is because it removes control from the patient, who can then be manipulated for political and social purposes. A second major issue that concerned Rosenhan was the **reliability** and **validity** of diagnosis: to what extent can the sane be consistently and accurately distinguished from the insane?

 **KEY IDEAS**

Abnormality is the term used by psychologists to describe a range of thinking and behaviours. There are many ways of defining abnormality. Two examples are:

- **Statistical infrequency** – behaviour that is rarely seen in the general population might be considered abnormal. An example of this is schizophrenia, a mental health disorder characterised by auditory or visual hallucinations, which typically affects less than 1% of the population.
- **Deviation from social norms** – behaviour that can be seen as a departure from what one society or culture defines as acceptable. This involves a judgment based on the context in which the behaviour occurs.

Figure 5.1 Jack Nicholson in the 1975 film version of Ken Kesey's One Flew over the Cuckoo's Nest, *which brought the anti-psychiatry movement to the popular masses*

KEY IDEAS

DSM – The Diagnostic and Statistical Manual of Mental Disorders (DSM) is published by the American Psychiatric Association and provides standard criteria for the classification of mental disorders. It is regularly revised. DSM-IV is currently in use, but a newer version (DSM-5) is due to be issued in 2013.

Reliability refers to how consistent a test or tool is. In this case, a diagnostic test is considered reliable if it can produce similar results when used again in similar circumstances.

Validity is the extent to which a test measures what it is intended to measure. In this case, the extent to which the diagnostic criteria can be used to accurately diagnose someone experiencing a mental illness.

ACTIVITY

When considering the accuracy of how we diagnose mental illness, it is useful to consider what is meant by 'abnormality'. Read the following examples and answer the questions below:

1 A maths teacher by day, who is also a cage-fighter and a transvestite dancer
2 An unmarried teenager who falls pregnant from a one-night stand
3 A 50-year-old man who in his leisure time wears a nappy, acts like an infant and drinks milk from a baby's bottle
4 A young man who hears the voice of god, and then wanders the desert for 40 years
5 A woman who takes 1–2 hours to leave her flat each day because she has to wash her hands 16 times, and check three times that each window in the house is locked and that switches are turned off.

Q

1 Which of these cases would you consider abnormal, and why?
2 To what extent are our ideas about what counts as 'abnormal' fixed and unchanging within different contexts?

IN BRIEF

Aim: To test the reliability of psychiatric diagnosis.

Method: Study 1 involved eight participants who presented themselves to 12 different psychiatric hospitals across five states in the USA as pseudo patients. This study can be considered to be a field experiment: the manipulation was the symptoms reported by participants when admitted (hearing voices); the dependent variable was their admission and the diagnoses they received. Once admitted, participants did not exhibit further symptoms of abnormality. The study was also a participant observation, as participants kept a written record of their personal treatment and the experiences of others on the ward. Study 2 consisted of a field experiment in a hospital whose staff were aware of the findings of the previous study. They were falsely briefed that, over three months, one or more pseudopatients would attempt to be admitted. They were then asked to score each new patient out of 10 as to the probability of their being a sane actor.

Results: In Study 1, all of the pseudopatients were admitted to hospital, and in all but one case they received a diagnosis of schizophrenia. They remained in hospital for between 7 and 52 days. The sanity of pseudopatients was not detected by staff, but other genuine patients were openly suspicious of the pseudopatients' sanity. Participants reported unpleasant experiences of depersonalisation and powerlessness. Study 2 found that many patients (approximately 10%) were judged to be pseudopatients by at least one psychiatrist and one other staff member.

Conclusion: The system for distinguishing the sane from the insane seems to be unreliable in this case, as neither sanity nor insanity was consistently identified. Patients who receive a diagnosis are 'labelled' as insane, which distorts subsequent perceptions of their behaviour.

AIM

The aim of the study was to investigate whether the sane can be reliably and accurately distinguished from the insane. In Study 1, this involved finding out whether normal, sane individuals would be admitted to psychiatric hospitals, to see if and how they would be discovered. In Study 2, this involved examining whether genuine patients would be misidentified as 'sane' by various hospital staff.

QUESTION SPOTLIGHT!

As you will see, Rosenhan's research is composed of two separate but related studies. This means you could be asked about either or both study in your exam. Ensure that you can clearly describe the aims, methods and results from each study.

STUDY 1: METHOD

Participants

Eight pseudopatients were adults over the age of twenty and included Rosenhan, a psychology graduate student in his twenties, psychologists, a pediatrician, a psychiatrist, a painter, and a housewife. Three were female, five were male. All used false names, and those with careers in mental health claimed to have an alternative occupation to avoid attracting any special attention from staff. Rosenhan was the first pseudopatient and his involvement was known only to the hospital administrator and chief psychologist.

The settings were also varied. To make the findings generalisable, pseudopatients sought admission to a variety of hospitals. Twelve hospitals were chosen, across five different states in the USA. They ranged from old and shabby, to modern and new, and included public, private and university-funded hospitals. Staff-to-patient ratios also varied greatly.

Design and procedure

After calling the hospital for an appointment, the pseudopatient arrived at the admissions office of the hospital and asserted that they had been hearing voices, which were unclear but were saying 'empty', 'hollow', and 'thud'. These words were chosen by Rosenhan as they were thought to imply a crisis about one's existence, but, at the time the study was conducted, there was no literature linking this to a known mental health disorder. Pseudopatients all reported that the voices were unfamiliar and were of the same sex. All other details of the pseudopatient's life, relationships and experiences were given truthfully to the doctoral staff, with the exception of their name, participation in the current study, and occupation. Pseudopatients entered the study understanding that they had to be released from the institution by their own means, by convincing staff they were sane.

Figure 5.2
Psychologist Dr David L. Rosenhan, who sadly died in February 2012

KEY IDEAS

The term '**labelling**' has a special meaning in this study. It is used to mean a tag that is attached to a person that refers to their mental illness. However, it is not just a description, it carries with it a negative social and personal meaning.

On the ward, the pseudopatients behaved 'normally' and attempted to engage others in conversation. They indicated to staff that they were no longer experiencing any symptoms, obeyed the rules and routines of the ward, and pretended to take prescribed medication without fuss. Although pseudopatients found the experience as a whole distressing and unpleasant, nursing staff recorded in their notes that they were friendly and cooperative.

This main study can be considered to be a field experiment. The IV was the symptoms of illness reported by participants upon admission to hospital. The DV was the admission of participants to hospital, the diagnoses they received, and the recordings of their experiences on the ward. The study was also a participant observation: researchers acted as genuine patients while keeping a written record of their personal experience in each institution. In four hospitals, the pseudopatients also observed staff responses to a specific request. They approached a member of staff and asked: 'when am I likely to be discharged?' Responses to this were recorded and compared to a control condition at Stanford University. This involved a researcher approaching a faculty member and asking a question such as 'Do you teach here?' and recording their responses.

STUDY 1: RESULTS

Both quantitative and qualitative data was gathered. Pseudopatients were successfully admitted at all 12 hospitals. Despite showing no symptoms of insanity once admitted, pseudopatients were not detected by staff in the hospitals. Failure to recognise sanity therefore was not related to the quality of the hospital. All except one received diagnoses of schizophrenia, and were discharged with a diagnosis of 'schizophrenia in remission'. In this way, patients discharged carry a **label** of mental illness beyond the hospital.

The length of stay in hospital ranged from 7 to 52 days, the average stay lasting 19 days. During the first three trials, 35 out of a total of 118 genuine patients voiced suspicions about the sanity of the pseudopatients. They made accusations such as 'You're not crazy ... you're checking up on the hospital', while none of the hospital staff raised such concerns. Rosenhan found a strong tendency towards a type 2 error in diagnosis, which is when a healthy person is diagnosed as ill.

Rosenhan found that, once admitted with a diagnosis of mental illness, subsequent behaviour by pseudopatients was interpreted in light of their diagnosis. He calls this the 'stickiness of psychodiagnostic labels'. Examples of 'pathological behaviour' from the observers' experiences included:

- When pacing in the hospital corridors from boredom, pseudopatients were asked by a nurse if they were nervous.

Figure 5.3
Rosenhan conducted the control trial for the first experiment on a university campus

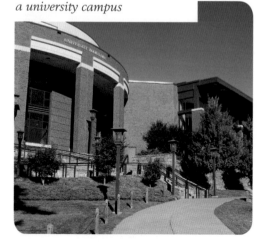

- When recording behaviour in notes on the ward, pseudopatients were desribed by the nurse as 'engaging in writing behaviour'.
- Waiting outside the cafeteria before lunch, pseudopatients were said to demonstrate the 'oral-acquisitive' nature of their conditions.

Experience of hospitalisation was overwhelmingly negative and unpleasant. Hospital staff avoided interaction with patients. On average, attendants spent only 11.3% of their time mixing with patients in the dayroom, and even during this time contact was minimal and might involve routine care-taking tasks, such as folding laundry or supervising tidying-up. The doctoral staff emerged even less often; on average, they left the separate staff areas only 6.7 times a day.

The results of the separate observation conducted in four of the hospitals directly measuring staff interaction with patients found that avoidance of a patient's questions was high. In many cases no response was given, in others only brief responses without eye contact were given while staff were 'on the move'. In contrast, in the university investigation, when staff members were directly approached by the researchers, virtually all stopped and answered their question.

Powerlessness was evident in each institution. In addition to the restricted contact with staff, personal privacy was inadequate. For example, patients' rooms could be entered and examined by any members of staff without warning or justification. There was a lack of confidentiality; patients' case notes were read openly by casual members of staff who had no therapeutic input. Patients' personal hygiene and waste evacuation were monitored, and toilet cubicles had no doors. Even the initial physical examinations were conducted in a semi-public room.

The **depersonalisation** of patients was also a key finding. There were instances where ward staff attendants physically abused patients in the presence of other patients. This behaviour ceased in the presence of any credible witnesses, such as staff. In one instance a nurse undid part of her uniform to adjust her bra in full view of male patients. A total of 2,100 pills were administered to pseudopatients (although they were not swallowed). Many other patients also disposed of their medication, unchallenged by staff as long as patients remained cooperative.

STUDY 2: METHOD

Participants

Psychiatric staff at one research and teaching hospital who had been briefed on the findings of the main study. Judgements were made on 193 patients who were admitted for psychiatric treatment.

Figure 5.4
Powerlessness and depersonalisation – patients experienced a continual lack of privacy: patients' rooms were entered without permission, and toilet cubicles were not fitted with doors

 **KEY IDEAS**

Powerlessness is a key idea used in this piece of research. It refers to the loss of authority or control an individual has to make their own legal or personal decisions. As well as a lack of control, the pseudopatients also experienced a loss of their sense of personhood: they ceased to be treated as individuals by staff. This can be described as **depersonalisation**.

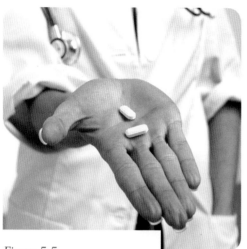

Figure 5.5
Pseudopatients accepted
their prescribed medication
without protest, and
disposed of it later. It was
found that many genuine
patients did the same.

Design and procedure

The staff were informed that at some point during a three-month period, one or more pseudopatients would attempt to gain admission into the hospital. Each staff member was asked to rate each patient – either at admission or on the ward – according to the likelihood that the patient was an imposter. A 10-point scale was used, with '1' reflecting the strongest belief that the patient was a pseudopatient, and '10' the strongest belief that that patient was genuine.

STUDY 2: RESULTS

All staff that had close contact or responsibility for patients made judgements on the 10-point scale. This included attendants, nurses, psychiatrists, physicians and psychologists. Of the patients admitted during the three-month period, 41 were rated with high confidence to be pseudopatients by at least one member of staff. Of these, 23 were suspected by at least one psychiatrist, and 19 were suspected by a psychiatrist and at least one other staff member.

No pseudopatients actually presented themselves to the hospital for admission during the period of this study. This secondary study lends evidence to Rosenhan's argument about the lack of reliability in diagnosis. In this instance, psychiatric staff committed a type 1 error by identifying mentally ill patients as healthy.

CONCLUSIONS

Rosenhan's study challenges the idea that psychiatric professionals can effectively distinguish between individuals who are sane and those who are insane:

- In Study 1, Rosenhan concludes that psychiatrists are unable to reliably identify sane pseudopatients (type 2 error: false positive).
- In Study 2, he claims to demonstrate that psychiatrists fail to reliably detect insanity (type 1 error: false negative).

These conclusions are consistent with Rosenhan's original scepticism about making diagnoses using the existing classifications of mental health disorders. Furthermore, within the 'insane' environment of the psychiatric hospital, an individual's behaviour is perceived in a distorted manner, which maintains their diagnostic label.

QUESTION SPOTLIGHT!

A typical question on Section A of the exam might check your understanding of what is meant by both a type 1 and type 2 error. Make sure that you can confidently explain the difference between the two, relating them to Rosenhan's study.

EXPLANATIONS FOR THE FINDINGS

Depersonalisation

Rosenhan argues that 'depersonalisation' has several causes. First, the staff's attitudes towards the mentally ill affected their treatment of the patients. They may have distrusted and feared patients, while also wanting to help them, and this combination of opposing feelings could have led them to avoid interaction with patients.

Second, the formal hierarchical structure of the hospitals could also have contributed to the depersonalisation experienced by patients. Those with the highest status within the hospital were those who had least contact with the patients. Average daily contact time with doctoral staff per patient was just 6.8 minutes. As doctoral staff serve as role models to the rest of the nurses and support staff, this could also have been a contributing factor.

There might be other practical considerations that contribute to the experience of powerlessness and depersonalisation, including financial pressures, staff shortages, and over-reliance on medication to treat patients.

Labelling

Rosenhan is highly critical of 'labelling' and describes the process as 'counter-therapeutic', suggesting that it actually does the patient more harm than good. He describes psychiatric hospitals as special environments, 'in which the meaning of behaviour can be easily misunderstood'. Instead of focusing on labelling an individual as 'insane', he supports alternatives such as community mental health centres and behavioural therapy programmes. These options could reduce the stigma while offering more personal treatment with an element of control for the individual.

Raising awareness of the issues faced by psychiatric patients in hospital staff could change the experience of hospitalisation. After such an experience, frontline mental health staff might increase their sensitivity to the position of hospitalised patients.

Importantly, Rosenhan maintains that there is a situational explanation for the powerlessness and depersonalisation experienced by psychiatric patients. Failures of the institutions studied were just that: institutional. The negative behaviour of staff towards patients as a whole reflected the culture and expectations within psychiatric hospitals. Therefore it makes sense that Rosenhan's explanations for these experiences and suggestions for how to improve conditions focus on educating staff and changing the fundamental methods of practice involved in the diagnosis and treatment of the 'insane'.

STRETCH & CHALLENGE ◎

Rosenhan's full study makes for an interesting read. You can access it at: www.psychology.co.uk (search for 'Rosanhan').

WEB WATCH @

BBC Radio 4 revisited Rosenhan's pseudopatient study, gaining access to his unpublished personal papers to discover how it changed our understanding of the human mind, and its impact 40 years on. You can listen to 'Mind Changers: The Pseudo-Patient Study' at: www.bbc.co.uk/iplayer/console/b00lny48

STUDY 1

ROSENHAN'S STUDY OF THE RELIABILITY AND VALIDITY OF PSYCHIATRIC DIAGNOSIS

SUMMARY

AIM

To investigate the reliability of diagnosis of psychiatric illness.

METHOD

Study 1: Pseudopatients presented themselves to different hospitals across the USA. On admission, they all reported the same symptoms (hearing voices). Once diagnosed, they were admitted and showed no further symptoms. Participants kept a written record of their own experiences and those of other patients in the hospital.

Study 2: In a different hospital, staff were made aware of the findings of Study 1. They were led to believe that over three months one or more pseudopatients would attempt to be admitted. They each scored new patients out of 10 as to the probability of their being a sane actor.

RESULTS

- All of the pseudopatients were admitted to hospital; none was detected as 'sane' by staff.
- Participants experienced depersonalisation and powerlessness.
- In Study 2, approximately 10% of genuine patients were judged to be pseudopatients by at least one psychiatrist and one other staff member.

CONCLUSIONS

- Psychiatric diagnosis lacks reliability.
- Labelling people as 'insane' can then change later interpretations of their behaviour.

EVALUATION OF THE STUDY

ETHICAL ISSUES

This study could be considered to be a field experiment, and it also used a participant observation to record data. In Study 1, staff at the hospital were unaware that they were taking part in a piece of research, which raises a number of ethical issues:

- **Consent.** People did not give their consent to take part in this study. Although pseudopatients were briefed on their task, staff at each hospital were unaware that research was taking place.
- **Deception.** People were deceived by pseudopatients who sought admission to the

hospital. Staff working with the pseudopatients were misled into administering medication and treatment to them as though they were genuine patients.

- **Harm/Distress.** The nature of the environment was potentially harmful for the researchers (as pseudopatients), who had to seek discharge from the hospitals by their own efforts. Pseudopatients witnessed physical and verbal abuse, which was not only highly distressing, but from which they had no immediate means of escape.
- **Withdrawal.** Participants could not ask to have

their data removed from the findings, as they did not know they had taken part in research. Staff did not give their consent to have their behaviour towards patients recorded and used in Study 1.

METHODOLOGICAL ISSUES
Sample and sampling method

The sample of hospitals in Study 1 was small, at only 12. However, Rosenhan took care to include different hospitals ranging in size, age, and staffing levels, and including both public and private institutions across the USA. This means that the negative experiences of patients could not be attributed solely to old, rural institutions, but equally to modern, smart hospitals. In Study 2, judgements were made on a sample of 193 admissions from one hospital. While the number of admissions is a fair amount for analysis, the results of this study could not be considered representative of other hospitals.

The research method

The main study was a field experiment. The key strength is the natural environment of the hospital in which the study was conducted, which allowed researchers to monitor the outcome of their admission in the real world. The typical difficulty of using this method is the lack of control over variables in the environment. Rosenhan and the other pseudopatients used certain controls to limit the effect of extraneous variables. One example of a control used would be the symptoms reported by the pseudopatients at admission, as they each reported hearing the same words. However, owing to the nature of the study, each hospital environment was different, and therefore it would have been impossible to control the many variables, such as staffing levels and expertise, or the institution's procedures and facilities.

Study 1 was also a participant observation. Researchers acted as patients and recorded their experiences in diaries during their period of hospitalisation. This is a strength of the study because it allowed them to experience life as a patient from the inside. However, it could be argued that conducting research as a participant observer compromises the validity of the research, as observers could lose their objectivity. For example, they might over-empathise with other patients and this could distort their reports of staff behaviour.

Ecological validity

This study would be considered to be high in ecological validity, as the environment of the psychiatric hospital was entirely natural. It was also clear that the hospital staff did not detect the sanity of the pseudopatients, so it can be assumed that they treated the researchers as typical patients. However, Rosenhan himself acknowledges that the researchers' experiences cannot be entirely valid, as they were not experiencing genuine symptoms of insanity.

Qualitative and quantitative data

Rosenhan collected both quantitative and qualitative data. Given that Rosenhan's approach was to explore the experience of hospitalisation, there is greater focus on qualitative findings. In Study 1, Rosenhan was interested in how many successful admissions would be made and the types of diagnosis that would be made, as well as the length of stay in hospital. Other quantitative data came from false negative ratings of patient admissions in Study 2, which was useful in identifying the significant proportion of type 1 errors made by staff.

Practical applications

This study raises important questions about the reliability of diagnostic processes and about how to treat patients. Rosenhan highlights problems with using classification systems through his fundamental challenge to the assumptions of psychiatry. Arguing that the criteria for disorders are too vague and arbitrary has paved the way for research into how subjective bias can undermine and distort diagnosis. In the UK, Loring and Powell (1988) found that psychiatrists were more likely to diagnose schizophrenia in black patients than white patients, based on identical case study descriptions. This shows how Rosenhan's findings can be applied to revealing racial bias in the diagnosis of mental illness.

EXAM FOCUS

We now show you some of the sorts of questions that could be asked about the Rosenhan study in your exam. We will then show you some examples of the sorts of answers we believe might be successful and less successful, and point out some classic traps to avoid.

SECTION A

1 From the Rosenhan study:

  (a) Give one example of how staff interpreted the behaviours of the pseudopatients. *(2 marks)*

  (b) How did the real patients interpret the behaviour of the pseudopatients? *(2 marks)*

2 In the study by Rosenhan, most of the pseudopatients were admitted to hospital with the incorrect diagnosis of schizophrenia. Give two possible explanations why the hospitals made these mistakes. *(4 marks)*

3 In the study by Rosenhan:

  (a) What was abnormal about the self-reports given by the pseudopatients on arrival at the hospital? *(2 marks)*

  (b) What is the difference between the self-reports given by the pseudopatients and the self-reports of the people who actually had schizophrenia? *(2 marks)*

4 From the study by Rosenhan, 'On Being Sane in Insane Places', give two features of life on the ward that was recorded by pseudopatients, and, for each feature, briefly outline what they observed. *(4 marks)*

5 From the first experiment in Rosenhan's 'On Being Sane in Insane Places' study:

  (a) Explain why the pseudopatients were falsely diagnosed as having a mental disorder. *(2 marks)*

  (b) Explain why people with real disorders were identified as pseudopatients in the second experiment. *(2 marks)*

6 Outline two ethical issues that could be raised in relation to Rosenhan's study 'On Being Sane in Insane Places'. *(4 marks)*

7 Explain one advantage and one disadvantage of conducting a field experiment in Rosenhan's study, 'On Being Sane in Insane Places'. *(4 marks)*

8 **(a)** In his study 'On Being Sane in Insane Places', what does Rosenhan mean when he writes about 'the stickiness of psychodiagnostic labels'? *(2 marks)*

  (b) Give one example of how the label 'schizophrenia' affected how hospital staff interpreted the pseudopatients' behaviour. *(2 marks)*

SECTION B

(a) What was the aim of Rosenhan's study? *(2 marks)*

(b) Describe the method in Rosenhan's study and suggest one advantage of using this method. *(6 marks)*

(c) Describe two ethical issues raised by Rosenhan's study. *(6 marks)*

(d) With reference to Rosenhan's study, explain one reason why the researcher needed to break ethical guidelines and one reason why they should not have done so. *(6 marks)*

(e) Suggest two changes to the study by Rosenhan to make it more ethical. *(8 marks)*

(f) Outline the implications of the ethical changes you have suggested for Rosenhan's study. *(8 marks)*

SECTION C

(a) Outline one assumption of the individual differences approach. *(2 marks)*

(b) Describe how the individual differences approach could explain the concept of abnormality. *(4 marks)*

(c) Describe one similarity and one difference between any studies that take the individual differences approach. *(6 marks)*

(d) Discuss strengths and weaknesses of the individual differences approach using examples from any studies that take this approach. *(12 marks)*

SOME ANSWERS AND COMMENTS

SECTION A 7 Explain one advantage and one disadvantage of conducting a field experiment in Rosenhan's study, 'On Being Sane in Insane Places'. *(4 marks)*

Martin's answer:

It was done in a real hospital and so was actually genuine but it was probably dangerous for them to be in there with no support as anything could happen.

Kai's answer:

The advantage is it has loads of ecological validity so this was good. A bad point is there were no controls in the field study and participants had no protection and could have been stuck in the institutions with the diagnosis of schizophrenia. They could have been in danger from real patients as well, which is more lack of control.

We say: 2 marks.
Martin, remember that for four marks the examiner is looking for some good explanation from you. Unfortunately, you have not achieved this here. You attempt to raise an advantage, but need to try to use terminology such as 'ecological validity' rather than just that it is 'real'. The disadvantage is really weak, and you forgot to have detail from the study to show that you know what it was about.

We say: 3 marks.
Kai, your answer adds in material from the study to make your disadvantage clear and it is explained well. The answer is a bit imbalanced, as the advantage is short, although accurate, and has no example from the study. You need just to add that they went to real institutions to get admitted with their fake symptoms.

SECTION A 5 From the first experiment in Rosenhan's 'On Being Sane in Insane Places' study: (a) Explain why the pseudopatients were falsely diagnosed as having a mental disorder. *(2 marks)*

Steph's answer:

They were writing diaries and this was said to be obsessive writing behaviour.

Hywel's answer:

They asked to be admitted saying they were hearing the word 'Thud' in their head. This symptom was deemed to be part of a mental disorder by the practitioner.

We say: 0 marks.
Steph, you have mixed up some of the symptoms here. The diary-writing happened after they were admitted to hospital and were on a ward. The question is asking about the symptoms they claimed they had, in order to get into the hospital, i.e. the voices they said they heard.

We say: 2 marks.
Hywel, this is a concise, accurate and clear answer. You identify the correct symptoms that lead to their diagnosis. You have learnt the study well.

SECTION B (d) With reference to Rosenhan's study, explain one reason why the researcher needed to break ethical guidelines and one reason why they should not have done so. *(6 marks)*

Liam's answer:

Rosenhan needed to be unethical in order to get people into the mental hospital. He shouldn't have done it because it put people in danger of being hurt.

Trevor's answer:

Rosenhan had to deceive the mental hospitals to get his pseudopatients inside. Without this deception the study could not have taken place and as such it was necessary. However, this should not have been done as it was reckless and carefree; it put the pseudopatients at risk of mental harm. This is unacceptable as people's lives aren't worth research findings.

We say: 2 marks.
Liam, you have made a couple of points here, but with six marks available I hope you can see that this is not enough? You have not made it clear why it had to be unethical to get people into hospital. If we have to ask 'why' when reading your answer, then you have not answered the question, and you do need to! After each of your sentences, clearly add in to your point the explanatory comment and discuss features of the study, as well as a more detailed example.

We say: 4 marks.
Trevor, your answer shows that you have thought through the ethical considerations. There is some discussion. Think about how you could incorporate some more detail from the study itself as support for your reasons, e.g. in the reason for breaking guidelines add that they needed to give fake symptoms or they would not be admitted and then it could not take place. Always show that you know a lot about the study alongside your specific answer to the question.

SECTION C (a) Outline one assumption of the individual differences approach. *(2 marks)*

Neema's answer:

One assumption is that not everyone is normal and we cannot really tell who is normal as it is difficult.

Carol's answer:

A key assumption is that everyone is an individual person and if we want to understand things about why we behave as we do then we need to look at how everyone's behaviour can differ. This means we can differ in things like personality and abnormality and these make us act in unique ways.

We say: 0 marks.
Neema, one of the studies looks at normal and abnormal behaviour, but there is more to the approach than this. You have not actually stated an assumption here, but partly mentioned conclusions from Rosenhan's study. This does not answer the question.

We say: 2 marks.
Nice explanation here, Carol. You have a clear, well-written outline that tells us about the approach and how it influences what we do. It gives a clear sense of what the explanation for our behaviour is.

THIGPEN AND CLECKLEY'S CASE STUDY OF A PATIENT WITH MULTIPLE PERSONALITY DISORDER

Thigpen, C.H. and Cleckley, H. (1954) A case of multiple personality. *Journal of Abnormal and Social Psychology*, **49**, 135–51.

CONTEXT

- Have you ever arrived at a friend's house with little recollection of how you got there?
- Have you ever got completely 'lost' in a book?

Most of us experience forgetfulness on a regular basis. We might forget something because we have become distracted and sometimes we can later recall the information we were trying to access. Some psychologists believe that these forms of dissociation occur on a continuum, with all of us experiencing occasional, mild dissociative episodes. However, the following study outlines a case of a woman with extreme **dissociation**, a disorder known as Multiple Personality Disorder (MPD).

MPD is a rare psychological condition. There are few cases, and so little is known about the disorder that some professionals doubt its existence at all. Nowadays, MPD is known as 'Dissociative Identity Disorder' (DID) in the Diagnostic Statistical Manual of Mental Health Disorders.

DID is defined by DSM-IV as the presence of two or more distinct identities, or distinct identities that each have their own way of perceiving and thinking about the environment and self. According to the diagnostic criteria, at least two of these personality states recurrently take control of the individual's behaviour. Although plural identities are present, it is important to remember that they all exist as manifestations of one person.

Two or more personalities co-exist, but only one is 'in control' of the person at a given time. The different personalities might not be aware

 **KEY IDEAS**

The term '**dissociation**' means that one's thoughts, perceptions and memories cease to be joined together in a meaningful way. DID, or MPD, is an example of a **neurotic** disorder; disorders of this type are characterised by anxiety and distress. On the other hand, **psychotic** disorders are those where individuals experience a loss of contact with reality – for example, schizophrenia.

Figure 5.6
The Strange Case of Dr Jekyll and Mr Hyde *is a well-known fictional tale by Robert Louis Stevenson of a man with two separate identities – one good, the other evil*

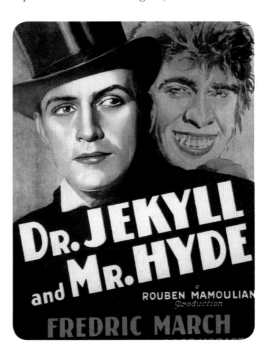

KEY IDEAS

A **fugue** state is an extreme but temporary type of amnesia in which a person forgets so much personal information that they lose their identity (though not their personality) entirely.

WEB WATCH @

Visit the following link to learn more about dissociative fugues: www.psychcentral.com/disorders

of one another's existence and experience. This means those with the disorder might experience dissociative **fugues**, and be unable to recall important personal information.

Dissociative fugues cannot be explained by everyday forgetfulness, and the disorder is not a physiological result of a medical condition or substance abuse. For example, blacking out and suffering memory loss owing to an epileptic seizure or excessive alcohol consumption, does not qualify as a dissociative fugue.

MPD is an example of a **neurotic** disorder – it is NOT a form of schizophrenia, although many people confuse the two conditions. Schizophrenia is a **psychotic** disorder that is characterised by the impairment of one's sense of reality, and can be accompanied by visual or auditory hallucinations or delusions. MPD is a neurotic disorder, where the sufferer does not experience a loss of contact with reality. (See key ideas, p. 189.)

As mentioned, the existence of MPD is highly contested. Not only is it very rarely diagnosed, but treatment of MPD often involves the use of hypnosis (which a controversial technique in itself). Some cases have become notorious, as the psychiatrists involved have been accused of exploiting their patients for their own purposes.

ACTIVITY

Read the following case study and consider the questions below:

THE CASE OF SYBIL

Shirley Ardell Mason, also known as 'Sybil', was a young woman who was diagnosed with multiple personality disorder in the 1950s. She was the daughter of a schizophrenic mother, and, as an adult, she became a teacher. As an adult she began suffering from frequent blackouts and had several breakdowns over the years. She decided to undergo psychotherapy with Cornelia Wilber, a Freudian trained psychoanalyst, to help her deal with her emotional problems.

The record of these sessions later formed the basis for the book about Sybil's life, which revealed that she alleged to have been the victim of physical and sexual abuse by her mother while she was a child. Wilber uncovered several different personalities within Sybil that emerged during therapy, leading to a diagnosis of Multiple Personality Disorder.

Wilber began to publicise the case and it was first turned into a book entitled 'Sybil' and, in 1979, into a film of the same name. However, many experts believed that Cornelia Wilber had made an incorrect diagnosis. One of these opponents was Herbert Speigel, who took over therapy sessions with Sybil on several occasions when Wilber was away. Speigel asserted that Wilber was in fact exploiting Sybil's case for personal gain. Along with others, he believed that Sybil was in fact a 'suggestible hysteric'.

Q

1 What factors might make Multiple Personality Disorder or Dissociative Identity Disorder a particularly difficult condition to diagnose?

2 What ethical issues does this case study raise?

IN BRIEF

Aim: To describe the experience and treatment of a young woman diagnosed as having multiple personalities.

Method: This was a case study of a 25-year old woman, known as Eve White, who was referred for treatment as she was suffering terrible headaches. Data was gathered from therapy sessions that involved interviews and hypnosis. Her family members were also interviewed about both her past and her recent behaviour.

After the emergence of a separate personality, the patient was subjected to psychometric and projective tests. Later, a third personality emerged, and all three personalities underwent an EEG recording to monitor neural activity as each different personality took control of the patient.

Results: At the start of treatment, some emotional problems were identified with Eve and she initially began to cease having such severe headaches. After several sessions, Eve showed additional symptoms, including a dissociative fugue wherein the psychiatrists received a letter written by her and, seemingly, another individual. This marked the emergence of a separate personality, Eve Black (EB). EB could be summoned through hypnosis at first, then of her own accord. She showed very distinctive character differences from Eve White (EW). EW was unaware of EB's existence prior to therapy. Psychometric and projective testing revealed distinctive variations in the personality and cognition of both identities. Further therapy revealed instances in Eve's past where EB had taken control and been involved in unconventional, mischievous behaviour, such as rebellion against Eve's parents and recklessness with money as an adult.

Over time, Eve seemed to be improving, until her headaches returned and were accompanied by blackouts that affected both personalities. Shortly afterwards, a third personality emerged, calling herself 'Jane'. Jane was more confident and interesting than EW, but lacked EB's character flaws. It was hoped that as Jane continued to take over and help EW in her work and home life, Eve's personality would finally reintegrate successfully.

Conclusion: The researchers concluded that they had observed the existence of three separate personalities in one individual. They doubted that this was all a clever act, as it would be so difficult for Eve to have kept up the pretence so convincingly over the 14 months the study had lasted.

AIM

To give an account of the psychotherapeutic experience of an individual who was considered to have multiple personalities.

METHOD

Participant

The participant was a 25-year old married mother with a four-year-old daughter; her real name was changed in Thigpen and Cleckley's report to 'Eve White' to preserve her anonymity. She was the oldest of three siblings and was employed as a telephone operator. This young woman was initially referred to Thigpen for therapy after complaining of 'severe and blinding headaches'. At her first interview she also mentioned experiencing blackouts following such headaches.

Figure 5.7
Eve White was originally referred for treatment for blinding headaches and blackouts

Figure 5.8
Hypnosis is a technique used to create
relaxed and trance-like mental states
within therapy; it is controversial because
some believe it makes the patient highly
suggestible, so they could be influenced by
the therapist's ideas or bias

WEB WATCH @

You can watch the original film trailer for 'The Three Faces of Eve' on IMBd: http://www.imdb.com/video/ screenplay/vi751895577

Design and procedure

This research is considered a classic case study. It focuses on one individual, Eve White, and explores her background, symptoms and therapy in great depth. Case studies employ a range of different methods for studying participants. Here, the case of Eve was explored primarily through psychotherapeutic interviews. Some of the interviews conducted with Eve were done under, or following, hypnosis, in order to 'draw out' different personalities. The study took place over a period of 14 months, and material was gathered from approximately 100 hours of interviews.

In addition, background information was obtained through interviews with family members, including Eve's husband. These were carried out in order to back up Eve's account of events from her childhood to adulthood. Quantitative measures were taken of Eve White and Eve Black. These included psychometric measures of memory and IQ. She also underwent two projection tests that were subjected to analysis by the researchers. These included an exercise drawing human figures, and interpreting Rorschach ink blots. Later in the case study, when the third personality 'Jane' appeared, all three were subject to an electroencephalogram (EEG).

RESULTS

Eve White

Initially, the therapists report some slight progress in treating Eve White's symptoms following discussion of some of her emotional problems. Eve was thought to be suffering from personal frustrations and difficulties with her husband (from whom she was currently separated). During the course of a session Eve was unable to recall details of a recent trip she had made. Hypnosis was induced and her memory was restored. Several days later, a letter from Eve was received about this therapy session written for the most part in her own handwriting, with the exception of the final paragraph, which was written in a childish scrawl.

The letter was the first indication that anything was unusual about Eve's case, as she had presented herself as a self-controlled and truthful person. At the next session, Eve denied sending the letter, but was distressed and agitated and finally asked whether hearing an imaginary voice would indicate she was 'insane'. She admitted she had occasionally heard a voice other than her own addressing her over recent months. Before any response to this was made, Eve held her hands to her head as if in pain and suddenly her entire manner and voice appeared to change. She smiled and said' Hi there, Doc!', and when asked who she was, introduced herself as 'Eve Black'. 'Black' was later found to be Eve's maiden name.

Eve Black

Eve Black (EB) now appeared mischievous, light-hearted and playful as she continued to be interviewed. She seemed to have existed independently from Eve White (EW) since childhood. She was found to have separate thoughts and feelings from EW, but also had awareness and access to EW's life while she herself was absent. Despite this access to EW's thoughts, EB had little sympathy for her. While EW loved and missed her daughter (from whom she was also separated), EB was unconcerned and glib about the suffering of EW. EW was totally ignorant of EB's existence, but came to be aware that she existed through the course of therapy. Initially, persuading EB to 'come out' required hypnosis, but over time this was no longer necessary. However, EB was never hypnotisable, and attempts to 'call out' both personalities simultaneously were unsuccessful and distressing to Eve.

While EB did not seem deliberately cruel, in early childhood she would emerge and cause trouble. EW was forbidden from playing in the woods as a child; one day EB took over and broke her parent's strict rule. Upon her return, EW was whipped for her disobedience, much to her confusion and dismay. Her parents corroborated this story and also expressed their puzzlement at such out-of-character behaviour in their normally obedient and honest daughter.

Similar instances occurred in Eve's adulthood. Her husband recalled an incident where he discovered she had spent an enormous sum of money of clothes; he had abused her for being so careless and indulgent. As it was EB who had indulged in the expensive shopping trip, EW was deeply bewildered and apologetic for such an irresponsible lapse in her behaviour. The therapists note that although it is unlikely Eve's marriage would have been successful even without her condition, there is no doubt EB's difficult behaviour contributed to the couple's difficulties.

To explore the extent of the psychological differences between the two personalities, Eve underwent several psychometric and projective tests (see Table 5.1). These revealed differences in IQ and memory, as well as key differences in the defence mechanisms of **repression** and **regression** that were underlying Eve's two different personas.

Eve Black's other distinctive behaviours included drinking to excess, hooking up with strange men and, allegedly, even committing to a prior secret marriage. EB claimed to be able to erase certain occurrences from EW's memory. 'I just start thinking about it very hard and after a while ... it doesn't come back to her anymore'.

After eight months of therapy, EW was no longer experiencing headaches or blackouts. EB had been causing less trouble and EW had had some encouraging successes in her work and social life. But suddenly

Figure 5.9
Eve Black recalled disobeying her parents and running off into the woods to play, leaving Eve White to take the blame

TABLE 5.1 RESULTS OF INDEPENDENT PSYCHOLOGICAL CONSULTATION ON EVE		
	Eve White	**Eve Black**
IQ test	110	104
Memory	Higher performance than IQ	Same performance as IQ
Projective tests	Repressed conflict and anxiety as a result of her role as wife and mother	Desire to regress to an earlier stage of life (i.e. before marriage)

Figure 5.10
An example of a Rorschach inkblot, one of
the projective tests used to reveal aspects
of the unconscious mind. Subjects are
shown a series of inkblots and asked to
describe what they see. This information
is then interpreted by the psychotherapist
and is supposed to offer insight into their
personality. Swiss psychologist Hermann
Rorschach died before the test came into
popular usage.

all this changed. The headaches, blackouts and fugues returned with greater frequency, and were now experienced by both EW and EB. The therapists feared she might be about to experience an episode of psychosis.

Jane

In a session after the headaches had restarted, EW was discussing a painful childhood memory when suddenly her head dropped back and her eyes closed. Two minutes later she looked around the room confusedly and asked where she was. Another transformation had taken place, with mannerisms and characteristics highly distinct from either EW or EB. 'Jane' – as she called herself – was more confident, interesting and assertive than timid EW, but without the personality faults of EB. She was aware of the behaviour of the other two personalities, but could not access their memories prior to her emergence.

The EEG conducted several weeks later on all three personalities traced 33 minutes of recording, including intervals of at least 5 minutes of each personality, and some transitions between individuals. Tenseness was most pronounced in EB, next in EW, and least of all Jane. Muscle tension was greatest in EB, and the test indicated it was easiest to transpose from EB to EW. EB's results were only borderline normal, with some records showing an association with psychopathic personality. Both EW and Jane's records were normal.

Jane continued to emerge through EW only, but became stronger over time. She took over many of EW's duties both at work and at home in an effort to help her, but was reluctant to fully take over as a maternal figure to EW's daughter as she did not wish to interfere with their relationship.

CONCLUSIONS

Despite the debate over the existence of MPD, Thigpen and Cleckley concluded that they were not tricked by a skilful actress but had observed the existence of three distinct personalities within one individual.

There will undoubtedly continue to be controversy over the existence of MPD/DID. Thigpen and Cleckley argue that what they witnessed was genuine because the length of time spent with Eve White, Eve Black and Jane meant that at least some mistakes or inconsistencies would have been noticed.

The researchers felt it right to speak of three different personalities inhabiting one body, rather than of three separate people. Later, an analysis was performed which revealed that despite considerable variations between the handwriting of each Eve, the material submitted was written by just one individual. It is clear to them that within each individual, personality can be seen as a 'complex process of growth or evolution'. The therapists hoped that over time Jane would show herself to be a reintegration of Eve's personalities and provide a successful outcome to the therapy, but they explicitly acknowledged it was not their role to select one of the personalities to survive as dominant.

EXPLANATIONS FOR THE FINDINGS

The researchers resisted offering an explanation for what led to Eve's experience of multiple personalities. There is a suggestion in the report they arranged, involving the psychometric and projective test, that rivalry with her younger twin sisters and a sense of parental rejection might have been contributing factors. However, Thigpen and Cleckley do not arrive at this analysis themselves. Instead they reflect on what is meant by our understanding of 'personality', while also calling for further study of multiple personality and a re-examination of past cases.

Figure 5.11
An electroencephalogram (EEG) was used to identify potential variations in brain activity between the three different personalities

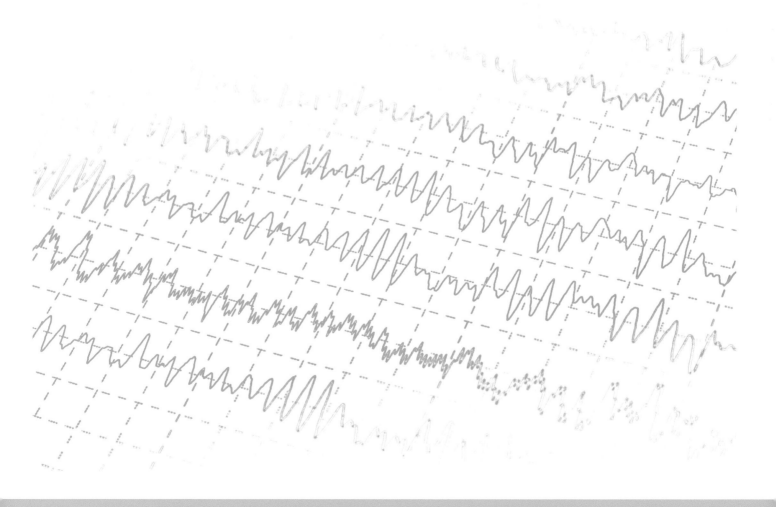

STUDY 2

THIGPEN AND CLECKLEY'S CASE STUDY OF A PATIENT WITH MULTIPLE PERSONALITY DISORDER

SUMMARY

AIM

To provide an account of an individual with multiple personalities.

METHOD

- A case study of a young woman suffering from headaches, which involved interviews and hypnosis to establish her background and current issues.
- Psychometric tests and projective tests were given to Eve White and Eve Black. An EEG recording was conducted on all three personalities.
- Eve's husband and family members were interviewed to corroborate her account.

RESULTS

- Eve Black, a hidden and mischievous personality, emerged in the course of therapy.
- Eve Black had a radically different set of traits and mannerisms, she was reckless and egocentric compared to the reserved and shy Eve White. Tests showed many differences between the two personalities.
- Over time, symptoms began to lessen, until a bout of blackouts and headaches preceded the emergence of Jane, a third distinct personality.
- Jane was considered a much more positive personality type and was aware of the two Eves.

CONCLUSIONS

- The researchers observed the existence of three different personalities within one individual.
- It was hoped that the emergence of 'Jane' might lead to a reintegration of Eve's personality and a resolution to the difficulties she was experiencing.

EVALUATION

ETHICAL ISSUES

Thigpen and Cleckley's case study was based on the therapy sessions undertaken by Eve White who was seeking help for her emotional difficulties. The notoriety of this case and subsequent dramatisations of Eve's life raise several ethical issues.

- **Consent.** Thigpen and Cleckley came to know of Eve's case through their work with her as a patient. Under the British Psychological Society (BPS) standards of conduct, we might question whether

Eve could be considered a vulnerable adult, whether sufficient attempts were made by the researchers to obtain her full and informed consent, and whether she was fully competent to give her permission to have her case published.

- **Harm/Distress.** The BPS ethical standards require that practitioners act in the best interests of participants and treat them with respect. It could be argued that Eve was treated more as a subject than a participant in this study. Furthermore, it could have

Figure 5.12
Joanne Woodward as Eve in the 1957 film, The Three Faces
of Eve, *a popular adaptation of Thigpen and Cleckley's*
book. The real Eve White revealed her true identity as
Christine Costner Sizemore in her 1977 book, 'I'm Eve'.

been distressing to Eve White to be told that she had
separate identities of whom she was unaware. When
attempts were made to draw out both EW and EB
simultaneously, this appeared to cause real distress
to the patient.

- **Confidentiality.** Eve's case was published by the
  researchers, which means details of her background
  and mental health that were discussed in confidence
  were made known to the general public. However,
  the researchers attempted to protect her identity by
  using a pseudonym in the published study.

- **Privacy.** Much of the information used in the study
  was taken from confidential disclosures made by Eve
  in the course of her therapy. In some cases this was
  done under hypnosis, which might have led to her
  making known to the therapists personal information
  that she might otherwise have preferred not to reveal.

METHODOLOGICAL ISSUES
Sample and sampling method
This is a classic case study, involving in-depth analysis
of one individual, 25-year old Eve White. Naturally, this
is a small and unrepresentative sample. However, MPD
is an extremely rare condition and an unusual example
of individual difference in psychology. It is difficult to

say to what extent Eve's case is representative of other
instances of MPD because there are so few. As Eve's
condition had occurred naturally and was a product of
her particular circumstances, it also makes it difficult
to compare to other known cases. This study involves a
self-selected or volunteer sample, as Eve was referred to
Thigpen and Cleckley for her severe headaches.

The research method
The case study has both advantages and disadvantages.
The key strength is that it provides researchers with a
unique opportunity to study an unusual psychological
condition. It also allows them to focus on studying the
individual in great detail. In this instance researchers
were able to analyse approximately 100 hours of
interviews with Eve. However there are issues with
using the case study method. One of these is that
working so closely with a patient might compromise the
objectivity of the therapists. Because they were aware
of the existence of the disorder, they might have led Eve
towards revealing new personalities or demonstrated
bias in their reporting of her case. Furthermore, much
evidence relied on testimony about past events, which
may not have been accurate and could even have been
distorted by Eve's current neurotic behaviour.

Validity and reliability
Thigpen and Cleckley used a range of techniques to
measure and analyse Eve's experience of MPD, including
interviews, psychometric and projective testing,
handwriting analysis and an EEG recording. Using several
different methods to collect data on Eve allowed them to
test the hypothesis that several personalities inhabited
the same body, which increases the validity of their claim
that Eve was in fact experiencing MPD. Independent
experts were used to conduct these assessments to
minimise bias. However, as Thigpen and Cleckley
themselves acknowledged, it was still (however remotely)
possible that the multiple personalities were presented
as an elaborate hoax by Eve. Owing to the nature of
the condition, there is no scientific way to confirm the
existence of the other personas.

This study can be said to have high ecological validity because it was a naturally occurring case of multiple personalities. Eve sought treatment herself and the disorder was assumed to be pre-existing. On the other hand, some psychologists would argue that it is possible that the techniques used by therapists might have provoked the emergence of Jane, Eve's third personality. A review by Fahy (1988) found that some psychiatrists are more liable to make a diagnosis of MPD or DID than others, and it is known that a disproportionate number of cases are found in North America. This might lead us to question the reliability of diagnosing MPD.

Qualitative and quantitative data

Thigpen and Cleckley collected both quantitative and qualitative data. As they wanted to gain insight into the experience of an individual with MPD, there is keener focus on qualitative data gained through interviews with Eve and her family members. An example of this data would be the dissociative fugue Eve experienced when running off into the woods as a little girl against her parent's wishes. This type of data helps us to understand the way in which Eve's personalities alternated in controlling her thoughts and behaviour. Quantitative data was also obtained in the study, for example through the psychometric testing undergone by EW and EB. This demonstrated differences in their memories and IQ scores, suggestive of two different individuals inhabiting the same body. Further quantitative data came from the EEG recording performed after the emergence of Jane. This type of data enabled the researchers to directly compare the separate identities and their individual characteristics.

Practical applications

Thigpen and Cleckley explored the case of Eve in their study and concluded that more research was required into the disorder in order to better understand it and, presumably, to provide more effective treatment for sufferers. Their later work goes on to explore underlying causes of the disorder, which are thought to lie in traumatic childhood experiences, including physical and sexual abuse. However, sceptics argue that MPD is actually a product of questionable therapeutic interventions performed on vulnerable, suggestible patients. If this is the case, it brings into question the usefulness of this research in helping those experiencing anxiety and dissociative symptoms.

EXAM FOCUS

We now show you some of the sorts of questions that could be asked about the Thigpen and Cleckley study in your exam. We will then show you some examples of the sorts of answers we believe might be successful and less successful, and point out some classic traps to avoid.

SECTION A

1. In their case study on multiple personality disorder, Thigpen and Cleckley used a number of ways of gathering data.
   (a) Identify two of these ways. *(2 marks)*
   (b) Outline one disadvantage of gathering data in one of these ways. *(2 marks)*

2. Thigpen and Cleckley used the case-study method to investigate the condition of multiple personality disorder. Give one strength and one weakness of the case-study approach and relate it to this particular study. *(4 marks)*

3. In the Thigpen and Cleckley study, give two differences and two similarities in the personalities of Eve White and Eve Black that were revealed by psychometric tests. *(4 marks)*

4. Suggest two pieces of evidence from the case study by Thigpen and Cleckley that indicate the patient really did have a multiple personality. *(4 marks)*

5. All studies raise some ethical dilemmas. Outline two ethical issues raised by the study of split personality by Thigpen and Cleckley. *(4 marks)*

6. Using information from the study by Thigpen and Cleckley, explain the difference between having a 'multiple personality disorder' and having different sides to your personality. *(4 marks)*

7. Outline two differences found between the personalities of Eve White and Eve Black in the study by Thigpen and Cleckley on multiple personality disorder. *(4 marks)*

8. **(a)** From the study on multiple personality disorder by Thigpen and Cleckley, describe one of the projective tests that were administered to Eve White and Eve Black. *(2 marks)*
   (b) Outline one problem with the use of such tests. *(2 marks)*

SECTION B

(a) What was the aim of the study by Thigpen and Cleckley? *(2 marks)*

(b) Describe the sample in the study by Thigpen and Cleckley and suggest one advantage of using this sample. *(6 marks)*

(c) Describe how data was collected in the study by Thigpen and Cleckley. *(8 marks)*

(d) Give one advantage and one disadvantage of using the self-report method in the study by Thigpen and Cleckley. *(6 marks)*

(e) Outline the results of the study by Thigpen and Cleckley. *(6 marks)*

(f) Suggest one way that the study by Thigpen and Cleckley can be improved and give reasons for your answer. *(8 marks)*

SECTION C

(a) Outline one assumption of the individual differences approach. *(2 marks)*

(b) Describe how the individual differences approach could explain multiple personality disorder. *(4 marks)*

(c) Describe one similarity and one difference between any studies that take the individual differences approach. *(6 marks)*

(d) Discuss strengths and weaknesses of the individual differences approach using examples from any studies that take this approach. *(12 marks)*

SOME ANSWERS AND COMMENTS

SECTION A 1 In their case study on multiple personality disorder, Thigpen and Cleckley used a number of ways of gathering data.
(a) Identify two of these ways. *(2 marks)*

Gloria's answer:
They asked Eve White and Eve Black things about their lives and thoughts in the psychologist's office.

Lloyds' answer:
Handwriting in a letter was analysed as there were two different styles that could be assessed for information, and Rorschach Ink Blots projective tests were done on the Eves.

We say: 1 mark.
Gloria, it does not count as two ways to get data by saying the same way but with two of the personalities! You mention the interviews, but this is just one way. You could also mention the EEG or the IQ tests as another different way to get both marks here.

We say: 2 marks.
Two clearly set out methods here, Lloyd, and both give data on the different personalities. You have done what you were asked!

6 Using information from the study by Thigpen and Cleckley, explain the difference between having a 'multiple personality disorder' and having different sides to your personality. *(4 marks)*

Pam's answer:
In the study Eve showed to be an erratic individual and constantly changing personality. It was uncontrollable and would occur after black outs. All personalities had names.

Alan's answer:
The difference is really that multiple personality disorder is much less brief, whereas people can have sudden mood swings showing different sides without any major long-lasting changes. The difference in tests, like handwriting, also shows the individual is completely changed more permanently with the disorder than a mood swing. Each personality is distinct from one another having names, so is very different to having a many-sided personality where they don't.

We say: 1 mark.
Pam – in any question that asks you to explain a difference you have to be very clear on what the actual difference is. Unfortunately you seem to describe what multiple personality is, and leave us to do the comparison for ourselves – not a good strategy. Make it crystal clear how you are comparing them. Take your point on how multiple personality occurred after blackouts, and then say this does not happen in mood swings so they are different. That is much more explicit.

We say: 4 marks.
Well Alan – this is a very detailed answer! You make several detailed points that very clearly point out differences between the two. What we like is that each one is a direct comparison so we can easily understand what the actual difference is and how it applies to either multiple personality or mood swings.

SECTION B (d) Give one advantage and one disadvantage of using the self-report method in the study by Thigpen and Cleckley. *(6 marks)*

Wyn's answer:

One advantage is you can have control over what the participant answers, as they are answering your particular questions on your topics, making it more accurate and reliable. The bad thing is it is not ecologically valid, as it is just talk and not something happening in the real world.

We say: 1 mark.
Wyn, you appear to have forgotten that the question is on Thigpen and Cleckley, as you have not mentioned them in your answer. Oh dear! Remember that it is important to read the question carefully, and it does say 'in the study by Thigpen and Cleckley', so you need to give examples from it. State your advantage/disadvantage, have some detail from the study to link it, and then add some more detailed comment overall. The point on ecological validity is not answering the question here.

Vanessa's answer:

An advantage is that you can get direct information from the individual who might be ill like Eve White. This is useful as it allowed the researchers to get an understanding of all the personalities, like Eve Black and Jane, and see how the responses differed. This is a kind of insight you get only with self-report. A disadvantage is that it is unreliable as you have to rely on what the participant is saying as true. Eve Black talked to the therapist for many hours but we cannot prove all that she said while talking about her life and Eve White.

We say: 5 marks.
Vanessa, this is straight to the point and explains the advantage in clear terms. We like how you go on to make clear why this is an advantage with an example from the study too. You show your examiners that you know what you are talking about! For the disadvantage you needed to add a further comment and expand on what you have written – you make the point and have some detail, but need to go a bit further.

SECTION C (d) Discuss strengths and weaknesses of the individual differences approach using examples from any studies that take this approach. *(12 marks)*

Bevan's answer:

One strength of the approach in Thigpen's study is that it shows how a woman got multiple personality disorder from a hideous experience as a child. It was useful for her doctor to know this. Another strength is in Rosenhan as it shows us it is actually easy to get into a mental hospital to see what the doctors and nurses do to the patients. A weakness is that in Griffiths he only studies gamblers using fruit machines and there are loads of other sorts of gambling that could be looked at and need investigation. A last weakness is that in Rosenhan, the pseudopatients could not just leave when they wanted to, so could not control their stay in the hospital.

We say: 0 marks.
Bevan, this is not a good answer, as this question asks you to look at the approach itself, whereas you look at the studies in the approach. This will not get you any marks and will not help your overall score. Do not evaluate the studies and their strengths and weaknesses; you should be doing this for the approach. The best way to tackle this question is to set out each strength (or weakness), explain it carefully for the examiner, and follow up by showing that you know the study by illustrating your point with some facts from the study.

GRIFFITHS' STUDY OF DIFFERENCES BETWEEN REGULAR AND NON-REGULAR GAMBLERS

Griffiths, M. (1994) The role of cognitive bias and skill in fruit machine gambling. *British Journal of Psychology*, 85(3), 361–9.

IN BRIEF !

Aim: To look for differences in skill, levels of irrationality and beliefs about the role of skill in gambling between regular and non-regular gamblers.

Method: 15 regular and 15 non-regular gamblers were each given £3 and instructed to try to play a fruit machine, staying on for at least 60 plays. Half the participants were also asked to think aloud, and their verbalisations were recorded and analysed. Afterwards, all participants were interviewed for evidence of their beliefs about the role of skill in gambling.

Results: Very little evidence was found for a difference in skill levels of regular and non-regular gamblers. However, the regular gamblers said more irrational things while gambling and they revealed a much greater belief in the role of skill in gambling compared to the non-regular gamblers.

Conclusion: There is no difference in skill between regular and non-regular gamblers. However, regular gamblers experience different cognitions when gambling and hold different beliefs about gambling.

CONTEXT

All gambling involves situations where the chances of winning are very much against the gambler. It is therefore quite an irrational way of trying to obtain money. Psychologists are always interested in irrational thinking and behaviour, and gambling has not escaped attention. However, not all gambling is the same. If you bet on horses, there is an element of skill in calculating the odds relative to the recent performance or form of the horses. Fruit machines are a particularly irrational form of gambling, because there is little or no skill involved.

Griffiths identifies two main theoretical approaches to understanding gambling behaviour.

1. Normative decision theory suggests that every gambling decision is logical and therefore possible to predict. Griffiths points out that actually most gamblers are not logical and that therefore predictions based on the theory tend to be wrong.

2. Wagenaar's **heuristics** and cognitive biases approach: Wagenaar (1988) suggests that regular gamblers have a set of cognitive biases. These include the following:
   a. *Illusion of control*: belief that the gambler can affect the probability of winning.
   b. *Flexible attributions*: taking personal credit for luck, and seeing failure as a near miss.
   c. *Representativeness*: seeing consistency or patterns in random events.
   d. *Availability bias*: overestimating the probability of winning because of attention to other peoples' winning events.

e *Illusory correlations*: beliefs that there is a relationship between two unconnected things, such as rolling a dice harder in order to obtain a higher score.

f *Fixation on absolute frequency of winning*: regular gamblers win more often because they play more often. They tend to interpret this as meaning they are more successful, but of course they lose more often as well.

In complex situations, where we have to make quick decisions in the face of many variables, we tend to rely on heuristics rather than more logical **algorithms**. Wagenaar suggests that, under pressure, gamblers tend to rely on heuristics for their decision-making. The problem is that these heuristics involve the cognitive biases listed above, so they lead to some dodgy decisions.

In his early research, Griffiths (1990) showed that many regular fruit-machine gamblers believed that they played with skill as well as luck. Interestingly, their intention was to use their money in order to stay on the machine for as long as possible, rather than to be ahead on money at the close of play. There was evidence of illusion of control: regular gamblers tended to believe that using nudge and hold buttons altered their chances of winning. The more pathological the gambler, the more they tended to believe that their success was affected by skill.

AIMS AND HYPOTHESES

The aims of the study were to investigate differences in behaviour and cognition between regular gamblers (RGs) and non-regular gamblers (NRGs). There were three specific aims:

1 To see whether there really are differences in skill between regular and non-regular gamblers. Skill was assessed in seven ways (see Table 5.2).

2 To see whether regular gamblers say more irrational things than non-regular gamblers while gambling.

3 To see whether there is a difference between perceptions of gambling skill in regular and non-regular gamblers.

The following hypotheses were tested:

1 There would be no differences in skill between regular and non-regular gamblers.

2 Regular gamblers would produce more irrational verbalisations while gambling than non-regular gamblers.

3 Regular gamblers would perceive more skill in gambling than non-regular gamblers.

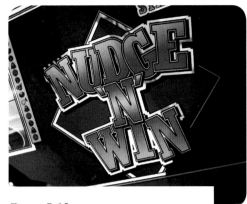

Figure 5.13
Nudge functions add to the illusion that fruit-machine gamblers can control the chances of winning

 **KEY IDEAS**

People can make decisions in two ways:
Algorithms are full logical reasoning processes. These are almost guaranteed to arrive at a logical decision, but take a lot of time and mental effort.
Heuristics are mental shortcuts. These simplify the world and so make decision-making a much quicker and easier process, but they might involve flawed logic.

Figure 5.14
Believing that the harder you roll the dice, the higher the resulting score, is an example of an illusory correlation

Figure 5.15
The study took place in a real amusement arcade rather than a laboratory

METHOD

PARTICIPANTS

Sixty people took part in the study (44 male, 16 female; mean age: 23.4 years). Half were regular gamblers, and half non-regular gamblers. Most were recruited through posters around a local university and colleges; a small number were introduced to the researcher by a regular gambler known to him. In the non-regular gambler group there were 15 males and 15 females. In the regular gambler group it was not possible to match numbers of males and females, as fruit-machine gamblers are almost entirely male. This group therefore contained 29 males and one female.

DESIGN AND PROCEDURE

For the sake of ecological validity the study was conducted in a local arcade rather than in a laboratory. Participants took part individually and, for the sake of experimental control, all used the same machine (called FRUITSKILL), unless they objected. Each participant was given £3, allowing them 30 free plays. They were told they could keep any winnings and were instructed to try to stay on for at least 60 gambles. After this, they could choose to stay on or to leave with any leftover money.

Half the participants (15 RGs and 15 NRGs) were asked to think aloud while playing. They were instructed to say, into a lapel microphone, everything that was going through their mind, whether it appeared sensible or irrelevant (see Box 5.1). What they said was recorded and later transcribed and analysed. This was to get an idea of the the cognitions

TABLE 5.2
SEVEN MEASURES OF GAMBLING SKILL

Dependent variable	NR/NTA	R/NTA	NR/TA	R/TA
Total plays	47.8	56.6	55.7	65.6
Total time	8.4	8.5	11.5	9.9
Play rate	6.5	7.5	5.3	8.4
End stake	4.0	0	7.3	13.9
Win	6.1	8.0	8.3	6.0
Win rate (time)	2.0	1.0	1.7	1.8
Win rate (plays)	12.5	7.5	8.0	14.6

(Source: Griffiths 1994, Table 3, p. 357)

that took place while gambling. A coding system was devised to classify what was said, which included irrational statements and questions:

- Personalisation of the machine, e.g. 'this machine likes me'
- Explaining away losses, e.g. 'I lost because I wasn't concentrating'
- Talking to the machine, e.g. 'aren't you going to pay out for me?'
- Swearing at the machine, e.g. 'you bastard'.

Also coded were more rational utterances such as: references to winning; references to not understanding what was happening; use of humour; references to numbers, e.g. 'I got a two there'; and references to luck. Following the session, participants were interviewed to see how regular and non-regular gamblers perceived the role of skill in fruit-machine gambling. The interviews were semi-structured, meaning that all participants received the same basic questions but, depending on the answers, they might be asked further different questions. All were asked:

- Is there any skill involved in playing the fruit machine?
- How skilful do you think you are compared to the average person?
- What skill (if any) is involved in playing fruit machines?

Figure 5.16
Swearing at the Fruitskill machine was classed as an irrational verbalisation

RESULTS

SKILL OF REGULAR AND NON-REGULAR GAMBLERS

The skill measures for the four groups are shown in Table 5.3. To make sense of this, remember that RGs are regular gamblers and NRGs are non-regular gamblers. TA refers to the thinking-aloud condition, and NTA to the non-thinking-aloud condition.

Overall, these results do not indicate that regular gamblers were more skilful than non-regular gamblers. The only significant differences were that RGs played faster and that regular gamblers thinking aloud had longer intervals between wins than the other three groups.

What RGs and NRGs said while gambling

- RGs referred significantly more often to numbers and to personification of the fruit machine.
- RGs swore and explained away losses more frequently than NRGs.
- The percentage of verbalisations classified as irrational was significantly greater in the RGs (14% compared to 2.5%).
- NRGs referred significantly more to confusion and to not understanding what was taking place.
- NRGs referred on occasion to their mind going blank and to experiencing frustration; RGs did not.

> **Box 5.1**
> **Instructions in the thinking aloud condition**
>
> The thinking aloud method consists of verbalising every thought that passes through your mind while you are playing. It is important to remember the following points:
> (1) Say everything that goes through your mind. Do not censor any of your thoughts even if they seem irrelevant to you;
> (2) Keep talking as continuously as possible, even if your ideas are not clearly structured;
> (3) Speak clearly;
> (4) Do not hesitate to use fragmented sentences if necessary. Do not worry about speaking in complete sentences;
> (5) Do not try to justify your thoughts.

(Source: Griffiths 1994, p. 356)

TABLE 5.3
RESULTS OF THE MEASURES OF GAMBLING SKILL

Dependent variable	Operational definition
Total plays	Total number of plays during the playing session
Total time	Total time in minutes of play during one playing session
Play rate	Total number of plays per minute during the playing session
End stake	Total winnings in number of 10 pence pieces after the playing session was over
Wins	Total number of wins during the playing session
Win rate (time)	Total number of minutes between each win during the playing session
Win rate (plays)	Total number of plays between each win during the playing session

(Source: Griffiths 1994, Table 2 p. 355)

WEB WATCH @

The gambling man? Read an interview with Mark Griffiths here:
http://www.psychblog.co.uk/interview-the-gambling-man-prof-mark-griffiths-119.html
Or listen to the interview on this podcast:
http://www.psychblog.co.uk/griffiths-cognitive-bias-and-skill-in-gambling-858.html

STRETCH & CHALLENGE ◎

This study has considerable practical applications in terms of informing how we treat addictions such as gambling. Research and design a leaflet outlining key findings of Griffiths' study and how irrational beliefs about gambling can be challenged through cognitive therapies such as CBT and REBT.

- RGs infrequently said things that suggested they were using heuristics of the type outlined by Wagenaar.

Post-experiment interviews
- Most RGs believed that there was an equal degree of luck and skill involved in playing fruit machines. However, most NRGs believed that luck was the more important factor.
- Most NRGs rated themselves as below average in fruit-machine ability, whereas most RGs rated themselves as above average.
- RGs referred to skills – such as judging when a payout was due, and judging when not to play because a payout was unlikely.

CONCLUSIONS

Referring back to the aims of the study:
1 Overall, there appear to be no skill differences between RGs and NRGs, although RGs did gamble faster and tended to gamble more times with the same money.
2 There are differences in the verbalisations of RGs and NRGs that suggest some differences in their cognitions. RGs do say more irrational things while gambling, suggesting that more irrational cognition is taking place. However, from these results RGs appear less irrational than has been suggested by previous studies, and most verbalisations are rational in both RGs and NRGs.
3 Regular gamblers are more likely than non-regulars to see success in fruit-machine gambling as a product of skill as well as luck.

The overall conclusion is that the major difference between regular and non-regular fruit-machine gamblers is cognitive. RGs believe there is more skill than there really is to gambling, and so they overestimate their ability to influence the outcome.

STUDY 3

GRIFFITHS' STUDY OF DIFFERENCES BETWEEN REGULAR AND NON-REGULAR GAMBLERS

SUMMARY

AIM

To investigate differences in skill and cognitions between regular and non-regular gamblers.
Three predictions were tested:

1 There is no difference in actual skill of RGs and NRGs

2 RGs produce more irrational verbalisations

3 RGs believe there is skill in fruit-machine gambling.

METHOD

Thirty regular gamblers and 30 non-regular gamblers were given £3 and instructed to try to remain on a fruit machine for at least 60 plays. The skill of the RGs and NRGs was judged by a number of measures. Half of each group were instructed to think aloud while playing, and their verbalisations were recorded and analysed. Afterwards, the participants were interviewed about the extent to which they thought skill was involved in fruit-machine gambling.

RESULTS

- There was little evidence of difference in skill between RGs and NRGs.
- The verbalisations differed between the two groups. RGs swore more than NRGs, and they personalised the fruit machine and explained away their losses more often.
- Interviews revealed that the RGs were much more likely than NRGs to see a role for skill in gambling.

CONCLUSIONS

RGs were no more skilled than NRGs. However, they believed much more in the role of skill in gambling and their cognitions differed from those of NRGs.

EVALUATION OF THE STUDY

Like most of the more recent studies reported here, this study does not raise the same kinds of serious ethical and methodological questions as some of the older ones.

ETHICAL ISSUES

By the 1990s there were tough ethical guidelines in place, and the Griffiths study was assessed against these before it was allowed to proceed. There were actually some clever features of the study that make it particularly strong on ethical considerations. For example, the control group comprised non-regular gamblers, rather than non-gamblers. This is important because it means that the researcher was not deliberately introducing people to gambling for the first time. That would have put their welfare at risk because they might have been vulnerable to gambling addiction. Because volunteers were sought, and adverts made the nature of the study clear, there was no issue of informed consent or deceit.

METHODOLOGICAL ISSUES
Sample and sampling
The overall sample size of 60 was fairly large for an experimental study in which participants took part one at a time, which is a strength. However, the sampling procedure – a mixture of self-selecting and snowball sampling – was a weakness because these are the methods least likely to produce a representative group. Here, this is understandable because gamblers are a hard-to-reach group. With 29 males and one female the sample of regular gamblers was probably representative, as few regular gamblers are female. However, this proportion of males to females was not well matched with the non-regular gamblers, so gender is an extraneous variable.

The research method
This study was carried out in a real amusement arcade rather than in a laboratory, so it is a field experiment. Field experiments come with their own set of strengths and weaknesses. The procedure is carried out in a real-life setting, so behaviour is likely to be lifelike. However, in a real-life environment it gets harder to control conditions. This is unlikely to be a problem in this study because all participants used the same machine in the same arcade.

Reliability
Remember that reliability means consistency. A procedure is reliable if it can be precisely replicated and if it consistently gives the same results when it is replicated. Reliability can be hard to achieve in real-life settings, where it is hard to make sure every participant has the same experience. However, this study was very well controlled for a field experiment because each participant went to the same arcade alone, and played on the same machine. Reliability was therefore good.

Ecological validity
Ecological validity refers to how lifelike a procedure is. There are two aspects to this: how realistic the environment is, and how realistic the tasks given to participants are. In this study, both aspects of ecological validity are very strong: the experiment was conducted in a real amusement arcade, so this was very lifelike; and the task – to play on a fruit machine – was also very realistic. The thinking-aloud condition was much less lifelike, but this was necessary to get an idea of differences in the cognition of regular gamblers and non-regular gamblers.

Quantitative and qualitative data
This study made very good use of both types of data. Generally, when we want to compare two groups, numbers can be useful. In this case, quantitative data was used to make judgements about the skill levels of regular and non-regular gamblers. Having numbers for such things as the amount of time spent playing, or the number of plays, allows us to be objective about the differences in skill levels. However, qualitative data comes into its own when we want to achieve a deeper understanding of what people are thinking. In this case, qualitative data was gained from the interviews, and this was very useful for understanding how regular and non-regular gamblers tended to think about the role of luck and skill in gambling.

Practical applications
One finding of this study is that gamblers are wrong to believe that there is a skill to fruit-machine gambling. This is useful information for professional gamblers who gamble to make money rather than for entertainment. Based on this study, we might advise professional gamblers to avoid fruit machines and focus their attention on some other form of gambling if they are looking to make money. This study also has implications for the treatment of gambling addicts. Regular gamblers showed evidence of unusual cognitions and incorrect beliefs. Cognitive therapies work by challenging and altering irrational beliefs and perceptions, so this study suggests that cognitive therapies might be very useful for treating problems relating to gambling.

EXAM FOCUS

We now show you some of the sorts of questions that could be asked about the Griffiths study in your exam. We will then show you some examples of the sorts of answers we believe might be successful and less successful, and point out some classic traps to avoid.

SECTION A

1 The study by Griffiths investigated cognitive bias and skill in fruit-machine gambling
   (a) Identify two pieces of quantitative data gathered in this study. *(2 marks)*
   (b) Outline one advantage of quantitative data used in this study. *(2 marks)*

2 Explain how Griffiths used the quasi-experimental method in his study into fruit-machine gambling. *(4 marks)*

3 In the study by Griffiths, each participant was given £3 to gamble on a fruit machine.
   (a) Describe the gambling task each participant was then set. *(2 marks)*
   (b) Explain why all participants were asked to use the same fruit machine. *(2 marks)*

4 From Griffiths' study on fruit-machine gambling:
   (a) Outline one way in which the sample may be considered representative. *(2 marks)*
   (b) Outline one way in which the sample may be considered unrepresentative. *(2 marks)*

5 The study by Griffiths on fruit-machine gambling had four hypotheses.
   (a) State one of the four hypotheses. *(2 marks)*
   (b) Explain how the results of this study support one of its hypotheses. *(2 marks)*

6 From Griffiths' study into fruit-machine gambling:
   (a) Describe one similarity between the results of regular and non-regular gamblers. *(2 marks)*
   (b) Describe one difference between the results of regular and non-regular gamblers. *(2 marks)*

7 In Griffiths' study on fruit-machine gambling, verbalisations from the thinking-loud group were analysed with a content analysis.
   (a) Give one result from this content analysis. *(2 marks)*
   (b) Outline one reason why this may not be considered to be a reliable method in this study. *(2 marks)*

8 In Griffiths' study on fruit-machine gambling, the content analysis of the results showed some irrational and some rational verbalisations.
   (a) Explain what is meant by an irrational verbalisation. *(2 marks)*
   (b) Give one example of an irrational verbalisation from the study. *(2 marks)*

SECTION B

(a) What was the aim of Griffiths' study? *(2 marks)*
(b) Describe how the sample in Griffiths' study was selected and suggest one advantage of using this sample. *(6 marks)*
(c) Explain why Griffiths' study can be considered a natural experiment. *(6 marks)*
(d) Give one advantage and one disadvantage of conducting a natural experiment in Griffiths' study. *(6 marks)*
(e) Give two suggestions as to how Griffiths' study can be improved. *(8 marks)*
(f) Outline the implications of the improvements you have suggested for Griffiths' study. *(8 marks)*

SECTION C

(a) Outline one assumption of the individual differences approach. *(2 marks)*
(b) Describe how the individual differences approach could explain the addictive behaviour of gambling. *(4 marks)*
(c) Describe one similarity and one difference between any studies that take the individual differences approach. *(6 marks)*
(d) Discuss strengths and weaknesses of the individual differences approach using examples from any studies that take this approach. *(12 marks)*

SOME ANSWERS AND COMMENTS

SECTION A 2 Explain how Griffiths used the quasi-experimental method in his study into fruit-machine gambling. (4 marks)

Sophie's answer: The arcade existed in real life so it is naturally occurring. This means it is good.

> **We say:** 0 marks.
> A bit of confusion here Sophie – the point about a quasi-experiment is that the groups of participants who are selected are naturally occurring, rather than where it is carried out as that is really ecological validity. Check your knowledge of key terms for methodology. The participants here were gamblers or non-gamblers already, so Griffiths used this as the basis for his quasi-experiment.

Louis' answer:

The experiment used people who were already regular gamblers on fruit machines or not in their real lives, and so naturally fitted into two groups to make a good comparison. Everyone who was there wasn't forced there so the groups weren't manipulated and thus the IV is naturally there in your experiment already and you just measure the DV.

> **We say:** 2 marks.
> Well explained here Louis. You have pointed out how groups naturally occur and what these groups are. Your last sentence gives some detail and expands well to answer clearly and concisely.

SECTION A 4 From Griffiths' study on fruit-machine gambling: (a) Outline one way in which the sample may be considered representative. (2 marks)

Leela's answer: There were non-gamblers and gamblers who had different levels of gambling.

> **We say:** 0 marks.
> Leela, your answer is just telling me who the two groups were in the study, i.e. what the IV is. You do not answer the question on how it may be representative. You need to look at the make-up of the sample and how many there were, and then decide how this is representative of the target population.

Anne's answer:

The sample looks poor as there were far more females in the group who gambled, but this is not a problem as gamblers doing fruit-machine gambling usually are men. This means it is accurate to what we find in real life so is representative overall.

> **We say:** 2 marks.
> A good answer here Anne. You have identified a relevant feature of the sample and outlined clearly how it is representative. Detailed knowledge of the study really does help answer the questions.

SECTION B (b) Describe how the sample in Griffiths' study was selected and suggest one advantage of using this sample. (6 marks)

Charlie's answer:

It was a self-selected sample as people chose to do it. There were some posters put up. This is good as it is really easy for the researcher to do, so Griffiths did not have to stand asking people.

Tasnia's answer:

Griffiths used a sample that was self-selected. Using some posters in a university and college, he asked for people to take part and they replied to him. He also got some more directly, as he knew a gambler who asked some other people if they might like to take part by contacting Griffiths. Self-selected can be good as a way to get a sample as you would get people who are really interested in what you are researching, so would be less likely to get bored or drop out.

We say: 2 marks.
Charlie, this is a very basic answer. You really do need to tell us a bit more about the study for the first part. There is not much specific detail from the study and you need to tell us how knowledgeable you are about it! Describe where the posters were and any other parts to the recruitment process. The advantage is too general and could apply to just about anything – focus on this study particularly.

We say: 5 marks.
You explain how the sample was selected really well, Tasnia. You name the actual sample type and explain exactly how this was carried out with detail from the study, showing knowledge and understanding. Your advantage was nicely explained, but you do need to explain this in the context of the study or it is just a general comment. Always remember do this!

SECTION C (d) Discuss strengths and weaknesses of the individual differences approach using examples from any studies that take this approach. (*12 marks*)

Pat's answer:

One strength of the approach is that it is not at all reductionist and allows us to take a more detailed approach at lots of reasons for behaviour. We can see how unique we all are.

Another good point is that is can be very useful and we can develop therapy and treatments from it to help others. This is because we can find out more detail and reasons for things as we look at each person and use this information.

A weakness is that it can sometimes use methods with quite small samples, like case studies, to get at the differences and so it may be not possible to generalise from the results. This is not very useful to us in understanding why we do things more generally.

Secondly a weakness is that if we point out how people are different and unique, people may notice this more and so become more prejudiced and discriminate against others. We use differences for the wrong things.

We say: 5 marks.
Pat, please do make sure you focus on all of the command terms in the question! Part of the key to doing well in this question was in the phrase 'using examples…', but you left out this part. Your points were appropriate to the approach and you did give some explanation of them. You have two strengths and two weaknesses so that's a nice balance, and clearly you understand and attempt to elaborate these points. However, the lack of really clear examples from the studies to illustrate these points lets you down. Always remember to illustrate a critical point with an example.

THE INDIVIDUAL DIFFERENCES APPROACH TO PSYCHOLOGY

We have explored in detail three important studies that follow the individual differences approach. Each core study has explored a unique aspect of the many ways in which human beings vary from one another. By considering these pieces of research we can outline some key assumptions behind this approach to psychology.

1   **Individuals differ in their personality, thinking and behaviour.** In many ways individual differences is a unique branch in psychology. Its key assumption is that the best way to understand the complexity of human behaviour and experiences is to focus on the differences between people. This is different from other approaches, which assume that we are all mostly the same, and that research should focus on studying universal aspects of human behaviour. Psychologists who adopt the individual differences approach are interested in a vast range of differences, including studying psychopathology, and theories of personality and intelligence. An example is Griffiths' study of the cognitive processes of regular and non-regular gamblers. Griffiths focused on collecting data that could directly compare the thought processes and behaviour of the two groups in relation to the gambling task. The approach also focuses on abnormality – those behaviours that are not observed in the majority of people. Rosenhan explores the idea of abnormality and how it is classified and diagnosed within psychiatry. His study mounts a challenge to our understanding of what is 'normal' and 'abnormal', by focusing on how different behaviours can stand out and attract fear, disgust or disapproval. The case study of Eve White, as described by Thigpen and Cleckley, is a good illustration of how the individual differences approach to psychology encompasses study of highly atypical behaviour, in the form of Multiple Personality Disorder.

2   **It is possible to measure and study individual differences.** All the studies we have considered from this approach have assumed that it is possible to form hypotheses about, measure, and collect data about the nature of individual differences in human behaviour. They also try to draw meaningful conclusions about aspects of behaviour that can vary from person to person. An area of the psychology of individual differences that continues to attract attention is research into intelligence. This is one of many factors that have traditionally been measured using standardised testing known as psychometrics. In their study of Eve White, Thigpen and Cleckley use a standardised Intelligence Quotient (IQ) test and scale to establish a disparity in intelligence between Eve White and Eve Black. It is assumed that intelligence is a quality that is unique to each person and can be quantified in a way that allows us to compare individuals, establishing a normal range of intelligence.

3   **We can understand human behaviour in terms of dispositional factors.** This refers to the idea that a person's behaviour could be explained by their personality or disposition, rather than it being a result of the situation that the person is in. The individual differences approach explores this in different ways. In Thigpen and Cleckley's case study, the occurrence of Multiple Personality Disorder in Eve was attributed to the fragmentation of her personality. It is a recognised dissociative disorder that is thought to occur as a result of the activity of one's defence mechanisms in response to trauma or abuse. This is a dispositional explanation, as it focuses on the character and temperament of an individual rather than on issues that might contribute to their diagnosis (for example, the influence of their gender or nationality on the likelihood of diagnosis). It could also be argued that Griffiths' study of gambling behaviour focuses on the particular

thinking patterns that regular gamblers exhibit, which lead to behavioural differences such as the increased number of irrational verbalisations. The researcher's explanation for these findings therefore focuses on a dispositional explanation, looking at individual cognition.

On the other hand, the study by Rosenhan highlights the weakness of this approach by showing how situational factors can cause us to misinterpret behaviour. In his study, the behaviour of the pseudopatients was wrongly thought to be a result of their mental illness, when it was actually a product of the hospital environment.

STRENGTHS AND WEAKNESSES OF THE INDIVIDUAL DIFFERENCES APPROACH
Strengths

1   **Research has practical applications.** All the studies in this chapter are highly relevant to improving our understanding of abnormal behaviour. Rosenhan's findings question the validity and reliability of psychiatric diagnosis, as well as raising concerns about the treatment received by patients in mental-health institutions. This has clear implications for the profession in terms of reviewing diagnostic processes and bringing to the forefront issues concerning patient experience. Griffiths' study of the cognitive processes of regular and non-regular gamblers provides a greater understanding of the faulty cognitions that underlie gambling behaviour. This can be applied to treatments for gambling addiction – for example, through cognitive therapies that effectively challenge dysfunctional thinking patterns. In this way, research from within the individual differences approach can be used to rehabilitate those with additive disorders.

2   **Different types of data used.** All the studies at in this chapter consider both quantitative and qualitative data. For example, Thigpen and Cleckley gathered extensive qualitative data on Eve's recollections and behaviour, which enabled them

to gain an in-depth insight into her unique case. They also gained quantitative data, including EEG recordings comparing the different brain activity exhibited by her separate identities. Measuring both types of data enables researchers to obtain comparable, measurable results, as well as explore the meaning of certain aspects of their enquiry.

Weaknesses

1   **Methodology is sometimes subjective.** Some techniques used in studies from this approach are not fully objective and might be open to bias. This is not to say that these techniques should not be used in psychology; in fact they might be the only methods available for studying some forms of individual difference. For example, Thigpen and Cleckley's data comes from extensive interviews with their patient. This might be the most appropriate way of investigating MPD and gaining insight into the lived experience of Eve White. However, it could be argued that they became too involved with Eve's case and might have lost their sense of objectivity. In Griffiths' study, some of the verbalisations made by gamblers might have been made in jest. However, they might have been interpreted as intended and irrational in line with the researcher's expectations.

2   **Ethical issues with the approach.** The three studies used to illustrate this approach have considerably different aims and methodologies. However, they all demonstrate ethical risks involved with labelling an individual as different or abnormal. Rosenhan acknowledges this issue in the findings of his research – indeed the pseudopatients assumed false identities partly in recognition of stigma that could result from their diagnosis. MPD sceptics suggest that Thigpen and Cleckley's diagnosis of Eve White with the condition was in part responsible for the emergence of further fragmentation of her identity. It seems possible that labelling individuals with mental health diagnoses can have a negative impact, and might in some cases lead to a self-fulfilling prophecy.

C6

PSYCHOLOGICAL INVESTIGATIONS

Part 1: Research methods

In this section we are going to explore the research methods that are used in psychological investigations – that is, the major techniques that psychologists use to explore behaviour, emotions and cognition. The major methods are the self-report, experiments, observations and correlations. We will look at each of these in detail.

A – THE SELF-REPORT

INTRODUCTION

In this section we will be looking at the way in which self-reports as a research method are used in psychology. Specifically, we will explore the use of rating and Likert scales, and two types of question – open and closed – in the collection of data in self-reports. We will also evaluate each of these techniques individually, and the method of self-reports overall.

THE SELF-REPORT

Self-report techniques are so called because the participant is reporting their own beliefs, thoughts or feelings to the researcher, rather than the researcher measuring aspects of the participant's behaviour (which reflect their thoughts or feelings). The methods include questionnaires and interviews. In both of these, the researcher presents the participant with questions. In a questionnaire, these are on paper (or on a computer) and the participant fills them in. In an interview, the questions are asked by the interviewer, usually face to face or by telephone. The methods share some basic question types, although there are some differences too.

 KEY IDEAS

Qualitative and quantitative data

Investigations using self-report can produce two types of data. Numerical data, or quantitative data, indicates the *quantity* of a psychological measure. Examples include time, or a numerical score on a personality test. These kinds of measures are associated with research methods, such as experiments and correlations. It is, however, possible to produce quantitative data from observations, questionnaires or interviews, for example by recording the number of times a behaviour is observed or by counting responses to closed questions. On page 293 we look in more detail at quantitative data and how they are analysed.

Qualitative data indicates the *quality* of a psychological characteristic, and comes from research that generates in-depth, descriptive findings. This is typical of observations in which particular behaviours are the focus of an observer's detailed account or questionnaires, interviews and case studies in which responses to open questions elicit elaborate reporting of feelings, beliefs or opinions. For example, rather than counting the number of times a behaviour occurs, behaviours may be described in detail.

 **KEY IDEAS**

Self-report methods are ways to obtain data by asking participants to provide information about themselves.

A **questionnaire** is a self-report method that uses written questions.

An **interview** is a self-report method in which participants reply verbally to questions asked by an interviewer.

Self-report can be a research method in itself, when the study consists solely of a questionnaire, for example. In other situations, self-report is used as a way to collect data. The latter approach is illustrated by the descriptions given by Little Hans to his father (Freud, 1909), by the recordings of dream content obtained by Dement and Kleitman, by much of the data collected by Thigpen and Cleckley, such as interviews of Eve and her family, and the responses to interview questions given by participants in Milgram's and Piliavin *et al.'s* studies.

ACTIVITY ✳

Devise rating scales to measure each of the following:
- How confident an eyewitness is that they saw a tattoo on a suspect's face
- The extent to which a bystander to an event feels obliged to help
- The likelihood that a participant believes that they would follow orders from someone
- The certainty with which an individual thinks they will win a particular game of poker.

RATING SCALES

A **rating scale** is a simple numerical scale on which a participant can indicate the extent or strength of some measure. They therefore generate quantitative data. Examples could include:
- indicating to what extent you agree with a statement by picking a number between 1 and 5
- identifying how likely you are to do something on a scale of 0–10
- stating your preference for something from a choice of 1, 2, 3 or 4.

To be valid, a rating scale should be able to discriminate between different responses. Participants' responses might tend to cluster in the middle so, to avoid this, the scale must offer a range of values (e.g. 11, as an odd number gives a middle score). If several rating scales are used, then there is a risk that participants might exhibit a response bias, tending towards one extreme or the other. Ideally, on some scales, the meaning of a high score should be reversed to reduce this (these are called positive and negative scales). However, in practice this can confuse participants and reduce the validity of the scale. When scales are used in this way, the numerical score must be reversed for the negative statements before analysis. The totals can then be added up to give a single score. Scales should also be reliable. To check this, a **pilot study** can be

QUESTION SPOTLIGHT! ⭑

Reicher and Haslam (2006) (see page 149) investigated organisational citizenship using a three-item scale:
- 'I am willing to do more than is asked of me by the guards.'
- 'I will do whatever I can to help the guards.'
- 'Whenever possible, I will try to make the guards' work difficult.'

The final item used reverse-scoring, which is often found in questionnaires using closed questions and rating scales.

Can you explain the purpose of having some items that are reverse scored?

done to test and retest the same participants to ensure that they do give the same answers. If there are scales that are unreliable (i.e. on which participants give different answers the second time), they should be amended or removed (see also page 291).

KEY IDEAS

A **pilot study** is a small-scale trial run of a method to identify any practical or ethical problems and resolve them.

TABLE 6.1 STRENGTHS AND WEAKNESSES OF RATING SCALES

Strengths	Weaknesses
• They are easy for participants to respond to, so large amounts of data can be collected quickly, making the data more reliable and, if a wide sample is found, more generalisible. • They produce quantitative data, which are easy to analyse, e.g. to find modes, medians and to use to plot graphs. • They can be tested for reliability (by test-retest or split-half techniques) and improved by changing or removing unreliable items.	• They produce only quantitative data, which lack detail, so participants cannot express opinions fully, lowering validity. • There is a risk of response biases, such as consistently giving answers in the middle of the scale or at one end. • The points on the scale are only relative (ordinal data), i.e. the gaps between the points are not equal. This means that the data should not be used to calculate a mean. • They cannot be used to measure complex variables that require more than a simple numerical response, such as attitudes.

LIKERT SCALES

We can elicit people's attitudes by asking them open questions, but their responses could be very varied, making them hard to compare. By using **Likert scales**, we can produce quantitative data that are much easier to analyse. A Likert scale begins with a statement and asks the participant to respond to the statement by saying how much they agree with it. For example, a statement might say 'I always throw a six when I need one' or 'I have a "good" day of the week for doing the Lottery'. The participant then chooses from 'strongly agree', 'agree', 'don't know', 'disagree' or 'strongly disagree' for each statement.

As with rating scales, it is important to prevent participants from developing a 'response set', such as always agreeing with the statement. To achieve this, about half of the statements should be 'reversed'. For example, when Likert scales are being used to measure attitudes to violent TV and aggressive behaviour, some should express a 'positive' opinion, such as 'I think an unnecessary fuss is made over the effect of violent TV', and others a 'negative' view, such as 'Violence on TV is to blame for the rise in crime'.

This ensures that similar, 'positive' or socially acceptable statements are neither always associated with agreement, nor always at the same side

KEY IDEAS

A numerical scale on which a participant indicates a choice by selecting one number, so providing quantitative data, is called a **rating scale**. Rating scales can be used to give a numerical answer to a question or to indicate the extent to which the participant agrees with a statement.

A **Likert scale** is a type of question that measures attitudes using a statement to which participants respond by choosing an option, typically from 'strongly agree', 'agree', 'don't know', 'disagree' or 'strongly disagree'.

of the page. The principle of reversing scales is applied to many other kinds of questions and helps to avoid bias in the way the participants respond.

Likert scales generate quantitative data because, although each participant's response is to a named category, the number of agreements and disagreements can be added up. Ultimately, this produces a single number for each participant for the attitude (or attitudes) tested. When the scales are scored, the responses are allocated numbers (from 1 to 5). For the negative scales, the scoring is reversed. So, in the examples above, responding 'strongly agree' to 'I think an unnecessary fuss is made over the effect of violent TV', would score 5. In contrast, for 'Violence on TV is to blame for the rise in crime', 'strongly agree' would score 1, whereas 'strongly disagree' would score 5.

TABLE 6.2 STRENGTHS AND WEAKNESSES OF LIKERT SCALES

Strengths	Weaknesses
• They are easy for participants to respond to, so large amounts of data can be collected quickly, making the data more reliable and, if a wide sample is found, more generalisible. • They produce quantitative data, which are easy to analyse, e.g. to find modes, medians and to use to plot graphs. • They can be tested for reliability (by test-retest) and improved by changing or removing unreliable items. • They allow the measurement of more complex attitudes than rating scales can.	• They produce only quantitative data, which lack detail, so participants cannot express opinions fully, thus lowering validity. • There is a risk of response biases, such as consistently giving answers in the middle of the scale or at one extreme end. • The points on the scale are only relative (ordinal data), i.e. the gaps between the points are not equal. This means that the data should not be used to calculate a mean. • The meaning of the middle value is ambiguous. It could indicate no opinion or undecided.

ACTIVITY ✳

Devise Likert scales to measure each of the following:
- The likelihood of helping someone in distress
- Attitudes towards regulations, such as mother-and-baby parking spaces
- A person's feelings towards their father.

QUESTION SPOTLIGHT!

Decide which of the following are rating scales, Likert scales or neither of these question types.

1   'I think all little boys are "mummy's boys".'
    strongly agree / agree / don't know / disagree / strongly disagree
2   On a scale of 1 to 7, how good are you at judging the speed of a vehicle? (1 = very good)
3   Describe your most recent dream.
4   Using the scale 1 to 5, rate how likely you would be to get lost when travelling to a place you have visited only once before.
5   Put a mark on this line to indicate how you are currently feeling:
    calm _____ tense
6   'Multiple personality disorder doesn't exist.'
    strongly disagree / disagree / don't know / agree / strongly agree
7   If you were a juror, would you trust evidence from an eyewitness?
    yes / no

OPEN AND CLOSED QUESTIONS

Both open and closed questions can be used in either questionnaires or interviews. A **closed question** gives the participant little choice and requires one of a small number of alternative answers. In a questionnaire these might be presented as words or numbers to circle, or as boxes to cross or tick (see Box 6.1, on page 220).

One advantage of using closed questions is that the results they generate are easy to analyse because they are simple numbers. For example, we could ask a group of mothers and fathers whether their children imitated specific behaviours, by using a yes/no format. This would allow us to say that x% of mothers and x% of fathers reported that children copied particular acts, such as cuddling a toy, playing with bricks or banging the computer mouse to make it work. Results that are numerical are called **quantitative data**.

An **open question** does not require a fixed response and gives the participant the chance to offer an extended answer (see Box 6.2). For example, an open question such as 'How does your autistic child express affection?' will supply much more information than ticking boxes about cuddling, play or talking would. Unlike the numbers produced by closed questions, the results generated by open questions are **qualitative**, that is, they are detailed and descriptive. This data is more difficult to analyse, the aim being to look for common themes across different participants' responses. For example, if the parents of normal and autistic children were

KEY IDEAS

Closed questions are questions that offer a small number of explicitly stated alternative responses and no opportunity to expand on answers. They generate quantitative data.

Open questions are questions that allow participants to give full and detailed answers in their own words, i.e. no categories or choices are given. They generate qualitative data.

KEY IDEAS

Numerical data collected as totals in named categories or on numerical scales is called **quantitative data** (see also levels of measurement, page 277). Descriptive data providing depth and detail is called **qualitative data**.

Box 6.1 Examples of closed questions

1 If you were trying to remember the details
   of a crime you had witnessed, would you: *Tick all that apply*

   a) write a list of the things that happened   ☐
   b) draw a map of where people and objects were   ☐
   c) repeat things over and over again   ☐
   d) tie a knot in your handkerchief?   ☐

2 Do you work in a legal or police-related occupation?

   Yes ☐   No ☐

3 Was the car involved in the accident: *Tick one*

   a) an estate   ☐
   b) a hatchback   ☐
   c) a sports car   ☐
   d) a people carrier   ☐
   e) none of the above?   ☐

Box 6.2 Examples of open questions

1 Thinking back to when you saw the accident, can you describe what other vehicles and people were around at the time?
2 Write an account of what you could hear at the time of the accident.
3 If you try to recall what happened immediately before the accident, what can you remember?

interviewed about how their children responded to play situations, different themes might emerge. For example, two opposing themes could suggest that the children predominantly played alone or with others. Another pair could suggest they played in imaginative ways or in predicable ways. Patterns emerging in the themes might show that there were differences in social or cognitive processing in the two groups.

Both qualitative and quantitative data can be collected using either questionnaires or interviews. In practice, researchers mainly use questionnaires to gather specific, quantitative information, and interviews to gather more in-depth, qualitative data.

QUESTION SPOTLIGHT!

Decide which of the following are open questions, closed questions or neither of these question types.

1 Which of the following do you think are important in affecting children's aggression: TV, the Internet, parents, teachers, friends, toys. (Circle all that apply)
2 Indicate how well you sleep normally on a scale of 1–11. (1 = well)
3 If you were a juror, would you trust evidence from an eyewitness? yes / no
4 Describe your most recent dream.

TABLE 6.3 STRENGTHS AND WEAKNESSES OF OPEN AND CLOSED QUESTIONS

	Strengths	Weaknesses
Open questions	• Open questions produce qualitative data, which provides detail, so participants can express opinions fully, raising validity. • Analysis retains detail of participants' answers, so information, such as variation in responses, is not 'lost' through averaging.	• They produce qualitative data, which are time consuming to analyse as themes need to be identified and extracted. • Interpretation of qualitative data can be subjective, leading to bias from individual researchers and potentially reducing inter-rater reliability. • Findings may be less generalisible.
Closed questions	• Closed questions are easy for participants to respond to, so large amounts of data can be collected quickly, making the data more reliable and, if a wide sample is found, more generalisible. • They produce quantitative data, which are easy to analyse, e.g. to find modes, medians and to plot graphs using data from many questions.	• They produce only quantitative data, which lack detail and meaning, so participants cannot express opinions fully, thus lowering validity. • There is a risk of response biases, such as consistently saying 'yes'. • The score for all participants on each question is only a total (nominal data), so the data can be used only to calculate a mode.

QUESTION SPOTLIGHT!

Figure 6.1

In Freud (1909) (see page 71), Hans's father asked both open and closed questions. The conversations reported by Freud included the following examples of open questions:

Open questions:
- 'Why did you come into our room?'
- 'What can it mean: a crumpled giraffe?'
- 'What did you do with the crumpled one?'
- 'Why did the crumpled one call out?'

Ensure that you can identify examples of open and closed questions from each relevant study.

QUESTIONNAIRES

In a questionnaire the questions are generally strictly ordered, so it is 'structured'. It is possible, especially using computers, to tailor questions to individual participants (e.g. when a questionnaire says 'Leave out this section if...'). However, in general, questionnaires are necessarily more structured than interviews.

A greater variety of closed questions can be used in a questionnaire than in an interview because it is possible to offer a variety of choices for responses in written form, including closed questions and rating scales as well as open questions..

QUESTION SPOTLIGHT!

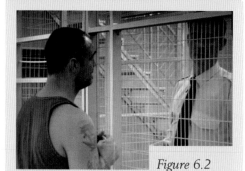

Figure 6.2

Reicher and Haslam (2006) (see page 149) investigated depression in the prisoners using a seven-item scale. The questions were:

- 'In general, how has your mood been over the last few days?'
- 'Do you ever feel low or depressed?'
- 'Do you feel hopeless about the future?'
- 'Do you have difficulty dealing with everyday problems?'
- 'Are you self-confident?'
- 'Do you think that you are a worthwhile person?'
- 'Do you think about harming yourself?'

Are these open or closed questions?

Questionnaires often end with an invitation that reads: 'Please tell us anything else you would like to about this topic'. This is an open question, allowing the researchers to collect some qualitative data. However, this is likely to be much less effective than qualitative research conducted through interviewing, as, in the absence of prompts from the interviewer, the participant might give very little information.

Finally, some questionnaires contain 'filler' and 'lie detector' questions. Fillers are questions that will not be used in the analysis. They are there simply to disguise the true purpose of the questionnaire, reducing demand characteristics. Lie detector questions are included to try to identify participants whose responses reflect a social desirability bias. For example, a questionnaire about drug use in teenagers included a closed question asking which drugs the individual had taken from a list of 11, one of which was made up. Results from participants who said 'yes' to the fictitious drug were ignored, as it was likely that they were lying about their drug use in general.

INTERVIEWS

The interview as a research method uses questions spoken by an interviewer to a participant. These questions might be **structured**, but can be much less so than a questionnaire. In an **unstructured** interview (or a **semi-structured** one) new questions can be incorporated in response to the participant's answers, which cannot be done in a questionnaire. This makes interviews particularly useful for gaining in-depth information about individuals and for new topics of investigation.

One advantage of an unstructured interview is that if new themes arise they can be thoroughly explored, whereas a questionnaire would

QUESTION SPOTLIGHT!

Reicher and Haslam (2006) (see page 149) investigated compliance using a two-item scale:

- 'I try to do what the guards want.'
- 'I try to comply with the guards' rules.'

Whether studies produce qualitative or quantitative data, it is important to be able to simplify and summarise the findings in order to draw conclusions. Responses on this test were averaged.

Is this simplification of results used when the data are qualitative or quantitative?

be unable to delve further. For example, in a questionnaire or structured interview about the behaviour of an adult with autism, relatives could be asked 'Does the individual display any evidence of failing to understand emotions?', followed by another saying 'If yes, indicate which of the following', with a list including items such as 'turning away at a key point in the conversation'. Here, the possible answers are limited, whereas an unstructured interview could pursue lines such as when the adult responds or fails to respond, what they do exactly, how other people react, etc. This would give a much fuller picture of the social interaction.

Structured interviews are the kinds of interviews you might have encountered outside supermarkets or in town centres. Everyone is treated in the same way, and numerical data are generated. In semi-structured and unstructured interviews, more open questions are used, generating detailed, descriptive responses, i.e. qualitative data. These are the type of interview that a patient has with a doctor, which might begin with 'How are you feeling?' The questions that follow depend on the symptoms the patient describes. The quantitative data produced by questionnaires and structured interviews is relatively easy to analyse because it is numerical. In contrast, the findings of unstructured interviews contain a great deal of information in the form of continuous speech. This has to be analysed by identifying themes, i.e. ideas within the respondent's comments that can be classified or interpreted, so are more difficult to analyse and are open to investigator bias as the responses might need interpreting.

 **KEY IDEAS**

A **structured interview** asks predominantly closed questions in a fixed order. The questions are likely to be scripted so they are standardised, and consistency might even be required for the interviewer's posture, etc.

A **semi-structured interview** uses a fixed list of open and closed questions, although the interviewer can introduce additional questions if required.

An **unstructured interview** generally begins with a standard question for all participants but from there on, questions depend on the respondent's answers. There might be a list of topics for the interviewer to cover.

QUESTION SPOTLIGHT!

Griffiths (1994) (see page 202) investigated cognition in gamblers. Participants in the 'thinking aloud' condition were given instructions to verbalise every thought they had while playing on the fruit machines. They were told the following important points:

1 Say everything that goes through your mind. Do not censor any of your thoughts even if they seem irrelevant to you.

2 Keep talking as continuously as possible, even if your ideas are not clearly structured.

3 Speak clearly.

4 Do not hesitate to use fragmented sentences if necessary. Do not worry about speaking in complete sentences.

5 Do not try to justify your thoughts.

These instructions will clearly produce very rich, qualitative data. As with many of the self-report tools used by other researchers (such as Reicher and Haslam, see above), these questions originated from another source (Ladouceur *et al.*, 1998).

Suggest one advantage and one disadvantage of using self-report tools that have previously been used by other researchers.

Griffiths notes that all the verbalisations made during each participant's gambling session were transcribed within 24 hours, to ensure that he could remember the context in which they were made.

Why is it important that the researcher could recall the context of the verbalisations?

Figure 6.3

Figure 6.4
Interviews tend to be more flexible than questionnaires as they can be unstructured

There are some potential problems with interviews as a research method. People might be less likely to be honest in an interview than in answering a questionnaire. Imagine how a respondent in a questionnaire study, compared to one in an interview study, might feel towards questions about punishing their child. There is likely to be a greater effect of social desirability when the respondent is face-to-face with the investigator. Conversely, participants in questionnaire studies might develop a different sort of response bias – one in which they tend always to give the same kind of answer (see page 216). Have you ever done a quiz in a magazine that asks you questions with answers 'a', 'b' or 'c'? After a few responses you might have decided which 'type' you are, which will colour the way you answer the remaining items.

Participating in a questionnaire or interview study requires time and effort from participants, and a willingness to divulge things about themselves. People can be reluctant to participate, especially if questions might invade privacy or be stressful: think about participants being asked about losing a parent, a severe addiction or about crime. This means that the people who do volunteer are probably not representative of the whole population. In a questionnaire study, participants also have to return the completed questionnaire. Even when given a postage-paid envelope, many potential participants do not return them. This adds a further bias to the sample.

ASSESSING RELIABILITY AND VALIDITY IN SELF-REPORTS

Reliability

Psychologists need to measure variables consistently. This is called **reliability**. If you are a reliable student, you regularly turn up to lessons or hand in your homework. Like a reliable student, a reliable psychological test or measure is also consistent: it will always produce the same results in the same situation. Reliability is used to assess both experimental procedures and 'tools' such as tests, interviews and behavioural categories in observations.

In self-reports we are concerned about the consistency of both the measure (i.e. the questions) and the researchers. With regard to the measure, in a reliable self-report the same person would give the same responses to the same questions each time. This can be assessed in two ways, by 'test-retest' and by 'split-half'. A test-retest assessment shows that the same participants will respond to the same test twice in a similar way. A split-half assessment shows that items within the self-report tool are measuring the same phenomenon. For example, a questionnaire testing extraversion might contain 20 questions. If scores from the first half of these are correlated with the scores from the second half, the measure has good reliability (see pages 243–7 for an explanation of correlations).

To maintain high reliability, researchers must interview in standardised ways and interpret the responses to open questions in consistent ways – this is **inter-rater reliability**. It is checked by each researcher assessing the same self-reports (e.g. producing a numerical score from each interview transcript) and then correlating their ratings. If there is a strong positive correlation, the researchers are reliable. Such correlational techniques can be used to identify specific items that that do not produce consistent responses. These unreliable items can then be removed, improving the overall reliability of the measure.

 **KEY IDEAS**

Test-retest is a measure of reliability that uses the same test twice. If the participants' two sets of scores correlate well, the measure has good reliability.

Split-half is a measure of reliability that compares two halves of a test, e.g. odd- and even-numbered questions. If the participants' scores on the two halves correlate well, the measure has good reliability.

Correlation coefficient is a measure of the strength of a correlation, usually expressed as an 'r' value between 0 and 1. A high value, e.g. $r=0.8$, means that there is a strong correlation, and $r=0$ means there is no correlation. This is often used to indicate reliability, so a higher value suggests better reliability.

Reliability is the consistency of a measure, e.g. whether results from the same participants would be similar each time.

Validity is the extent to which a test or tool measures what it claims to measure.

Inter-rater reliability is the extent to which two researchers will interpret and therefore score the same responses in the same way.

QUESTION SPOTLIGHT! ⭐

*Which is face validity and which
is concurrent validity?*

- An interview about addiction to
  gambling genuinely measures
  betting and risk-taking behaviours
  in the context of slot machines or
  card games, rather than eliciting
  socially desirable responses.
- Clinicians working with patients
  who have mental-health disorders
  use a range of standardised
  diagnostic self-report tools that
  make the same diagnoses.

Validity

To be valid, a questionnaire or interview must be reliable, but other factors affect the validity of self-reports too. **Validity** is the extent to which a technique is capable of achieving the intended purpose: if a questionnaire measures the aspect of beliefs or behaviours it is supposed to, it is valid. If a score in an experiment task is a valid indicator of the DV, it measures the variable under scrutiny rather than varying because of demand characteristics, fatigue or the effect of the experimenter.

Internal validity refers to the test being used, e.g. whether changes in the DV are caused by the IV rather than sources of error. This includes **face validity** (whether a measure appears, at face value, to test what it claims to) and **concurrent validity** (whether a measure will produce a similar score for a particular individual as another test that claims to assess the same phenomenon). This can be assessed by comparing the results to a measure known to be effective. **External validity** relates to issues beyond the investigation, such as ecological validity (see page 260).

TABLE 6.4 STRENGTHS AND WEAKNESSES OF SELF-REPORT TECHNIQUES

	Strengths	Weaknesses
Questionnaires	• They are relatively easy to administer and can be sent or emailed to participants, making them time- and cost-efficient. • Respondents might be more truthful than in an interview, especially if their answers are personal or socially sensitive. • Data is relatively easy to analyse as it is quantitative.	• Response biases – such as tending always to answer 'no', or always ticking the box on the left – can lead to invalid results. • They are limited because, unlike unstructured interviews, there is no flexibility to allow for the collection of useful but unexpected data, as new questions cannot be added.
Interviews	• Structured interview data is relatively easy to analyse as it is quantitative. • Semi-structured or unstructured interviews enable the researcher to gain specific and detailed information from the respondent that could be missed in structured techniques. • Face-to-face, an interviewer can respond more flexibly to gain useful, detailed information when this is difficult to obtain.	• Structured interviews are limited by fixed questions. • Investigator bias can be a problem, as the expectations of the interviewer can either alter the way in which they ask questions, thus unconsciously affecting the respondents' answers, or affect they way in which responses are interpreted.
Both questionnaires and interviews	• Generate quantitative or qualitative data. • Structured questionnaires and interviews can be easily repeated to generate more data or check findings. • Structured questionnaires and interviews can be readily assessed for reliability and improved by removing inconsistent items.	• Participants can be affected by biases such as social desirability, and might be influenced by leading questions. • As only some people are willing to fill in questionnaires or be interviewed, the participants might not be representative of the majority of the population.

EXAM FOCUS

We now show you some of the sorts of questions that could be asked about the self-report research method in your exam. We will then show you some examples of the sorts of answers we believe might be successful and less successful, and point out some classic traps to avoid.

QUESTION 1

A study investigating factors influencing inter-personal attraction was conducted by psychologists using the self-report method. This involved asking people questions about how important age, appearance, personality, occupation and money were when forming romantic relationships. People were approached in a local shopping centre one weekday morning and asked if they would take a questionnaire home to complete, and return it using a pre-paid envelope.

(a) Identify two ethical issues in this study. *(4 marks)*

(b) Suggest how one of these ethical issues could be addressed. *(3 marks)*

(c) Evaluate the reliability and validity of this research. *(10 marks)*

(d) Name and describe an alternative sampling method for this study. *(3 marks)*

QUESTION 2

A researcher is interested in studying stress associated with driving. She wishes to conduct an investigation to assess stress levels of motorists in England using the self-report method.

(a) Identify one strength and one weakness of using the self-report method in this study. *(4 marks)*

(b) Describe and evaluate an appropriate sampling technique for this study. *(10 marks)*

(c) Suggest an appropriate question using a rating scale that the researcher could use in this study. *(2 marks)*

(d) Evaluate the validity of using this question in this study. *(4 marks)*

QUESTION 3

Researchers conducted an investigation about dreaming using a self-report. Some examples of what participants were asked are presented below.

> *On average, how many dreams do you remember having each week?*
> *Briefly describe the best dream you have ever had.*

> *Do you appear in your own dreams?*
> *Never / Sometimes / Always*

(a) Identify one open and one closed question from this investigation. *(2 marks)*

(b) Outline one strength and one weakness of the closed question you have identified. *(6 marks)*

(c) What is qualitative data? *(2 marks)*

(d) Identify how qualitative data would be obtained from one of the questions used in the investigation. *(3 marks)*

(e) The table below shows the results from ten participants (five males and five females aged 16 to 25) when asked the question about the number of dreams they remember each week.
Outline two findings from the data in this table. *(4 marks)*

Participants	The number of dreams that people remember having each week.
1	1
2	3
3	2
4	3
5	1
6	12
7	2
8	2
9	3
10	2

(f) Evaluate the sample used to obtain the data presented in this table. *(3 marks)*

SOME ANSWERS AND COMMENTS

QUESTION 3 (a) Identify one open and one closed question from this investigation. *(2 marks)*

Jo's answer:

An open question is 'briefly describe the best dream you have ever had' and a closed is 'On average, how many dreams do you remember having each week?'

We say: 1 mark.
The open question is correct Jo, but the closed one isn't. A closed question needs to show the categories that you can choose the answer from. Although you choice of closed question looks like you can give only a number, there are no categories, and so people could actually say whatever they want to here.

Matt's answer:

The closed question is 'Do you appear in your own dreams? Never / Sometimes / Always' and the open one is 'On average, how many dreams do you remember having each week?'

We say: 2 marks.
Well chosen, Matt, these are both correct, with the closed question having set categories for you to choose one, and the open question allowing for any response the participant wants to give.

QUESTION 3 (b) Outline one strength and one weakness of the closed question you have identified. *(6 marks)*

Terri's answer:

My closed question is good because there are not many responses to choose from, so it is easy to do. It is bad because we do not get a lot of information about the person answering as they just tick their choice and don't say anything else at all.

We say: 3 marks.
Your answer is really too brief and lacks detail and explanation, Terri. To get more marks here, you should have a really clear statement and explanation of the strength you are using and you must put in it context. This means relating it to the investigation on dreaming – so you could include the question or say it is from the self-report investigation into dreaming. The weakness is nicely explained but, again, it lacks context and could be about any question in any investigation – and you are being asked about the investigation on dreaming!

Theo's answer:

Closed questions have strength as they are easy to analyse as you can count up the number of people who chose each response and so you would get quantitative data to analyse.
The weakness is that you do not get any idea of the reasons that the person chose that answer as it is just one category they pick with no chance to give any explanations or detail.
In the closed question on appearing in your own dreams they can say Never / Sometimes / Always, but we don't know anything else, like what they are doing in the dreams, or are they with other people. This doesn't give us much detail.

We say: 5 marks.
Overall, you have some good explanation and psychological knowledge here, Theo. Your strength is well set out and you show us that you understand it. You did not put it in the context of the specific investigation in the question, so cannot get full credit here. Do not forget to include the context. The weakness was really clearly outlined and expanded on, with a detailed example from the context of the study. Good work.

QUESTION 3 (c) What is qualitative data? *(2 marks)*

Ed's answer:

It is words, not numbers and has description of things.

Becki's answer:

This is data where a person expresses their own thoughts and feelings to a researcher so they gain more understanding. It is detailed and has a description of their thoughts.

We say: 1 mark.
Ed, this is basically correct as it is true that qualitative data is description. However, to get the two marks, tell us what it is a description of – 'things' is just too vague. You need to explain it is people's own thoughts and feelings to get both marks.

We say: 2 marks.
Your answer had the key points here Becki, and captures the idea that it is rich data from your participants. Well done.

QUESTION 3 (d) Identify how qualitative data would be obtained from one of the questions used in the investigation. *(3 marks)*

Brian's answer:

When they answer the question on briefly describing the best dream you have ever had.

Farhana's answer:

Asking participants to describe the best dream they have ever had is qualitative data because people can say whatever they want to. They have to put in detail and personal information to describe clearly what their dream was about. The researcher could get the answers from lots of people, and their dreams will not be the same so that they would have a huge range of material describing different dreams. They can analyse this to look at what people dream about.

We say: 1 mark.
Brian, you seem to have partly misread the question. The question you have picked out would indeed give qualitative data – but that it not all that is required for this three-mark answer. You need to explain how exactly we get the data from this, i.e. explain that people will describe dreams in their own way so we get insight from this written detailed information they provide. That will fully address the requirements of the question.

We say: 3 marks.
A detailed answer, Farhana, which shows that you understand types of data. You clearly identify an appropriate question and then go on to say very clearly how responses to this will allow the researcher to get the qualitative data they want. Nice work!

QUESTION 3 (e) Outline two findings from the data in this table. *(4 marks)*

Polly's answer:

The highest score anyone got was 12. The mode of the scores was just 2, which is quite low.

Niall's answer:

The range was from 1–12, which is 11 for the dreams that people reported in one week.

There was nobody who said that they had no dreams at all in the week, as there were no scores of zero in the table.

We say: 2 marks.
Polly, you have done some good analysis of the data in the table and have identified two correct findings. The problem with your answer is that nowhere does it refer to the fact that these figures are the number of dreams people have! You need to clearly relate the findings you pick out to the context of the source – which is number of dreams per week. So you should say 'the highest number of dreams anyone recorded was 12', rather than just that the highest score was 12. You have lost marks by being too general.

We say: 4 marks.
Niall, you have clearly identified two findings from the table which are correct. There is also a nice link to the context of the question – i.e. dreams per week – so full marks. You do not have to write really long answers if you focus on the question, give a clear explanation and relevant links or context back to the source.

QUESTION 3 (f) Evaluate the sample used to obtain the data presented in this table. *(3 marks)*

Dave's answer:

There were only 10 people as there was just data from 10 people's number of dreams in the table. This is really small and not very good.

Brenda's answer:

If it is a weekday morning in a shopping centre when you ask people to be in the study on dreaming, then it is quite a limited sample of people. Many people would be at work or at college, so the sample is quite specific and might have more retired people or mothers with little children and it is difficult to say that it is representative of everyone in the population, as not everyone would be out shopping then.

We say: 2 marks.
Dave, you have the basis of a good point here – there were just ten people – but you need to expand your point to say that it might not be representative or that it would be hard to generalise from. A small sample could be good in some situations, so, as you have identified a small sample as a weakness, just go on to show more understanding and say why that is bad by expanding on it.

We say: 3 marks.
Well thought-out here, Brenda. You have identified a relevant weakness and explained in some detail. We like the clear link to the context of the study, as you mention dreaming and how they selected people in the shopping centre. You have covered everything you need to get the points.

B – THE OBSERVATIONAL METHOD

INTRODUCTION

In this section we will be looking at the way in which the research method of observations is used in psychology. Specifically, we will look at participant observations, structured observations, and time versus event sampling. We will also evaluate each of these techniques and the observational method overall.

 **KEY IDEAS**

The **observational method** is used when watching participants (human or animal) directly in order to obtain data and gather information about their behaviour.

THE OBSERVATIONAL METHOD

Observation can be a research method in itself, when the study consists solely of a means to collect data by watching participants and recording their behaviour directly to provide data. Alternatively, observation can be used as a technique to collect data about variables within other research methods. For example, observations might be used to measure the dependent variable in an experiment. In this situation, the data collected would be quantitative, although qualitative data can also be collected if appropriate.

QUESTION SPOTLIGHT!

Bandura *et al*. (1961) studied aggression in children (see page 61). *Suggest two behavioural categories that could be used to make observations of a child's aggressive behaviour towards a toy.*

ACTIVITY

Find an animal to watch, such as a pet cat or dog, or a bird or squirrel out of the window. Try to record everything it does, in sequence. What problems did you have?

Possibly, you found that:

- Behaviours happen too fast for you to keep track of them.
- It is hard to break the stream of behaviour into discrete events.
- Even when discrete behaviours can be identified, they may overlap.
- You were tempted to record states (which can only be inferred, not actually observed) in addition to behaviours (which can be seen).
- Your presence altered the behaviour of the animal.

Observational techniques attempt to overcome problems such as these.

Figure 6.5
Observations can be used with animals as well as humans

KEY IDEAS

Participant observation is a way of collecting data such that the participants' behaviour is recorded by a researcher who is engaged with them as part of the social setting.

Overt observation (or disclosed observation) is research in which the role of the observer is known to participants.

Covert observation (or non-disclosed observation) is research in which participants are unaware that they are being watched.

Figure 6.6
The dangers of participant observation

QUESTION SPOTLIGHT!

In Bandura *et al.*'s study (see page 61), behaviours were observed through a one-way screen.

Is this participant or non-participant observation?

Observations were the main way in which data was collected in several of the core studies. For example, observations were used to monitor the chimps' language development in Savage-Rumbaugh *et al.*'s study. They were also used to measure the DV in Bandura *et al.*'s experiment on aggression, and in Piliavin *et al.*'s study of helping behaviour. In Dement and Kleitman's study of dreaming, the recordings of eye movements were observations, and in Milgram's study, observational records were kept of participants' behaviour in addition to the measure of obedience.

Initially, recordings in an observational study tend to be non-focused, that is, the observer looks at the range of possible behaviours to investigate. Subsequently, in **structured observations**, this is narrowed to a smaller set of clearly defined behaviours. The **behavioural categories** must be observable rather than inferred, internal states. For example, behaviours such as smiling or laughing can be observed, but 'being happy' cannot. This might seem to be a disadvantage of observations, but it can also be seen as a strength – helping to make data recording objective.

PARTICIPANT OBSERVATIONS

The role of the observer in the social setting might be either participant or non-participant. A **participant observer** is part of the social setting, for example, a researcher investigating social roles in a simulated prison who is both an observer and a prisoner. Alternatively, a non-participant observer is not involved in the situation being observed, for example, a researcher entering a simulated prison situation daily to record the behaviour of prisoners and guards.

In some respects, Savage-Rumbaugh *et al.*'s work included conducting participant observation, as the researchers played with the chimps and communicated with them in order to find out about their language and understanding. This was a participant observation because the researchers were involved with the participants in the activities being observed.

In addition, an observer may be either **overt** or **covert**. Often a participant observer is overt, for example, when the researcher is holding a clipboard. Alternatively, they might be covert, for example, if they are disguised as a member of the social group (such as the observer acting as a prisoner described in the example above), or if they are physically hidden (e.g. when using CCTV). As a consequence, the participants would not know that they were being watched. This increases validity as it is unlikely that participants would be affected by demand characteristics or social desirability. However, it raises practical issues, as the observer must be either

TABLE 6.5 STRENGTHS AND WEAKNESSES PARTICIPANT OBSERVATIONS

Strengths	Weaknesses
• Being involved in the social group can give the observer insight into the real participants' emotions and motives. • If the participants are unaware of the observer's dual role they might behave more normally than they would otherwise, thus increasing validity. • If the participants are unaware of the observer's dual role, they might reveal more than they would otherwise.	• It is difficult to record observations accurately when also engaged in the social activities of the group. • Being involved in the social group can make the observer subjective. • If a participant observer has to be hidden, this raises practical and ethical issues, as the participants cannot give informed consent.

hidden, far away or disguised in their role. Covert participant observation also presents ethical problems as the participants cannot give informed consent, and if they work out the observer's role this can cause distress.

Participant observations are harder to conduct than non-participant ones as the observer cannot concentrate exclusively on recording behaviours – they must engage in social behaviour as well. They might also find it difficult to focus on one individual or behaviour and actually record behaviours, as they might draw attention to their role as an observer. It is also harder for the observer to remain objective if they are participating – that is, they risk becoming biased as they develop a personal viewpoint. However, their involvement can also be a benefit: by engaging in the social situation, they might be able to gain greater insight into the participants' feelings and motives than a non-participant observer could.

STRUCTURED OBSERVATIONS

The environment in which observations take place can be natural, such as in a familiar work environment, or contrived, such as in a university laboratory. Savage Rumbaugh *et al.*'s observations of chimpanzees (see page 24) were mainly set in what had become their normal environment but also in test settings. In either situation, observations may be structured, i.e. restricted to pre-decided and defined behavioural categories. These behavioural categories must be operationalised, i.e. clearly defined. For example, Bandura *et al.* (see page 61) studied aggression in children by exposing them to a fixed sequence of behaviours performed by an adult model. They then gave the children toys, such as a large inflatable 'Bobo doll', a mallet and a dart gun, and recorded specific aggressive behaviours. Their behavioural categories included:

- striking the Bobo doll with the mallet
- sitting on the doll and punching it in the nose
- kicking the doll

ACTIVITY ✳

Figure 6.7
Observations can be used with animals as well as humans

Imagine the following studies. Would each be a participant or a non-participant observation?

1 A study of eyewitness testimony in which the researcher interviews witnesses to real crimes.

2 An investigation into navigation in an unknown environment in which a researcher who is part of a rambling group goes out for a walk with them and records the group's decision-making processes as they find their way.

STRETCH & CHALLENGE ◎

For each study that is not a structured observation, describe how it could be changed so that it is structured.

QUESTION SPOTLIGHT! ☆

Suggest two other behavioural categories that could have been used by Bandura et al. to collect data about aggressive behaviour towards the Bobo doll.

QUESTION SPOTLIGHT! ☆

Photographs and videos of behaviour can be analysed after the event. This is useful as analyses can be revisited and shared between observers.
Suggest one other advantage and one disadvantage of using a camera compared to simply watching.

- tossing the doll in the air
- repeating the phrases: 'Sock him', 'Hit him down', 'Kick him', 'Throw him in the air', or 'Pow'
- striking, slapping or pushing the doll aggressively
- shooting darts with the gun
- aiming the gun and firing imaginary shots.

The way in which data is recorded within these behavioural categories is also important. Techniques can include photographs, video, audio recordings (of spoken descriptions), hand-written notes or direct records inputted into a computer. Hand-written and computerised data collection can take the form of descriptions, ratings or codings (checklists).

If there is more than one observer they should record the same information when observing the same events. To achieve this, they are trained in the use of the behavioural categories. They practise the data-gathering techniques by simultaneous observation or repeated use of recorded video sequences, as well as by discussion of the definitions, so that they achieve a high level of agreement before the collection of data for the study begins. This serves to improve the data collected by raising inter-rater reliability.

TABLE 6.6 STRENGTHS AND WEAKNESSES OF STRUCTURED OBSERVATION

Strengths	Weaknesses
• Operational definitions can be developed in a pilot study before data collection begins to be certain that they include all the key actions. This improves validity. • Operationally defined behavioural categories agreed between observers are likely to be reliable. • Practising the use of data-collection techniques further improves inter-rater reliability. • Photographic and video data collection allows re-analysis of data, which improves validity as rapidly occurring behaviours are less likely to be missed.	• Simple definitions of behaviour may not convey sufficient meaning, e.g. 'lifting a hand' could be a friendly wave or an intimidating threat. This lowers validity. • Total numbers of behaviours within a category may be relatively meaningless without the context in which they occurred. This lowers validity. • Having predetermined behavioural categories may be limiting if new behaviours become apparent during the study. • Hand-written notes are subjective as they are based on the observer's personal perspective.

ACTIVITY ✳

Imagine the following studies. Would each one be a structured observation or not?

1   A study of taxi drivers' navigation in which a researcher sits beside the driver on specified, complex routes and notes the number of times they frown or scratch their heads.

2   A study of split-brain patients that observes any difficulties they have in day-to-day life.

3   A researcher investigates whether children understand that volumes and numbers stay constant even if the shape or layout changes. They watch as parents cut their child's food up to see whether the child eats more or less of the food.

4   An observer who studies obedience by pretending to be a new army recruit and watching what the other recruits do when ordered to do impossibly difficult physical tasks.

Figure 6.8
"But now there are even more sprouts!"

DATA COLLECTION IN OBSERVATIONS: EVENT AND TIME SAMPLING

Data collection may be driven by the occurrence of, or changes in, the events, with each occurrence of a behaviour being tallied. This is called **event sampling**. Alternatively, data collection may be driven by time, i.e. recording *when* events happen. This is called **time sampling**.

 **KEY IDEAS**

Event sampling is a data-collection technique that uses a checklist of possible activities, which are tallied as they occur.
Time sampling is a data-collection technique that uses a limited list of possible activities. The occurrence of these activities is recorded in relation to short, specified time intervals.

Box 6.4 Observation checklist for event sampling

Imagine a rabbit which, over the course of one minute, eats, hops, eats, hops, stands still for a long time, hops, hops again, eats, stands still for a long time, runs down into its burrow, runs out again, hops, hops again, eats, sniffs, eats, then stands still until the end of the minute.
The checklist would look like this:

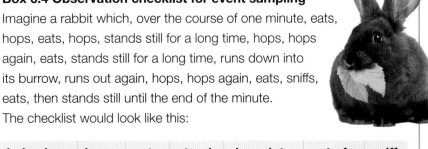

behaviour	hop	eat	stand	down into burrow	out of burrow	sniff
tally	6	4	3	1	1	1

In its simplest form, event sampling involves using a **checklist**, and each time an event happens it is ticked on an observation sheet (or keyed in directly on a computer). This generates total occurrences for

 **KEY IDEAS**

A **checklist** is a list or table of behavioural categories used to tally each event as it occurs.

KEY IDEAS

A **structured observation** is one in which behaviours are recorded in pre-decided and pre-defined categories.

Inter-observer reliability is the extent to which two observers will produce the same records when they watch the same event.

Behavioural categories are the operationally defined units of events used in a structured observation to break a continuous stream of activity into discrete recordable events.

each behavioural category. However, this technique does not indicate how long each event lasted or when in time they occurred. For example, an event sample of students' behaviour in the classroom might indicate how often each member of the class looked out the window or yawned, but it wouldn't tell us how long they spent gazing or whether the yawns were all towards the end of the lesson.

There are several different ways to conduct time sampling, although all involve dividing the observation period into recording intervals such as every ten seconds. A mechanism for timing the interval must be used in addition to an observation sheet. In general, fewer behaviours can be time-sampled in any one session than can be event sampled. In **instantaneous scan sampling** only the action being performed at the start of each preset interval is recorded. For example, if an observer was watching one child's aggressive behaviour in the playground, they might record at 10, 20, 30, 40 seconds, etc., whether he or she was behaving aggressively, non-aggressively, or was not interacting with others, and they would ignore the child's activity at any other time. In **predominant activity sampling**, the same time periods and behavioural categories can be used, but instead of recording only the single behaviour occurring at the moment the time interval ends, the observer watches throughout the interval and records the behaviour that the individual performed the most during that time. In **one-zero sampling**, again the same time periods and behavioural categories can be used, but here the researcher would record each occurrence of a behaviour within the time period. This is like event sampling divided into time slots.

TABLE 6.7 STRENGTHS AND WEAKNESSES OF EVENT AND TIME SAMPLING		
	Strengths	**Weaknesses**
Event sampling	• It can record every occurrence of each behaviour to give a complete record. • Records are easy to obtain and to analyse as they are just totals.	• It gives no indication of the relative time spent on each behavioural category. • It gives no indication of the order in which events from each behavioural category occur.
Time sampling	• It can give an indication of the order in which events happen. • It can give an indication of the relative time spent on each behaviour. • Instantaneous scan sampling can be highly reliable. • Predominant activity scans provide a estimate of time spent on each behaviour. • One-zero scans can record the occurrence of infrequent behaviours.	• Even with computerised systems, it is difficult to record as many different behaviours in time sampling as can be recorded in event sampling. • Records are more difficult to obtain as timings have to be precise and if they are indicated by a timer that makes a noise, this can lead to demand characteristics. • Predominant activity scans provide only a relative estimate of time spent on each behaviour, not an actual measure.

Box 6.3 Time-sampling techniques compared

Imagine the rabbit again. Here are three possible time-sampling records:

INSTANTANEOUS SCAN						
Time interval	10	20	30	40	50	60
Hop						
Eat	✓		✓	✓		
Stand		✓			✓	✓
Sniff						

PREDOMINANT ACTIVITY SCAN						
Time interval	10	20	30	40	50	60
Hop						
Eat				✓		
Stand	✓	✓	✓		✓	✓
Sniff						

ONE-ZERO SCAN						
Time interval	10	20	30	40	50	60
Hop	✓	✓		✓		
Eat	✓		✓	✓	✓	
Stand	✓	✓	✓	✓	✓	✓
Sniff					✓	

Note that:

- in the instantaneous scan, no record is made of hopping or sniffing because they didn't happen to occur at the precise moment of the end of any intervals
- only the predominant activity scan shows that the rabbit spent most of its time standing still (although this is only an estimate)
- only the one-zero scan records the occurrence of sniffing, as it was infrequent and brief.

ASSESSING RELIABILITY AND VALIDITY IN OBSERVATIONS

RELIABILITY

Remember that reliability is about consistency (see page 225). A single observer must record their observations consistently from one participant to another. They can improve this by working with operational definitions of behavioural categories and using sampling methods such as instantaneous scan time sampling, which offers high reliability. Where there is more than one observer, high inter-rater reliability is important. This is achieved by observers working together on their operational definitions and practising the use of the data-collection technique prior to the study. This is usually done by each observer scoring the same section of recorded behaviour on video.

Figure 6.9
Rosenhan (1973) conducted a participant observation of the reactions of hospital staff to pseudopatients

QUESTION SPOTLIGHT! ⟩

Observations are commonly used in developmental psychology.
Can you suggest why this is the case?

VALIDITY

Remember that validity is about being sure that you are measuring what you intended to measure (see page 225). To produce valid data in an observational study, a researcher must be confident that the behaviours they are recording are a true representation of the participants' normal behaviour. It is therefore important that appropriate behavioural categories are chosen, and that the definitions reflect the intended activities. To achieve this, behavioural categories should be mutually exclusive, i.e. a particular activity of interest would appear in one and only one category. For example, returning to the observation of a rabbit on page 235, if the rabbit hopped down into its burrow, would that be recorded as a 'hop' or as going 'down into the burrow'? Valid operational definitions of the categories would overcome this problem, for example by saying that 'down into the burrow' is any activity resulting in movement that takes the rabbit's ears past the burrow entrance. The 'hop' would therefore be scored as 'down into the burrow'.

Several other factors can reduce validity, including demand characteristics and social desirability. To reduce the effects of these, observers can keep their role hidden – as in a covert participant observation – so the participants are unaware that they are being observed. Finally, using a realistic setting is important so that the behaviours reflect normal activities.

TABLE 6.8 STRENGTHS AND WEAKNESSES OF OBSERVATIONAL TECHNIQUES

Strengths	Weaknesses
• Participant observers may benefit from being involved in the social experience by gaining insights into the emotions or motivation felt by participants making the data more detailed and more valid. • In naturalistic settings and with covert observers behaviour is likely to be highly representative of real life, unlike questionnaires or interviews in which people might report different behaviours than they would actually do in real life. • The technique allows for data collection from participants who are unable to contribute to interviews, questionnaires or experimental testing, such as animals and children. • Observations can be preferable when direct methods are impractical, e.g. because they would induce demand characteristics or because they would be unethical, e.g. if they deliberately produced a stressful situation.	• Participant observers may be biased if they become involved in the social situation they are observing. • If multiple observers are used, inter-observer reliability may be low. • Ethical issues arise when participants are unaware that they are being observed. • It is harder to control extraneous variables, even in a structured observation, than in a laboratory experiment.

EXAM FOCUS

We now show you some of the sorts of questions that could be asked about the observational method in your exam. We will then show you some examples of the sorts of answers we believe might be successful and less successful, and point out some classic traps to avoid.

QUESTION 1

A researcher conducted a study using the participant observation method to investigate the behaviour of people waiting in a bus queue. The observation took place on a weekday between 8 am and 10 am using event sampling. The table below shows the number of times different behaviours were observed.

Reading (magazine, newspaper, book, etc.)	Talking to other people	Listening to music through headphones	Using a mobile phone	Waiting quietly doing nothing
31	11	18	26	8

(a) What is participant observation? *(2 marks)*
(b) Identify one strength and one weakness of using the participant observation method in this study. *(4 marks)*
(c) What is event sampling? *(2 marks)*
(d) Identify one strength and one weakness of using event sampling in this study. *(4 marks)*
(e) Sketch an appropriate graph or chart to display the findings from this study. *(4 marks)*
(f) Outline two findings from the data displayed in this graph or chart. *(4 marks)*

QUESTION 2

A group of psychologists are interested in conducting an observation study of people's behaviour as they walk past a shop window. The psychologists want to see if people pay any attention to their own reflection and, if so, what they do.

(a) Describe an appropriate procedure that could be used in this study. *(6 marks)*
(b) Evaluate the reliability and validity of carrying out the study in this way. *(6 marks)*
(c) What is time sampling? *(2 marks)*
(d) Describe one strength and one weakness of time sampling if it were to be used in this study. *(4 marks)*
(e) Identify one ethical issue in this study. *(2 marks)*

QUESTION 3

Researchers want to conduct an observation study of shopping behaviour at a large local supermarket.

(a) Describe and evaluate a suitable procedure for this observation study. *(10 marks)*
(b) Describe one ethical issue that the researchers need to consider when conducting this observation study and suggest how this could be dealt with. *(4 marks)*
(c) Explain what is meant by inter-rater reliability in observation research. *(2 marks)*
(d) Suggest how the researchers could ensure that this observation has good inter-rater reliability. *(4 marks)*

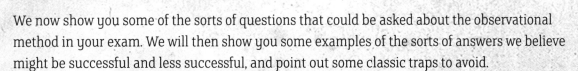

QUESTION 2 (a) Describe an appropriate procedure that could be used in this study. *(6 marks)*

Sharon's answer:

To do this study I would go to a high street in the nearest large town to me on a busy weekend on Saturday. Saturday is a day when lots of people go and do their shopping. I would stand where I can see a big shop window and have a notebook with me. I would watch what people do as they go by and if they look at themselves at all I would note down all the facts about them, but if they do not stop then I would write nothing down and ignore them. I would observe the shoppers going past who stop but not children, as that is not ethical.

Colin's answer:

I would go to the high street of my local town on Saturday at lunchtime as it is busy then. This would be from 12–2pm. I would sit on a bench in the middle of the precinct where I can see a shop clearly. I would prepare a chart to use with categories of behaviour on it that people might do, e.g. smiles at themselves, touches hair, pokes out tongue, admires their reflection. I would have space to put in other categories if needed for other behaviours. I would start observing at 12 noon and wait for a person to look at themselves and see what they are doing. I would tick my relevant categories off for each person. They might do more than one thing but that would be alright as I would tick several categories. When they have passed on I would wait for the next person. I would have a magazine to pretend to read so people would not notice me observing. My sample would be anyone shopping at this time that came past, so is an opportunity sample. I will not know their ages in advance. Being there for two hours should give me enough people, but I would stay longer if needed to ensure I got 30 people.

QUESTION 2 (b) Evaluate the reliability and validity of carrying out the study in this way. (6 marks)

Kristin's answer:

My study would be reliable as if I were to do it again I would get the same results, so it is very reliable. I could improve the reliability by doing it in another town as well. The ecological validity is good as I used real

We say: 3 marks
Sharon, the description of the procedure here is worth six marks. For your answer to be worth the full six marks, someone should be able to copy exactly what you have done. If you look at what you have written, you may notice that there are a few details missing! You do identify where you are going and what day, but you should specify how long you plan to carry out the observation for. Is it one hour, the morning or the whole day? You have some brief detail on the sample and the procedure but this lacks clarity. The description suggests you are gathering qualitative data, so you do not need to explain any behavioural categories, but you should say a little more about what exactly you will be recoding descriptively about each participant. It would be possible to replicate your procedure, but the omissions would make this a bit difficult; if you had included more detail, then it would be easy to do so.

We say: 6 marks.
Quite a clear description of what you plan to do here Colin. You give detailed comments on where you are going, what time you will be there and where you will be to do the observation. The use of the magazine to 'blend in' is a sensible idea. You suggest some appropriate categories to use and how you would use your coding chart. The sample is nice and clear and you say how many people you would have as your minimum sample. Someone could go out and copy this quite easily, owing to your well-explained and clear outline.

We say: 2 marks.
Kristin, when asked to evaluate in a question, try to explain the points more fully to show that you are able to take a critical look at research. Your point on reliability is not really correct here. Your observation would be reliable if you could carry it out in exactly the same way with the same procedure and you were clear about exactly what data you were recording and exactly how you recorded it, so all

shoppers in a shopping centre on Saturday so they are doing natural behaviours of shopping.

Joshua's answer:

The validity is good in this study as the participants do not know I am observing them looking in the shop windows at their reflections. This means that there aren't any demand characteristics and they don't change their behaviour. I am measuring their real reactions to looking at their reflections, so this means it is very valid overall.

I have made it very reliable as I have got some clear categories of behaviour in my chart. I thought carefully about what people do and about what each category is, so that when I watch a participant I will be certain which category to tick. They are not ambiguous and I did a pilot study to check I knew how to use my chart.

observers record in the same manner. Just repeating it on its own does not make it reliable, as you may not be observing in the same way as before. Your comment on validity was in the context of your procedure – which it needs to be, but it was a little short.

We say: 5 marks.
You seem to have reliability and validity sorted here, Joshua. Well done. The first point on validity was well written, expanded on and had a nice link back to the context of your procedure. This is very important for all your answers. Unfortunately, you then forgot this for reliability! While your point on clear categories and interpretation of these was fine, especially checking them in a pilot study, there was no link. Without a link you could be talking about any study and you are being asked about the one you have just designed.

QUESTION 2 (c) What is time sampling? *(2 marks)*

Dan's answer:

This is where you look at the participants at a certain particular time to see their behaviour.

Ina's answer:

Time sampling is where you decide on a time period such as every 2 minutes and then look to see what participants are doing at that point in time and make a note of this on your recording chart.

We say: 1 mark.
You have tried to communicate the main point of time sampling here, Dan, but it could be clearer. Your answer needs to communicate the idea that we look at behaviours for a fixed amount of time, e.g. for 30 minutes but at several set times during a day, or that it is at a fixed point, e.g. every 60 seconds for a set period such as two hours.

We say: 2 marks.
Ina, your answer is focused and clear. You have obviously done your revision!

QUESTION 2 (d) Describe one strength and one weakness of time sampling if it were to be used in this study. *(4 marks)*

Ceri's answer:

A strength is it is not very tiring as you are not recording information from the passers by the shop window all the time so you can rest in between. A weakness is that you could miss some behaviour in between your time intervals, so you don't get all the data.

We say: 1 mark.

Ceri, remember that this is a psychology exam. Your strength is not very appropriate to time sampling, and is not really a psychological criticism. This is a pity, as you have made a link back to the context, but the point itself is not credit worthy. Revise your methodology notes again. Your weakness is fine and is clearly explained, but has no context. You need to have a clear psychological point and then the context to get the marks.

Salma's answer:

A strength of time sampling is that you can get to see how the behaviour could change over time when you are sampling. If you look at people every 5 minutes for three hours in a morning you could see whether they stare at the shop window more in the early morning or more at lunch time and so spot patterns and trends you couldn't with just event samples. A weakness is that there might be observer bias as the observer looking at the shoppers' behaviour in the reflection might misinterpret what they are doing and so we get inaccurate data.

We say: 2 marks.

Do check carefully what the question is asking, Salma, to avoid losing marks. Your strength is really spot on. It is appropriate, related specifically to time sampling, plus it has a clear link to the context of the study. Your weakness was not specific to time sampling, but is more of a comment on the problems of observation in general. This is not what the question requires and so cannot gain any credit. Be sure to check the exact detail of the question to avoid this in future.

QUESTION 2 (e) Identify one ethical issue in this study. *(2 marks)*

Jay's answer:

One issue is that the participants do not know that they are taking part in a study, so they do not get the right to withdraw, which all participants should have in any research.

We say: 1 mark.

Jay, you have a well-described ethical issue, but remember the question says 'in this study', which is a clue that you need to provide context – and you did not do so. It is important to remember this, as you can quickly lose marks if you keep forgetting to do so.

Sian's answer:

Debriefing is an issue here. Everyone should get a debrief to reassure them at the end of the study and prevent any harm. This was not done here because it was in a shopping centre and people were observed as they passed by the window looking at their reflection. They walked away so no one told them there was a study or explained it to them.

We say: 2 marks.

Sian, you give an appropriate and clearly described ethical issue, which does what the question asks, and you clearly provide some context from the study when you mention the shopping centre and their reflection in the window. Keep this up.

C – THE CORRELATIONAL ANALYSIS

INTRODUCTION

In this section we will be looking at the way in which the research method of correlational analysis is used in psychology. Specifically, we will explore positive and negative correlations and the production and interpretation of scattergraphs. We will also evaluate the method of correlational analysis.

CORRELATIONAL ANALYSIS

A **correlational analysis** aims to investigate whether two variables are related. In order to do this, each variable must exist over a range and it must be possible to measure them numerically, i.e. the data must be quantitative. This means that the participants' scores cannot just be in named categories (nominal data – see page 277). Although the scales for each variable may be different, they both need to be numerical (or it must be possible to convert them to numbers).

For example, variables such as 'brain weight' or IQ are numerical and could be used in a correlation, as could scores from rating scales (see page 216). However, responses to the question 'What's your favourite colour?' would produce data only in named categories, which could not be used in a correlation. Similarly, the question 'What is your employment status?' could generate answers of 'employed', 'self-employed', 'student', 'retired' or 'at-home mum', and although this gives a range of responses, we cannot put them in order so they could not be used in a correlation.

A correlational design is useful in situations in which it is only possible for the variables to be measured, rather than manipulated or compared, i.e. when it is not possible to conduct an experiment. This might be the case where changing the variables would not be practical, such as attempting to vary the amount of pre-school exposure to TV, or where it would be unethical, such as increasing real-life exposure to violence.

It is important to note that a correlational analysis looks for a link between two measured variables. These are sometimes called co-variables because a correlation cannot investigate which of them is causing the

 **KEY IDEAS**

Correlational analysis is a technique used to investigate a link between two measured variables.

Figure 6.10
*My goldfish lives in a tank on my desk. The more fizzy drinks I consume, the more active my fish is. It's tempting to assume there is a causal relationship – seeing the bubbles in my glass makes her excited. In reality, there is no **causal relationship**; both variables are affected by a third factor – temperature. The hotter the weather, the more I drink, and fish are more active in warmer water.*

Figure 6.11
Correlations cannot
tell us about causal
relationships

other to change (or whether variation in both of them is caused by a third factor). Although we might have a strong suspicion which variable is responsible, a simple correlation cannot help us to be sure: it can tell us only whether the two variables are related. As a consequence, you must not refer to them as the independent variable and dependent variable!

We cannot say from one correlation that an increase in one variable has caused an increase (or decrease) in the other, because it is possible that the changes in both variables could be the result of another factor. Suppose we measure two variables – memory and number of GCSEs – and find that they are positively correlated. It might be tempting to say that a good memory is responsible for getting better grades, but we cannot be sure of this. It is possible that both of these factors depend on another variable, such as the amount of practice at learning and recall the individual has had in their lifetime. All we can conclude is that the two factors we have measured vary together, not that there is a cause-and-effect relationship between them. If we want to make judgments about causality, we need to conduct an experiment in which we can be sure that it is the manipulation of one variable that is responsible for the change in the other. Of course, if we conduct a correlational analysis and find that there is no link between two variables, then we can conclude that there is no **causal relationship.**

KEY IDEAS

A relationship between two variables such that a change in one is responsible for a change in the other is known as a **causal relationship**.

STRETCH & CHALLENGE ◎

Dan and Alysha set up a company for the Young Enterprise scheme and have been washing cars in the local town. When they study the variation in their takings over time they discover a pattern. Dan thinks it matches one he's seen in the local police station about car theft. When they look at the incidence of thefts and of their car washing, there is a clear positive correlation. The more cars they wash, the higher the number of thefts. Alysha wonders whether the thieves are more likely to steal clean cars!

In reality, it is unlikely that this apparent relationship is causal. Suggest a third factor that could increase both the incidence of car theft and the likelihood of people having their car washed.

QUESTION SPOTLIGHT!

Remember that correlations find *links* between variables, not causal relationships, so we don't use the terms IV and DV.
Judging only by the way these sentences are worded, decide which are proposing correlational relationships, and which are proposing causal relationships:

1   Age affects a child's ability to understand that volume stays the same even when shape changes.
2   The duration of eye movements in sleep are related to the perceived the length of a dream.
3   There is a link between the size of the hippocampus in the brain and a person's navigational ability.
4   Children are more likely to copy the behaviour of same-sex adults than that of opposite-sex adults.

POSITIVE AND NEGATIVE CORRELATIONS

The findings of a correlational analysis are used to assess the nature of the relationship between the two variables. This can be described in two ways, by the *direction* and the *strength* of the link. In a **positive correlation**, both variables increase in the same direction – that is, higher scores on one variable correspond with higher scores on the other. For example, we would expect to find a positive correlation between exposure to aggressive models and violent behaviour, such that greater exposure to models is linked to a higher incidence of violence. When two variables are **negatively correlated**, higher scores on one variable correspond with low scores on the other. For example, we might predict a negative correlation between number of years of education and level of obedience, such that as the amount of education increases, the likelihood of blind obedience decreases. Alternatively, there might be no relationship at all between two variables; this is called a zero correlation.

QUESTION SPOTLIGHT!

Maguire *et al.* (2000) (see page 85), investigated several correlational relationships between the volume of different brain areas and time spent working as a taxi driver.
Identify whether the following were positive or negative correlations:

1   As posterior hippocampal size increased, so did years spent driving a taxi.
2   As years spent driving a taxi increased, the size of the anterior hippocampus decreased.

ACTIVITY ❋

Look at the two sets of correlational data below.
Which one do you think is a positive correlation, and which one do you think is a negative correlation?

TABLE 6.9A									
Reaction time (secs)	78	71	69	86	98	65	70	69	71
Hours of sleep	6	9	7	5	4	7	8	9	8

TABLE 6.9B									
Attendance (%)	41	19	85	90	54	82	79	89	61
Exam score	3	3	9	10	5	9	8	8	6

💡 KEY IDEAS

A **positive correlation** is a relationship between two variables such that an increase in one accompanies an increase in the other.
A **negative correlation** is a relationship between two variables such that an increase in one accompanies a decrease in the other.

ACTIVITY ❋

Using the two sets of correlational data from the activity above, sketch a scattergraph for each correlation, labelling the variables on each axis.

SCATTERGRAPHS

The different relationships can be illustrated visually on a **scattergraph** (or scattergram). This is a graph with one variable along each of the axes on which each point represents one pair of scores. These two scores

KEY IDEAS

A **scattergraph** is a graph used to display the data from a correlational study. Each point on the graph represents the participant's score on scales for each of the two measured variables.

QUESTION SPOTLIGHT!

On page 245, two correlational relationships from Maguire *et al.* (2000) are described.

Sketch a scattergraph for each correlation, labelling the variables on each axis.

usually relate to one participant. However, in some situations they might not, e.g. when comparing data from pairs of twins or when testing reliability between two researchers scoring or rating the same observation or interview (see pages 234 and 225).

A scattergraph readily indicates whether a correlation is positive or negative. For example, if we were to collect data on the variables of brain volume and braininess, we might expect both to increase together. This would be a positive correlation and the line of 'best fit' between the points would slop upwards from left to right (see Figure 6.12a). Alternatively we could measure brain volume and reaction time. Now we would expect faster speeds (i.e. smaller reaction times) with bigger brains. This would be a *negative* correlation and the line of 'best fit' between the points would slop downwards from left to right (see Figure 6.12b).

Another aspect of the findings of a correlation is the strength of the relationship. If a correlation is very strong, the two variables are closely linked. This can also be readily seen on a scattergraph. The closer the points are to the line, the stronger the correlation (see Figures 6.12c and d). This measure of 'strength' can also be described numerically, as a correlation coefficient (see page 225).

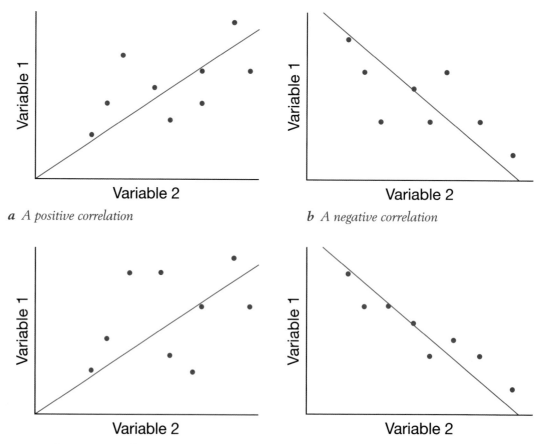

Figure 6.12
A scattergraph is used to represent the results of a correlational analysis

a A positive correlation

b A negative correlation

c A weak positive correlation

d A strong negative correlation

ASSESSING RELIABILITY AND VALIDITY IN CORRELATIONS

RELIABILITY

Remember that reliability is about consistency (see page 225). In correlational analyses we are concerned about the consistency of the measures used. The findings of a correlational analysis will be reliable only if the measures of both variables are consistent. Thus, for some correlations, such as those using scientific scales (such as volume or time), the measures will be highly reliable. In other cases, such as studies correlating variables measured using self-reports, observations or estimates, reliability will potentially be lower.

VALIDITY

Remember that validity is about being sure that you are measuring what you intended to measure (see page 225). To be valid, a correlational analysis must be reliable, but other factors affect validity too. As with reliability, the findings of a correlational analysis will be valid only if the measures of both variables measure real phenomena in effective ways. To achieve this, the variables must be defined and measured effectively.

WEB WATCH @

Look at the scattergraphs on the following websites:
www.intropsych.com/ch01_psychology_and_science/01drinkingandgpanegcorrelation.jpg
http://origin-ars.sciencedirect.com/content/image/1-s2.0-S0738399199000476-gr2.gif
www.holah.co.uk/images/correlationquestion2.png
www.ecs.org/html/educationIssues/Research/images/primer/example_understanding7.gif
Which are positive correlations and which are negative?
Which of the correlations look the strongest and the weakest?

ACTIVITY ✳

How would you operationalise the two variables in each of the possible correlations described below?

1 A link between the language ability and age of a chimp.
2 An increase in aggressiveness and the amount of internet use.
3 A relationship between eyewitness accuracy and post-event exposure to media reports about the crime.

TABLE 6.8 STRENGTHS AND WEAKNESSES OF OBSERVATIONAL TECHNIQUES

Strengths	Weaknesses
• A correlational study can be conducted on variables that can be measured but not manipulated, i.e. when experimentation would be impractical or unethical. • A correlation can demonstrate the presence or absence of a relationship so is useful for indicating areas for subsequent experimental research.	• A single correlational analysis cannot indicate whether a relationship is causal, so when a relationship is found this might be due to one of the measured variables or alternatively another, unknown, variable might be responsible. • Correlational analysis can be used only with variables that can be measured on a scale.

EXAM FOCUS

We now show you some of the sorts of questions that could be asked about correlational analyses in your exam. We will then show you some examples of the sorts of answers we believe might be successful and less successful, and point out some classic traps to avoid.

QUESTION 1

Psychologists want to investigate if there is a correlation between how interested a person is in cars and their driving skills.

(a) Suggest an appropriate null hypothesis for this study. *(4 marks)*

(b) Describe and evaluate a way to measure 'driving skills' that could be used in this study. *(10 marks)*

(c) Identify one strength and one weakness of using the correlation method in this study. *(6 marks)*

QUESTION 2

A psychologist conducted a correlation study to investigate the relationship between the number of friends people claim to have on social networking sites, and the number of times they go out socialising each month. The data was obtained from students in a psychology class who left the classroom one at a time to provide details to a researcher sitting outside.

The findings from the study are presented in the scattergraph below.

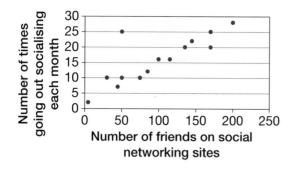

(a) How many participants was data collected from in this study, and how do you know this? *(2 marks)*

(b) Name and briefly describe the sampling method used in this study. *(2 marks)*

(c) Identify one strength and one weakness of using this sampling method for this study. *(4 marks)*

(d) From the scattergraph presented, what is the mode for the 'number of times going out socialising each month', and how do you know this? *(2 marks)*

(e) Outline two other findings from the scattergraph. *(4 marks)*

(f) What is qualitative data? *(2 marks)*

(g) Give two examples of qualitative data that could have been collected in this study. *(4 marks)*

QUESTION 3

Researchers conducted a study investigating the correlation between amount of sleep and concentration. First the researchers asked participants how long they had slept the previous night in minutes. This was then recorded as 'total minutes slept'. Researchers then used a letter cancellation task to assess concentration. The participants had two minutes to read from a book. They had to count how often the letter 'f' appeared. The data is presented in the table below.

Participant (initials)	Total minutes slept the night before	Number of times the letter 'f' was identified
MM	480	14
MJ	270	12
JW	420	24
CC	390	20
EP	450	25
HA	180	8
MH	300	16
JD	360	18

(a) Identify one strength and one weakness of the correlational method. *(4 marks)*

(b) Suggest an appropriate alternate hypothesis for this study. *(4 marks)*

(c) Identify two findings from the data in this study. *(4 marks)*

(d) Outline one strength and one weakness of the way that researchers measured concentration in this study. *(6 marks)*

(e) Explain what is meant by a positive correlation. *(2 marks)*

SOME ANSWERS AND COMMENTS

QUESTION 1 (a) Suggest an appropriate null hypothesis for this study. (4 marks)

Declan's answer:

There won't be any correlation between the variables in the study.

Ben's answer:

There will be no correlation between the amount of interest someone has in cars and what their driving skills are when assessed.

We say: 1 mark.
Declan, as hypotheses are meant to be specific predictions of what you think will happen in your study, you need to make them really clear. You have not communicated much about what you are doing as you have not clearly identified either of your variables. You really must do so. You did say there would be no correlation so get some credit, but you need to say more than that.

We say: 4 marks.
A clear and well set out null hypothesis, Ben. You identify that it is a null hypothesis by correctly stating 'no correlation'. You also have identified the two variables and stated them quite explicitly. Nicely written!

QUESTION 1 (b) Describe and evaluate a way to measure 'driving skills' that could be used in this study. (10 marks)

Hywel's answer:

I would use a popular computer game on driving skills and take it to college with me. I would set it up in the social area and get people to use it. They would have two goes on it as the first is just practice in case they have not used it before. I would see what their score was on the second go as my measure of driving skill.

This would be good as it is quite a realistic game and so has a lot of ecological validity. The computer game would give me the score so it would be quite accurate as well, as I would not make any mistakes over scoring. It is easy to get. I think people would find it fun so I would get lots of participants so I would have a bigger sample so I could generalise.

We say: 4 marks.
Hywel, the measure you chose was a good one to use, but as you provide very little detail it would be really difficult for anyone to replicate your study. If you have to describe a way to measure something, or a procedure or sample for instance, then it is important to give enough detail so that another researcher could copy exactly what you did. This means you should try to describe it exactly in your answer. Tell us the type of game or name used, how long they will be using it, what the scores will be, i.e. times or amount of errors? This would give more detail and demonstrate how you would take a measure of driving skill. Your evaluation was not particularly detailed, and remember there are 10 marks available here – so don't waste them. Your point on ecological validity was not really correct, because however realistic a game is, it is still a game and not like driving a car on a road. Your point on scoring is fine, but you then discuss sample which is not actually about specifically measuring driving skills. Check the wording of the question carefully so that you know exactly what to discuss and evaluate.

Becki's answer:

One way to measure driving skills would be to use a questionnaire with a range of questions on it that could examine what participants know. It could give a score and the higher it is the better their skill. I would have 20 questions in it on different aspects of driving. It would be multiple-choice and they would have to select the right answer.

One question would be: If you are going down a steep hill should you be in – (a) low gear, (b) high gear or (c) neutral?

Another one could be: What would you do if the car was in a skid? (a) speed up (b) brake quickly or (c) steer carefully the way you are skidding

They would get a point for each one correct and high scores out of 20 mean more skill, so it is quantitative data. I would test all aspects of driving that relate to skill and what to do in tricky situations, such as when children run into the road, in bad weather, etc.

This is a good way, as it is quite quick to do and very easy. I would not need anything other than the questions on driving skill. My way has good validity as it is easy to see that the questions all relate to aspects of driving, and to be a good driver you would have to know all about these types of difficult areas. Therefore, it has high face validity as it is on driving skills and how good a driver you are, so measures what it sets out to. It may not be valid if people guess the answers to the questions, as then it is not measuring how they really drive or their skill, but how good they are at guessing. This makes it not accurate as it is not genuine skill.

We say: 10 marks.
You have chosen an interesting way to measure skills, Becki, and it would work. You have given a good idea of the type of questions you would use, and how you would get an overall score to measure people's driving skill. You evaluation shows that you can take a critical view, and you have clearly identified some relevant issues. You explained these issues nice and clearly, showed how they applied to your chosen measure, and related them clearly to this. There were three separate points that you clearly understood. Good work here, Becki, as this question is worth a lot of marks.

QUESTION 1 (c) Identify one strength and one weakness of using the correlation method in this study. (6 marks)

Paul's answer:

Correlation has a strength that it is very easy to see what the data looks like on a graph to see what it tells us. You could see if driving relates at all to if you like cars and find them interesting. The weakness is that you cannot say that one thing causes another.

Nadia's answer:

A weakness is that a correlation is just a relationship between two things, so you cannot say one has caused another. Other variables might affect them, which we have not identified. Being interested in cars does not mean this causes you to be a good driver, as you may have had lots more driving lessons. A strength is that correlations can be used to find out about how things go together and you can then use all this information to plan a specific investigation in a experiment to test them in a more controlled way once you have seen that there is a link. You could compare people who don't find cars interesting to those that do, and measure their driving skills in an experiment with two conditions.

We say: 3 marks.
Paul, you have studied psychological research methods for some time in your class, so try to show us all this in your answers. That would get you more marks. Your strength is a little vague and could include the fact that it is the scattergraph that allows us to see this relationship clearly, rather than just talking about a graph more generally. You explained what the variables were, so good thinking there. You weakness is basically correct, but is too brief and a bit unclear, and you also need to relate this point to the specific variables in the question to add to your marks.

We say: 6 marks.
Nadia, you have obviously studied correlation carefully, and this shows in your detailed answer. You have a very clearly discussed strength and weakness, which shows your understanding. Both of these included a point on what the correlation in this question was about (i.e. driving skills/interest in cars) – so you had a nice link. You get all the marks here as there is nothing else you could add.

D – THE EXPERIMENTAL METHOD

INTRODUCTION

In this section we will be looking at the way in which the experimental method is used in psychology. Specifically, we will explore three types of experimental design and evaluate them. We also evaluate the experimental method in general.

EXPERIMENTS

An experiment is a way to carry out an investigation in which one variable is manipulated by the experimenter and the effect of this change on another variable is observed or measured. In this way, the experimenter can see whether the variable they are manipulating causes the other variable to change too. If it does, there is said to be a cause-and-effect relationship between the two variables.

In an experiment, the situation allows the effects of one variable on another to be observed and measured. In a true experiment (see page 259) the variations in the first factor, the one causing the difference, are deliberately created by the researcher; in a quasi-experiment these variations arise naturally. In either case, the variable causing the change is called the **independent variable** (or **IV**). The variable being measured, that varies as a consequence of the changes in the IV, is called the **dependent variable** (or **DV**). The measure of the DV provides quantitative data. An experimenter can be sure that it is only the IV that is causing a change in the DV, as all other variables are closely controlled.

An experimental investigation usually has two (or more) conditions or **levels of the IV**, and the DV is measured in each of these situations. To be certain that any changes in the DV arise only because of changes in the IV, the experimenter uses controls to keep constant any other factors that could affect the DV. It is this that ensures they can conclude whether or not there is a cause-and-effect relationship. For example, in a study investigating the effects of hunger on concentration, students could be tested before and after lunch. The time of day would be the IV, with two conditions 'before lunch' and 'after lunch'. The DV (of concentration) would be measured in each condition. It is possible for there to be several levels of the IV. In the first experiment in Loftus and Palmer's study (see page 6), there were five levels – five different verbs were used in a leading question (hit, smashed, collided, contacted, bumped). Each of these was an experimental condition, i.e. one in which the IV was being actively changed. The DV (being measured) was the participant's estimate of speed. In contrast, the second of Loftus and Palmer's experiments used a **control condition**, that is, a condition from which the IV is absent. In this case, they compared two conditions, one in which they used a leading question (the experimental condition), and another which used a non-leading question (the control condition). The DV was again the participant's estimate of speed.

QUESTION SPOTLIGHT!

For each of the following experiments, decide whether the conditions are all experimental or whether one or more experimental conditions is being compared to a control condition:

1   A study looks at the difference between eyewitness recall when there are delays of 1, 2, 3 or 4 days between the event and giving the testimony.

2   A test of whether people are more likely to help a stranger who is struggling to get up some steps when the stranger either does or doesn't have a pushchair.

Figure 6.13

3   An investigation looking at recall for shopping trips in people with mental health problems, including addiction to shopping, amnesia and multiple personality disorder, and people with no mental disorder.

STRETCH & CHALLENGE ◎

For each of the situations above, identify the IV and DV, and explain how you would operationalise them.

QUESTION SPOTLIGHT! ⭐

Maguire *et al.* (2000) (see page 85) investigated several differences using experimental designs.
Identify the IV and the DV in each of these experiments:

1   A comparison was made between anterior hippocampal volume in taxi drivers and in non-taxi drivers.

2   Total brain volume was measured in taxi drivers and non-taxi drivers.

3   The size of the left and right hippocampus in taxi drivers was compared.

💡 KEY IDEAS

An experiment characterised by the absence of the IV is known as the **control condition**. It is used as a baseline for comparison with an experimental condition.

QUESTION SPOTLIGHT! ⭐

Identify whether these experiments used a control condition or only experimental conditions:

1   Dement and Kleitman (1957) (see page 97). Consider approach 1 only.

2   Piliavin *et al.* (1969) (see page 162). There are four IVs and two measures of the DV.

3   Samuel and Bryant (1984) (see page 48). There are three levels of the IV, as well as the three types of material to assess judgments of mass, number and volume.

KEY IDEAS

The definition of variables so that they can be accurately manipulated, measured and replicated is called **operationalisation**.

QUESTION SPOTLIGHT!

It is important that you can define variables, as well as identify them. Consider again the IVs and DVs you identified in the question spotlight above. *How was each variable operationalised?*

1   Dement and Kleitman (1957) (IV and DV).
2   Piliavin *et al.* (1969) (4 IVs, 2 DVs).
3   Samuel and Bryant (1984) (3 IVs, 1 DV).

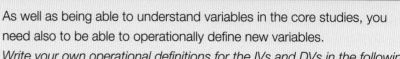

QUESTION SPOTLIGHT!

As well as being able to understand variables in the core studies, you need also to be able to operationally define new variables.
Write your own operational definitions for the IVs and DVs in the following studies:

1   In a test of memory, recall of long and short words was compared.
2   An investigation aimed to measure whether attachment of five year old boys was stronger to their mother or their father.
3   Some students conducted an experiment to find out if there was a difference in the labelling of mental health patients as 'insane' depending on the diagnosis they had received.

Figure 6.14

OPERATIONALISING VARIABLES

In order to be certain about the findings of an experiment we must be sure that we know exactly what has changed. For the IV this means knowing precisely how the variable was manipulated. For the DV this means being confident that any variation has been measured accurately. To achieve this, the researcher **operationalises** both variables. For example, in an experiment testing the effect of leading questions on recall we can identify the two variables: the IV is leading questions and the DV is recall. However, these are not sufficient as definitions – another researcher wouldn't be able to tell what had been changed or how the effect had been observed, hence the need for operationalisation. To operationalise the IV we could state that there were two levels of the IV, one that used leading questions, saying 'Did you see the...' and one that used non-leading questions, saying 'Did you see a...'. This could be expanded by giving examples of the items in the questions. Operationalisation of the DV would be the number of questions incorrectly answered, i.e. errors in recall.

KEY IDEAS

The term **'experimental design'** refers to the way in which participants are allocated to levels of the IV.

Independent groups design is an experimental design in which different participants are used for each level of the IV.

Repeated measures design is an experimental design in which each participant performs in every level of the IV.

Matched pairs design is an experimental design in which participants are arranged into pairs. Each pair is similar in ways that are important to the study and the members of each pair perform in the two different levels of the IV.

EXPERIMENTAL DESIGN

In an experiment, participants may be tested in all, or only one, of the levels of the IV. The different ways that participants are allocated to the levels of the IV are called **experimental designs**. Three common experimental designs are:

- **independent groups design**
- **repeated measures design**
- **matched pairs design**.

INDEPENDENT GROUPS DESIGN

In this experimental design, a separate group of participants is used for each level of the IV. This means that the set of data gained for each condition is 'independent' because it is not related to any other pieces of data – they have come from different people. Note that this is not the same use of the word 'independent' as in the 'independent variable'. If we wanted to know if age affected memory, we could test recall in a group of young people and then wait for them to grow old. However, it is much quicker to compare them to a group of older adults to look at the effect of age. This would be an independent groups design.

This design has the advantage that the participants experience the experimental setting only once. This means that they are less likely to notice clues that might tell them the aims of the experiment (**demand characteristics**) and to respond to them. One disadvantage is that there might be individual differences between participants that could influence the findings. For example, in a study on the effect of repetition, all the people with good memories might end up in the 'no repetition' group. If so, it might look as though repetition was less important than it is in reality. This effect can be reduced by randomly allocating participants to different conditions. This should even out the differences between individuals across the levels of the IV. In order to randomly allocate participants, each is given a number, and the numbers are then randomly divided into two groups. This can be done by putting cards with numbers on into a hat and drawing out two sets, or using a random number generator (e.g. on a computer) to do the same thing.

Figure 6.15
Randomly allocating participants to conditions can help to overcome bias caused by individual differences

 **KEY IDEAS**

Demand characteristics are features of an experimental setting that indicate to participants the aims of the study and so can influence their behaviour.

QUESTION SPOTLIGHT!

1   Bandura *et al.* (1961) (see page 61) used different children to test the effects of male and female models.
Why was it better to do this than to use the same children?

2   Baron-Cohen *et al.* (1997) (see page 15) used an independent groups design to compare normal participants and those with Asperger's syndrome/high-functioning autism on the eyes test. *Why?*

ACTIVITY

Find the website for the Ignobel awards and have a look at their publications ('The Annals of Improbable Research' and 'MiniAir'). As the title suggests, they publish all kinds of improbable research (not all of which is psychological).
Find an interesting psychology experiment and design a poster or presentation about it, indicating the type of experiment used, the IV and DV, the experimental design and what controls were implemented.

KEY IDEAS

A **single blind** experimental procedure ensures that participants are unaware of the level of the IV in which they are performing. This helps to reduce the effect of demand characteristics.

A **double blind** experimental procedure protects against both demand characteristics and experimenter bias. It ensures that neither the researcher working with the participants nor the participants themselves are aware of which condition an individual is in.

QUESTION SPOTLIGHT!

1   Maguire *et al.* (2000) (see page 85) compared the left and right side of taxi drivers' brains using a repeated measures design. *Why did they use this design?*

2   Dement and Kleitman (1957) (see page 97) asked people to recount their dreams following waking from REM and from nREM. They could have used different people for REM and nREM wakings. *Why did they choose this design?*

In order to hide the purpose of the experiment, the researcher may deceive the participants about the aims of the study. For example, in a test on the effect of leading versus non-leading questions on eyewitness memory, the researcher might not want the participants to know it is a test of memory at all, because that would cause them to focus on the task. Instead, the participants might be told that it is a test of hearing or concentration and that they are to watch a film. This would reduce the risk of demand characteristics affecting performance, but it also raises ethical issues (see page 296). There is clearly a dilemma for researchers between, on the one hand, the need to conduct rigorous studies in which variables are effectively controlled, and on the other, the need to keep participants informed about the aims and methods of a study.

If possible, only the researcher, and not the participants, should know which condition each individual has been allocated to. This is called a **single blind** procedure and it helps reduce the risk that participants will try to produce the results that they believe the experimenter wants. If possible, someone other than the experimenter should allocate the participants to groups. This arrangement, called **double blind**, means that even the experimenter dealing directly with the participants is unaware of the level of the IV to which each participant belongs. This ensures that the experimenter will not affect the participants' performance by treating them (even unconsciously) in biased ways.

REPEATED MEASURES

When the same group of people participate in each level of the IV, this is called a repeated measures design. You can think of this as the participants 'repeating' their performance under different conditions. For example, we could conduct a study to investigate the effects of an orienteering course on hippocampal size. We would measure hippocampal volume in the same group of people before and after the course.

A repeated measures design has the advantage that each person effectively acts as their own baseline. Any differences between participants that might influence their performance will affect both levels of the IV by the same amount, so this is unlikely to bias the findings. Supposing in our experiment on hippocampal volume, one person was already very good at orienteering and navigation and another quite poor. This could be a problem if they happened to be in different groups in an independent groups design. In a repeated measures design, however, initial differences between the participants are less important, as both could show an improvement. Individual differences between participants are called **participant variables**. These variables, such as age, gender or intelligence, can affect the participants score on the DV. It is therefore important to make sure that such differences do not hide, or exaggerate, differences between levels of the IV.

The main problem with this design arises because if each individual participates in every level of the IV they will perform the same or similar tasks two or more times. This repetition can lead to **order effects**. Specifically, repeated performance could cause the participants to improve because they have encountered the task before – a **practice effect**. This would matter because participants who were tested on one of the conditions second would perform better than those who did it first. Alternatively, repetition might make performance worse, perhaps because the participants get bored or tired – a **fatigue effect**. Furthermore, the participants have more opportunity to work out what is being tested, and see both levels of the IV, and are therefore more likely to respond to demand characteristics.

Order effects can be overcome in two ways: by randomisation or **counterbalancing** (see page 258). Let's assume that there are two conditions in a memory experiment: 'delay' (D) and 'no delay' (N). In randomisation, participants are randomly allocated to do either condition D followed by N, or vice versa. As some will do each order, any advantage of doing one of the conditions first will probably be evened out in the results. To be more certain that possible effects are evened out, counterbalancing can be used. Here, the group of participants is divided into two and one half will do D followed by N, the other half N followed by D. If on the second test there was a risk of participants muddling up items remembered from the first test, this would be a problem for exactly half the participants in the 'delay' condition, and exactly half in the 'no delay condition'. Of course, another alternative would be to use a different design.

KEY IDEAS

Participant variables are individual differences between participants (such as age, skills, personality) that could affect their responses in a study.

In a repeated measures design, **order effects** (either practice or fatigue effects) can produce changes in performance between conditions that are not due to the IV, so can obscure the effect of the DV.

The **practice effect** refers to the situation where participants' performance improves because they experience the experimental task more than once. They might become more familiar with the task or recall their previous answers.

The **fatigue effect** refers to the situation where the participants' performance declines because they have experienced an experimental task more than once. They might be bored or tired.

QUESTION SPOTLIGHT!

You need to be able to decide which experimental design to use in different situations.

Would you use an independent groups or repeated measures design in each of these studies and why?

1 A study into eyewitness testimony looking at the difference between answers to untagged questions ('Did you see the burglar's gun?') and tagged ones ('You saw you the burglar's gun, didn't you?').

2 A test of vocabulary development comparing chimpanzees and gorillas learning sign language.

3 An investigation looking at split-brain patients' comprehension of TV programmes compared to people without split brains.

4 A comparison of the amount of dreaming reported after drinking coffee or not drinking coffee.

Figure 6.16
Should you use two separate groups to test the effects of coffee on dreaming?

Figure 6.17
Identical twins make ideal
matched pairs

MATCHED PAIRS

One way to overcome the problems associated with both independent groups and repeated measures designs is to use a matched pairs design. In this situation a different group of participants is used for each level of the IV. However, each participant in one group is matched to a corresponding participant in the other group. This matching is done on relevant variables. For example, in a study looking at the effect of amnesia by measuring recall of words it would be ideal to compare each amnesic to an unaffected person who was similar in other respects (such as the same age, intelligence or vocabulary). While some factors, such as age or gender might be important characteristics for matching in many studies, others, such as vocabulary or attitudes, might be very important in specific investigations but unimportant in others. When possible, identical twins make ideal matched pairs.

 **KEY IDEAS**

Counterbalancing is used to overcome order effects in a repeated measures design. Each possible order of levels of the IV is performed by a different sub-group of participants. This can be described as an ABBA design, as half the participants do condition A then B, and half do B then A.

TABLE 6.11 STRENGTHS AND WEAKNESSES OF EXPERIMENTAL DESIGNS

	Strengths	Weaknesses
Independent groups	• Different participants are used in each level of the IV so there are no order effects. • Participants see the experimental task only once, reducing exposure to demand characteristics. • The effects of individual differences can be reduced by random allocation to levels of the IV.	• Individual differences could distort results if participants in one level of the IV differ from those in another. • More participants are needed than with repeated measures (may be less ethical or harder to find).
Repeated measures	• Individual differences unlikely to distort the effect of the IV, as participants do both levels. • Counterbalancing reduces order effects. • Uses fewer participants than repeated measures so is good when participants are hard to find. • Blind procedures can reduce demand characteristics.	• Order effects and extraneous variables could distort the results. • Participants see the experimental task more than once, increasing exposure to demand characteristics.
Matched pairs	• Participants see the experimental task only once, reducing exposure to demand characteristics. • Controls for individual differences – e.g. identical twins – are excellent matched pairs. • No order effects.	• The similarity between pairs is limited by the matching process, which might be flawed. • Matching participants is time-consuming and difficult and may not be possible.

TRUE EXPERIMENTS AND QUASI-EXPERIMENTS

In some experiments it is possible for the researcher to allocate participants to levels of the IV, for example in a laboratory experiment on the effects of group size on bystander apathy in which the participant is surrounded by a larger or smaller group (of confederates). These are called **true experiments**. In other situations the level of the IV for a participant might be determined before the study, such as having a mental disorder or not, or doing a certain job, or the species of animal. This is called a **quasi-experiment** because it is not truly experimental, in that the experimenter cannot be absolutely sure that the only difference between the groups is the IV, as they are not actually manipulating the variable themselves.

THE LABORATORY EXPERIMENT

A **laboratory experiment** is a study in a contrived environment such as a laboratory (but can include other artificial settings). The participants come into this setting in order to be part of the study – they would not be there normally. By creating the situation artificially, the experimenter can control many variables that might influence the participants' behaviour. For example, they can readily ensure that every participant is treated in the same way by using **standardised instructions**. This control of **extraneous variables** is central to a laboratory experiment. It is one of the main reasons that researchers choose to conduct laboratory experiments – they can be confident that if the IV does appear to affect the DV, then the

KEY IDEAS

A **laboratory experiment** is a study conducted in an artificial environment in which the experimenter manipulates an IV and measures the consequent changes in a DV, while carefully controlling extraneous variables.

Standardised instructions are a set of learned, written or recorded instructions presented to participants to tell them what to do. This ensures that all participants receive identical treatment and information, so differences between their performance on the DV are more likely to be due to the IV.

Extraneous variables are factors other than the IV which could affect performance on the DV (and so distort the results).

Situational variables are factors in the environment surrounding participants that can affect their performance on the DV, and so could obscure the effect of the IV.

KEY IDEAS

In a **true experiment** a researcher can randomly allocate participants to different levels of the IV.

In a **quasi-experiment** an experimenter makes use of an existing change or difference in situations to create levels of an IV, and then measures the DV in each condition.

A **field experiment** is a study in which the researcher manipulates an IV and measures a DV in the natural setting of the participants for the activity being tested.

Ecological validity is the term given to the extent to which findings generalise to other situations. This is affected by whether the situation (e.g. a laboratory) is a fair representation of the real world and whether the task is relevant (see mundane realism, page 263).

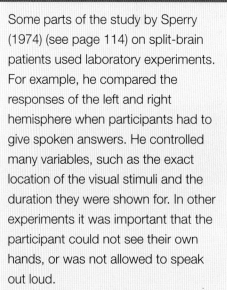

QUESTION SPOTLIGHT!

Some parts of the study by Sperry (1974) (see page 114) on split-brain patients used laboratory experiments. For example, he compared the responses of the left and right hemisphere when participants had to give spoken answers. He controlled many variables, such as the exact location of the visual stimuli and the duration they were shown for. In other experiments it was important that the participant could not see their own hands, or was not allowed to speak out loud.

All of these controls were implemented by standardised procedures for the experimenter and instructions for the participant. *Why are these important?*

QUESTION SPOTLIGHT!

Which of the following studies were laboratory experiments and which were field experiments?

1 Loftus and Palmer (1974) (see page 6): eyewitness testimony study.
2 Samuel and Bryant (1984) (see page 48): asking children only one question about conservation.
3 Reicher and Haslam (2006) (see page 149): BBC TV prison study.
4 Piliavin *et al.* (1969) (see page 162): good Samaritan study.
5 Griffiths (1994) (see page 202): gambling study.
6 Baron-Cohen *et al.* (1997) (see page 15): the eyes test study.
7 Rosenhan (1973) (see page 177): mental hospital study.

Figure 6.18
What extraneous variables might affect student performance in the classroom?

relationship is a causal one. One important variable to control in memory experiments is distractions –rehearsal is important and can be prevented by interference, so in laboratory experiments factors such as noise and the presence of other people is regulated. Factors in the surroundings that can disrupt an experiment, such as noise or light, are called **situational variables**. All the features that make the procedure of laboratory experiments so rigorously controlled also make them easy to replicate. Doing this allows researchers to be more confident about their findings.

THE FIELD EXPERIMENT

An alternative approach to using a laboratory is to conduct a **field experiment**. In this case, there is still an IV that is manipulated by the experimenter, and a DV that is measured. However, the setting is the participants' normal environment in relation to the behaviour being investigated. For example, the effect of different revision methods on memory might be tested in a classroom. The investigator could set up a situation in which a teacher uses revision diagrams for one topic and revision songs for another. The IV would be the revision strategy, either visual (diagrams) or auditory (songs). The DV would be measured using tests of each topic. As the situation would be familiar to the students, they should be relatively unaffected by being in an experiment compared to a similar test in a laboratory. They may not even know that they are in an experiment at all, so would be unlikely to respond to demand characteristics. When participants are unaware of the experiment, their behaviour is more likely to be representative of real life, and therefore the findings are more likely to generalise to other situations, i.e. to have high **ecological validity**. Of course, the lack of awareness does raise ethical issues.

One clear disadvantage of the field experiment is that it is difficult to maintain control over **situational variables**. This means that changes in the DV might be caused by factors other than the IV. In the case of the classroom example, the different topics could have been more difficult or interesting, or could have been taught at times in the term when the students were more or less tired. Any of these variables could have caused differences between conditions that would look as though there was an effect on the DV caused by the IV.

THE QUASI-EXPERIMENT

A quasi-experiment (or natural experiment) differs from a true experiment because the experimenter does not set up the levels of the IV. Quasi-experiments make use of 'natural', i.e. not artificially produced, changes or differences in circumstances to provide the experimental conditions. They can be conducted in laboratory or field settings. Researchers use quasi-experiments when it would be impractical or unethical to generate the conditions necessary for the different levels of the IV. For example, when comparing witnesses to real crimes who have been frightened or not, we cannot randomly allocate people to the 'frightened' and 'not-frightened' conditions. Instead, we would have to search for people who either had or had not had frightening experiences as eyewitnesses and use them as separate groups of participants.

Where quasi-experiments are conducted in the field, they have the benefit that the participants are in their usual environment so their behaviour is more likely to be representative of real life. As the participants are not actively allocated to conditions, it is more possible that the existence of the experiment can be hidden from them. This reduces the risk of demand characteristics affecting behaviour. Of course, because participants are not randomly allocated to different levels of the IV, it is difficult to distinguish the effects of any existing differences between groups of participants and those differences that are due to the experiment. For example, if we were to investigate the effects of organisation on revision using a quasi-experiment we might compare people who revise using cue-cards and mindmaps (high organisation), and those who revise using a highlighter pen to go through their class notes

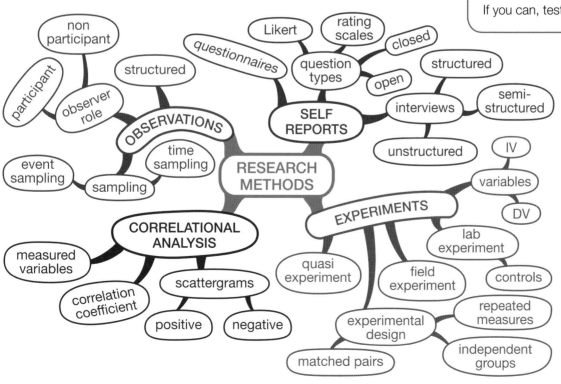

Figure 6.19
How well do different revision strategies work?

KEY IDEAS

Mundane realism is the extent to which an experimental task represents a real-world situation.

Generalisability is the extent to which findings from one situation or sample will apply to other situations or people.

(low organisation). Although the people who used the high-organisation techniques might get better results (i.e. there may be a difference in the DV) we wouldn't know if this was really caused by the revision method (the IV) or whether the participants in the high organisation group were simply more intelligent, or spent more time working, than those in the low organisation group.

ASSESSING RELIABILITY AND VALIDITY IN EXPERIMENTS

RELIABILITY

Laboratory experiments are conducted in an artificial setting, so the researcher can impose controls, for example through standardised procedures. These increase reliability as they ensure that all participants are treated in the same way. As field experiments (and some quasi-experiments) are conducted in the participants' normal environment for the situation or activity being explored, variables within the setting are harder to control, so there is likely to be greater variation between the precise circumstances under which the DV is measured between participants, which lowers their reliability relative to laboratory experiments. Remember, however, that it is still possible to impose some controls. Controls in any experiment make replication easier as researchers can be confident that they are following exactly the same procedure, for example giving identical instructions, using the same stimulus materials and the same timings, and measuring the DV in the same way. If replications produce the same results – i.e. if they demonstrate the same differences between the levels of the IV – a researcher can be confident that their findings are reliable. However, this is likely to be difficult in a quasi-experiment.

VALIDITY

In laboratory experiments, extraneous variable are controlled, so the researcher can be sure that any changes in the DV can have been caused only by the IV. This certainty is important because it means that the validity of the study is high. The measurement of the DV is typically very accurate, also increasing validity. Although these factors raise confidence that the influence of the independent variable is being measured, rather than the effects of extraneous ones, this does not necessarily mean that the findings really reflect the intended aim of the study. A problem with laboratory experiments is that, in general, the measure of the DV tends to be quite artificial, in other words the participants' responses are being measured in a way that doesn't reflect day to day life. This is described as a lack of **mundane realism**. For example, Loftus and Palmer asked participants to estimate the speed of a filmed car, but we aren't usually asked to respond to film clips in this way. Furthermore, the artificial setting of the laboratory means that the participants will almost certainly be aware that they are participating in a study (although they might be unaware of its aims), which means that their responses might not be representative of the way they would behave in other situations. This means that the results might not **generalise** beyond the laboratory setting; if so, the findings would be said to lack ecological validity.

The ecological validity of field experiments is likely (but is not guaranteed) to be higher than for laboratory studies as they use less artificial settings, so the participants are more likely to behave in true-to-life ways. Instead, field experiments face a different problem. Precisely because they are set in more authentic environments, situational variables are harder to control, so there is likely to be greater variation between the exact circumstances under which the DV is measured. Importantly, there might be uncontrolled variables arising between levels of the IV, which confound the results. For example, a study about helping behaviour might be conducted in a shopping centre. If the researchers were investigating the effect of crowding on helping, they might compare Saturday mornings (crowded) to Thursday mornings (not crowded). However, a potential confounding variable would be the type of people who were in the shopping centre on those days. Perhaps the shoppers at the weekend would be predominantly families, who might be more helpful, whereas those in the week would be business men and women, who might be too busy to stop and help, or older people who had a greater sense of community and might be more likely to help. Such effects could skew the results so that it *looked* as though crowding made people either more or less helpful – in which case neither would be true.

However, in field experiments the effect of demand characteristics would also be lower, as the aims of the study would be less apparent, and because participants mght be unaware that the experiment is taking place, their behaviour is also more likely to be realistic. Both of these points increase validity. Nevertheless, not telling the participants about the experiment in advance has disadvantages in terms of ethics. On one hand, it means that they have not been given the opportunity to give their informed consent to participate (see page 296), although conversely there is no need to deceive them about the aims.

In quasi-experiments it is more difficult, if not impossible, to impose controls on the sample. There is therefore less certainty that any observed changes in the DV have necessarily arisen as a consequence of the IV,

Figure 6.20
How sure can you be that the IV is the only factor that differs in a field experiment?

STRETCH & CHALLENGE ◎

You might have already looked at the website for the Ignobel awards (http://improbable.com/ig/) and have seen their publications ('The Annals of Improbable Research' and 'MiniAir').
Search through the research for some that is psychological in nature. Find an experiment and evaluate it in terms of its reliability and validity.

which potentially lowers validity. However, if the contrasting situations are chosen carefully, there could be very few extraneous variables. As with field experiments, there are advantages in comparison to contrived situations. Because the difference is naturally occurring, it is less likely that demand characteristics will be apparent (although this will also depend on how obviously the measure of the DV is taken). In addition, the ecological validity of the situation is necessarily high, because the change or difference is a real one. It is likely, therefore, that the test will be a valid one and that the findings will be highly representative.

TABLE 6.12 STRENGTHS AND WEAKNESSES OF THE EXPERIMENTAL METHOD

	Strengths	Weaknesses
Laboratory experiments	• Good control of extraneous variables. • Causal relationships can be determined. • Strict procedures allow them to be replicated, so researchers can be more confident about their findings. • In a repeated measures design, counterbalancing can be used to reduce order effects.	• The artificial situation could make participants' behaviour unrepresentative. • Participants could respond to demand characteristics and alter their behaviour.
Field experiments	• As participants are in their normal situation, their behaviour is likely to be representative. • Participants could be unaware that they are in a study, so demand characteristics are less problematic than in laboratory experiments.	• Control over extraneous variables is more difficult than in a laboratory, so they are less reliable and replication is more difficult. • The researcher cannot be sure that changes in the DV have been caused by changes in the IV. • Participants are likely to be unaware that they are in a study, which raises ethical issues.
Quasi-experiments	• They can be used to study real-world issues. • If participants are in their normal situation, their behaviour is likely to be representative. • If participants are unaware that they are in a study, demand characteristics will be less problematic. • They enable researchers to investigate variables that could not practically or ethically be manipulated.	• They are only possible when naturally occurring differences arise. • Control over extraneous variables is often very difficult. • As the researcher is not manipulating the IV, they can be less sure of the cause of changes in the DV, i.e. a causal relationship cannot be established. • They are generally hard to replicate.
All experiments	• Using a repeated measures or matched pairs design helps to reduce participant variables. • Using an independent groups design helps to avoid the influence of demand characteristics and of order effects.	• If participants are unaware that they are in a study, this raises ethical issues. • The researcher's expectations could lead to biased results.

EXAM FOCUS

We now show you some of the sorts of questions that could be asked about the experimental method in your exam. We will then show you some examples of the sorts of answers we believe might be successful and less successful, and point out some classic traps to avoid.

QUESTION 1

Psychologists wanted to investigate why we don't laugh when we tickle ourselves. One idea is that tickling is a social act that is out of our control and must be done by another person. To investigate this, participants had the soles of their feet tickled by another person at any time during a 30-second period. Later on, the same participants had to tickle themselves. They put their feet on a tickling machine (a feather on a rotating turntable) at any time they chose during a 30-second period. The volume of laughter was recorded in decibels.

(a) Identify the experimental design used in this study. *(2 marks)*

(b) Outline one strength and one weakness of using this experimental design in this study. *(6 marks)*

(c) Identify the independent variable (IV) and the dependent variable (DV) in this study. *(2 marks)*

(d) Describe and evaluate one other way to measure the dependent variable (DV) in this study. *(10 marks)*

QUESTION 2

Researchers conducted an experiment to investigate the ability of 10 males and 10 females to recognise emotions displayed on the face. A set of 12 photographs of the same person displaying the six primary emotions (happiness, sadness, anger, surprise, fear and disgust) was used. Participants had 10 seconds to look at each photograph and had to identify the emotion displayed before moving on to the next. One mark was awarded for each correct response, giving a total out of 12.

(a) Explain what is meant by the descriptive statistic called the mean. *(2 marks)*

(b) Explain how the mean would have been calculated for the males and females in this study. *(4 marks)*

(c) When would the descriptive statistic called the 'median' be more appropriate, and why? *(4 marks)*

(d) Evaluate the reliability and validity of the way the dependent variable (DV) has been measured in this study. *(10 marks)*

QUESTION 3

Researchers conducted an experiment using an independent measures design to investigate whether people rate the friendliness of other people more highly if they receive physical contact.

They did the experiment between 11am and 2pm on a Wednesday in a coffee bar, as customers were paying. The cashier touched some customers lightly on the upper arm, but did not touch others. Afterwards, outside the coffee bar, the customers were asked how friendly they thought the staff were on a scale of 1 (not very friendly) to 10 (extremely friendly).

(a) Identify the sampling technique used to obtain participants for this study and suggest one weakness with it. *(4 marks)*

(b) What is an 'independent measures' design? *(2 marks)*

(c) Identify two controls that researchers could have used in this study, and explain why they would have needed them. *(6 marks)*

(d) Identify the dependent variable (DV) in this study. *(2 marks)*

(e) Outline one strength and one weakness of the way that the researchers measured the dependent variable (DV) in this study. *(6 marks)*

QUESTION 4

Researchers conducted a matched pairs design experiment to investigate whether background noise can interfere with a person's concentration when performing a cognitive task.

They placed an advert in the local paper asking interested people to turn up at a local college on a particular day. On arrival, participants were matched for age (as near as possible) and had to complete a difficult word-search task. Half had the noise from a radio station playing loudly in the background and the other half had silence while completing the word-search task. The results obtained are presented in the table below.

Participant	Condition 1 (silence) Time to complete word search (seconds)	Condition 2 (noise from radio) Time to complete word search (seconds)
1	210	275
2	190	225
3	300	285
4	245	470
5	225	305
6	205	250
7	310	405
8	195	335

(a) Suggest an appropriate alternate hypothesis for this study. (4 marks)

(b) What is a 'matched pairs design'? (2 marks)

(c) Give one strength and one weakness of using a matched pairs design in this study. (4 marks)

(d) Name and describe an alternative sampling method for this study. (4 marks)

(e) Sketch an appropriate graph to display the findings from this study. (4 marks)

(f) Describe how the dependent variable (DV) has been operationalised in this study. (2 marks)

SOME ANSWERS AND COMMENTS

QUESTION 3 (a) Identify the sampling technique used to obtain participants for this study and suggest one weakness with it. (4 marks)

Ceri's answer:

The sample was whoever went to the coffee shop that day. This is a poor sample as not everyone likes coffee so they would not go in, so it's not representative.

Hugh's answer:

It is an opportunity sample as you only got to be in it if you went into the coffee shop when they were testing the friendliness ratings on Wednesday from 11–2pm, so not everyone has the opportunity. They are not good samples as they are not representative. Only people who have lots of free time to go out at this time of day to a coffee bar would be in the sample, which leaves out loads of people. These may be much friendlier people but they do not have a chance to be in your sample, so it can't be generalised from.

We say: 2 marks.
Ceri, if asked to identify the sampling technique then you need to actually state what type it is rather than just describe it. You say that it is whoever went into the coffee shop, so you understand that it is opportunity sampling – but you forget to name it! You should also explain your weakness a little more clearly and relate this in more detail to the context of the study, i.e. customers in the coffee shop between 11am–2pm on a Wednesday. Look at the description of the study and use as much context as you can from it that is relevant to each answer.

We say: 4 marks.
You have named the correct sampling technique here, Hugh, and put it into a clear context. The weakness you gave is a good one, as it is really well explained and expanded on, making it clear that you know what you are talking about. Good psychological knowledge here.

QUESTION 3 (b) What is an 'independent measures' design? *(2 marks)*

Neema's answer:

This is where people do only one half of the experiment and not all of it.

> **We say:** 1 mark.
> Neema, try to explain key terms a little more clearly. Your answer does not communicate the idea of separate groups of participants in each of the experimental conditions. You need to go over the types of design again.

Ruth's answer:

It is where in an experiment you have two groups of different people and they do only one of the conditions each, and not both of them.

> **We say:** 2 marks.
> Clear and to the point – a good explanation of this design, Ruth.

QUESTION 3 (c) Identify two controls that researchers could have used in this study, and explain why they would have needed them. *(6 marks)*

Kai's answer:

Two controls would be that you should have the same cashier touching the customers on the arm all through the study. Second is that the cashier must be the same in their manner to all customers and not be smiley to some and grumpy and miserable to others. You need controls in an experiment so that everything is exactly the same and standardised so nothing else affects the study.

> **We say:** 3 marks.
> Kai, always read the questions through very carefully in your exams to make sure that you are doing exactly what the examiner wants. Here, you identify two really good controls, but then have a general point as to why controls are needed. If you look at the question, you can see that you need to explain why each of them individually would be needed, not to give a general comment as to why controls in a general way are required.

Carol's answer:

First, they should have a control of how busy the coffee bar was or not, and try to do the study when it was roughly the same amount of other people. This is a good idea because if it was really busy so people were squashed at their tables sometimes and had to queue for ages they would be feeling annoyed compared to people who go in when it is quiet. They may rate friendliness less if they were annoyed by being squashed. Another control is that the cashier in the coffee bar should try to touch people on the arm in the same way all the time as they leave. If they nearly hit them sometimes and were very

Continued

> **We say:** 6 marks.
> Carol, you show a sound knowledge of methodology and experimental design in this answer. You have picked out two very relevant controls and showed very clearly why they are needed. You explanation included examples from the study to show how you were thinking of this particular study and the features of its design – not just giving general comments on any procedure or methods. Nice work.

lightly touching other people this would not be a fair test. It would make people angry to be pushed on the arm and make them give bad ratings of friendliness compared to others who were touched much more gently than this. This makes it not standardised very well.

QUESTION 3 (d) Identify the dependent variable (DV) in this study. *(2 marks)*

Gavin's answer:

The DV is friendliness.

Aisha's answer:

The DV in the study is the friendliness rating that the customers gave on the 0-10 rating as to how friendly they thought staff were in the coffee bar.

We say: 1 mark
Gavin, it is true generally that the DV is friendliness, but you need to say whose friendliness, i.e. that of the staff as rated by the customers. You were just not clear enough here.

We say: 2 marks.
A well-explained and clear outline of the DV here, Aisha, with all the relevant points. Explaining a DV must be exact and very specific – and this was.

QUESTION 3 (e) Outline one strength and one weakness of the way that the researchers measured the dependent variable (DV) in this study. *(6 marks)*

Tom's answer:

It would be really quick and simple to get people to give a score from 0–10, so they would not mind doing it for you. A weakness is that the people would probably be in a hurry when leaving and not want to be bothered by a researcher so just put down any number without thinking about it, so it is not accurate about what they really think.

We say: 3 marks.
Tom, having six marks available for a question on one strength and one weakness should suggest to you that you should explain your answer a little more than you have done here. Your points were basically fine and were correct, but to show your examiner your psychological knowledge, tell them a little more about the points by expanding and explaining them. Your examiner will not know what you know, if you don't tell them! Add detail to both your points to make them clearer and remember you must always have plenty of context from the experiment, as the question does say 'in this study' – that should be a hint for you.

Aina's answer:

The good point is that you do get numbers from the rating scale so it is very easy to analyse and compare. You can see how many participants in each condition thought staff in the coffee shop were really friendly with high scores, or not friendly with low scores. It is quantitative data.

A bad point is that customers might feel bad if they rate staff with low scores as they might go in the coffee shop a lot and know the staff there. This means they might give a socially desirable answer of a high rating which is not their true feeling on friendliness, so their rating scale score is not accurate and the scores are not really any good.

We say: 6 marks.
Evaluation is obviously something you have been working on, Aina. You have given an appropriate and detailed answer for both the strength and weakness. They are really well explained and have comment and detail from the actual study, i.e. context, rather than just being general points.

QUESTION 4 (a) Suggest an appropriate alternate hypothesis for this study. *(4 marks)*

Millie's answer:

People will do worse on the word search when there is noise on the radio.

We say: 2 marks.
Always remember the key to writing a clear hypothesis is that you have to fully identify both your variables Millie. You have not completely done this, so your hypothesis is not fully clear. Saying they will 'do worse' does not make the DV very explicit. It is measured using timings, so you could include that. You have only really mentioned half of the IV by saying 'noise', but have left out the other condition of silence, and the hypothesis should have both of these. Practice writing a few hypotheses to get them more specific.

Jake's answer:

Participants will take a longer time, as measured on a stopwatch, to find all the words in the word search when they have a radio on very loud, compared to when it is silent conditions.

We say: 2 marks.
You give a really specific prediction in this hypothesis of what you expect to happen in the study, Jake. You clearly say what the variables are. Nicely written.

QUESTION 4 (b) What is a 'matched pairs design'? *(2 marks)*

Richard's answer:

The participants are all very similar to each other in the different conditions of the study. You choose them for this reason to be similar.

We say: 1 mark.
You appear to have got the basic idea here, Richard, but it is not particularly well explained. Always make it easy for your examiner to give you marks by giving clear explanations and setting out your points in a straightforward way. The participants are similar, as you have actually chosen a relevant characteristic to match them on in each group. You need to tell us that, rather than being vague.

Aoife's answer:

This is where in an experiment you try to make sure that the people in your two groups for the experiment are as similar as they can be. If you had someone who was 25 years old in one group, you would get someone else this age for the other group. You can choose what particular thing you want to match them with.

We say: 2 marks.
You provide us with a very explicit outline of what matched pairs means, Aoife – you clearly know your designs.

QUESTION 4 (c) Give one strength and one weakness of using a matched pairs design in this study. *(4 marks)*

Mike's answer:

The strength is that they are really very similar people to each other in the conditions, which is good for your experiment as it is a type of control. A weakness is that they are still not the same people, even though they are very similar. This means that the results in the two conditions might be different because of this fact and not what you are investigating in your study.

We say: 2 marks.
Mike, lots of students lose marks in exams as they fail to read the question carefully to see what the examiner wants them to do. You failed to spot the part of the question that says 'in this study'. This meant that you needed to refer to details from the outline of the study in the question (i.e. the context), such as the two conditions of noise and silence and matching on age for them. Your two points were appropriate, but lacked this link.

Yvonne's answer:

One strength is that there are fewer differences between your participants in the two groups, so overall there are less participant variables affecting the score. People might get better at doing a word search as they get older, so matching for age means that it is only the radio noise or silence affecting them, rather than age. However, it can take be difficult to get people who match each other that well for the groups, so it could be quite a problem to actually do. You don't know who will apply to take part and if they were all different ages it would be hard to match them on age into the radio noise and silence groups to do the word search.

We say: 4 marks.
Some good psychological knowledge here, Yvonne. We like your well-expressed points, which show you fully understand this type of design. There was quite a bit of detail from the study itself, showing you have addressed all parts of the question – a good strategy if you want to do well.

QUESTION 4 (d) Name and describe an alternative sampling method for this study. *(4 marks)*

Gwen's answer:

An alternative would be instead of putting the advert in the local paper you put up posters around the town and get people to ring you if they want to take part as you give your mobile number on the poster. You could get lots of people this way as they would easily see the poster in town.

Eshe's answer:

Another sampling method would be to do an opportunity sample. This is where you get people who are where you are as the researcher when you are recruiting the sample. They have the opportunity to take part if they are there. I could actually go to the local town centre and stand in a busy spot on a few lunchtimes in the week from 12–2 pm. I could ask passing shoppers if they would like to take part. If they do I would tell them to come to the local college to take part and give details of when it would be.

We say: 0 marks.
Gwen, you have misinterpreted the question here, unfortunately. You are asked for an alternative sampling method, not an alternative way of gathering the same type of sample. In the study they use a self-selecting sample using an advert in the local paper. You should then identify an alternative sampling method, such as opportunity sampling, and describe how that could be used. You have described another way of getting a self-selected sample. Read questions a couple of times to make sure you are certain what they are asking.

We say: 3 marks.
Eshe, you have identified another sampling method that would be appropriate to use in this study. We like the detail in your answer explaining exactly how you could use this method to actually gather some participants. Another researcher could easily carry this out.

QUESTION 4 (e) Sketch an appropriate graph to display the findings from this study. *(4 marks)*

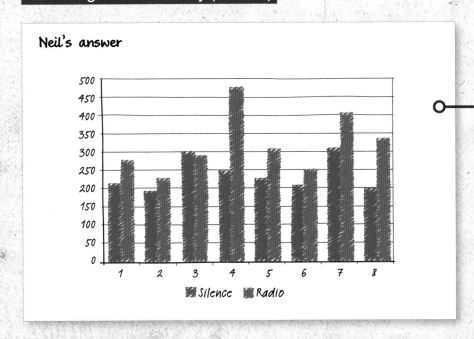

Neil's answer

We say: 2 marks.
Neil, while your graph does show the two conditions from the study, and you have identified these on your graph, there are several things missing from it. You do not have a title, and it is really important to specify what the data on the graph actually shows. Put a clear title on every graph or chart that you draw in psychology. The other point to remember is that you need to label the axes clearly, to show that one is the time in seconds to complete the word search, and the other is the participants. Without this detail the graph is incomplete. Whenever you draw a graph, check your labeling carefully to avoid missing out on marks.

QUESTION 4 (f) Describe how the dependent variable (DV) has been operationalised in this study. *(2 marks)*

Nessa's answer:

It is operationalised by seeing how the noise affected them completing the word search and if it made the task more difficult. We can see how much more difficult it was from their scores.

Amir's answer:

The DV was how long people took to do the word search. The researchers used a timer to see this and they then wrote down how many seconds it was, so they could compare the conditions of noise and silence.

We say: 0 marks.
Nessa, you should try not to be vague and general when talking about features of an experiment. Focus on being really precise. A dependent variable is what you measure to see if the independent variable has had an effect. This means that you need to state clearly the actual measure of performance used. In this study, participants were timed, in seconds, while doing the word search – so you need to say exactly that. You said how the noise affected participants, but you need to specify what was done to find that out!

We say: 2 marks.
Amir, you clearly understand what is meant by operationalising a variable and have told us exactly what was measured (the time to do the word search) and how it was measured (in seconds). This is very precise and just what is needed, as your examiner is looking for specific details to show you can identify the parts of an experiment.

C6

PSYCHOLOGICAL INVESTIGATIONS

Part 2: Understanding research

In this section we will explore the planning and evaluation processes that are common to all psychological investigations and the particular design decisions required in planning investigations using each of the four research methods. Specifically, we will look at different types of hypotheses, and at how to respond to investigations described in a source, including: variables, samples and sampling techniques, forms of measurement and procedures for investigations, and the strengths and weaknesses of different approaches to these issues. We will also look at design decisions in experiments, correlational analyses and self-report studies, including issues of reliability, validity and ethics.

E – AIMS, HYPOTHESES AND PROCEDURES: DESIGNING AND EVALUATING INVESTIGATIONS

 KEY IDEAS

A **hypothesis** (or **plural hypotheses**) is a testable statement that predicts a relationship between variables, such as in an experiment where a change will produce an increase or a decrease in the DV, or, in a correlation, whether an increase in one variable will be linked to an increase or a decrease in another variable.

An **alternate** (or **alternative**) **hypothesis** is a testable statement that predicts that there will be a relationship between variables in an investigation.

A **one-tailed** (or **directional**) **hypothesis** is a statement that predicts the direction of a relationship between variables, for example in an experiment whether a change will produce an increase or a decrease in the DV, or, in a correlation, whether an increase in one variable will be linked to an increase or a decrease in another variable.

A **two-tailed** (or **non-directional**) **hypothesis** is a statement that predicts how one variable will be related to another, for example whether there will be a difference in the DV between levels of the IV (in an experiment), or whether there will be a relationship between the measured variables (in a correlation).

INTRODUCTION

This section explores the details you need to design and evaluate your own studies and those presented in a source in an examination.

HYPOTHESES

A **hypothesis** is a testable statement of the investigator's predictions about the results of their study. In most published research the hypotheses are not stated, so you are unlikely to have encountered them even if you have read original journal articles. However, they are useful in the process of drawing conclusions from research, which you need to understand them.

The alternate hypothesis

Most studies have a hypothesis as well as an aim, but some, for example some observations, are not testing a particular idea, so they do not. In contrast, the aim in an experiment is very specific. If you conduct an experiment to find out whether increasing arousal with loud music improves or worsens recall of words, your aim would be to test this effect. You would need a corresponding hypothesis, for example: 'There is a difference between the number of words recalled when listening to loud or quiet music.' This is called your alternate (or 'alternative') hypothesis. An **alternate hypothesis** states the difference you expect to find between levels of the IV.

Direction in hypotheses: one-tailed and two-tailed hypotheses

The alternate hypothesis (sometimes written as HA) above is a **two-tailed hypothesis**. In an experiment, we expect that the IV will change the DV, but we might not be sure whether the effect will be an increase or a decrease, in which case we use a two-tailed hypothesis. We would probably choose this type of hypothesis if we were testing the effect of a variable that had not been investigated before – for example, if we were investigating the effect of eating jelly babies on recall. They might help us to remember, or they might distract us. If most previous research suggests that we can be confident about the nature of an effect we can use a **one-tailed hypothesis**. In a test of how post-event information from talking to other witnesses affects testimonies, we could be confident that talking would make them less accurate. This is a one-tailed prediction, so a hypothesis might be: 'Testimonies from eyewitnesses who have discussed events with others are less accurate than those of witnesses who have not discussed events.' The corresponding two-tailed hypothesis would have been: 'There is a difference in the accuracy of testimonies from witnesses who have and who have not discussed events.'

A two-tailed hypothesis in a correlational study simply predicts that there will be a relationship between the two measured variables. A one-tailed hypothesis states whether this relationship will be a positive or a negative correlation. For example, in a study looking for a relationship between brain volume and braininess, we might say: 'There will be a relationship between brain volume and braininess'. This would be a two-tailed hypothesis. Alternatively, we could suggest a one-tailed hypothesis, such as: 'There will be a positive correlation between brain volume and braininess'. We could also say: 'As brain volume increases braininess increases'. This would be a one-tailed hypothesis too. Remember that we cannot say that one factor *causes* the change in the other. One-tailed hypotheses for negative correlations follow the same pattern, for example: 'As brain size increases, reaction time decreases'. This could alternatively be written as: 'There will be a negative correlation between brain size and reaction time'.

The null hypothesis

As well as the alternate hypothesis, you also need to be clear about the **null hypothesis**. This states that any difference in the DV between levels of the IV is so small that there is a high probability that it has arisen by chance. This is an important idea because it is used in statistical testing. These tests (which you will study at A2 level) help you to decide whether it is likely that the null hypothesis is correct. A typical null hypothesis (H_0)

QUESTION SPOTLIGHT!

The aim for approach 1 of Dement and Kleitman (1958) (see page 97) is written as a hypothesis.
Is it one or two tailed?
The experiments by Loftus and Palmer (1974) (see page 6) expected eyewitness testimony to be less accurate with leading questions.
Explain whether the hypotheses would have been one- or two-tailed.

KEY IDEAS

A **null hypothesis** is a testable statement saying that any difference or correlation is the result of chance, i.e. that no pattern in the results has arisen because of the variables being studied.

Figure 6.21
Is brain size related to brainiess?

1   Imagine an experiment testing the effect of eating either healthy or unhealthy food on concentration. *Write a two-tailed hypothesis for this study.*

2   I predict that listening to music will make students quicker at completing dot-to-dot puzzles. *Write a one-tailed hypothesis for this experiment.*

3   A teacher thinks that there might be a correlation between the amount her students have eaten and their concentration. She isn't sure whether eating more will make them less hungry, so they will concentrate better, or that eating more will make them sleepy, so they will concentrate less. *Write a two-tailed hypothesis for her study.*

4   A watch-dog organisation is concerned about a possible relationship between eyewitness accuracy and the amount of post-event exposure to media reports about the crime. *Write a one-tailed hypothesis for this correlation.*

would be: 'Any difference in the accuracy of testimonies from witnesses who have and have not discussed events is due to chance.'

The null hypothesis basically says that 'any difference in the DV between condition X and condition Y is due to chance'. If we were investigating the effect of age on eyewitness memory, a suitable null hypothesis would be: 'Any difference in recall between older and younger witnesses is due to chance.' So that the sentence makes sense, it is sometimes better to swap the order around – but always make sure that you state both of the levels of the IV and the DV. So a slightly different way to write this null hypothesis would be: 'Any difference between older and younger witnesses' recall is due to chance.' You can also express this by saying that there will be no difference between the DV between different levels of the IV, e.g. 'There will be no difference between recall by older and younger witnesses'. But beware – there is a risk of saying that there is no difference between the IV and the DV, which is incorrect!

STRETCH & CHALLENGE

Which of the alternate hypotheses above are one-tailed and which are two-tailed?

Operationally define the variables in each of the null hypotheses.

QUESTION SPOTLIGHT!

Read each of the following hypotheses.
Which are alternate and which are null hypotheses?

1   Any difference between test scores of students who have learned using mindmaps or mnemonics is due to chance.

2   There will be a difference between the helpfulness of people who own pets and people who do not.

3   Any correlation between time spent doing homework and achievement is due to chance.

4   Students who do their homework on the bus or train will get lower scores than those who sit at a desk.

5   There will be a negative correlation between number of hours spent doing a part-time job and module grades.

6   Students who play a musical instrument will concentrate better in class than those who do not.

As with experiments, correlational studies need a null hypothesis. This predicts that any relationship could have occurred by chance. A typical null hypothesis for a correlational study reads: 'Any relationship between variable X and variable Y is due to chance.' For example, 'Any relationship between brain volume and braininess is due to chance.'

VARIABLES

The key things you need to remember about variables are that experiments have independent and dependent variables, and that correlations have two measured variables.

Operationalising and measuring variables: the independent and dependent variable

Experiments investigate changes or differences in the DV between two or more levels of the IV, which are set up by the experimenter. In an experiment, the IV must be clearly defined, or 'operationalised', so that the manipulation of the conditions is a valid representation of the intended differences. For example, in a study with an IV of age, with 'young' and 'old' groups, it is important to know how old the groups are. The DV must also be operationalised, so it can be effectively measured. In a study comparing recall of old and young witnesses, we might measure the DV by counting the number of things they remember correctly, or the number of errors they make.

Measuring variables: the levels of measurement

Experiments and correlational analyses produce quantitative data, i.e. generate one or more or numerical 'scores' for each participant. The different types of data differ in their relative strengths and weaknesses and in the way that they are analysed (see page 294).

Quantitative data can be recorded in many different ways. Although it is usually numerical, sometimes this is not obvious. For example, when a researcher uses Likert scales (see page 217), the results are points on a scale, usually from 'strongly agree' to 'strongly disagree'. However, these scores can still be counted up, making the data quantitative. There are four different types of numerical data, referred to as different **levels of measurement**. These are:

- Nominal data
- Ordinal data
- Interval data
- Ratio data

(Note that their initial letters spell 'NOIR', a helpful way to remember them.)

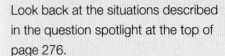

QUESTION SPOTLIGHT!

Look back at the situations described in the question spotlight at the top of page 276.

1 *Identify the IV and DV in each experimental study.*

2 *Operationalise each of these variables.*

KEY IDEAS

Levels of measurement refers to the type of quantitative data obtained (see nominal, ordinal, interval or ratio data).

Nominal data – data as totals of named categories, such as the number of participants saying 'yes' or 'no'.

Ordinal data – data as points along a scale, for example a rating or Likert scale, such that the points fall in order but there are not necessarily equal gaps between those points.

Interval data – data as points on scale that has equal gaps between the points but does not have a real zero, e.g. standardised measures such as IQ tests.

Ratio data – data as points on scale that has equal gaps between the points and a real zero, e.g. centimetres, beats-per-minute, etc.

What level of measurement was used to score the DV in each of the following studies?

1 Maguire *et al.* (2000) (see page 85) measured hippocampal volume in taxi drivers.

2 Piliavin *et al.* (1969) (see page 162) measured time for train passengers to respond.

3 Samuel and Bryant (1984) (see page 48) recorded whether children responded correctly or incorrectly to a question about the changing appearance of materials.

4 Dement and Kleitman (1957) (see page 97) recorded the number of words in participants' dream narratives.

5 Reicher and Haslam (2006) (see page 149) used seven-item scales with end-points labeled 'not at all' and 'extremely' to measure social identification in the prison study.

Nominal data

Results that are just totals in two or more named categories that are unrelated are called **nominal data**. This includes answers to simple questions, such as saying 'yes' or 'no'. There can be more than two categories, for example if eye-movements are classified into 'horizontal', 'vertical' or 'both horizontal and vertical'. The important idea is that these scores are not related in a way that would allow them to lie along the same scale. Closed questions in interviews or on questionnaires often generate nominal data.

Ordinal data

In **ordinal data**, the results are points on a scale. The results themselves might be numbers or words, but the points relate to one another, so they could be put in order, for example from smallest to biggest, or from worst to best. There needs to be a clear increase in the value of points along the scale but the size of each increase does not have to be equal, i.e. the gaps between the points on the scale do not have to be the same. For example, we could ask participants to rate how good they think their memory is on a scale that reads: 'very poor', 'poor', 'average', "quite good', 'very good'. We would know that people who rated themselves as 'very good' were much better than average, but we would not know for sure if they were twice as good as people who said they were 'quite good'. Numerical scales can also produce ordinal data, for example, if an eyewitness indicates how certain they are that their recall is accurate on a scale of 1 to 10. Because the participants are only estimating, we cannot be sure that one person's interpretation of the scale is the same as another's, so the absolute value of each point might not be the same. To help you to remember that ordinal data is points in order along a scale, look at the first three letters.

Interval data

Like ordinal data, **interval data** has scores on a linear scale; the points increase in value. However, on an interval scale, the divisions between the points are equal. For example, if participants in a memory test have to recall nonsense items, such as FZC, DMP, WBR, HTG, LXV, SQJ, each one is equally memorable, as they are all unfamiliar. The same might be true for some words lists, such as ant, cat, dog, hen, fox, pig, as they are all familiar three-letter, one-syllable animal names. These would be interval scales. However, on a word list that included rhinoceros or porcupine, it is unlikely that each item would be equally memorable, so the gaps between the points on the scale of 'the number of words recalled' would not all be equal, and so the scale could not be described as an interval level of measurement. In psychology, commonly used intervals scales include measures of intelligence and personality. To help you to remember interval scales, remember that there are equal intervals between the points.

Ratio data

Ratio data, like interval data, has equal intervals between the points. They differ because ratio scales also have a real zero. Although it might not be possible for a participant to score zero, that is where the measurements on the scale start. For example, in an experiment on anxiety in eyewitnesses we might measure pulse rate to indicate how anxious the participants were. Even the most relaxed people wouldn't score zero for their pulse rate, but the scale of 'beats per minute' would be measuring from this baseline. Think back to the example of

QUESTION SPOTLIGHT! ⟩⟨

Look back to your operationalisation of the DV for the situations described in the question spotlight on page 276. *Were your proposed measures of the DV in each study nominal, ordinal, interval or ratio data?*

TABLE 6.13 STRENGTHS AND WEAKNESSES OF DIFFERENT WAYS TO MEASURE VARIABLES

	Strengths	Weaknesses
Nominal	• Easy to generate from closed questions, so large amounts of data can be collected quickly, thus increasing reliability. • Quick to find the mode to assess central tendency.	• Without a linear scale, participants might be unable to express degrees of response. • Points are not on a linear scale, so medians and means cannot be used to assess central tendency.
Ordinal	• More informative than nominal data, as it indicates relative values on a linear scale rather than just totals. • Easy to generate from Likert and rating scales. • Points are on a linear scale, so a median can be used as well as a mode to assess central tendency.	• As the gaps between the points are only relative, comparisons between participants might be invalid, as they may interpret the scale differently. • Gaps between the points are not equal, so means cannot be used to assess central tendency.
Interval	• More informative than nominal and ordinal data, as the points are directly comparable because all the points are of equal value. • Easy to generate from closed questions. • Points are on a linear scale, with equal gaps between the points, so a mean can be used as well as the mode and median to assess central tendency.	• There is no absolute baseline to the scale, so scoring zero might not mean that the participant does not demonstrate that variable at all – it might merely indicate that the scale does not measure it.
Ratio	• More informative than any other level of measurement, as the values are absolute (because the scale has a real zero). • Scientific measurements are highly reliable. • Points are on a linear scale, with equal gaps between them so a mean can be used as well as the mode and median.	• Scientific scales do not exist for many psychological phenomena, so it might not be possible to generate ratio data.

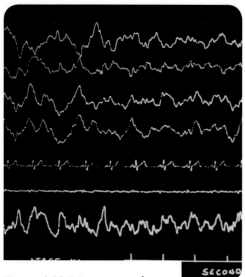

Figure 6.22 Measures such as frequency and amplitude of brain waves measured with an electro-encephalograph (EEG) are ratio scales.

remembering a word list. If a person scored zero for recall of words, it wouldn't necessarily mean they had no memory (they might just be poor at remembering animal names). However, if a participant had a pulse rate of zero, it *would* mean that they had no pulse at all. All physical measures, such as centimetres, kilos and degrees Centigrade are all ratio scales. To help you remember that ratio scales are often mathematical units, think of working out *ratios* in maths.

Samples and sampling

The group of participants in a study are called the **sample**. They are selected from the target population and should represent that population. Details about the sample that indicate its diversity – such as age, ethnicity and gender – are important in most investigations. Depending on the study, many other characteristics of the sample may be relevant, such as socio-economic status, education, employment, geographical location or occupation. Sample size is also important. Small samples are less reliable and less likely to be representative. In addition, different sampling methods produce samples that vary in their representativeness.

Opportunity sampling

Researchers often choose a sample simply by using those people who are around at the time. This is called **opportunity sampling** and is unlikely to fairly represent the population. Think about any studies you have done. You probably conducted them on your class, friends, family or students in the canteen. These people will all tend to be very alike – they won't include the variety that exists in the population from which they come. For example, your classmates are probably all in the same year, doing the same subjects, and might be predominantly of one gender. This means your results will not reflect the scores that people of different ages and interests at your school or college might produce. Despite this potential problem, opportunity sampling is the most common method, even for professional psychologists, many of whom rely on university students for participants. This is acceptable where the results are unlikely to be affected by features such as age, education or socioeconomic status.

Self-selected sampling

Rather than asking people directly, you might request volunteers. This might be done by putting up a notice, making an announcement or posting a request on the Internet. The people who respond and become participants choose to do so, and are described as a **self-selected sample**. This sampling technique is also unrepresentative of the population. Volunteers are likely to have more free time than average and, apart from being willing, tend to have other characteristics in common, such as being better educated. However, it is a very useful technique when looking for participants who are unusual in some way – for example, in Sperry's study of split-brain patients (see page 114).

Random sampling

Both opportunity and self-selected samples run the risk of being biased – they will probably contain very similar people and are unlikely to include a spread of characteristics of the population. A better way to obtain participants is by **random sampling**, which ensures that each person in the population has an equal chance of being chosen. This means that the sample is much more likely to be representative. This is quite different from an opportunity or self-selected sample. If you place an advert for volunteers on the library notice board, students who never go to the library cannot be included. If you find people by opportunity at the start of the day, the students who are always late cannot be included. If, however, you start with a numbered list of all students and use a random number generator to chose the sample, any individual is equally likely to be chosen. For a small population, this can be done by allocating each person a number, putting into a hat pieces of paper with each number on, and drawing out numbers until there are enough for the sample.

QUESTION SPOTLIGHT!

Which sampling method was used in each of the following studies?

- Reicher and Haslam (2006) (see page 149) recruited participants to their prison study though adverts in the national press and leaflets.
- Maguire *et al*. (2000) (see page 85) used a group of taxi drivers who volunteered for the study.
- Piliavin *et al*. (1969) (see page 162) observed train passengers who happened to be in the carriage.

TABLE 6.14 STRENGTHS AND WEAKNESSES OF SAMPLING TECHNIQUES

	Strengths	Weaknesses
Opportunity sample – participants are chosen because they are available, e.g. university students selected because they are around at the time.	Quicker and easier than other methods, as the participants are readily available in the same location as the researcher.	Non-representative, as the kinds of people available are likely to be limited, and therefore similar, making the sample biased.
Self-selected sample – participants are invited to participate, e.g. through advertisements or via email or notices. Those who reply become the sample.	Relatively easy because the participants come to you and are committed, e.g. they are likely to turn up for repeat testing.	Non-representative, as the kinds of people who respond to requests are likely to be similar, e.g. the might be better educated or have free time.
Random sample – all members of the population (i.e. possible participants) are allocated numbers, and a fixed amount of these are selected in a unbiased way, e.g. by taking numbers from a hat or using a random number generator.	Should be representative, as all types of people in the population are equally likely to be chosen. Findings are therefore more likely to generalise to a wider population.	Difficult, as everyone in the population must be equally likely to be chosen, but this is hard to achieve, e.g. through lack of information or access, and even then the sample might be biased, e.g. if only girls happen to be selected.

THE PROCEDURE: DESIGNING PSYCHOLOGICAL INVESTIGATIONS

When designing the procedure of a study, researchers have to consider the relative importance of ethics (see page 296) and scientific rigour. In the previous sections we discussed four different research methods:

- The self-report (see pages 215–30)
- The observational method (see pages 231–42)
- The correlational analysis (see pages 243–51)
- The experimental method (see pages 252–72).

In this section, we will remind you about these and explore how an appropriate technique is selected and applied to a research problem. The most commonly used method is the experiment. This is a study in which an independent variable (IV) is manipulated, and consequent changes in a dependent variable (DV) are measured, in order to establish a cause-and-effect relationship. Different experimental designs might be used in which participants are allocated to levels of the IV in different ways. These include:

- *Independent groups design* – different groups of participants are used for each level of the IV.
- *Repeated measures design* – each participant performs in every level of the IV.
- *Matched pairs design* – participants are arranged into pairs; each pair is similar in ways that are important to the study and the members of each pair perform in the two different levels of the IV.

In Table 6.15, a range of research methods is briefly described to remind you about how they can be used.

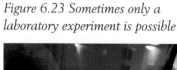
Figure 6.23 Sometimes only a laboratory experiment is possible

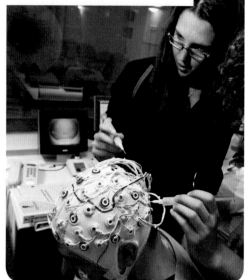

Design decisions in experiments
Laboratory, field or quasi-experiment?

The first decision is whether the IV can be manipulated at all. If the IV will change during the experiment, but this is not under the control of the researcher, then it will be a quasi-experiment. This method tends to be used when it is unethical or impractical to manipulate the IV. Here is an example of a quasi-experiment: a researcher believes that high stress levels will lead to a greater incidence of depression. It would clearly be unethical to deliberately increase stress with the intention of inducing depression. However, the incidence of depression in students could be measured immediately before their exams and some time afterwards.

In true experiments, the researcher actively allocates participants to conditions or manipulates the situation to create different conditions.

TABLE 6.15 WHEN ARE DIFFERENT RESEARCH METHODS USED?	
	When is the method used?
Laboratory experiment	When looking for differences, comparisons or cause-and-effect relationships. It must be possible to actively change the levels of the IV, i.e. to allocate participants to conditions, and to record the DV accurately. It is important that the behaviour is likely to be relatively unaffected by a contrived environment.
Field experiment	When looking for differences, comparisons or cause-and-effect relationships. It must be possible to actively change the levels of the IV and record the DV accurately. It is preferable when it is likely that behaviour could be affected by a contrived environment.
Quasi-experiment	When looking for differences or comparisons between variables that cannot be artificially controlled or manipulated.
Correlational analysis	When looking for relationships between variables. Can be used when it is unethical or impractical to artificially control or manipulate variables. There must be two variables that can be measured.
Structured observation	When seeking to record specific observable behaviours rather than inferred states. This might also include variables that cannot be measured by asking questions.
Questionnaire	When aiming to collect data about opinions or attitudes from a large sample, and when the questions to be asked are largely straightforward and the same for every participant. Also if face-to-face contact might reduce the response rate or honesty.
Interview	When aiming to collect data from individuals using questions that might require explanation or when the questions might need to vary between participants.

These conditions might be set up either in a contrived environment (a laboratory experiment), or in the participants' normal surroundings for the activity being tested (a field experiment). A laboratory environment is used when a high level of control over the situation is required, as well as accurate measurement of the DV and the potential to use specific apparatus. For example:

- Presenting stimuli at a fixed distance or for a specific length of time can practically be achieved only in laboratory conditions.
- Timing participants' reactions requires precision that can be achieved only in the laboratory.
- Using a brain scanner requires participants to come to a laboratory.

A laboratory experiment is therefore chosen when practicality or the need for experimental rigour exceeds the importance of reducing demand characteristics. When, however, it is more important that the participant is responding without the influence of an artificial setting, or should be unaware that they are participating in an experiment at all, a field experiment would be chosen if this were possible.

If a researcher conducts a laboratory experiment, they have the advantages of rigorous control over the situation and their participants.

Which type of experiment would you choose to use in each of the following studies and why?

1 Do problem gamblers behave in more risky ways in their everyday life than non-problem gamblers?

2 An investigation into the way children respond when parents ask them a question twice, for example: 'Did you eat the last biscuit? Did you *really* eat the last biscuit?' or 'Are you going to bed now? You are going to bed now, aren't you?'

3 Does watching a physically violent TV programme lead to immediate increases in verbally aggressive behaviour?

4 Are five-year-old children are more likely to talk about their fantasies to their mum or to their dad?

They can control precisely the nature and presentation of stimuli, sources of distraction and the order of conditions (see 'counterbalancing', below). However, they also have some hurdles. Demand characteristics can be a risk, as they indicate to the participants the aims of the study which, in turn, affects the participants' behaviour. Clearly this should be avoided. A researcher can minimise the effects of demand characteristics by disguising the purpose of the experiment, for example by using 'filler' questions between the critical ones in a questionnaire. Such distractions make it harder for participants to correctly guess the experimental aims. Alternatively, participants can be deliberately deceived about the aims. This is likely to be effective but also raises ethical issues (see page 296).

A **pilot study** is often conducted prior to an experiment (see page 217). The purpose of this is to investigate whether there are any problems with the procedure (it is not to assess ethical issues or to see if the results are likely to be as expected). It enables the experimenter to establish that their operational definition of the IV does produce two different conditions, and that they can measure the DV over a range of scores. Importantly, it also allows them to identify and introduce controls for any extraneous variables that could confound the results.

Another risk in laboratory studies is that of experimenter bias – for example, the distortions that arise because the experimenter responds differently to participants in the different levels of the IV. This response might be unconscious but it can subtly alter responses, creating or hiding patterns in the results. Imagine a researcher who is looking for differences between participants with or without an eating disorder, and who acts in a kindlier way to those with mental health problems. This might make them feel more confident or positive about completing the experimental task, so they try harder or persist for longer. Any differences in the results could be caused by experimenter bias, so would be erroneous.

Which experimental design?

In any true experiment, a decision has to be made about the allocation of participants to levels of the IV. There are good reasons for choosing each design. By having different participants in each level of the IV, an independent groups design, the researcher avoids order effects. In addition, the participants have less opportunity to become aware of the aims, so they will be less likely to respond to demand characteristics. It is also possible for all conditions to be tested simultaneously. This is sometimes an advantage. Imagine a field experiment comparing attention in gamblers who are recovered-addicts and never-addicted participants, which relies on a particular social context, such as a staged distraction. As

QUESTION SPOTLIGHT!

Re-read the example of a comparison between recovered-addicts and never-addicted participants in the text.
What possible variables could affect attention?

Imagine that an experimenter wanted to compare attention in a real-life situation for people with gambling addiction who were undergoing treatment and those who were untreated.
Why might it be better to conduct a laboratory experiment than a field experiment?

Figure 6.24 A repeated measures design runs the risk of a fatigue effect

there may be many variables that *could* affect attention, it might be better to have all the participants, from both levels of the IV, together.

Sometimes a repeated measures design is preferable, as it overcomes problems with individual differences. If there are different participants in each level of the IV, any differences found between these conditions could be due to the people rather than to the variable being manipulated. In a repeated measures design any differences between performance in each level of the IV should be due to the experimenter's manipulation. However, there is a problem here. It is possible that differences could arise because an individual experiences the same (or similar) tasks more than once, i.e. order effects. These cannot be avoided, but they can be cancelled out using counterbalancing.

Ideally, researchers would like to avoid the problems of both individual differences and order effects. This is possible, to an extent, with a matched pairs design. To set up a study using matched pairs the researcher decides on the important ways in which participants could differ. Consider a study about eating disorders that is investigating the influence of a big meal on body image. What design would be best? In repeated measures, the aim would be obvious, so demand characteristics would be a problem. Using an independent groups design would be possible but variables other than the meal size – such as age, gender, educational level or socio-economic group – could affect vulnerability to eating disorders. In a matched pairs design, participants are identified who share important characteristics, so that one of each similar pair can be placed into each level of the IV. So, in this case, if two 25-year-old female students from the same socio-economic group were found, one would be allocated to each group. As you can imagine, this procedure is time-consuming and is not without risk – it relies on the assumption that the criteria being used for matching are those which are most important, and this might not be the case. Nevertheless, once established, the two

QUESTION SPOTLIGHT!

You need to be able to suggest appropriate controls. *Identify the variables you would control in each of the situations below and explain how and why you would do this. Give examples where appropriate.*

1. Designing a word list to use in a memory experiment on the effect of a delay.
2. Writing questions for a study on the effect of leading questions on recall accuracy.
3. Selecting images for a study on factors affecting gambling addiction.
4. Choosing music for a study on the effects of music on concentration, comparing classical and pop.
5. Deciding on objects to use for recognition by touch alone in a test on split-brain patients.

matched groups have the advantages both of independent groups and of repeated measures designs.

Design decisions in correlational analyses

Remember that a correlational study looks for relationships between two variables. Both variables must exist over a range and it must be possible to measure them numerically. This means that the participants' scores cannot be just in named categories, they must be on an ordinal, interval or ratio scale, i.e. one that is, or can be converted to, numbers. The two can, however, be different. The choice of scales will depend on the variables being tested. Ideally, interval or ratio scales would be used, as the data from these allows more detailed statistics to be conducted on the results. However, many psychological variables cannot be measured in this way. For example, the amount of dream sleep can be measured in hours and minutes (a ratio scales) but the detail in a dream report can only be estimated (e.g. from the length of a participant's dream narrative), which gives an ordinal score.

A researcher is likely to choose to conduct a correlational study when the variables they are investigating cannot be manipulated for practical or ethical reasons. This would apply to variables such as the length of time a person has had a mental illness, or its severity. A correlational design is also used to measure inter-rater reliability, i.e. to see whether two researchers are consistent in their rating of responses from participants in a self-report or observational study. Correlations are also used to assess the reliability of tools such as questionnaires. If participants are assessed on the same variable twice, the two sets of scores should correlate.

Design decisions in observations

Observations are chosen when records are needed of actual behaviours rather than, say, what people think they would do, which they would report in a questionnaire. Having access to physical responses rather than verbal ones, scores on tests, or performance on experimental tasks, means that researchers can investigate participants who cannot follow instructions or give spoken responses, for example, animals, very young children or non-verbal adults.

One ethical concern in designing an observation is the need to protect people's privacy. Participants should either give their consent to be observed, or observations should take place only in situations where the individuals would reasonably expect to be watched by others.

A researcher has to decide whether to observe in a naturalistic or contrived situation. If the behaviour is very infrequent and its appearance is dependent on a certain set of circumstances, a contrived situation will employ deliberate manipulation of the setting to ensure that the behaviours are seen. This would be preferred, e.g. when recording the responses of gamblers to winning and losing, or scoring changes in aggressive behaviour following pro- or anti-social television programmes.

Participant or non-participant observation?

If the researcher knows that their participants will be affected by being observed, they might conduct a covert observation, where the participants are unaware that they are being observed. We are more likely to obtain representative information about the behaviour of a gambler by observing them covertly than if they are aware of our role, as they might change their behaviour (e.g. they might 'play safe' or take even bigger risks).

Clearly, covert observations raise both ethical and practical issues. In general, a covert observer is physically hidden (e.g. they are far away). However, awareness of the observer can also be avoided if the observer is 'disguised' within the observed group, i.e. in a participant observation. In the gambling situation, the observer could appear to be another gambler, or the croupier. This is advantageous for the researcher as they can more easily conduct a controlled observation, for example, changing their betting strategy to observe the effect on the participant. Participants can alternatively be made aware that they are going to be observed. This is an overt observation. This raises fewer ethical issues. Participants can be asked for their informed consent so can be observed in a greater range of environments.

A non-participant design helps the observer to concentrate on the behaviours of interest, as they do not have to pay attention to maintaining their role in the social situation. It is also easier for the non-participant observer to remain objective so when subjectivity is a potential risk this is preferable. In contrast, participant observation might be more useful

ACTIVITY ✳

Look back at the correlational ideas on page 276.
Design and conduct a correlational analysis to test one of these ideas. Your answer should state a hypotheses, operationally define the two variables, describe the procedure, and explain how you would obtain your sample. Justify your decisions, such as the choice of variables and whether you are predicting a positive or negative correlation.

Figure 6.26
Participant observers become part of the social situation being observed

ACTIVITY ✳

Staff on a psychiatric ward want to investigate whether patients copy the bizarre behaviours they see in each other.

Design an observation to test this. Your answer should state a hypothesis, the procedure, and how you would obtain your sample. Justify your decisions, such as the choice of behavioural categories and whether the observation will be participant.

ACTIVITY ✳

Felicity is planning the timetable in a college and think each subject should have some morning and some afternoon lessons. This is because she believes that students don't concentrate as well in the afternoon as they do in the morning.

Design and conduct an observation to test this. Your answer should define the behavioural categories, describe the procedure, including whether the observers will be participant and why. Justify your choice of behavioural categories and sampling strategy (time or event sampling).

for exactly the opposite reason – by becoming involved in the social situation, the observer might gain greater insight into the participants' feelings or motives than a non-participant observer.

Preparing to collect data

In an observation, design decisions also have to be made about how data will be collected. These include:

- the sampling strategy
- behavioural categories.

In event sampling, the observer uses a checklist and tallies each occurrence of a behaviour, while in time sampling, records can be taken at fixed time intervals (e.g. every 10 seconds). In either case, each behaviour or 'behavioural category' should be operationally defined. This ensures that the observer is consistent in their recording of each type of event and that, if there is more than one observer, their records are also consistent (see inter-observer reliability, page 236). It is important at the design stage that each behavioural category is independent and observable, that is, that they can be readily separated from the continuous stream of events and are reliably identifiable – they must be directly observable and not inferred. For example, recording a gambler 'getting excited' would not be a valid category, as 'excitement' itself cannot be seen, whereas an observable product of excitement, such as tapping the fingers, would be a valid category.

For time sampling, the researcher has to make decisions about:

- the time-sampling technique
- the length of the time intervals.

The choice of time-sampling technique (instantaneous scan, one-zero or predominant activity) will be determined in part by the type of information required (e.g. about duration versus frequency of behaviours) and in part by the nature of the behaviours themselves. When some frequent and some infrequent behaviours are of interest, instantaneous scan sampling would not be used, but it would be ideal when there are many behaviours of similar duration. This can be assessed in a pilot study. The ideal length of the time intervals can also be determined in a pilot study. They should be long enough to gather data over a range of behaviours, but short enough to detect changes in patterns of behaviour.

Design decisions in self-report studies

In self-report studies, participants report their beliefs, thoughts or feelings to the researcher. They include questionnaires and interviews. In both techniques, the researcher presents the participant with questions.

Interview or questionnaire?

The first decision to be made is whether to collect data face-to-face (by interview) or on paper (using a questionnaire). If the nature of the investigation is socially sensitive, a questionnaire might be preferable. Respondents are less likely to be affected by social desirability, or to lie or omit answers, if they do not feel judged because they are not face-to-face with a researcher. For example, interviewees might under-report childhood abuse because they are embarrassed. Conversely, spending time building up a trusting relationship can help an interviewer to elicit more information.

Structured, semi-structured or unstructured?

Although different questions *can* be given to different individuals in a questionnaire, in general everyone's questions are identical. This is an example of a structured design because the structure remains the same for every participant. In a semi-structured design, the same questions are used for each respondent, but additional questions can be used, so there is some tailoring of the questions to the individual on the basis of the answers given. Interviews can alternatively be unstructured – these are entirely variable so the interviewer can respond to the answers a participant gives with different questions. This adaptable technique is more likely to gain useful, detailed information when this is difficult to obtain. For example, with a reticent participant with mental health problems, more is likely to be learned using a flexible approach than by sticking rigidly to a set of predetermined questions.

Open or closed questions?

A researcher might choose to use closed questions because the results are easy to analyse as they generate simple numbers. For example, we could ask 'Do you believe that you would help a stranger in distress in the street?' using a yes/no format. Alternatively, we could ask a forced-choice question: *'How many of the following strangers have you ever helped: an elderly person, a child, a person with a pushchair, an ill person?'* This would allow us to say that X% of participants reported particular altruistic behaviours. Another kind of closed question is the Likert-style question. This is used to elicit attitudes. When using Likert scales, some of the statements must be 'reversed' so that the 'positive' or socially acceptable response is not always at the same side of the page.

Closed questions, including Likert and rating scales, all produce results that are numerical or 'quantitative' (see page 215). However, if the nature of the research requires detailed, in-depth answers, then open questions are more appropriate as they can elicit extended answers.

Figure 6.27 If people are likely to clam up under the scrutiny of an interviewer, a questionnaire is a better choice

ACTIVITY

Derek is a careers officer and is deciding what career guidance to offer students on different courses. He suspects that science students have clearer career goals than arts students do.

Design a self-report to test this. Your answer should state the hypothesis, whether you are planning a questionnaire or interview, the procedure, and how you will obtain your sample. Justify your decisions, such as the choice of question types and questions.

QUESTION SPOTLIGHT!

Look back to your answers to the question spotlights on page 276.

1   Using your operational definitions, describe what apparatus or materials would be needed to create the levels of the IV, and measure the changes in the DV in each case.

2   Suggest at least two controls for each study and explain why they are necessary.

An open question such as 'How do you feel when you have the urge to gamble?' will supply much more information than ticking boxes about excitement or desperation. Unlike the numbers produced by closed questions, the results generated by open questions are qualitative – that is, they are detailed and descriptive. This data is therefore more difficult to analyse, and this would be a consideration for researchers who wanted to collect a wide range of information from a large sample of participants.

Both qualitative and quantitative data can be collected using either questionnaires or interviews. In practice, researchers would generally choose questionnaires to gather specific, quantitative information, and interviews to gather more in-depth, qualitative data.

DEVELOPING A PLAN

When designing a study, a researcher needs to work through several important steps to plan effectively. They should:

* decide on their aim and, if appropriate, develop hypotheses to test
* select the most appropriate research method
* identify and operationalise the variables
* make design decisions (including considering what controls are necessary)
* ensure the design is ethically sound
* devise appropriate materials or apparatus
* use a pilot study to resolve any practical issues
* identify the target population
* decide which sampling method to use and the sample size they will need.

Finally, the researcher should decide how the results will be analysed, choosing which descriptive statistics they will use once the data have been collected (see pages 293–6).

IMPROVING INVESTIGATIONS

Once a study has been designed, and a pilot study conducted, the procedure can often be refined to improve reliability and/or validity.

In order to be reliable, a measure must be consistent. Imagine trying to work out the dimensions of a box with a ruler that can only measure 'short' and 'long', or that is was made of elastic. These would be nominal and ordinal measures respectively. Because the elastic ruler might stretch by different amounts each time you used it, your judgments would lack consistency – a reliability problem. The short/long ruler wouldn't tell you what you wanted to know (i.e. how big the box was) a problem of validity.

One way to raise reliability and validity is to change the way in which variables are measured. If possible, 'better' levels of measurement can be

TABLE 6.16 USING A PILOT STUDY TO CHECK THE METHOD: WHAT TO LOOK FOR

	Check:
Experiment	• Can the participants follow the standardised instructions? • Are the apparatus and materials appropriate? • Does the DV cover the full range of scores? • Are there any possible extraneous variables that need to be controlled? • Will any aspects of the procedure lead to demand characteristics? • Are there any order effects in a repeated measures design?
Self-report	• Do the participants understand the questions and are they prepared to answer them? • Do closed questions offer suitable options? • Are open questions also needed to elicit unpredictable responses? • Are response biases limited, e.g. through the use of filler questions and reversal of positive and negative 'ends' of Likert and rating scales? • Is the reporting method appropriate, e.g. if a face-to-face interview is too intimidating should it be changed to a questionnaire?
Observation	• Do observers agree on operational definitions of behavioural categories? • Inter-observer reliability – do they need practice? • Do behavioural categories include all the important behaviours? • Do behavioural categories not overlap? • Are the participants are affected by the observers? Should they be non-disclosed?
Correlation	• Can the participants follow the standardised instructions? • Are the apparatus and materials appropriate? • Do the measures of the two variables cover the full range of scores?

used. For example, in a study investigating chimp language, they might be assessed by asking questions and recording whether they answered correctly or not (a nominal measure). Alternatively, the researchers could record how many relevant words the response contained (an ordinal scale) and how quickly it was given (a ratio scale). These data would be more informative than simply whether the chimp answered correctly or not. However, such changes are only improvements if they are genuinely more useful. It might be, for example, that factors other than linguistic competence affect how quickly chimps respond, such as how motivated they are – a chimp might well respond more quickly to the question 'Would you like a banana or an apple?' than to 'Are you brushing your teeth or your toes?' So, although as a measure it would be more reliable, it might not necessarily be more valid.

In questionnaires, reliability can be raised by improving the questions used. If test-retest or split-half analyses reveal a lack of reliability in particular questions, these can be removed from the questionnaire or amended and tested again to ensure they are consistent. Filler and lie-detector questions also help to improve the validity of questionnaires (see page 222).

QUESTION SPOTLIGHT! ⭐

Remember that quantitative data can come from nominal, ordinal, interval or ratio levels of measurement – nominal (categories) being the least infomative, and ratio (mathematical scales) the most informative.

Which is which of the following levels of measurement?

- 'How hard do you work when you revise? (very hard/quite hard/averagely/less than most people/hardly at all)'
- Answers to the question 'Which revision techniques do you use? (tick all that apply)'
- How long do you spend revising each day?

Improvements often affect both reliability and validity. It is therefore important when answering a question to explain how your proposed change tackles issues of either consistency (reliability) or relevance (validity).

For each of the studies below, suggest an improvement and explain whether it would improve reliability, validity or both, and why.

1   Phil is using points on a scale of 1 to 10 to measure how aroused people feel in an experiment looking at exposure to violent films versus exciting fantasy ones. He wants a better measure of arousal.

2   Alysha is exploring whether mathematical ability is better in musical or non-musical students. She asks them if they play a musical instrument to divide them into the levels of the IV, and then whether or not they have GCSE maths. How could you improve the measure of the DV?

Design two experiments to investigate whether people with a gambling addiction have poor memories. One should have high mundane realism and the other should have rigorous controls.

For each of the proposed improvements below, decide whether they would improve reliability, validity or both, and explain why.

1   Gerry is investigating sleep and asks people how well they slept last night on a scale of 'very well / well / okay / badly / very badly'. He decides that this isn't informative enough and changes it to record the number of hours of sleep.

2   Steph starts off recording her DV of dream content by asking people: 'Did you have a nice dream last night?' She revises this to: 'Select which of the following you dreamt about last night: eating, flying, dancing, running, falling, aliens, animals, talking'.

3   Jenny is investigating mother-love fantasies in five-year-old boys. She asks them: 'Do you ever want to sleep in your mother's bed?' She decides to abandon this question and asks instead: 'Do you ever hope that you will spend the rest of your life with your mother?'

There is at least one problem with each of the proposed changes, Identify these too and explain whether they are issues of reliability or validity.

Reliability and validity can also be improved by refining the way in which variables are defined. For example, in an experiment recording aggressive behaviour (such as Bandura *et al.*'s study, page 61), *fighting* might include 'pushing, pulling or hitting another individual'. However, such behaviours might also be seen in play. A good operational definition would distinguish between these, perhaps by adding 'in the absence of smiling or laughter'. This would increase the consistency of observations, as some researchers might have been including play and others not, thus raising reliability. It would also mean that the records reflected purely aggressive behaviours rather than a mixture of aggression and play, so it would also improve validity.

In experiments, several other procedures can improve validity. These include imposing more controls, using standardised instructions, blind and double-blind procedures, random allocation in independent groups designs, and counterbalancing in repeated measures designs (or, alternatively, using a matched pairs design). In any study, if the sample is unrepresentative, an improvement in sampling method to obtain a larger and/or wider sample will make the findings more representative. In general, improvements to mundane realism and ecological validity work against these changes which improve other aspects of the study, so a balance must be achieved between scientific rigour and validity in terms of real life.

F – DEALING WITH DATA AND ETHICS

INTRODUCTION

The purpose of research is to test hypotheses. To do this, investigations generate data and this must be analysed to decide whether the findings support the alternate hypothesis. This section looks at some ways to present and analyse data, and considers ethical issues in designing studies.

QUANTITATIVE AND QUALITATIVE DATA

Quantitative data, mainly associated with experiments and correlations, is numerical. The strengths of quantitative data tend to come from having high **objectivity** and reliability. Qualitative data in contrast, being in-depth and descriptive, is typically more **subjective** but can often be more representative and therefore higher in validity (see page 215 for more about the distinction between qualitative and quantitative data).

 **KEY IDEAS**

A personal viewpoint that is likely to be biased as it is not independent of the situation is **subjective**. Being unbiased in conducting a study, so that the data collected are independent of the researcher's individual perspective, is being **objective**.

TABLE 6.17 STRENGTHS AND WEAKNESSES OF QUALITATIVE AND QUANTITATIVE DATA

	Strengths	Weaknesses
Quantitative	Tends to be collected using objective measures. Data collection tends to be highly reliable.	Method of measurement can limit participant's responses, making the data less valid, e.g. if appropriate response options are not available.
Qualitative	Tends to be collected using objective measures. Data collection might be highly valid as it is likely to be possible for participants to express themselves exactly as they want to.	Tends to be collected using relatively subjective measures. Data collection might be invalid as recording or interpretation of participants responses might be biased by the researcher's opinions or feelings.

DESCRIPTIVE STATISTICS

Psychological investigations that collect quantitative data tend to generate quite a lot of results – one or more scores from each participant. In order to summarise these – to make any patterns easy to see – researchers use descriptive statistics including averages, the range, tables and graphs.

KEY IDEAS

Measure of central tendency is a mathematical way to describe a typical or average score from a data set (such as using the mode, median or mean). The **mode** is worked out as the most frequent score(s) in a set of results. The **median** is worked out as the middle score in the list when the data are in rank order (from smallest to largest). If there are two numbers in the middle they are added together and divided by two. The **mean** is worked out by adding up all the scores and dividing by the number of scores. The **range** is a measure of dispersion that tells you how spread out the data in a set are. It is worked out by taking the smallest score in a set away from the largest score.

QUESTION SPOTLIGHT! ⟩

In the study conducted by Rosenhan (see page 177), the pseudopatients recorded qualitative data about the way in which they were responded to by nurses, doctors and other patients, for example, writing down what was said to them. They also collected quantitative data, for example, recording the total number of times they were spoken to or ignored by staff. *Which data could be used to calculate a measure of central tendency?*

QUESTION SPOTLIGHT! ⟩

Calculate the mode for the two sets of scores in the section on the median above right.

AVERAGES: MEASURES OF CENTRAL TENDENCY

One way to analyse quantitative data is to work out the measure of central tendency or 'average'. This is a single number that indicates the 'middle' or typical point in a set of data. There are different measures of central tendency to use with different levels of measurement: the mode, median and mean.

The mode

The **mode** is the most frequent score in a set of results. If two (or more) scores are equally common there will be two (or more) modes. For example, if a researcher asks participants to decide whether their last dream was active, inactive or mixed, and finds that out of 50 people, 36 say active, 12 say inactive and 2 say mixed, the modal dream content type is active. The mode can be used with any kind of data but it is the only measure of central tendency that can be used with nominal data.

The median

The **median** is found by putting all the scores in a set into order from smallest to largest and finding the one in the middle of the list. When the scores in a group with an even number of participants are put in order (i.e. 'ranked'), there will be two numbers in the middle. These should be added together and divided by two to find the median. The median cannot be used with nominal data but can be used with data of any other level of measurement, such as with data generated from rating and Likert scales. For example, a researcher might measure self-reported navigational ability in bus drivers and non-bus drivers. If they used four rating scales, each ranging from 1 to 10, and added each participant's scores together, the median would be calculated in the following way:

- **Bus drivers:** 11, 12, 13, 15, 20, 22, 25, 26, 28, 30

$20 + 22 = 42, \frac{41}{2} = 21$, so the median = 21

- **Non-bus drivers:** 1, 4, 9, 15, 20, 24, 25, 30, 37, 39

$20 + 24 = 44, \frac{44}{2} = 22$, so the median = 22

The medians for the two sets of data above are very similar. This suggests that there is no difference in navigational ability of bus drivers and non-bus drivers.

The mean

The **mean** is the measure of central tendency we usually call the 'average'. It is worked out by adding up all the scores in the data set and dividing by the total number of scores (including any that were zeros). The mean is the most informative measure of central tendency because it takes every score into account, but it should be used only with interval or ratio data. As many memory studies use interval scales from carefully controlled lists of stimuli, such as numbers, nonsense syllables or equal frequency and length words, the mean is often used as the measure of central tendency. For example, a researcher might measure navigational ability in bus drivers and non-bus drivers by timing how long they take to find their way through a virtual maze in the laboratory. The mean from their time in minutes would be calculated in the following way:

- **Bus drivers:** 2, 15, 6, 8, 14, 19, 9, 4, 8, 13

total = 98, $\frac{98}{10}$ = 9.8, so the mean is 9.8 minutes

- **Non-bus workers:** 14, 3, 6, 18, 2, 18, 13, 5, 1, 15

total = 95, $\frac{95}{10}$ = 9.5, so the mean is 9.5 minutes

The means for the two sets of data above are very similar. This again suggests that there is no difference in navigational ability of bus drivers and non-bus drivers.

GRAPHS AND TABLES

Tabulations and graphical representations of data are used to illustrate the findings of studies. They may illustrate totals or frequencies, percentages and any of the measures of central tendency. Different graphs are used for different types of data. You need to know which to choose and how to sketch them.

Tables

So that other people can clearly see the outcome of a study, a summary of the findings is usually presented in a table. Tables should always have an informative title and clear headings for each row and column, including units of measurement if appropriate. Results such as totals or frequencies, percentages, means, medians and modes can all be tabulated. The medians and means from the data above would be presented as in Table 6.18.

Bar charts

A bar chart is used when data are in discrete categories, that is, when scores are not on a continuous scale. For example, bar charts would be used for the totals of nominal data and for all measures of central tendency (modes, medians or means). The bars on a bar chart must be separate. This is because the x axis represents distinct groups, not a linear scale. If you are plotting the results of an experiment, the levels of the IV go along the bottom (on the x axis), and the DV goes on the vertical y axis (see Figure 6.28 on page 296).

STRETCH & CHALLENGE

Calculate the means for the two sets of scores in the section on the median.

Why is it an unsound procedure mathematically to calculate the mean on these data, but okay to calculate the mode?

QUESTION SPOTLIGHT!

Calculate the mode, median and mean for the set of data below about obedience to Police Officers and Community Police Officers (CPOs).

Authority figure	Seconds to obey
Police officer	6, 5, 3, 8, 3, 7, 9, 2, 3, 4
CPO	12, 14, 2, 6, 9, 5, 8, 2, 10, 15

STRETCH & CHALLENGE

Look at your answers to the Question Spotlight above. How does the mode distort the apparent difference?

TABLE 6.18 NAVIGATIONAL ABILITY IN BUS DRIVERS AND NON-BUS DRIVERS

navigational ability	bus drivers	non-bus drivers
median	21	22
mean	9.8	9.5

QUESTION SPOTLIGHT!

Tabulate the modal scores from the example about dreaming on page 227.

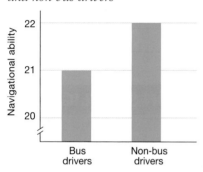

Figure 6.28
Navigational ability in bus drivers and non-bus drivers

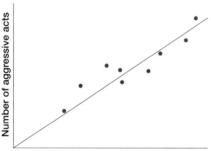

Hours of violent TV viewed per day

Figure 6.29

1   *How strong is the positive correlation shown in the scattergraph compared to the one in Figure 6.12c (see page 246)?*
2   *What conclusion would you draw from these data?*

QUESTION SPOTLIGHT!

The range of the IQ data in the table opposite would be calculated as
132 – 98 = 34
so the range is 34 IQ points.
Calculate the range for the memory test scores in the same table and for the two sets of data on page 295.

Scattergraphs

Scattergraphs were discussed on page 00. They are used to display the findings of correlational studies. To construct a scattergraph, a dot is plotted at the point where each individual's scores on each variable cross. A line of best fit is then drawn at an angle so that it comes close to as many points as possible (see Figure 6.29). In a strong correlation all the data points lie close to the line, in a weak correlation they are more spread out. Where there is no correlation, the points do not form a clear line at all.

Remember that you cannot draw a causal conclusion from a correlational study, so the scattergraph in Figure 6.29, which shows a positive correlation, tells us that there is a relationship between aggression and TV viewing of violent TV, but not which (if either) of these variables is the cause of this link. We would have to conduct an experiment to find this out.

ETHICAL ISSUES RELATING TO PSYCHOLOGICAL RESEARCH WITH HUMAN PARTICIPANTS

You will already have encountered ethical issues raised in earlier chapters. Here we will look at the ethical dilemmas that psychologists face and how they can deal with them effectively.

BPS GUIDELINES

To help psychologists to cope with ethical issues arising in research and professional practice, the British Psychological Society (BPS) regularly updates its ethical guidelines. As psychologists are concerned with people's welfare, it is important that these guidelines are followed. When research is conducted at institutions such as universities, the planned study must be approved by an ethical committee. This ensures that these guidelines are being followed. While the primary concern is for the welfare of individuals, another issue is the perception of psychology in society. Participants who are deceived or distressed might not want to participate again, might portray

QUESTION SPOTLIGHT!

1   *Draw a scattergraph using the data below.*
2   *Does the scattergraph show a positive or a negative correlation?*
3   *What conclusion would you draw from these data?*

IQ	103	119	98	121	101	125	109	132
memory test score	14	17	11	17	9	16	16	19

psychology in a poor light to others, and are unlikely or trust the findings of psychological research. These are all outcomes we would want to avoid.

Consent and deception

As we saw on page 255, it is important in experiments to hide the aims from participants, or even to deceive participants, in order to reduce demand characteristics. However, potential participants also have the right to know what is going to happen so that they can give their informed consent. These two opposing needs mean that it can be hard to get genuine consent. Ideally, researchers should obtain full and *informed consent* from participants by giving them sufficient information about the procedure to decide whether they want to participate.

However, there are some situations in which the researcher cannot ask for consent. This is often (but not always) the case in naturalistic observations, field experiments and laboratory experiments where deception is essential to the aims. In these situations, a researcher can attempt to decide whether participants in the sample would be likely to object by asking other people. Using a group of people similar to those who will become participants, the researcher can ask whether they would find the study acceptable if they were involved. This is called **presumptive consent** because it allows the researcher to presume that the actual participants would also be happy to participate.

Deception should be avoided. If used, participants should be told the real aim as soon as possible and allowed to take their results away. When participants know they have been in a study they should be **debriefed** quickly and should leave in at least as positive a mood as they started.

Right to withdraw

Participants have the right to leave a study at any time if they wish. This is their right to withdraw and it must be observed, even if this means data are lost. While participants can be offered incentives to join a study, these cannot be taken back if they leave – so they do not feel compelled to continue. Nor should researchers should use their position of authority to encourage participants to continue beyond the point where they want to stop. In practice, this means that researchers must make the right to withdraw explicit to participants and be prepared to relinquish data if a participant chooses to withdraw. So, if a participant leaves between the first and second testing in a repeated measures design, their data from the first condition cannot be used.

KEY IDEAS

Gaining agreement to participate in principle from a similar group of people to the intended participants by asking them if they would object to the procedure is called **presumptive consent**. It can be used when gaining informed consent from the participants themselves would lead to their working out the aim of the study. A **debrief** is the information given to participants *after* a study. It serves to explain the aim and to return them to their previous state to ensure that they have not been affected by participation. Debriefing is *not*, however, an excuse for deceiving participants.

WEB WATCH @

Look on the BPS website for the most up-to-date Ethical Guidelines. *Why is it necessary to update the guidelines?*

QUESTION SPOTLIGHT!

Rosenhan (1973) (see page 177) investigated the behaviour of hospital staff towards patients who had a diagnosis of schizophrenia based on pretend symptoms. *Why was it necessary to use deception in this study?*

QUESTION SPOTLIGHT!

A researcher is working with a person who has multiple personality disorder.
What steps should they take to ensure:
- that the individual has given informed consent
- their confidentiality
- they are given the right to withdraw?

Privacy and confidentiality

Studies that ask for personal information, or observe people, risk invading privacy. A researcher should make clear to participants that they have a right to ignore questions they do not want to answer, thus protecting their privacy. When completing a questionnaire in a laboratory situation, participants should be given an individual space and assured of the confidentiality and security of their data.

All data should remain confidential (e.g. by not storing names with data) unless participants have agreed otherwise. Participants' identities can be protected by allocating each person a number or letter, and using this to identify them. In experiments with an independent groups design this helps to identify and keep a record of which condition each participant was in. In repeated measures designs participant numbers are essential for pairing up an individual's scores in each condition.

In observations, people should be watched only in situations where they would expect to be on public display. When conducting a case study, including those of larger groups such as institutions, confidentiality is still important and identities must be hidden. For example, the identities of schools or hospitals should be concealed.

The only exceptions to this general principle are that personally identifiable information can be communicated when the individual gives their informed consent to do so, or in exceptional circumstances when the safety or interests of the individual or others may be at risk.

Protection from harm

Studies have the potential to cause participants psychological harm (e.g. distress) or physical harm (e.g. engaging in risky behaviours such as taking drugs). In these situations, participants have the right to be protected and should not be exposed to any greater risk than they would be in their normal life. Experienced researchers should be used in risky procedures and studies should be stopped if unexpected risks arise. If participants have been negatively affected by a study, the researcher has a responsibility to return them to their previous condition. This is one of the functions of the debrief, but this is not an alternative to designing an ethical study. It is therefore important to consider all the ways in which a study could cause distress and to minimise them.

QUESTION SPOTLIGHT!

A researcher is designing a field experiment about emotions and death in which participants will see a staged violent crime in which someone appears to be shot dead.
How should they deal with the following ethical issues:
- informed consent
- privacy
- protection from harm?

TO A2 AND BEYOND!

As you get to the end of your AS year, and exams are out of the way, this is a good time to start thinking about careers. If you're applying to University in the Autumn, time will soon creep up on you, and it is advisable to prepare an early application. If you're going to manage that, you need to get planning now.

MAKING THE MOST OF THE A2 YEAR

Psychology is one of the most popular and competitive subjects at degree level, and obtaining a place to study psychology is now as tough as obtaining a place to study medicine or law. Any offers you are given next year will be conditional on your overall A-level grades, so it is critical to get the highest grades that you can next year. You won't want to be preparing for January units at the same time as you are completing your UCAS application, so get your careers research done now, and send in your application as early as possible in the Autumn.

A2 level is a step-up in level from AS level, but what does that mean in practice? It does not mean that the psychology you will study will be harder to understand than what you have already been studying, so don't let yourself be frightened off! You will probably notice an increase in pace, and perhaps there will be more to learn for exams, depending on which options you take. You might also find that you have to learn more theory, but fewer studies (again, depending on your options).

The main difference between AS and A2 is in the exam questions. A2 exam questions differ from AS questions in two important ways. First, they require longer answers. Second, more marks will be allocated for analysis and evaluation, and fewer for straight description. Be prepared to start writing more extended prose than you are used to, and to applying the general evaluation skills you have learned this year to a range of question types. If you are prepared to have a good go at both these things, then you are well on the way to making the transition from AS to A2.

UNDERGRADUATE PSYCHOLOGY

Although we recommend studying psychology, you should be aware that most psychologists who teach undergraduates don't think that A-level psychology is particularly good preparation. Many psychology undergraduates are surprised at how scientific university psychology is. There will be little or no Freud! You will spend a lot of time carrying out experiments and other types of study, and a considerable amount of time learning about research methodology and statistics. There is also less opportunity at first- and second-year undergraduate level to choose interesting-sounding options, and you may come to realise that your A-level teacher has chosen the most interesting and 'sexy' options that protect you from some of the more dry and technical aspects of psychology.

The other key difference between studying at A-level and undergraduate level – in any subject area – is the particular requirement for independent study. The emphasis at A-level is on learning and knowing well a particular body of information, and being able to demonstrate that you can think analytically about this material. This necessarily means that your teacher will provide you with everything you need to know, or will at least prescribe reading that will give you all the answers. At undergraduate level, there is far greater emphasis on your locating and processing information for yourself and developing your own skills.

Psychology careers

Do you want to be a professional psychologist? If the answer to this is 'yes', then you really need to start with a psychology degree. If, however, you don't yet have a firm career plan, but you are looking for an interesting degree that is well regarded by a range of employers, then you would also do well to consider a degree in psychology. It is important to know that the vast majority of people with psychology degrees never go on to become professional psychologists. This means that you don't have to worry that you are limiting yourself to a career as a psychologist if you take a psychology degree. People who study psychology at degree level can end up working in a huge variety of fields, including health, sport, education, criminal justice or business. Detailed information about different psychology careers can be found here:

www.heacademy.ac.uk/assets/documents/subjects/psychology/Employability_Guide.pdf

CHOOSING A PSYCHOLOGY DEGREE
Accredited degrees

At the time of writing there are 388 degrees in the United Kingdom accredited by the British Psychological Society. Some of these are straight psychology, but you can also opt for a range of joint or combined honours courses, if that suits you better. If you are likely to want to be a professional psychologist it is important to choose a degree that is accredited by the British Psychological Society. You can see a list of these here:

www.bps.org.uk/careers-education-training/accredited-courses-training-programmes/accredited-courses-training-progra

Entry requirements

Psychology is now extremely popular, and you will find that entry grades are correspondingly high. For the most popular courses, this can mean up to three A grades at A level. You can see an up-to-date list of entry requirements here:

www.ucas.com/students/coursesearch

You will see that there is wide variation in entry grades from one course to another. Remember that the most sought-after courses are not necessarily those that will suit you best as an individual. The courses that are hardest to get into are likely to be those where the most famous researchers work. This may or may not be important to you; you might place more emphasis on quality of teaching.

It is also worth remembering that the popularity of a course might be determined as much by the location of the university, as by the quality of the course itself. Pretty campus universities in the home counties are most popular – but beware that rural campuses can be miles from the nearest pub! If you're willing to live in the rougher part of a city, at a university that has no landscaped grounds, you might be able to get into a decent course with lower grades (and perhaps have more fun).

Measures of course quality

There are two major published figures that are used to define the quality of a university department.

- The Research Assessment Exercise (RAE) grade. This is a measure of how successful the department is in publishing influential research. Grades are on a scale of 1 to 5*, with the highest grade being 5*. RAEs are available here:

www.rae.ac.uk/pubs/2009/ov

(Note that the RAE is due to be replaced in 2014 by the Research Excellence Framework (REF), so from then on you will need a different source for department ratings.)

- The National Student Surveys. These provide a statistical record of how highly psychology undergraduates rated their courses. Scores are out of 5 for several criteria, including quality of teaching and feedback. You can see student satisfaction ratings here:

www.thestudentsurvey.com

We hope you have enjoyed AS psychology and that you will decide to take it further.

Matt, Julia, Lizzie and Penny

INDEX